The British School at Athens

MOSAIC

FESTSCHRIFT FOR A. H. S. MEGAW

MOSAIC
Festschrift for A. H. S. Megaw

edited by
Judith Herrin, Margaret Mullett and Catherine Otten-Froux

BRITISH SCHOOL AT ATHENS
STUDIES 8

Published and distributed by
The British School at Athens
Senate House, Malet Street, London WC1E 7HU
© individual authors, and the Managing Committee, the British School at Athens

First published in Great Britain 2001
ISBN 0 904887 40 5

This book set in Ehrhardt and Palatino OSF by WM Pank, King's College London.
Printed in Great Britain by Technical Print Services Ltd, Nottingham

Tabula Gratulatoria

Gunila Åkerstrom-Hougen
†Seka Allen
Aristodemos Anastasiades
Richard Anderson
Pamela Armstrong
Charalambos Bakirtzis
Susan A. Boyd
Sebastian and Helen Brock
Anthony Bryer
Gerald Cadogan
Hector and †Elizabeth Catling
Richard Catling
J. N. Coldstream
†R. M. Cook
Anthony Cutler
Bank of Cyprus, Cultural Foundation
Oliver Dickinson
Suzy Dufrenne
George Galavaris
Andreas Georgiades
Phryne Hadjichristophi
John Hayes
Judith Herrin
Tony and Meg Househam
Miss H. F. Hughes
Joan Hussey
Irmgard Hutter
George Huxley
Marina Ieronymidou
Ruth Keshishian
P. M. Kitromilides
Peter Lock
Franz Georg Maier
Georgios Magginis
Eunice Dauterman Maguire
Henry Maguire

Anne McCabe
Shelagh Meade
J. V. S. Megaw
Demetrios Michaelides
Margaret Mullett
Ino Nicolaou
Catherine Otten–Froux
Tassos Papacostas
A. Papageorghiou
Demetra Papanikola–Bakirtzi
Kika Papapetrou
Georgios Philotheou
T. C. Potts
Denys Pringle
†Jane Rabnett
Raleigh Radford
Jean Richard
John Rosser
Mossman and Charlotte Roueché
Hugh Sackett
Guy Sanders
Jean–Michel Spieser
Karin M. Skawran
Ken Storer
R. Tanner
†Homer Thompson
Joan Thornton
A. D. Trendall
Yoram Tsafrir
Demetrios Triantaphyllopoulos
C. and E. Vermeule
Vera von Falkenhausen
Marie–Louise von Wartburg
Gill Webster
†Marjorie Wilde

Contents

List of illustrations

List of abbreviations

Abbreviations used in this volume, in addition to those observed in BSA publications.

Introduction

In this volume several of A. H. S. (Peter) Megaw's friends speak for a much wider circle who wish to congratulate him as he celebrates his ninetieth year. His lifetime's devotion to the archaeology, art history and culture of the Greek world, especially of the Byzantine period, is reflected in the wide range of papers published, from specialists in early Christian inscriptions to those skilled in the modern techniques of kite flying for aerial photography. From earliest times to the present, Peter has always maintained a curiosity about structures, forms of decoration and artistic styles, regardless of the medium in which they occur. His lengthy bibliography published here is witness to his ability to study and publish whatever finds he excavated. But it is as the master of *panta ta byzantina* that he is most cherished and to this sphere of his expertise that many of the following papers are addressed.

Yet Peter Megaw was not trained as a Byzantinist. Being an aspirant architect at the height of the Depression did not promise great prospects, and so the suggestion that he might visit Greece and offer his services as a site architect brought him into direct contact with the monuments that were to determine his career. This move also launched a particularly significant relationship: his meeting with Eleni Elektra Mangoletsi, then an art student. Their courtship blossomed into marriage, celebrated in Athens in 1937, and a long and successful partnership, which flourished despite the demands of both diplomatic life and the rigours of quite primitive dig houses.

For many of us who worked with Peter on Cyprus, both during his tenure as Director of the Antiquities Service and after, the island will always be associated with Peter and Elektra, whose warm welcome coloured all our memories. Their determination that visitors should experience its innumerable glories to the full meant that a season of excavation was regularly enlivened by a Sunday *ekdrome*, when we drove to a newly opened archaeological site, stopping at an interesting Byzantine church, or calling at a local museum, or went up into the Troodos mountains in search of a particular wild flower which Elektra wished to draw. Each will sustain a special memory—of parties at St. Hilarion under the moonlit profile of the castle before '74, or magical late afternoon swims from remote beaches, or Saturday evening dinners on the harbour at Kato Paphos with the pelican. While most excavators know it is important to look after their student staff and encourage them to explore unfamiliar sights, Elektra and Peter took this responsibility to heart in a quite extraordinarily generous way: they gave us family outings, without any of the strains attached to real families.

After his move to Athens as Director of the British School another group of students with interests in quite different periods benefitted from Peter's dedication. Through his close attention and care, many were saved from unsuitable research topics, were guided through the complex procedures of obtaining a permit to excavate, and helped to get started on their ancient surveys, Bronze Age or Classical sites. Again, expeditions organised by the Director as well as Christmas parties at the School are remembered with particular fondness to this day. Others have additional reasons for recalling Peter and Elektra's stay in the Upper House: at least four courtships evolved into marriage under their watchful eyes.

Still later, the monuments of Cyprus called Peter back to Paphos and the house on Exo Vrysi became a miniature centre of Byzantine Studies as teams arrived to work either at the castle of Saranda Kolones, or up the road at Kourion. Peter's interest in all the other periods of Cypriot history never flagged, and he and Elektra were regular and most welcome visitors at many sites. At Palaia Paphos (Kouklia), the German-Swiss team still continues the work of a British team which had been the first to include German students in the '50s, and has extended its activity from the classical temple site to the excavation of a medieval water mill. Everywhere excavators were urged to take care of their Turkish and Byzantine pot sherds, to wash and classify them like any other valuable archaeological find. Peter patiently encouraged the study of these often unlovely fragments, with such success that a whole new generation of medieval pottery specialists are now engaged, with his help, in advancing the most sophisticated technical analysis, pioneered at the Fitch laboratory attached to the British School at Athens. Some of the results of their work feature in this volume and reveal the way in which Peter's influence has altered perceptions of a particular field and has born such important fruit.

The editors deeply regret the length of time which has elapsed between their first proposal for the volume and its realisation. They thank Wendy Pank and Bill Cavanagh for ensuring its appearance in print. While it is by no means an adequate tribute, we hope that the contributors and all those who supported the venture will feel that it forms an appropriate ninetieth birthday present for Peter.

Chronia polla!

Judith Herrin

12

1

The Transition from Paganism to Christianity as revealed in the Mosaic Inscriptions of Cyprus

Ino Nicolaou

The Edict of Milan, published in AD 313 in the joint names of Constantine I and Licinius and reaffirmed by Constantine as sole emperor in AD 323, accorded to the Christians complete freedom of worship. By the middle of the fourth century, Emperor Julian (AD 361–363), the last champion of paganism, and most determined opponent of the new religion, had to admit that the ultimate victory of Christianity was assured.

This new religious order had its repercussions in Cyprus. There were three Cypriot bishops present at the First Ecumenical Council held at Nicaea in AD 325,[1] twelve at the Council of Sardica in AD 343[2] and five at the Council of Constantinople in AD 381,[3] indicating the existence of at least twelve episcopal sees in Cyprus by the end of the fourth century. This number appears to have increased to fifteen by 400, according to the synodical letter of Theophilos, Patriarch of Alexandria.[4] It seems therefore, that Christianity was firmly established on the island by the end of the fourth century. This is supported further by the archaeological remains, which provide 'ample evidence for large-scale church building in the 4th century in many different parts of the island'.[5] But although a great number of these Early Christian churches have been located, few have been excavated and not one complete monument of this period survives.[6] Some of these basilica churches had decorated mosaic floors and there are examples where mosaic inscriptions have been inserted in their decoration.[7] These inscriptions will form the subject of this paper.

Of all these inscriptions one betrays a paganistic aspect. Inscribed in a *tabula ansata*, with one small cross inscribed in a circle on each *ansa* and an imposing jewelled cross above, it was inserted in the mosaic decoration in the nave of a late fourth century basilica, which lies under the modern church of Hagios Spyridon at Tremithous (Tremetousha).[8] (PLATE 1.1) The inscription reads:

Ψηφίδι γραπτῆ ποικίληται τὴν χρόαν
τόπον κοσμῆσαι Ἁγίων Ἐπισκόπων
Καρταιρίου χερσὶν προσέταξεν ἀγαθὲς
μνήμης Σφυρίδων μεταίχων ἁγίας
ἴσος ὁμοίῳ δυνάμι πνευματική +

The church of the Hagioi Episkopoi was adorned with decorative and multicoloured *tesserae* (mosaics) by the hands of (by the mosaicist) Karterios instructed by Sphyridon who, being equal (to the bishops, i.e. bishop himself) and endowed with similar vigour, shares their pious memory.

This inscription testifies that the basilica was dedicated to the Hagioi Episkopoi and that Sphyridon, who ordered this mosaic floor from the mosaicist Karterios,

PLATE 1.1: *Hagios Spyridon, Tremithous, mosaic in the nave*

was a bishop himself. Sphyridon has been correctly identified with Bishop Spyridon (Hagios Spyridon), who attended the Council of Nicaea and who signed, in 345, the Acts of the Council of Sardica.[9]

The less than impeccable iambic metre and the quasi allegoric expression of this inscription, with its colourless style and its shocking orthography, is characteristic of the period. In essence we are reading the dying influence of the pagan literary form on Early Christian writing. But even later, at the dawn of the following century an atmosphere of tolerance still persists, which is suggestive of a gradual transition from paganism to Christianity. This is what can be deduced from the mosaic inscriptions, this time of a secular building, that is known as the Complex of Eustolios at Kourion.[10] This complex, originally built probably in the reign of emperor Valens, was remodelled during the reign of Theodosius II (*c.*AD 408-450)[11] and its pavements were adorned with mosaics. In the recreation rooms' mosaics inscriptions were inserted, three of which are of unique importance because they relate not only to the gradual transition from paganism to Christianity but also to a prevailing spirit of tolerance at Kourion in the early fifth century, otherwise a period of great intolerance.

i) In a rectangular panel on the threshold of the passage from the South to the East Hall, there is the following inscription in dactylic hexameter (PLATE 1.2):[12]

’Αντὶ λίθων μεγάλων, ἀντὶ στερεοῖο σιδήρου
χαλκοῦ τε ξανθοῖο καὶ αὐτοῦ αὐτ’ ἀδάμαντος
<ο>ἴδε δόμοι ξώσαντο πολύλλιτα σήματα Χριστοῦ

In place of big stones (walls) and solid iron, bright bronze or even adamant, this house has girt itself with the much venerated symbols of Christ.

In this inscription the name of Christ is openly expressed. The πολύλλιτα σήματα Χριστοῦ, 'the much venerated symbols of Christ', have been depicted by the mosaicist on the floor in eight circles in two rows, but the composer of this text, as well as of the two which follow, could not stop his ears to the Pagan Siren. Indeed the dactylic hexameter and the archaising verbal style recall Homeric verses. The propaganda of the new religion was being made through the traditional pagan means of expression.

ii) On the mosaic floor of the East Hall of this complex, in a rectangular panel the following fragmentary inscription can be read in three elegiac couplets (PLATE 1.3):[13]

PLATE 1.2: *Complex of Eustolios at Kourion, on the threshold of the passage from the South to the East Hall*

PLATE 1.3: *Complex of Eustolios at Kourion, in the East Hall*

] το πα .... παντὶ π..ρ.τας
] ων ἐκ ποδὸς Εὐστόλιος
]ρης ἐπελήσατο ἀλλ' ἄρα καὶ τῆς
]ως λουτρὰ χαρισσάμενος
]διζε το Κούριον ὥς ποτε Φοῖβος
] υχ ... θηκεν ὑπηνεμίην

In line 6, Y and X appear almost complete on D. C. Fales' and Mitford's photos.[14]

I fully agree with Bagnall and Drew-Bear's criticism of Mitford's 'in main *exempli gratia*' restoration of the text and of the inaccuracies in his facsimile. I shall refrain from restoring the text by giving other *exempli gratia* readings, thus adding further false impressions! I shall confine myself to discussing Mitford's restorations in line 5: [αὐτός δη τότ ʹἐ] δίζετο Κούριον ὥς ποτε Φοῖβος. The verb δίζημαι in no way means 'to visit' ('visiting the city in person', p.357), but 'to seek out', 'to look for', 'to enquire'.[15] Mitford, by restoring αὐτός (i.e. Eustolios) as subject of the verb [ἐ]δίζετο, puts Eustolios and the god Phoebus Apollo on equal footing. Considering that this text originates from the same complex as the previous inscription, where an open declaration of the new faith is made, I would restore Χριστός. This not only maintains the balance between the ruling power of the past and that of the time of the inscription, but also keeps to the spirit of the message that these inscriptions were meant to convey, namely the triumph of Christianity over paganism. In the past Phoebus had his temple and sanctuary at Kourion—he was worshipped there since the 8th century BC—his cult represented the pagan religion; at the time when the inscription was laid down, Christ is the ruler, and so Christian symbols adorn this structure. It is clear that verse 5 comes into the passage as a parenthesis and it was meant to give this very message. Megaw[16] rightly observes that this inscription 'illustrates the ambivalent state of a society still on the threshold of Christianity'. There is nothing in the inscription which shows that Eustolios lived abroad or that he held an imperial office, as Mitford thinks. The inscription in its fragmentary condition simply attests that Kourion enjoyed Eustolios's beneficence.

iii) On the mosaic floor, at the entrance of the southern room of the Eustolios Complex, in a rectangular panel one may read the following elegiac couplet (PLATE 1.4):[17]

'Εξέδρην θάλαμόν τε θυώ[δεα τοῦτο]ν [ἀδ] ελφαὶ
Αἰδώ<ς> Σωφροσύνη τε καὶ [Εὐσεβίη] κομέουσιν

The sisters Reverence, Prudence (or Temperance) and Piety to the God tend (look after) this exedra and the fragrant hall.

Examining this inscription we realise that its poetic form and means of expression are those of pagan poetry. The Homeric source of this couplet is made evident both by its dactylic hexametre and by its vocabulary. The θάλαμόν τε θυώδεα finds its parallel in the Homeric θαλάμοιο θυώδεος (Od. iv. 121), εἵματα ... θυώδεα (Od. v. 264), θυώδεος ἐκ θαλάμοιο (Hymn to Demeter 244, 288). As a matter of fact this couplet, as such, could very well have been of pre-Christian date. It has, however, been archaeologically proven that this inscription is contemporary with the above (i), where the name of Christ is explicitly invoked, and with (ii), in which the restoration Χριστός is imposed by the context of line 5. It is thus reasonable to prefer Mitford's[18] original restoration Εὐσεβίη to his final Εὐνομίη, the former expression is more in the spirit of nascent Christianity. It should be interpreted : 'Piety to God', 'Reverance towards the God'.[19] But even if Εὐνομίη is to be preferred, it should have the meaning 'Loyalty, Obedience to the law of God',[20] so important for the new faith.

PLATE 1.4: *Complex of Eustolios at Kourion, entrance to the southern hall*

In order to understand the meaning and the purpose of the three inscriptions in the Eustolios Complex we must examine them in their context as a group.[21] All three were laid down and composed contemporarily. They were all incorporated into the mosaic borders of the long halls on the south-east side of the garden (courtyard). These halls were the recreation rooms for the public using the nearby baths,[22] as mentioned in inscription (ii). The inscriptions were meant to be read by this public and to instruct them, to give them a message. Inscription (i) forms the main axis of the three: this building has girt itself, is invested with the power of (Christ) the Cross, the emblem of the Christian faith. Inscription (ii) informed the visitors that Eustolios was the founder of the bathing establishment and of another building (?) (mentioned in the missing part of line 6), and reminded them that Christ was now ruling(?) there as Phoebus Apollo did in the past. Inscription (iii) instructs the public in three of the main principles of the Christian faith: Reverence, Prudence and Piety to God (or Obedience to the Law of God).

There was no better place for exercising the propaganda for the new religion than those recreation halls. What is worth emphasizing in these inscriptions is that the pagan literary forms were still used to express the message of the new religion. Pagan temples may have been left to decay, if not destroyed, but literary culture could not be changed over-night and it continued to be at the service of the new faith. Literature may be considered indeed the last stronghold of paganism (for the cultivated classes) both in the East and the West. It was one of the silent means of reconciliation between Christianity and paganism.

44 Metochiou Avenue
Cyprus 1101 Nicosia

NOTES

1. J. Hackett, *A History of the Church of Cyprus* (London 1901) 7
2. Ibid.
3. G. Hill, *A History of Cyprus*, I (Cambridge 1949) 251 and n.1
4. Ibid., n.2.
5. D. Michaelides, *Cypriot Mosaics* (Nicosia 1992) 6
6. A. H. S. Megaw, 'Early Christian Byzantine monuments in Cyprus in the light of recent discoveries', *Akten des XI Byz.-Kongress* 1958 (Munchen 1960) 345–351; A. Papageorghiou, 'Η Παλαιοχριστιανική καί Βυζαντινή Αρχαιολογία καί Τέχνη εν Κύπρω κατά τό 1963', *Απόστολος Βαρνάβας* (1964) 3–13; Id., 'L'architecture paléochrétienne de Chypre', *Corso di Cultura sull'arte Ravennate e Byzantina*, (1985) 300; D. Michaelides, ibid., 6–10.
7. Id., ibid., Nos. 34–37, 48
8. A. Papageorghiou, ''Ερευνα εις τόν ναόν του Αγίου Σπυρίδωνος εν Τρεμετουσία', *Κυπριακαί Σπουδαί* 30 (1966) 17–33, esp. 23–29; D. Michaelides, ibid. no. 38; cf. A. H. S. Megaw, 'Byzantine architecture and decoration in Cyprus: metropolitan or provincial', *DOP* 28 (1974) 61; Id., 'Interior decoration in Early Christian Cyprus', *Actes du XVe Congrès International d'Études Byzantines* (Athens 1976) 12.
9. See n.8
10. Preliminary reports in *Bulletin of the University Museum, Philadelphia*, (hereafter *UPMB*), 7.2 (1938) 4–10, pl.III; 13.3, (1948) 12 (J. F. Daniel); 14.4, (1950) 27-37, pl.VII (De Coursey Fales); G. H. McFadden, *AJA*, 55, (1951) 167; D. Soren and J. James, *Kourion, A Search for a Lost Roman City* (New York 1985) 20-23.
11. A. H. S. Megaw, *DOP* (n.8), 60 and n.5
12. T. B. Mitford, *The Inscriptions of Kourion* (Philadelphia 1971) 353–354 and n.202; I. Nicolaou, 'The Epigraphic Evidence', *An Archaeological Guide to Ancient Kourion at Akrotiri Penninsula*, ed. H. W. Swiny (Nicosia 1982) 97
13. T. B. Mitford, ibid., 356–357 and n.204; (D. C. Fales, ibid., PL.VII; D. Soren and J. James, ibid., 21, for photos); cf. R. S. Bagnall and Th. Drew-Bear, 'Documents from Kourion: a review article', *Phoenix*, 27, (1973) 239–241.
14. Ibid.
15. *LSJ* s.v.
16. A. H. S. Megaw, *DOP* (n.8), 59.
17. T. B. Mitford, ibid., n.203; I. Nicolaou, ibid., 97.
18. Ibid., 355 and n.1
19. *LSJ* s.v.
20. Ibid., s.v.
21. Cf. R. S. Bagnall, and Th. Drew-Bear, ibid., 238-239
22. J. F. Daniel, ibid., 30-32; D. C. Fales, ibid., 33

2

Two Syriac Translations of the Life of Epiphanios

Sebastian Brock

Any scholar who writes about the great basilica at Salamis/Constantia is likely to have occasion to cite the Life of Epiphanios[1], where a description is provided of the inception of the building works during Epiphanios' episcopacy.

The Greek Life of Epiphanios consists of two main parts, the first of which (*BHG*596; chapter 1–69) purports to be by Epiphanios' Arab disciple John. John takes the narrative up to the time shortly after Epiphanios' consecration as bishop of Constantia. In the course of this first part we are told (ch.54) that when some Palestinian bishops had, at an earlier date, wanted to make Epiphanios a bishop they sent a young monk by name of Polybios to fetch him; Polybios, however, was persuaded by Epiphanios to abandon his mission and stay on with him as a disciple. It is this Polybios who is entrusted by John on his deathbed with some notebooks, with the help of which he is to take on the story from where John had had to leave it. Thus it is in the part attributed to Polybios (*BHG*597; chs 70–127) that we learn of Epiphanios' building activities (chs 73, 83), his visit to bishop John of Jerusalem, during which he surreptitiously sells off John's best silver dinner service for the benefit of the poor (ch 77–80), and his journey to Constantinople and encounter with the empress Eudoxia in connection with the case of John Chrysostom (chs 112–17). This second part of the Life is followed by an exchange of letters (*BHG* 598–9; chs 128, 129–32) between Polybios and Epiphanios' successor as bishop of Constantia, Sabinos. This gives the hagiographer the opportunity to provide information on Epiphanios' funeral, which Polybios had missed, having previously (in obedience to Epiphanios' instructions) set out for Egypt, where he ended up as bishop of Rhinokouroura.

Although the *Life*, which probably dates from the fifth/sixth[2] century, is not a reliable historical document, Sabinos is independently known, from a passing mention in the *Acts of the Council of Ephesus* (431),[3] to have been Epiphanios' successor, whereas no mention elsewhere of a Polybios, bishop of Rhinokouroura, is to be found.

The Greek text of the *Life*, lacking the final letter from Sabinos to Polybios, was first published in 1622 by Petavius (D. Petau), and then reprinted in vol. 41 of Migne's *Patrologia Graeca*.[4] Although the final letter had been known since 1558 in a Latin translation made by Aloysius Lipomanus, it was not until 1833 that the Greek was made available for the first time.[5] A much needed new edition of the entire Greek text has recently been prepared by C. Rapp and should be published in the near future.

Besides the Greek text, preserved in eleven extant Greek manuscripts (of which the oldest may go back to the ninth century), four oriental translations are known: an Arabic version in several manuscripts, of which the oldest is dated 885;[6] an extensive Coptic fragment, probably of the seventh century, covering most of the first and second parts;[7] two Georgian manuscripts, one (dated 981/3) containing all four parts, and the other with only Sabinos' Letter to Polybios;[8] and two Syriac manuscripts, which provide the occasion for the present contribution.

Both Syriac manuscripts are today in the British Library, having reached there last century from the Syrian Monastery in the Nitrian Desert. Both are dated by Wright in his *Catalogue* to the ninth century,[9] which means that they are at least contemporary with, if not earlier than, the earliest Greek manuscript.[10] Since the Syriac translation, or rather, as we shall see, translations, will belong to at least a couple of centuries earlier, this means that these manuscripts are potentially of considerable interest as witnesses to a form of the Greek text prior to that exhibited by the earliest Greek manuscripts.

British Library Add. 14657, consisting of 25 folios, contains only the *Life of Epiphanios*, with the contents distributed as follows:

ff.1v - 15r: Part I, by John;
15r - 25r: Part II, by Polybios;[11]
25r: Letter of Polybios to Sabinos;
25rv: Letter of Sabinos to Polybios.

The first and last folios have been written in a much more cramped style, though probably the copyist was the same person who wrote the rest of the manuscript.[12] The significance of this curious feature will emerge below.

The second manuscript, British Library Add. 17192, contains a great variety of monastic texts, notably Evagrios and Mark the Hermit; what had seemed to be an otherwise unknown work by Gregory of Nyssa, on Poverty, has recently been shown to be an abbreviated version of one of the monastic discourses by Philoxenos of Mabbug.[13] The only other piece of hagiography in the manuscript is the *Life of John of Rome.* In contrast to Add. 14657, Add. 17192 provides only the first part of Epiphanios' Life, on ff. 231v-254v.

Comparison of the two manucripts in the first part, to which they are both witnesses, at once throws up a remarkable feature. For the first three and a half chapters both manuscripts attest what is basically the same translation; variations between them are of a minor character. From about the middle of chapter 4 onwards, however, the two manuscripts part company and each goes its own way, Add. 14657 providing a rather close rendering of the Greek text, and Add. 17192 giving what is generally a slightly abbreviated paraphrase. Now the point at which the two texts start to diverge comes in Add. 14657 precisely at the transition from folio 1v to 2r. Since the first folio of this manuscript (and above all its last five lines) has been written in a much more cramped style than the rest of the manuscript, it is an obvious deduction that the manuscript from which the scribe was copying lacked the opening paragraphs, and so the scribe had to provide them at a subsequent point from another source. If we look at the style of translation on f.1 of Add. 14657 it becomes clear that, in contrast to the situation in the main part of the manuscript (i.e. folios 2–24), the rendering is much freer, and every now and then abbreviated.[14] In other words, the scribe of Add. 14657 copied the *Life* primarily from a source that contained a rather close rendering of the Greek text, but supplied the missing opening from another manuscript, which happened to provide a much freer translation; this freer translation we have preserved in full for the first part in Add. 17192.

In Add. 14657 the final folio, containing the end of chapter 123 onwards, to the conclusion of the two letters, is also written in the same cramped fashion as the first folio. This suggests that the scribe of Add. 14657 copied this page at the same time as folio 1, and that the manuscript from which he was copying had lost its ending as well as its opening; to remedy this situation it is likely that he again had recourse to his subsidiary source; confirmation that this was indeed the case comes when one observes that the translation of these final chapters abandons the rather literal rendering of the main part of the *Life* in this manuscript, and takes on a much more abbreviated character (above all in chapters 124–7). We are thus usefully provided with evidence that the more paraphrastic translation once spanned the entire *Life*, and not just the first part (as in Add. 17192). As will become clear below, this freer rendering was the earlier of the two translations, and the more literal one is a revision of this. In order to provide samples of the two different Syriac translations I select chapters 1–5, 17 and 55–6. Chapters 1–5 cover the first folio and beginning of the second in Add. 14657: on the first folio (i.e.sections 1–4a of my

paper) the translation will be seen to be very close to that of Add. 17192, whereas from the beginning of folio 2 of Add. 14657 (section 4b onwards) the two translations diverge. In chapter 17 the alleged author John speaks of his baptism by Hilarion, while in chapters 55–6 we hear of Epiphanios' visit to Paphos to see Hilarion.

In order to facilitate comparison of the two Syriac versions the following typographical conventions are employed:

(+) denotes omission in Syriac of material present in Greek

boldface denotes additional material in Syriac, absent from Greek.

<u>underlined</u> (in 4b–5, 17,55–6) denotes wording in common between Add. 17192 and 14657.

Since Add. 14657 in these sections is a very close translation of the Greek, the material in ordinary typeface in 17192 here will be paraphrasing the Greek.

(a) Chapters 1–5

Add. 17192 and 14657:[15]

1. The blessed Epiphanios **was from the people of the Jews**; he was born in a village belonging to the *chora* of Eleutheropolis, at a distance of three miles from the town, and located in the region of Phoinike. This man's father was a farm-worker, while his mother wove linen. (+) He also had a sister, whose name was Kallitropos, **which means 'beautiful in manners'.** It happened that his father departed from the world, and Epiphanios was left at the age of ten with his mother.

2. His mother was hard pressed (to find) sustenance for herself and her children, for they were poor in their livelihood. Now they had an unruly colt, the offspring of an ass, and his mother said to Epiphanios, "My son, seeing that we are lacking (+) in provisions, take this colt and go (+) and sell it, so that **from its price** we can meet the requirements for our sustenance". The young man said, "Mother, you know the unruly nature of this donkey. When I bring it to be sold, people will see its unruliness and they will gather round in that place and bring me to an evil end, (+) in accordance with the law". His mother says to Epiphanios, "Go, my son; may the God of our Fathers, of Abraham, Isaac and Jacob, grant to the donkey a peaceful disposition so that we may be provided for out of its price".

Epiphanios, having called upon God who gave grace to Moses to perform mighty miracles in the sight of Pharaoh, set off in full obedience to his mother.

3. (+) When he stood the colt (there), **ready to be sold**, it was very calm. (+) A man came along, a Jewish merchant named Jacob, and spoke to Epiphanios. "Do you want to sell me this donkey?" He said to him, "Yes,

father; that was why I brought it here". Jacob said to Epiphanios, "To which religion do you belong?" He said, "I am a Jew". The man said, "Since we are from the same people, let us not introduce sin into our midst, but seeing that we belong to a just God, let us settle fairly on a price for this colt, so that you do not lose out, and I do not get defrauded—lest we bring a curse upon ourselves and anger God over this matter. Rather, let us bring a blessing upon ourselves, for (Scripture) has said, 'Blessed is he whom I shall bless, and cursed is he who curses'"[16]

Once Epiphanios had heard these words from Jacob he was greatly afraid and said, "I do not want to sell you this colt". The man said to him, "What is the reason, my son?" He told him, "Because it is unruly. **I should tell you**, father, that our home is in bitter affliction: I have a mother and a sister, and my father has departed this world. My mother's intructions were that this donkey be sold, to provide for the needs of our sustenance. But now I have heard from you that it is wrong for someone to cause his fellow to go short, and I am afraid of God, lest God destroy me as a result of your curse which will come upon me".' When Jacob heard this **apologia** from the boy, he was astonished. He produced three *darics* and gave them to him, saying these words by way of intruction, "My son, take this blessing; go to your mother and stock up provisions for your household. And take this colt as well: if it ceases from its evil disposition, let it stay in your household, but if it remains unruly, get rid of it, lest it should happen that it causes the death of one of you".
4a. When Epiphanios heard these words, taking the three *darics* from Jacob he led off the donkey with him as well. He went home to his mother, but when he was (still) a mile away from the village, a man who was a Christian, named Kleobios, met him and said, "Are you selling this donkey, my son?" "No, father", he replied. The blessed man again said to Epiphanios, "If you (are willing to) sell it, take its value and give it to me". While they were speaking to one another, the colt, with a violent movement (typical) of its unruly nature, pushed Epiphanios, knocking him to the ground; it then dashed off and left the road.[17] [Add. 14657 folio 2 begins here, and at this point the two manuscripts provide different translations].

Add. 17192:

4b. As a result of the violence of the fall, the boy was hurt in his thigh and could not get up. Instead, there he lay crying bitterly on the ground. Kleobios approached Epiphanios and took hold of his thigh in the place where he had been hurt and he made the sign of the cross over it (lit. sealed it) three times **and the pain fled**—whereupon (Epiphanios) stood up healed. The blessed man approached the donkey (+) and said to it, "Because you sought to kill your master, I tell you in the name of our Lord Jesus who was crucified, do not come any closer from where you are". At these words

it collapsed on the ground and died.[18]

Epiphanios asked Kleobios, saying to him, "Father, who is this Jesus who was crucified, whose name can effect these things?" He replied, saying, "Jesus is the Son of God, whom the Jews crucified". Now Epiphanios was afraid that the blessed man might realize that he was a Jew.

Kleobios went on his way, while Epiphanios returned home to his mother, who received him with great joy. He related to her what had happened to him as a result of that bad donkey.
5. After a short time had passed his mother said to him, "My son, our fields are uncultived" (+). Now they had a little land which his father used to cultivate very diligently **while he was alive**, and from it they obtained what they needed for their sustenance. His mother says to Epiphanios, "Let us hand over the land to someone who can cultivate it. As for you, go to some God-fearing man and be learning a craft, one from which, as you work, you can sustain yourself from it and provide me and your sister with provisions."

Now there was a Jew, a teacher of the Law, in that town, an admirable God-fearing man, (living) in accordance with the Law of Moses, (+) who had known his father and mother as well as Epiphanios and his sister. He owned **farm-workers and** lands in the village where Epiphanios had been born, and one day he went out to inspect them. On entering the village he called on Epiphanios' mother and said to her, "Woman, give me your son, so that he may be a son for me, and you and your daughter will be provided for out of my household **all the days of your lives.**" On hearing these words from the scribe Epiphanios' mother was extremely happy: she took the boy and gave him over to the man to be a son to him. Now the scribe's name was Tryphon, and he had an only daughter, whom he sought to marry off to Epiphanios.

Add. 14657 = Greek:

4b. Epiphanios, as a result of the violence of the donkey's unruliness, was hurt in his thigh, and lay sprawled on the ground, weeping bitterly and unable to get up. Kleobios approached Epiphanios, and took hold of him by his thigh, the place that had been injured by the unruliness of the donkey. He made the sign of the cross over it (lit. sealed it) three times, and straightway he stood up, not harmed in any bad way. Kleobios said to the donkey, "Be off, I tell you, donkey full of every kind of unruliness; because you wanted to bring about the death of your master, in the name of Jesus Christ who was crucified, you shall not henceforth move away from this place." At Kleobios' words, the donkey straightway collapsed and died. Epiphanios asked Kleobios. "My father, who is the Jesus who was crucified, that such things should take place in his name?" Kleobios answered and said to Epiphanios, "This Jesus is the Son of God whom the Jews crucified". Now Epiphanios was afraid to reveal to Kleobios that he was a Jew. Kleobios went on his way, while Epiphanios returned to his mother. On seeing him his mother received him with joy, and Epiphanios related to his mother all that had happened to him as a result of the unruliness of the donkey.

5. When some time had passed, his mother said to Epiphanios, "My son, [...][19] and we have no produce from it to comfort us." Now their piece of land was small, and his father had laboriously used to cultivate it, gathering from it a small crop. His mother said to him, "Let us give this piece of land to a man who is a farmer; as for you, go to a God-fearing man and learn a craft, from which you will be enabled to sustain our lives with bread, adequately for both me and your sister". Now there was Jew, a teacher of the Law in Eleutheropolis, an admirable man, a God-fearer (who lived) in accordance with the Law of Moses. This man possessed lands in the village where Epiphanios had been born, and he knew his father and mother, as well as Epiphanios and his sister. Having gone out to inspect his lands this man said to Epiphanios' mother, "Woman, are you willing to give me your son as a son (to me)? (If so,) your requirements, and your daughter's, will be provided from my household". On hearing this from that scribe. Epiphanios' mother was very happy. She took Epiphanios and readily(?) gave him over to the scribe (to be his) son. Now the name of that scribe was Tryphon, and he had an only daughter, whom he wanted to marry off to Epiphanios.

(b) Chapter 17

Add 17192:

17. I, the writer who has written these words, was one of these men. Remaining behind with him (sc. Epiphanios), I was instructed by him (+). After we had lived in that cell for six months the blessed Epiphanios took me and we went to the great Hilarion, to his monastery. (+) We spent three days there, and he asked him to baptize me, seeing that he (sc. Hilarion) held the priestly rank. (+) So the blessed Hilarion baptized me (+), and we stayed there another ten days. The brethren were urging Epiphanios to remain with them and live with them, but he did not wish to do so. Instead, he took me and we returned to that former location.

Add. 14657 = Greek:

17. Now I, who am one of them, stayed behind with Epiphanios and I was instructed by him in the word of truth; and I lived with him, passing a period of six months. Epiphanios led me off and we went to the monastery, to the great Hilarion. And when all the brethren saw Epiphanios they rejoiced greatly. We remained in the monastery for three days, and Epiphanios urged the great Hilarion to give me the seal of Christ, seeing that Hilarion had been held worthy of the rank of priesthood. The great Hilarion therefore took me and instructed me in the entire service (*akolouthia*);

and he baptized me in the name of the Father, Son and Holy Spirit. We remained with them for ten days, and the brethren were urging Epiphanios that we should live in that place with them, I and he. But he did not wish to do so, wanting again to live in that same place where he was previously living.

(c) Chapters 55–6

Add. 17192:

55. (+) That night we left to go to Jerusalem, taking with us Polybios. We went off, and entering Jerusalem we worshipped the Cross of our Saviour. We stayed there three days. Epiphanios said to us, "Come, my children, let us go and receive a blessing from our great father Hilarion, for I have heard that his abode is on the island of Cyprus (+)".

56. Having gone down to Caesarea we arrived at the harbour where we found a boat from Cyprus, from the town called Paphos. Epiphanios was questioning the master of the boat concerning Hilarion. (+) The man told him, "He is in a cave near the town of Paphos." On hearing this, and learning that the boat was near to that place, Epiphanios and I got on board. That night we set off by sea and we reached Cyprus. On our entering the blessed Hilarion's presence he received us with great joy. We stayed with him for two months.[20] (+)Epiphanios made the judgment in himself to move away from that place. Hilarion said to him, "My son, where is it you wish to go?". He replied, "To Ascalon and Gaza. and from there to the desert". The blessed man said to him, "Not so! Rather, go to the town of Salamis, for it is there that you ought to live". Epiphanios however did not submit to Hilarion's words, and he (Hilarion) said to him again, "Go where I told you, and do not argue, lest a storm encounter you at sea".

Add. 14657 = Greek:

55. Epiphanios therefore took me and Polybios (ms Qolybios!) that night and we left the monastery and went to Jerusalem to worship (the source of) our life, that is, the honoured Cross. We entered and stayed in the city for three days. And Epiphanios said to me and to Polybios, "Come, my children, let us go to Cyprus and receive a blessing from our great father Hilarion: for I have heard concerning him that he is in Cyprus". And God guided and brought Epiphanios to Cyprus.

56. We went down to Caesarea and found a boat there which was going on the home journey, from the town of Paphos, which is in the island of Cyprus. Epiphanios questioned the master of the boat concerning the great Hilarion and where he was living. He announced to him, telling him that he was living in a cave on the outskirts of Paphos, and that the boat was going there, to Paphos.

That night, then, we got on board and set sail for Paphos. Once we had left the ship we asked for, and came to, the great Hilarion. As we entered there was great joy at our meeting each other. We stayed with him in that place for two days. Hilarion had a great deal of toil and trouble as a result of those who thronged to him. When Epiphanios had decided to leave Paphos, Hilarion said to Epiphanios, "Where are you going, my son?". Epiphanios said to Hilarion, "To Ascalon and Gaza, and from these to the desert." Hilarion said to Epiphanios, "Go to Salamis, my son, and you will find a place to live there." Epiphanios however did not want to listen to Hilarion's words. Hilarion again said to Epiphanios, "I told you, my son, it is right that you should go there: there you shall live, so do not argue against my words lest you incur some peril at sea."

If we compare the characteristics of the translation in sections 1–4a (the same in both manuscripts) with the two translations beginning at 4b, it soon becomes clear that the single translation preserved for 1–4a accords in style with that of Add.17192 from 4b onwards. The following are some of the more noteworthy features:

(a) in 1–4 there is frequent rephrasing and reordering of the Greek, e.g.

1 Greek: Ἐπιφάνιος γένος μὲν ἦν Φοινίκων τῆς περιοικίδος Ἐλευθεροπόλεως, ἀπὸ σημείων τριῶν τῆς αὐτῆς πόλεως ὑπάρχων ἀπὸ κτήματος.

Add. 17192 = Add. 14657: The blessed Epiphanios was from the people of the Jews. He was born in a village belonging to the chora of Eleutheropolis, at a distance of three miles from the town, and located in the region of Phoinike.

Exactly the same sort of thing occurs in Add. 17192 later on, where Add. 14657 conforms closely to the Greek, e.g.

55 Greek = Add. 14657: Τῇ οὖν νυκτὶ ἐκείνῃ λαβὼν Ἐπιφάνιος ἐμὲ καὶ τὸν Πολύβιον, ἐξήλθομεν ἐκ τοῦ μοναστηρίου καὶ ἐπορευθῆμεν ἐν Ἱεροσολύμοις τοῦ προσκυνῆσαι τὴν ζωὴν ἡμῶν τὸν τίμιον σταυρόν.

Add. 17192: That night we left to go to Jerusalem, taking with us Polybios. We went off, and entering Jerusalem we worshipped the Cross of our Saviour.

The same feature can be observed in the text on the final folio of Add. 14657.

(b) In sections 1–4a there are a number of short omissions and additions, just as in Add. 17192 (but not Add. 14657) from 4b onwards. These can be readily located typographically from the sample translations above, where (+) denotes the omission in Syriac of a phrase or sentence in the Greek, while bold face denotes added material in the Syriac. Omissions and additions of this sort again recur in Add. 14657 on the final folio of that manuscript.

(c) In sections 1–4a, where verbs of saying occur, the subject and indirect object in the Syriac have often been altered from those found in the Greek, e.g.

2 Greek: Epiphanios said to his mother
Add. 17192 = Add. 14657: The young man said

3 Greek: Jacob said to Epiphanios
Add. 17192 = Add. 14657: The man said to him.

The same phenomenon continues to occur in Add. 17192 later on (but not in Add. 14657, which adheres closely to the Greek over this matter), e.g.

4b Greek = Add. 14657: Kleobios answered and said to Epiphanios
Add. 17192: He replied saying

56 Greek = Add. 14657: Hilarion again said to Epiphanios
Add. 17192: The blessed man said to him.

(d) In sections 1–4a the epithet 'blessed' is several times added (1, 4a); it likewise occurs in Add. 17192 (but not Add. 14657) in the sample sections 17, 56, as well as often elsewhere in that manuscript. The added epithet is also to be found in Add. 14657 on its final folio, e.g.

130 Greek: τοῦ ὁσίου πατρός
Add. 14657: the blessed man

132 Greek: ἐπὶ τῆς θήκης
Add. 14657: + of the blessed man.

(e) In section 1 the name of Epiphanios' sister, Kallitropos, is glossed 'which means "beautiful in manners"'. The glossing of Greek names can also be found elsewhere in Add. 17192, e.g. 49 '(Hierax), which means "falcon"'; 63 '(Drakon), which means "dragon"'. Similarly on the last folio of Add. 14657 we have: 128 '(Kalliopas), which means "handsome"'.

(f) In section 3, νομίσματα is translated 'darics', which conforms with Add. 17192 in sections 63–4, against Add. 14657 ('denarii').

While the translation in Add. 17192 remains paraphrastic from 4b onwards, in Add. 14657 ff.2–24 it conforms very closely with the Greek. Since there is, nonetheless, quite a lot of phraseology in common (as will have been readily seen from the underlined passages in the sample translations above), it is evident that the two translations must be related, and not independent. This leaves us with two possibilities: either the translation in Add. 17192 is an abbreviating rephrasing of that in Add. 14657, or Add. 14657 represents a revision, on the basis of the Greek, of an earlier translation preserved in Add. 17192. Everything would seem to point to the latter as being the correct interpretation of the evidence. This is suggested above all by the fact that Add. 17192 and 14657 on occasions, each represent a different Greek text (a good example occurs in section 55; see note 20). If the translation in Add. 17192 was rephrasing that in Add. 14657 this situation would be inexplicable, whereas if Add. 14657 represents a revision of an earlier translation, preserved in Add. 17192, then there is no difficulty in explaining how this could have come about.

If, then, Add. 17192 represents the earlier translation, can anything be said of its date or place of origin? A combination of several small details suggest that this original translation can hardly be earlier than the sixth century.[21] And since most revisions of earlier Syriac translations from Greek belong to the seventh century, it would seem entirely reasonable to allocate the revision preserved in Add. 14657 to that century as well.

Unfortunately there are no such pointers as far as the place of origin of the two translations is concerned. The fact that in Add. 17192 the true authorship of a text by Philoxenos of Mabbug has been disguised, attributing it to Gregory of Nyssa, might possibly suggest that the manuscript is of Melkite origin, in which case a south Syrian or Palestinian location for the original translation would be plausible (but by no means necessary).[22] In the case of the revision, it might at first sight seem tempting to try and link this with another work of revision which is known to have taken place in Cyprus in the early seventh century, namely that of Paul bishop of Edessa, who revised the sixth-century Syriac translation of Gregory of Nazianzos' homilies in 623/4 in Cyprus, having fled thither during the Persian occupation of his see.[23] However, the style of the two revisions is very different when one examines them in detail, and so we are left with no justification for suggesting that the revision of earlier Syriac *Life of Epiphanios* was undertaken by Syriac-speakers in Cyprus.

Though the places of origin for the Syriac translation and its subsequent revision remain unknown, the dates suggested above for the two undertakings seem reasonably assured, which means that our two surviving witnesses, Add. 17192 + Add. 14657, ff. 1, 25 for the original translation, and Add. 14657, ff.2–24 for the revision, clearly deserve to be taken into account[24] in establishing the Greek text of the *Life* of one of Cyprus' most celebrated saints.

Oriental Institute, Oxford

NOTES

1. E.g. A. H. S. Megaw, 'Byzantine architecture and decoration in Cyprus: metropolitan or provincial?', *DOP* 28, (1974) 61–2.

2. C. Rapp, *The Vita of Epiphanius of Salamis—an Historical and Literary Study*, D. Phil. Thesis Oxford, 1991, I, 100–102, 214, argues for a mid fifth-century date. I am most grateful to Dr. Rapp for kindly providing me with a copy of her thesis. See now also her 'Epiphanius of Salamis: the Church Father as Saint', in A. A. M. Bryer and G. S. Georghallides (eds), *The Sweet Land of Cyprus* (Nicosia 1993) 167–87; and especially 178.

3. *ACO*, I.V, 359. Since we learn from this passage that Sabinos' successor Troilos had recently died, the inscription (*SEG* 20, (1964) 259) mentioning, along with bishop Photeinos, the 33rd year of Sabinos' ἀρχιερωσύνη must refer to the second bishop of Constantia of that name, who features in a post-Chalcedonian document of 457, *ACO* II. V, 23 (The Photeinos of the inscription will be Photeinos bishop of Kytrea who was present at the Council of Chalcedon; cf *ACO* II.II.II, 77). The revelant episcopal lists can be found in G. Fedalto, *Hierarchia Ecclesiastica Orientalis* II (Padua 1988) 875–88; his list for Cyprus, however, ignores the epigraphic evidence, e.g. of bishop Ploutarchos of Constantia in the early seventh century, for whose building inscriptions see T. B. Mitford 'New inscriptions from early Christian Cyprus', *Byzantion* 20, (1950) 116–25; see also note 22 below. What may be an acclamation of Epiphanios at Salamis can be found in T. B. Mitford and I. K. Nicolaou, *The Greek and Latin Inscriptions of Salamis*, Salamis 6 (Nicosia 1974) 84 no. 55.

4. Cols 24–113.

5. A. Mai, *Scriptorum Veterum Nova Collectio* 7 (Rome 1833) 178-80; the final letter also features in G. Dindorf, *Epiphanii Episcopi Constantiae Opera* I (Leipzig 1859) xxxi–xxxv.

6. Vatican, Arabic 71, ff.3r–40r. This contains parts I–II together with an abbreviation of parts III–IV, (Information kindly provided by Kate Leeming). Some other, later, manuscripts are listed by G. Graf, *Geschichte der christlichen arabischen Literatur*, I, Studi e Testi 118 (Rome 1944) 358.

7. T. Orlandi, 'Les papyrus coptes du Musée Egyptien de Turin', *Le Muséon* 87, (1974) 126 (Codex XV); Rapp, n.2, II, 33–4.

8. The complete text (Sinai, Georgian 6 = Tsagareli 71) is described by G. Garitte, *Catalogue des manuscrits littéraires géorgiens du Mont Sinai*, (Corpus Scriptorum Christianorum Orientalium 165, Subsidia 9 [Louvain 1956]) 16–18; he notes there that Part IV alone is in Jerusalem, Georgian 3. The Arabic and Georgian texts are both of Palestinian provenance.

9. W. Wright, *Catalogue of the Syriac Manuscripts in the British Museum Acquired since the Year 1838*, II (London 1871) 780 (Add. 17192); III (London 1872) 1150 (Add. 14657).

10. Athos, Vatopedi gr. 84, which has variously been dated between the ninth and eleventh centuries.

11. Single folios have been lost between the present f. 11 and f. 12, and f. 19 and f. 20 (with the loss of ch. 51 (end) to 53 (mid), and ch. 93 (end) to 97 (mid)). On folio 14 a tear in the middle of the page has resulted in the loss of the end of chapter 64 and the middle of chapter 66, while on folio 17 another tear at the top of the page involves the loss of the end of chapter 77 and the beginning of 80.

12. Wright (n.8), III, 1150, held that folios 1 and 25 were written by a later hand; this seem to me unlikely.

13. See M. Parmentier, 'Pseudo-Gregory of Nyssa's Homily on Poverty', *Aram* 5 (1993) 401–26.

14. See below for the evidence.

15. The translation is from Add. 17192; it does not seem worth indicating here the few minor variations in Add. 14657 (apart from that mentioned in note 17).

16. cf. Gen. 12:3,27:29 (not an exact quotation).

17. Add. 14657 (at the very end of f.1v) has a slightly different wording here: 'the colt reared up, in its unruliness, against Epiphanios, threw him on the ground, kicked him and left the road for (lit. in) the fields'.

18. The words 'on the ground', absent from Add. 14657, are nevertheless in the Greek: this is one of the very rare cases where Add. 17192 = Greek against Add. 14657 (possibly the words have fallen out in Add. 14657).

19. The text in Add. 14657 is corrupt at this point.

20. Instead of 'months' (so most Greek manuscripts), Add.14657 has 'days'.

21. E.g the use of the Greek loanwords μάλιστα (38) and συντυχία (38), neither of which is found in Syriac writers before the sixth century.

22. In passing it is worth recalling that Philoxenos of Mabbug's nephew, Philoxenos of Doulichion, became Chalcedonian some time after 532 and ended up in Cyprus as archbishop (his high rank is attested by an inscription): see C. Hadjipsaltis, 'Un archévêque inconnu de Chypre: Philoxène (VIᵉ siècle)', *Byzantion* 31 (1961) 215-6, and 'Εἰδήσεις ἱστορικαὶ περὶ τοῦ Ἀρχιεπισκόπου Κύπρου Φιλόξενο', *Κυπριακαὶ Σπουδαί* 27 (1963) 76–74. There is no reason for supposing, however, that Philoxenos of Doulichion was the person responsible for introducing some of his uncle's works to a Melkite readership, let alone for sponsoring, once he had arrived in Cyprus, a Syriac translation of the *Life of Epiphanius.*

23. See my *The Syriac Version of the Pseudo-Nonnus Mythological Scholia* (Cambridge 1971) 28–30.

24. As indeed they are in the forthcoming edition by Claudia Rapp. It should be noted that the chapter numbering of her edition (rather than that of *PG*) has been adopted in this article.

3

The Propriety of Peter. On the Nature and Authenticity of the Bryn Athyn Apostle Plaque

Anthony Cutler

Like the reputation of scholars, that of the objects that they study is subject to a pendular motion. As against, say, the often uncritical, late nineteenth-century acceptance of works that we now know to be forgeries,[1] the late twentieth century has witnessed a rush to expose as modern creations objects that are, in fact, 'good' but which fail in one way or another to conform to preconceived iconographical and/or stylistic limits on such works.[2] The note that follows, devoted to an ivory that has been known since (at least) 1897 and which has recently come under attack,[3] might prove of interest to the scholar who made so fertile a use of Roman and early Byzantine examples in this medium when, together with Ernest Hawkins, he published the early sixth-century church of Lythrankomi and its mosaics.[4] The plaque in question represents St. Peter, identifiable by the key that he holds in his left hand, striding to the right and, with his right hand, grasping a long cross that is planted on a mound diagrammatically carved with the four rivers of paradise (PLATE 3.1). This action is set between and in front of a pair of grooved columns supporting 'a conch with an exaggeratedly scalloped edge'.[5]

Many scholars have written about the object but few seem to have examined it directly, an omission epitomized by the lack of information concerning the four cuttings toward the left edge of its reverse and the absence of any photograph of this side, here published for the first time (PLATE 3.2). These incisions, which do not perforate the fabric, bear no relation to the way

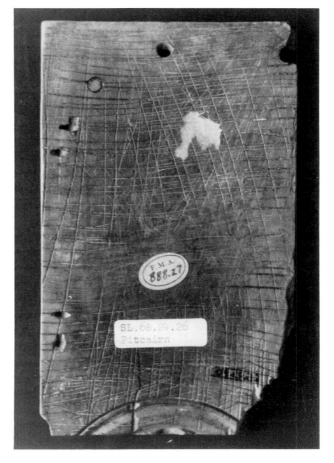

PLATE 3.1: *Bryn Athyn, Pa., Glencairn Museum. Peter ivory (photo: author)*

PLATE 3.2: *Reverse of* PLATE 3.1 *(photo: author)*

in which late antique diptychs were joined by means of hinges let into the *edges* of leaves,[6] and almost certainly represent a secondary (or rather, as we shall see, a tertiary) use of the plaque. This re-use is perhaps to be associated with the striations intended to help the reverse adhere to an alien surface (such as a bookcover). At any rate, nothing on this face requires that the plaque originally had an 'adjoining wing'.[7] Nor, given the crudeness of these marks, do they suggest the hand of 'uno scultore dell' 800'[8] aiming to lend an air of antiquity to his new creation. As opposed to the neglect of these later cuttings, the presence of a portion of a roundel, preserved as a series of concentric arcs at the bottom of the reverse, has been noted and the plaque consequently interpreted as the re-used leaf of a consular diptych.[9] This is unlikely. First, those consular diptychs that do make use of roundels[10] never display an uncarved space of some thirteen centimetres above or below such medallions. Instead, we are here confronted with a 'trial piece', a reject turned to secondary use. What went wrong we shall never know for the problem evidently occurred in that area of the plaque which originally lay below the surviving arcs. These arcs, moreover, are in a finished state and have not been levelled, further evidence that our plaque was cut from a larger, unfinished artefact, but not one that had been planed down.[11]

If such technical niceties are tiresome, they yet help to establish the history of the Bryn Athyn ivory, a past which, for all that it lacks in persons, places and dates, extends backwards through a series of uses[12] to which human beings put an ancient creation. How far this past reverts can, with some greater degree of precision, be assessed by consideration of the front of our plaque, for it is here that the craftsman's original deliberations and his audience's presuppositions came together on the field of shared experience. This experience is normally treated by art historians under two heads, the style in which the piece was carved and the iconography in which the beholder's expectations were answered. I shall deal with these discrete events as if they were one, since only if they can be seen to converge can the mentalities responsible for both the object's creation and its initial employment be recognized as socially entwined and chronologically concurrent. Yet in addition to this desirable coincidence, there is another factor, the techniques employed in the plaque's production, that must be taken into account, if only because this allows us to define the age and nature of the arena in which maker and user met. In this respect, the single most striking aspect of the Bryn Athyn apostle is the skill with which the carver exploited the natural properties of his raw material in order to flesh out the effects that he intended, effects to which the

PLATE 3.3: *Detail of* PLATE 3.1 *(photo: author)*

PLATE 3.4: *Detail of* PLATE 3.1 *(photo: author)*

ivory's purchaser may surely be presumed to have responded. It goes without saying that the domain of craftsmanship is a condition of the content perceived in the object by its beholder; equally, it is prior to the object's style, which is less an inherent characteristic of the individual artefact than an *ex post facto* reaction in the historian's mind and a learned attitude addressed primarily to an object's relation with others of its kind.

Now, like other organic materials, the appearance (though not the structure) of elephant ivory differs from one instance to another as a function both of natural variation and of the way in which a section is cut from a tusk.[13] We may thus infer the craftsman's skill at work in his selection of the material from which he fashioned his plaque as in the means that he employed to serve his own and his client's purposes. Whether we choose to look at the way the grain is used to model Peter's forehead and cheek (PLATE 3.3), the form of his right hand (PLATE 3.4), or the plastic complexities of his tunic and *pallium* (PLATE 3.5), the Bryn Athyn ivory presents not only a choice and an expertise that are alien (to the best of my knowledge) to nineteenth-century ivory carving but firmly grounded in the art of the fifth-sixth centuries. The ellipses that animate the apostle's head attained their apogee in the Archangel ivory in the British Museum (PLATE 3.6),[14] while the cascades of often contrary arcs that enliven the debate between the figure of Peter and the ground from which he and his clothing emerge is found supremely in a well-known, if anonymous, plaque in the Louvre (PLATE 3.7).[15] All three examples exploit to the full the fact that in some sections of some tusks the *lamellae* that represent the fundamental growth patterns of dentine are sufficiently pronounced to be seen as possessing aesthetic qualities in their own right. The evidence for delight in such frozen movements in late antique Italy and Justinianic

Byzantium requires no better witness than the marble revetments of church interiors.

But the argument against forgery need not rest on an account of period taste. What is *lacking* in the Bryn Athyn ivory also testifies to its differences from even the best work of the nineteenth century. First, the absence of true undercutting, a favourite technique achieved with what the Victorians called an 'inside parting-tool'[16] (and, by present-day cabinet-workers, a scorper). Had the plaque been a modern creation the illusion of volume so ingeniously foisted on the apostle's garments (PLATE 3.4), the fronds of the vault above him (PLATE 3.3) and his cross would almost certainly have been achieved by this means rather than by the prodigious investment of time and energy involved in cutting straight back to the ground in a body of relief up to five millimetres deep.[17] It may also be argued that no forger, torn between the desire to make his artifact 'authentic' and the need to make it attractive, would have carved and then abraded portions of the nose and lips (PLATE 3.3) to the point where Peter displays an almost simian aspect. Instead, these areas, by no means the most prominent on the ivory, are shaped by devotion over the *longue durée*, possibly by kissing the holy figure.[18]

Uninformed by unmediated knowledge of our plaque, its indictment has been couched in terms of iconography. The sculptor, it is urged, made a gross mistake in creating a Peter who bears the cross not as a symbol of his martyrdom but as a symbol of Christ.[19] Quite apart from the fact that the cross was a widely venerated symbol of Christ and of the Church until the end of Iconoclasm,[20] the merits of the charge rest entirely upon the assumption that the cross which the apostle touches on the Bryn Athyn ivory is *his* cross. Yet on at least two sarcophagi Peter touches a long cross that is held by Christ as the latter stands upon the

PLATE 3.5: *Detail of* PLATE 3.1 *(photo: author)*

mound from which flow the four rivers.[21] Indeed, the 'inspiration' hypothesized for the Bryn Athyn ivory is a fragment of a sarcophagus 'from which the Christ has been lost, leaving St. Peter and the cross on the hill with the rivers'.[22] Conversely, on other sarcophagi, such as one in Verona (PLATE 3.8),[23] the apostle may shoulder the cross of his martyrdom even while, with Paul, he attends Christ raised on the paradisal mound. Both combinations are thus attested in the fourth and fifth centuries and, in the face of this diversity, there is a certain unconscious arrogance in the postulate that, because no exact analogue exists for the version found on our plaque, it must therefore be modern. Precisely because St. Peter was so widely depicted in late antiquity one would expect considerable variety in his representations. And such expectations are fully rewarded: standing beside Christ, Peter may hold a long cross, as on a slab in Istanbul;[24] Christ may hold such an object, even as he confronts Peter on the ivory 'Passion plaques' in the British Museum;[25] the *crux gemmata*, without an accompanying Christ, may be set on the mound from which the rivers issue as on a silver-gilt paten in St. Petersburg.[26] In other words, the richness of invention in the era in question—one thinks of the originality of the image of the Incarnation in the apse of Lythrankomi, and the incomprehension that it

encountered until it was explicated by Megaw[27]— suggests that, whatever the subject matter, restrictions set by modern scholars on the iconographical fecundity of a period from which they are removed by one and a half millennia may say more about their own limits than about those of the fifth and sixth centuries. Peter imagery in particular was subject to creative substitution and innovation, whether in the fourth century we find him performing a water miracle that supplants Moses striking the rock[28] or, much later, carrying his keys in an unprecedented fashion around his neck.[29] In the face of such mutations, it ill behoves us to equate invention with forgery.

The meaning of the Bryn Athyn plaque may be hard to establish if indeed it was one of a pair or part of a series. As Ševčenko pointed out, the representation of Christ on an adjoining leaf would likely have been superfluous.[30] Yet to limit the possibilities in this way may again be too restrictive. Given the demonstrable closeness in this period between monumental sculpture and ivories—the scallopped conch on our plaque is matched on a late fourth-century sarcophagus in Arles[31]—the evidence of objects carved on a larger scale may be useful. Among frieze sarcophagi the water miracles worked by Peter occur more frequently than any other scenes involving the apostle[32] and here, as on

PLATE 3.6: *London, British Museum. Archangel ivory, detail, head (photo: author)*

PLATE 3.7: *Paris, Louvre. Apostle ivory (photo: courtesy of D. Gaborit-Chopin)*

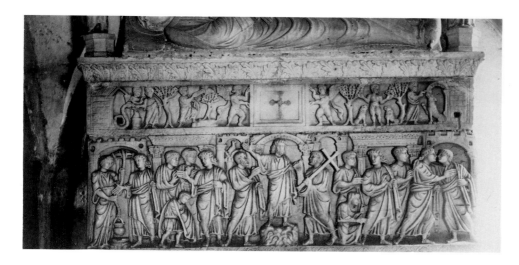

PLATE 3.8: *Verona,
S. Giovanni in Valle.
Sarcophagus 'of SS. Simon
and Judas Thaddeus'
(photo: courtesy of
J.-P. Caillet)*

ivories, serve as antitypes to the *Quellenwunder* of Moses.33 Striking water from the rock, the Jewish patriarch is shown to parallel the acts described in the Petrine apocrypha in which the apostle works his spring miracle and baptizes his guards with its water. In both cases, the rock is cleft and the saving stream issues from it as, in the mid-fifth century, Leo I, the occupant of the Cathedra Petri, was regarded as the issue of the apostle to the Gentiles: Leo was Peter's vicar as Peter was Jesus'.34 Any image of Christ in association with our ivory would be redundant, for the gemmate cross, planted in the mountain from which the rivers flow, is the Lord's sign; and the cross is the image, par excellence, of his Resurrection. It may be that Moses appeared on an 'adjoining wing', but it would be hard to find a more telling glorification of Peter, to whom Christ appeared on the day of his Resurrection (Luke 24:34; I Cor. 15:5), and of his earthly successors. Like the physical fabric of the ivory, the mental process involved in the conceit smacks much more of the fifth than of the nineteenth century.

Pennsylvania State University

NOTES

1. A striking example is the large bone plaque showing Christ enthroned, now in the Museo Civico Medievale at Bologna. On the reception of this object and its exposure as a fake, see A. Cutler, *The hand of the master. Craftsmanship, ivory, and society in Byzantium (9th–11th Centuries)* (Princeton 1994) 64–5 and fig. 71.

2. A characteristic instance is the recent charge against a well-known diptych leaf in the Victoria and Albert Museum: J. M. Eisenberg, 'The Symmachi ivory diptych panel: a nineteenth-century interpretation of a lost original?' *Minerva*, 4:2 (1993) 12–18, and its vindication by D. Kinney, 'A late antique ivory plaque and modern response', *AJA*, 96 (1994) 457–72, and A. Cutler, 'Suspicio Symmachorum', ibid. 473–80.

3. See the study by the lamented I. Nikolajević, 'Un San Pietro inconsueto. La placca d'avorio della Glencairn Foundation, Bryn Athin [*sic*] Penn.' in *Studi in memoria di Giuseppe Bovini*, (Ravenna 1989), ii, 429–41. Since the majority of this paper (429–38) is devoted to a survey of the literature on the Bryn Athyn ivory, and only its last three pages to the argument that the object is a forgery, I ignore all but the essential bibliography in favour of discussion of the question of authenticity.

4. A. H. S. Megaw and E. J. W. Hawkins, *The church of the Panagia Kanakaria at Lythrankomi in Cyprus. Its mosaics and frescoes* (Dumbarton Oaks Studies 14; Washington, D. C. 1977). On ivories, see 65, 88, 93 and notes 195–6, 321, 349, 373, 440.

5. N. P. Ševčenko in K. Weitzmann (ed.), *Age of Spirituality: late antique and early Christian art, third to seventh century* (New York 1979), no. 485, which remains the best description of this face of the ivory. The plaque, Glencairn Museum inv. no. 04 CR36, measures 14.3x9.0cm and has been cut down, probably by no more than a centimetre or two, at the top and sides, where the frame, invariably present on complete late antique and early Byzantine ivories, is lacking. I am grateful to Dr. Ševčenko who was the first to draw my attention to Nikolajević's article.

6. R. Delbrueck, *Die Consulardiptychen und verwandte Denkmäler* (Berlin-Leipzig 1924), 19

7. Ševčenko (n.5).

8. Nikolajević (n.3), 439. That the plaque is much older than the 19th century is further suggested by the contrast between the deep, rust-coloured patina of the reverse and the whiteness of the dentine in a small area where the surface of the reverse has been damaged

9. Eadem, 438, following Ševčenko.

10. Delbrueck (n.6), nos. 16–20, 29–34.

11. The absence of planing and of saw-marks in the vertical plane

of the reverse further shows that we do not have here a 'reduced' consular diptych. The normal thickness of such diptychs is 10mm, while the Bryn Athyn plaque at its thickest (in the area of the central frond above Peter's head [PLATE 3.3]) measures 7mm.

12. This must include the three holes (one now plugged) that puncture the upper part of the plaque to secure its attachment in secondary and/or tertiary use. For examples of later holes driven into the body of plaques (none of them of contested authenticity) see W. F. Volbach, *Elfenbeinarbeiten der Spätantike und des frühen Mittelalters* (3rd edn; Mainz 1976) nos. 5, 19, 21, 31, 36, 41, 45. Instances in which later attachment holes were driven through the frame are of course much more numerous.

13. A. Cutler, *The craft of ivory. Sources, techniques, and uses in the Mediterranean world: AD 200–1400* (Washington, D. C. 1985) 1–19, 37–42.

14. On which see D. H. Wright, 'Justinian and an Archangel', in O. Feld and V. Peschlow (eds.), *Studien zur spätantiken und byzantinischen Kunst Friedrich Wilhelm Deichmann gewidmet* (Mainz 1986) iii, 75–9.

15. Volbach (n.12) no. 123.

16. C. Holtzapfel, *Turning and mechanical manipulation* (London 1864) ii, 517–20.

17. True undercutting was of course extensively used on some late antique ivories. See, e.g., A. Cutler, 'Barberiniana', in *Tesserae. Festschrift für Josef Engemann* (Jahrbuch für Antike und Christentum, Ergänzungsband 18 [1991]) 334 and esp. PLS. 55–6.

18. For this Christian practice, see Cutler, *Hand of the master* (n.1) 25–6. Similar wear seems evidenced by the Peter ivory at Kykko, which Volbach, *Elfenbeinarbeiten*, no. 135, associates with the Bryn Athyn plaque but which I have not examined.

19. Nikolajević (n.3) 439.

20. See the entry 'Cross, cult of the' in *The Oxford Dictionary of Byzantium* (New York 1991) i, 551–3 (R. F. Taft and A. P. Kazhdan).

21. G. Bovini and H. Brandenburg, *Repertorium der christlich-antiken Sarkophagen. I, Rom und Ostia* (Wiesbaden 1967) nos. 57, 671 and pls. 18, 107. These sarcophagi are reproduced by Nikolajević as figs. 2, 3. For Ravennate examples employing variations on the same theme, M. Lawrence, *The sarcophagi of Ravenna* (New York 1945) 34–36 and esp. figs. 1–3. The identification of the base on which Christ stands as a rock rather than, as is customary, a mountain is firmly grounded in literature of the fifth century (Paulinus of Nola). See J.-M. Spieser, 'Remarques complémentaires sur la mosaïque de Osios David', Διεθνὴς Συμπόσιο: Βυζαντινὴ Μακεδονία, 324-1430 μ.Χρ. (Thessaloniki 1995) 295–306.

22. Nikolajević (n.3) 440.

23. G. Stuhlfauth, *Die apokryphen Petrusgeschichten in der altchristlichen Kunst* (Berlin 1925) fig. 1; P. L. Zovatto, *Antichità cristiane di Verona* (Verona 1950) 46–53; and, most recently, J.-P. Caillet and H. N. Loose, *La vie d'éternité. La sculpture funéraire dans l'Antiquité chrétienne* (Paris–Geneva 1990) 62–64, 80–82.

24. A. Grabar, *Sculptures byzantines de Constantinople (IVᵉ–Xᵉ siècle)* (Paris 1963) 129 and pl. XVI.1. See also the relief in Berlin on which a figure identifiable as Peter holds a long cross (A. Effenburger and H.-G. Severin, *Das Museum für Spätantike und Byzantinische Kunst* [Berlin 1992], no. 34). In this healing scene Peter does not hold a key but has the same head-type and costume as on our ivory.

25. Volbach, *Elfenbeinarbeiten* (n.12) no. 116.

26. *Age of Spirituality* (n.5) no. 482 (J. L. Schrader).

27. Megaw and Hawkins, *Panagia Kanakaria* (n.4) 61–79.

28. As on the fourth century glass patera in St Petersburg (P. C. Finney, *The Invisible God. The Earliest Christians on Art* [New York 1994] 284–5 and fig 7.4).

29. K. Weitzmann, *The St. Peter Icon of Dumbarton Oaks* (Washington D.C. 1983). The type recurs among the frescoes of the Peribleptos church in Ohrid.

30. See n.5 supra.

31. Caillet and Loose (n.23) fig. 65. An even closer analogue is found on the so-called Kaiserpriester diptych (Delbrueck, *Consulardiptychen*, no. 57) in Paris.

32. E. Dinkler, 'Die ersten Petrusdarstellungen. Ein archäologischer Beitrag zur Geschichte des Petrusprimates', *Marburger Jahrbuch für Kunstwissenschaft*, 11–12 (1938–39) 22.

33. H. L. Kessler, 'Scenes from the Acts of the Apostles on some early Christian ivories', *Gesta* 18 (1979) 109–19. See also E. S. Malbon, *The Iconography of the Sarcophagus of Junius Bassus* (Princeton 1990) 78–81.

34. E. Dinkler (n.32) 5 and passim.

4

Evidence for a Justinianic garrison behind Thermopylae at the Dhema Pass

John Rosser

Located in the mountains behind Thermopylae (FIG. 4.1), the fortifications at the Dhema Pass (FIG. 4.2; PLATE 4.1*a*) consist of simple walls, quite unsophisticated as compared to the Frankish castle in Paphos, which Peter Megaw and I have excavated. However, their importance was quite considerable, since they guarded the entrance to a natural corridor through central Greece, one that outflanks the coastal route by Thermopylae. That this natural corridor existed and was used in historic times as the easiest and quickest route through central Greece to the Peloponnesos is a thesis argued in the work of the Phokis-Doris Expedition.[1]

Dhema's strategic importance in Late Antiquity has been argued chiefly by Professor W. Cherf, who has analyzed all the available literary evidence for the history of Dhema in Roman times, through to the period of Justinian I.[2] He has used radiocarbon-dates from the lime mortar of these walls (PLATES 4.1*b*, 4.2) to provide a firm chronological framework for their construction. His analysis suggests that the initial work was done in the late fourth century, and refurbished during the reign of Theodosius II (408–50),[3] a conclusion that challenges the nature and extent of

Justinian's program of fortification for Greece as presented by Procopius. However, *De Aedificiis* must be read critically, and some of its attributions taken with a grain of salt.[4] Thus, we are left with no direct evidence for supposing that any of the fortifications at Dhema, including the cross-wall discovered by Dr. E. W. Kase in 1977, are of Justinianic origin. Some refurbishment of these walls by Justinian cannot be ruled out, but it must be doubted that Justinian built the walls *de novo*.

Professor Cherf has also argued that a portion of the 2000 man garrison that Justinian brought to Thermopylae was stationed at Dhema. This can be further argued on the basis of archaeological evidence, not heretofore published, from the Phokis-Doris Expedition. In doing so, the place to begin is the year 540. In that year, 'Hunnic' raiders[5] entered Greece, outflanking the defenses of Thermopylae, in much the same way that Xerxes did in 480 BC, using the Dhema Pass, which must not have been well defended. However, when they were unable to cross the Gulf of Corinth, they contented themselves with ravaging central Greece.[6] Justinian's response to this was to reinforce the fortifications around Thermopylae, not

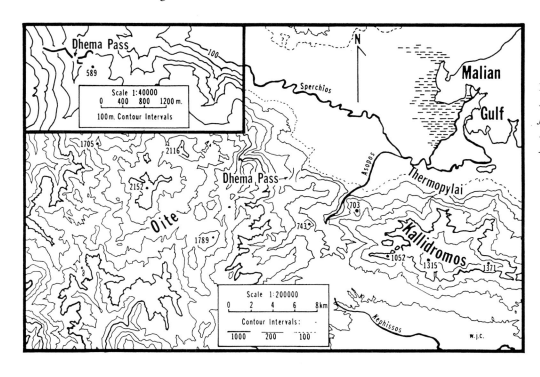

FIG. 4.1: *The Dhema Pass, located in the foothills of the Malian Basin* (from Cherf, *AJA* 88 [1984] 595)

just the coastal defenses. This can be demonstrated by analyzing the testimony of Procopius, as well as the evidence from trial excavations at the Dhema Gap.

There is a long passage in his work on Justinian's buildings[7] in which Procopius describes the emperor's refortification of the Thermopylae region. Here, he seems well informed, perhaps first-hand by the *logothete* Alexander 'Psalidius', who supervised the project, as we know from another of Procopius' works.[8] Certain specific points are made, which bear on the archaeological evidence from the Dhema Pass. First of all, Justinian realized that coastal defenses at Thermopylae could be easily outflanked, just as Xerxes had done. Procopius refers to this particular event, but points out, quite rightly, that there is not just one way to outflank the coastal defenses, but many. There were ascents from the coast, previously unguarded and unwalled, which Justinian walled off.[9] Some of these ascents he fortified were really roads, almost wagon-roads.[10] Where walls already existed, Justinian strengthened them by adding double battlements.[11] Thus, Justinian's work at Thermopylae was not just at the famous coastal defenses, but throughout the entire region, and particular concern was given to the fortification of paths and roads[12] that had allowed invaders to outflank those defenses. This important task was given to the *logothete* Alexander 'Psalidius'. It was he who installed a garrison of 2000 men for the defense of the region.[13]

It seems clear that this garrison's use can only be understood within the context of Procopius' more general discussion of Justinian's realization that the paths and roads that allowed the coastal defenses to be outflanked had to be better fortified. Along with this plan of fortification must have been a plan to distribute

the garrison accordingly, as opposed to placing all the soldiers in one location. As confirmation of this, note that in the same sentence where Procopius mentions the garrison, he writes of the establishment of granaries and reservoirs of water in safe places everywhere.[14] If the garrison was placed in only one location, why were granaries and reservoirs placed everywhere? It seems obvious that they were meant to defend the newly fortified (or refortified) strongpoints.

It cannot be ruled out that Dhema is associated with Myropoles, one of Justinian's fortresses in central Greece.[15] It is possible, certainly, that wall section D, next to the Xirias River (more a mountain stream), is the wall that Procopius mentions in connection with Myropoles.[16] The fact that the radiocarbon dates from what is left of Dhema's fortification walls are pre-Justinianic[17] does not, necessarily, exclude that possibility.[18] Whatever Dhema's name in the Justinianic period, it was quite obviously a key part of the defenses behind Thermopylae, a place that Justinian may have refortified, given his interest in strengthening all of the region's strongpoints. It had to be, given its obvious strategic value. Even if he did not refortify it, there is ample evidence of a garrison there in the mid-sixth century, one that can be connected with Procopius' testimony.

The evidence for a garrison at Dhema in the mid-sixth century is demonstrated by pottery and other small finds (PLATES 4.3–4.4, FIG. 4.3) from trial trenches at the site in 1977. The crucial ones for our purposes are trenches II, III and IX. Trench II was located at the north end of the site, within the fortification wall. The upper 0.65–0.95m of the fill (Level 1, Passes 1–8, and Level 2, Passes 1–2 = Level 5) contained many large, worked limestone blocks, fallen from the

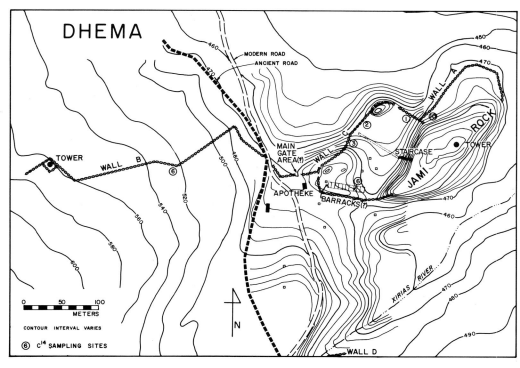

FIG. 4.2: *The fortifications at the Dhema Pass,* (from Kase *et al.,* *Explorations of the Phokis-Doris Expedition,* Vol. I [Dubuque, Iowa 1991] fig. 4–21)

PLATE 4.1*a*: *Looking SE towards the Dhema Pass. Mt. Oite is in the upper right.* (From Kase *et al., Explorations of the Phokis-Doris Expedition,* Vol. I [Dubuque, Iowa 1991] pl. 1–7)

PLATE 4.1*b*: *Wall B.* (From Kase *et al., Explorations of the Phokis-Doris Expedition,* Vol. I [Dubuque, Iowa 1991] pl. 4–61)

fortification walls. One huge block, *c.*1.50x1.20m., covered the entire southeast corner of the trench and proved impossible to move. This upper stratum contained a mix of prehistoric pottery, Late Roman pottery, including the rim of a red-slipped plate (Cat. No. 7), cooking ware jar and stewpot fragments (Cat. Nos. 8–9), amphorae fragments (Cat. Nos. 22–24)...(etc.), and incised coarseware (e.g., uncataloged DII.1.3–4:31-34), in addition to some later glazed Byzantine sherds, a small piece of glass, a small bronze pendant-cross, all datable to the late eleventh century.[19] In addition, there are a number of roof tile fragments (e.g., uncataloged DII.1.3–4:26), and a large assortment

of uncataloged ovicaprid, pig and cattle bones. Essentially, this stratum ended at the bottom of the fallen blocks, below which there was an almost complete absence of historic sherds, tile fragments, and animal bones. The pottery and most of the small objects could be defined as either Late Roman or Byzantine, but the animal bones and roof tile fragments could not. Trench III helped to define the tile fragments as Late Roman in date; Trench IX would demonstrate the same for the animal bones.

Trench III was a 2.0 x 2.0m trench about 30m to the south of the fortification wall, the uppermost stratum (Level 1, Pass 2=Level 2) of which produced a mixture

PLATE 4.2*a* (ABOVE): *Wall C.* (From Kase *et al.*, *Explorations of the Phokis-Doris Expedition*, Vol. I [Dubuque, Iowa 1991] pl. 4–62)

PLATE 4.2*b* (BELOW): *Wall B, south face* (From Kase *et al.*, *Explorations of the Phokis-Doris Expedition*, Vol. I [Dubuque, Iowa 1991] pl. 4–63)

of prehistoric and Late Roman coarsewares. The roof tiles (Cat. Nos. 27–28) associated with this stratum are thus obviously Late Roman in date.

Since the possibility existed that some of the sherds from the upper stratum of Trench II were washed down the slope from higher up, it was decided to lay out another trench (IX) farther up the slope of the hill, but still inside the fortification walls. Trench IX contained a single stratum 0.70m in depth, filled entirely with Late Roman incised and combed coarseware, animal bones, nails, tacks (e.g., PLATE 4.4*b*) and an iron-socketed spear point (PLATE 4.4*a*), suggesting that the area may have been used as a dump in Late Roman times. What is so significant about the material from this single stratum is that whereas in Trench II there is a mixture of prehistoric, Late Roman, and Byzantine sherds, here we are dealing with a single deposit of mid-sixth century date. The absence of roof tile fragments from Trench IX (as opposed to Trench II) may indicate that what is represented is a rubbish heap for items of daily use.

The pottery from the Late Roman deposit in Trench IX (Cat. Nos. 1–5, 7, 10–15, 17–21, 25–26) includes probable cooking ware similar to the pottery found in excavations on Kythera, dated to the late sixth and early seventh centuries, and described as casseroles and *chytras* by the excavators. John Hayes examined the Dhema examples and dated them to the mid-sixth century AD, or at least no later than 600 AD.[20] Amphora fragments from the deposit include some body sherds with wavy incisions that are of the same date.[21] Also contemporary are the fragments of Central Greek Painted Ware. The fabric[22] is uniformly fine in texture, varying from red to reddish yellow, with decorated red to gray matt paints in designs that often consist of radiating leaf sprays. Plates are common in this ware,

and the Dhema fragments are from plates, one of which has a leaf spray. Another has a central medallion that may imitate a Late Roman African Slip Ware stamp. The small finds from this deposit are dated by the pottery, and include an iron socketed spearpoint, a lamp fragment, and some glass fragments. It seems likely that here indeed is evidence of the Justinianic garrison which Procopius states that Justinian sent to 'Thermopylae'. It is suggested that this was done after the 539/40 raid of the Huns, and that the garrison was maintained until it was withdrawn in 552 to fight the Ostrogoths in Italy.[23] How it was garrisoned after that is not known. But in 559 a Kotrigur raid on central Greece was stopped at Thermopylae, indicating that the garrison, or some elements of it, may have returned.[24] It is possible that the garrison continued to function until Dhema was abandoned in the face of the massive Slavonic invasions of Greece that began in 578.[25] Some elements of the pottery assemblage at Dhema resemble finds from Argos dated to a destruction layer of 585 AD.[26] In other words, since the pottery evidence from Trench IX at Dhema is roughly dated to the period framed by the 'Hunnic' raid of 540 and the Slavonic invasions, it seems reasonable to think that these events influenced the creation (and demise) of the garrison there.

CATALOGUE OF LATE ROMAN FINDS

A. *Fine Wares*

Central Greek Painted Ware is a sixth century ware described by Hayes[27] as uniformly fine in texture, varying from red to reddish yellow, with decorated red to gray matt paints in designs that often consist of radiating leaf sprays, such as our cat. no. 3. Plates are common in this ware.[28] A central Greek origin seems likely for this ware, although examples have appeared as far away as Constantinople and Abu Mena in Egypt.[29] That this ware was used well into the second half of the sixth century is indicted by its occurrence at Argos in a destruction layer dated to 585.[30] The red slipped wares are regional types, none of which can, as yet, be connected securely with imported fine ware shapes.

1. RIM OF PLATE FIG. 4.3.1.
Rim fragment of Central Greek Painted Ware plate. Approx. diam. 28 cm. Red matt paint (2.5 5/6) on int. and ext. Reddish yellow fabric (5YR 6/6)[31] throughout. Text.[32] fine.
Trench IX, Level 1. Inv. No. DIX.1.4–6:9

2. BOTTOM OF PLATE PLATE 4.3*b*, lower right
Bottom fragment of Central Greek Painted Ware plate. Painted central medallion of two concentric rings, radiating from which are alternate hatched bands and decorated circles. The medallion may imitate a Late Roman African Slip Ware stamp. Int. paint dark gray (5YR 4/1); entire ext. painted weak red (10R 4/2). Fabric reddish yellow (7.5YR 7/6). Text. fine.
Trench IX, Level 1. Inv. No. DIX. 1.6:4.

3. BOTTOM OF PLATE PLATE 4.3*b*, top
Bottom fragment of a Central Greek Painted Ware plate. Int.

has leaf spray with ribs turned upwards in weak red (2.5YR 4/2) paint. Ext. and core fabric light red (2.5YR 6/6); int. reddish yellow (5YR 6/6). Text. fine.
Trench IX, Level 1. Inv. No. DIX. 1.4–6:18.
There is a plate from Delphi with similar decoration.[33] A similar leaf spray was found in a destruction layer at Argos, dated to 585 AD.[34]

4. BOTTOM OF PLATE
Bottom fragment of Central Greek Painted Ware plate. Int. has daub of dark gray (5YR 4/1) paint; fabric light red (2.5Y 6/6) throughout. Text. fine.
Trench IX, Level 1. Inv. No. DIX.1.4–6:20.

5. BOTTOM OF PLATE
Bottom fragment of a Central Greek Painted Ware plate. Int. has streak of reddish brown (5YR 5/3) paint. Ext. fabric reddish brown (5YR 5.3); int. light reddish brown (5YR 6/4); core reddish brown (2.5YR 5/4). Text. fine.
Trench IX, Level 1. Inv. No. DIX. 1.4–6:6.

6. RIM OF A SMALL BOWL FIG. 4.3.2.
Rim of a small, red-slipped bowl. Approx. diam. 8 cm. Red (2.5YR 4/8) slip; fabric throughout reddish yellow (5YR 6/8). Text. fine.
Trench II, Level 1. Inv. No. DII.1.3–4:1.

7. RIM OF A PLATE FIG. 4.3.3.
Flaring rim of a red-slipped plate, with three grooves on ext. Approx. diam. 14 cm. Light red slip (10R 6/6). Fabric color throughout light red (5.YR 6/6). Text. fine.
Trench IX, Level 1. Inv. No. DIX.1.4–6:19.

B. *Cooking Ware Jars or Stewpots*

Among the Late Roman cooking wares at Stobi, jars and stewpots are common, and the two-handled stewpot is the most common.[35] The Dhema examples come closest to nos. 1262–63 from Stobi, which are described as stewpots.[36] On Kythera, similar cooking ware, described as *chytras*, are dated to the late sixth/early seventh century.[37] As with the parallels from Stobi, our rims are flattened and out-turned, with diameters from about 12–16cm. A single handle, perhaps two, is common. However, no complete profile of this ware could be assembled, so it is impossible to ascertain if the Dhema jars had one or two handles. Bases are flat and range in diameter from 10–12 cm. The exterior and interior colors range from shades of red to gray; the cores are mostly gray. The use of wavy-incised decoration on jars and rough combing on amphorae is consonant with a mid to late sixth century date.[38]

8. RIM OF A COOKING WARE JAR OR STEW-POT FIG. 4.3.4.
Approx. diam. 12 cm. Very dark gray (5YR 3/1) throughout. Text. coarse.
Trench II, Level 1. Inv. No. DII.1.3–4:13.

9. RIM OF A COOKING WARE JAR OR STEW-POT FIG. 4.3.5.
Approx.diam. 14 cm. Reddish brown (2.5YR 4/4) throughout. Text. coarse.
Trench II, Level 1. Inv. No. DII.1.1–2:6.

10. RIM AND HANDLE OF A COOKING WARE JAR OR STEWPOT FIG. 4.3.6.
Flattened, out-turned rim fragment with band of incised, wavy lines. Approx. diam. 14 cm. Strap handle has two slight vertical

ridges. Handle width 3 cm. Ext. and int. light red (2.5YR 6/6); core gray (5YR 6/1). Text. very coarse.
Trench IX, Level 1. Inv. No. DIX. 1.4–6:41.

11. RIM OF A COOKING WARE JAR OR STEW-POT FIG. 4.3.7.
Flattened, out-turned rim fragment. Approx. diam. 16 cm. Ext. and core pinkish gray (7.5YR 6/2); int. light red (2.5YR 6/6). Text coarse.
Trench IX, Level 1. Inv. No. DIX. 1.4–6:7.

12. RIM OF A COOKING WARE JAR OR STEW-POT FIG. 4.3.8.
Out-turned, flattened rim fragment. Approx. diam. 16 cm. Ext. alternates between light red (2.5YR 6/6) and gray (5YR 6/1), the latter being the color of the int. and core. Text. coarse.
Trench IX, Level 1. Inv. No. DIX. 1.4–6:12.

13. RIM OF A COOKING WARE JAR OR STEW-POT FIG. 4.3.9.
Out-turned, flattened rim fragment. Approx. diam. impossible to estimate. Gray (2.5Y N5/) throughout. Text. coarse.
Trench IX, Level 1. Inv. No. DIX. 1.4–6:14.

14. BASE OF A COOKING WARE JAR OR STEW-POT FIG. 4.3.10.
Flat base fragment. Approx. diam. 12 cm. Ext. and core gray (5YR 5/1); int. very dark gray (2.5YR N/3). Text. coarse.
Trench IX, Level 1. Inv. No. DIX.1.1–3:12.

15. BASE OF A COOKING WARE JAR OR STEW-POT FIG. 4.3.11.
Flat base fragment. Approx. diam. 10 cm. Ext. and core reddish gray (10R 5/1); int. light red (2.5YR 6/6). Text. very coarse.
Trench IX, Level 1. Inv. No. DIX. 1.1-3:16.

16. BODY OF A COOKING WARE JAR OR STEW-POT PLATE 4.3a, lower right.
Body fragment of an amphora with three horizontal bands of incised lines. Ext. light red (2.5YR 6/6); int., core brown (7.5R 5/2). Text. medium.
Trench II, Level 1. Inv. No. DII.l.3–4:34.

17. BODY OF A COOKING WARE JAR OR STEW-POT
PLATE 4.3b, lower left.
Body fragment of an amphora with three bands of horizontal lines and band of wavy incision.
Ext./int. gray (5YR 5/1); core very dark gray (2.5YR N/3). Text. medium.
Trench IX, Level 1. Inv. No. DIX.1.1–3:13.

C. Amphorae

Amphorae and cooking ware jars of Justinianic date are often decorated with combing and wavy incision. Those body fragments (nos. 20–24) with combing find parallels from the Justinianic fortress at Isthmia,[39] and from the Justinianic harbour at Anthedon.[40] The shallower, more finely incised decoration (no. 26), including wavy incised bands (no. 25), find a parallel of Justinianic date at Tiryns.[41]

18. RIM OF AMPHORA FIG. 4.3.12.
Rim fragment of amphora. Approx. diam. 12 cm. Horizontal rib at level of handle attachment, part of which remains. Ext. reddish yellow (5YR 7/6); int. and core red (2.5YR 5/6). Text. coarse.
Trench IX, Level 1. Inv. No. DIX.1.4–6:31.

19. RIM OF AMPHORA FIG. 4.3.13.
Rim fragment of amphora. Approx. diam. 11 cm. Ext. and int. reddish yellow (5YR 7/6); core red (2.5YR 5/6). Text. coarse.
Trench IX, Level 1. Inv. No. DIX.1.4–6:30.

20. BODY OF AN AMPHORA
Body fragment of an amphora with horizontal combing. Color ext., int. and core light red (2.5YR 6/8). Text. coarse.
Trench IX, Level 1. Inv. No. DIX.1.4–6:2.

PLATE 4.3a: *Coarseware Sherds: Cat. Nos. 16 (lower right), 22 (upper left), 23 (Upper right), 24 (lower left)*

PLATE 4.3b: *Central Greek Painted Ware Sherds: Cat. Nos. 2 (lower right), 3 (top), Incised Cooking Ware: Cat No. 17 (lower left)*

PLATE 4.4*a* (ABOVE): *Iron Spearpoint (Cat. No. 31)*

PLATE 4.4*b* (LEFT): *Iron Tack (Cat. No. 34, top) and Iron Nail (Cat. No. 35, bottom)*

21. BODY OF AN AMPHORA
Body fragment of an amphora with horizontal combing. Ext., int. and core light red (2.5YR 6/8). Text. coarse.
Trench IX, Level 1. Inv. No. DIX.1.4–6:4.
22. BODY OF AN AMPHORA PLATE 4.3*a*, upper left.
Body fragment of an amphora with horizontal combing. Ext., int. and core light red (2.5YR 6/8). Text. coarse.
Trench II, Level 1. Inv. No. DII.1.3–4:31.
23. BODY OF AN AMPHORA PLATE 4.3*a*, upper right.
Body fragment of an amphora with horizontal combing. Ext., int. and core light red (2.5YR 6/6). Text. coarse.
Trench II, Level 1. Inv. No. DII.1.3–4:32.
24. BODY OF AN AMPHORA PLATE 4.3*a*, lower left.
Body fragment of an amphora with horizontal combing. Ext. and int. reddish yellow (5YR 7/8); core light red (2.5YR 6/8).
Trench II, Level 1. Inv. No. DII.1.3–4:33.
25. BODY OF AN AMPHORA
Body fragment of an amphora with wavy-incised decoration between two parallel bands of incised lines. Ext. and int. light red (2.5YR 6/8); core gray (5YR 5/1). Text. medium.
Trench IX, Level 1. Inv. No. IX.1.4–6:35.
26. BODY OF AN AMPHORA
Body fragment of an amphora with three parallel bands of incised lines. Color ext., int., core gray (5YR 5/1). Text. medium.
Trench IX, Level 1. Inv. No. IX.1.4–6:33.

D. Roof Tiles

27. ROOF TILE
Pan tile fragment. Reddish yellow throughout (5YR 6/8). Text. granules.
Trench III, Level 1. Inv. No. DIII:1.2:15.
28. ROOF TILE FIG. 4.3.14.
Pan tile fragment. Light red throughout (2.5YR 6/8). Text. granules.
Trench III, Level 1. Inv. No. DIII.1.2:16.

E. Minor Objects

Only the finds from Trench IX, Level 1 are included, since they come from a uniform deposit that can be dated from roughly the mid to late sixth century. The objects all have a domestic use that indicate a settlement at the site, presumably a garrison, as would be suitable for a settlement within an important fortification. The iron spearpoint further indicates this.

29. GLASS BOWL FIG. 4.3.15.
Three non-joining rim fragments from a small glass bowl. All have the same approx. diameter, 8 cm., the same rim thickness, 0.2 cm., the same color (light green), the same fabric, and the same profile.
Trench IX, Level 1. Inv. No. 1977:D66, a–c.
30. LAMP
Fragment of a lamp discus, decorated with a pair of concentric circles in a field of smaller circles. Color ext. reddish yellow 5YR 7/6; core gray 5YR 6/1.
Trench IX, Level 1. Inv. No. 1977:D70.
31. IRON SPEARPOINT PLATE 4.4*a*.
Iron spearpoint, much corroded, with tip missing. Round, hollow socket for shaft; midrib along blade. Length 9.4 m.; max. width 1.7 cm.; shaft thickness 0.5 cm.
Trench IX, Level 1. Inv. No. 1977:D52.
32. IRON BLADE
A fragmentary iron blade, much corroded. Maximum preserved length 3.8 cm.; maximum preserved width 1.1 cm.; preserved thickness 0.3 cm.
Trench IX, Level 1. Inv. No. 1977:D42.

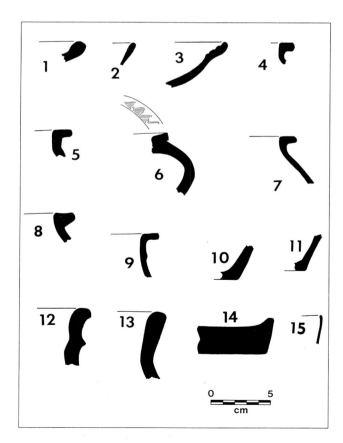

FIG. 4.3 (ABOVE): *Late Roman Pottery (1–14) and Glass (15)*

33. IRON BLADE
A slightly curving iron blade, much corroded. Preserved length
5.3 cm.; maximum preserved width 1.5 cm.; maximum
thickness 0.35 cm.
Trench IX, Level 1. Inv. No. 1977:D51

34. IRON TACK PLATE 4.4*b*.
Iron Tack. Head and upper part of shank preserved. Preserved
length 2.3 cm.; maximum width of oval head 1.6 cm.;
maximum thickness of shank (square in section) 0.3 cm.
Trench IX, Level 1. Inv. No. 1977:D10.

35. IRON NAIL PLATE 4.4*b*; bottom.
Iron nail, intact except for missing tip. Pres. length 11 cm.;
head 2.2 cm. square; maximum thickness of shanke (square in
section) 0.8 cm.
Trench IX, Level 1. Inv. No. 1977:D11.

Boston College, Massachusetts

NOTES

1. This is the central thesis argued in E. W. Kase, G. J. Szemler, N. C. Wilkie, P. W. Wallace (eds.), *The Great Isthmus Corridor Route: Explorations of the Phokis-Doris Expedition* (Center for Ancient Studies, University of Minnesota, Publications in Ancient Studies, 3; Dubuque, Iowa 1991) i.

2. Most important are W. J. Cherf, *The Dhema Pass and Its Early Byzantine Fortifications* Ph.D. Diss., Loyola University of Chicago, 1984; id. 'Lime Mortar C14 and the Late Roman Fortifications at Thermopylai', *AJA* 88 (1984) 594–98; id. 'Dhema', in E. W. Kase, G. J. S. Szemler, N. J. Wilkie, P. W. Wallace (eds.), *The Great Isthmus Corridor Route*, 56–59; ibid., 'The History of the Isthmus Corridor During the Roman Period: The First Through the Mid-Sixth Centuries AD', 134-55.

3. This was probably part of a larger response to Alaric's pillage of Greece in 396, ibid., 138–39. See also P. A. Clement, 'Alaric and the Fortifications of Greece', *Ancient Macedonia* ii, 135–37.

4. See W. J. Cherf, *Sixteenth Annual Byzantine Studies Conference. Abstracts of Papers* (Baltimore 1990) 16–17. The deficiencies in Procopius' treatment of Justinianic fortifications are well known, and have also been commented on by A. Cameron, *Procopius and the Sixth Century* (Berkeley and Los Angeles 1985) 84–112, especially 109–110. See also M. Whitby, *The Emperor Maurice and His Historian: Theophylact Simocatta on Persian and Balkan Warfare* (Oxford 1988) 74-5. Chief among these deficiencies is Procopius' exaggeration of the extent of Justinian's building program, especially his tendency to claim repairs as new constructions. Moreover, his knowledge of geography is often so deficient that it is often difficult to identify Justinianic fortification walls. The radiocarbon dates from the Dhema fortifications only reinforce the nature of this problem, since the upper portion of these walls, which might have been Justinianic repairs, are destroyed.

5. Procopius, *Wars*, ii.4.10–11, where they are referred to as Huns. They were probably Bulgars; see Cherf, in E. W. Kase *et al.* (n.2) 139; see also J. Rosser, 'The Role of the Great Isthmus Corridor in the Slavonic Invasions of Greece', *Byzantinische Forschungen* 9 (1985) 247–48; id., 'The Dark Ages', in Kase *et al.* (n.2) 145–46.

6. Procopius (ibid.) states that as a result of finding the wall at Thermopylae well defended, the 'Huns' found the path up the mountain and 'destroyed almost all the Greeks except the Peloponnesians, and then withdrew'. The reference to the 'Huns' not having access to the Peloponnesos may not refer to the Isthmus being well defended, but to the fact that the Gulf of Corinth was itself an impediment, once they reached Galaxeidi, at the end of the Great Isthmus Corridor. However, in the tenth century when Tsar Samuel invaded central Greece, the Great Isthmus Corridor was used and the Gulf of Corinth was crossed; see J. Rosser, 'The Dark Ages', (n.5) 148–51, and id., 'Byzantine Isles of Refuge in the Chronicle of Galaxeidi', Peter Lock and G. D. R. Sanders (eds.), *The Archaeology of Medieval Greece*. Oxbow Monograph 59 (Oxford 1996) 139–45.

7. *De aedificiis*, v. 2. 1–22.

8. *Anecdota*, xxvi. 29–34.

9. *De aedificiis*, iv. 2. 7.

10. Ibid., iv. 2. 8.

11. Ibid., iv. 2. 3.

12. Ibid., ii. 9. Here, Procopius seems to refer to a single road, which is to say a main route to outflank those defenses.

13. The figure of two thousand is mentioned ibid., iv. 2. 14, and in the *Anecdota*, xxvi. 32–33.

14. *De aedificiis*, iv. 2. 14.

15. Ibid., iv. 2. 21–22. See Cherf, in Kase *et al.* (n.2) 140–41; see also Rosser, *Byzantinische Forschungen* (n.5) 251–52.

16. Cherf, (n.2) 140–41, pl. 4–65.

17. Cherf, *AJA* 88 (see n.2).
18. Cherf has expressed doubts about the Justinianic contribution to any of Dhema's fortifications; see n. 4 above. However, Procopius makes it clear that much of Justinian's work in the Thermopylae region was refortification. Thus, any Justinianic work on the Dhema fortifications could have been in the form of an added double battlement, which no longer exists, as suggested by Cherf, *AJA* 88 (above, n.2) 598, n.16. The radiocarbon dates from Dhema are, of course, from only the preserved (lower) part of the fortification walls. Until such radiocarbon analysis is done on more of the oft-presumed Justinianic walls in the Thermopylae region, it is premature, in my view, to use the Dhema radiocarbon dates to speculate about the overall truthfulness or falsehood of Procopius' account of Justinian's work in the region as a whole.
19. A glazed rim sherd (Inv. No. DII.1.3–4:8) appears to be from a chafing dish at Corinth. These were common in the eleventh century; see C. H. Morgan II, *Corinth* XI fig. 24b for a parallel. There is also a rim sherd of sgraffito ware, which can hardly be earlier than the late eleventh century. The bronze pendant cross is similar to one from Corinth that is dated to the tenth or eleventh century; see G. F. Davidson, *Corinth* XII 258, pl. 110, no. 2077. Thus, a late eleventh-century reoccupation of the site is suggested by this evidence.
20. J. W. Hayes, personal communication to E. W. Kase, July 3, 1983.
21. For parallels, see O. Broneer, 'Excavations at Isthmia, Fourth Campaign, 1957–1958', *Hesp.* 28 (1959) 336–37, nos. 15–16; H. Schläger, D. J. Blackman, J. Schäfer, 'Der Hafen von Anthedon mit Beiträgen zur Topographie und Geschichte der Stadt', *AA* 83 (1968) 87, fig. 88.
22. Described by J. W. Hayes, *Late Roman Pottery* (London 1972), 413.
23. Procopius, *Wars*, v. 26. 1–3.
24. Agathias, *History*, v. 23. 6. Presumably the garrison, or some part of it, returned to Thermopylae after the defense of Croton. See also Whitby, *The Emperor Maurice and His Historian* (n.4) 78-80, where the effectiveness of Justinian's strategy in the Balkans is evaluated.
25. See P. Charanis, *Studies on the Demography of the Byzantine Empire* (Variorum Reprints, Collected Studies 8; London 1972) xxi, 15; also J. Rosser, 'The Dark Ages' (note 5) 146.
26. Notably several examples of Central Greek Painted Ware, one of which has a painted leaf spray that resembles our cat. no. 3; see P. Aupert, 'Objets de la vie quotidienne à Argos en 585 ap. J.-C.', *BCH, Suppl.* VI *Etudes argiennes* (1980), 420–21. fig. 37, no. 159a). The combed and wavy-incised amphorae (ibid., 438–41) resemble our own cat. nos. 18–21); the presence of red slipped ware fragments (Ibid., 415–20; our cat. nos. 6–7) is also consonant with an occupation of Dhema that continued up to the Slavonic invasions of central Greece.
27. Hayes (n.22) 413.
28. Ibid. pl. xxiii, b (from Delphi).
29. Ibid. 413.
30. Aupert (n.26) 420–21, fig. 37.
31. Fabric descriptions are from the *Munsell Soil Color Charts* (Baltimore 1988).
32. Texture descriptions are from the Wentworth Scale.
33. See n.27.
34. Aupert (n.25) 420–21, fig. 37, no. 159a.
35. V. R. Anderson–Stojanović, *Stobi: The Hellenistic and Roman Pottery* (Stobi. Results of the Joint American-Yugoslav Archaeological Investigations, 1970–1981, I; Princeton 1992) 130, fig. 3.10.
36. Ibid. 141, and pl. 146.
37. J. N. Coldstream, G. L. Huxley (eds.), *Kythera* (Park Ridge, N.J. 1973) 173, nos. 67–70, fig. 52, pl. 49.
38. For parallels, see ibid. pl. 48, no. 38, pl. 49, nos. 49–53;

Broneer (n.21) 336, no. 15; Schläger-Blackman-Schäfer (n.21) fig. 88; Aupert (n.26) 438–42.
39. Broneer (n.21) 336–37, pl. 72, a, b.
40. Schläger-Blackman-Schäfer (n.21) 87, fig. 88.
41. *Tiryns. Forschungen und Berichte* V (Deutsches Archäologisches Institut Athen; Mainz am Rhein 1971) 102, pl. 44, no. 31.

5

The Ambo of Basilica A at Cape Drepanon*[1]

Demetrios Michaelides

It was the great savant of Paphos, Loizos Philippou, who, in 1949, informed the then Director of the Department of Antiquities of Cyprus, A. H. S. Megaw, that damage was being done to a hitherto unknown site on Cape Drepanon on the western coast of the island. The people responsible for this damage were the blacksmiths of Paphos who had discovered that this site was particularly rich in marble, a substance very much in demand in their profession, because, in powder form, it was an excellent flux for the fusion of metals.[2]

A small-scale investigation in the same year brought to light part of what was clearly an important early Christian basilica, and this led to the systematic investigation of the area between 1952 and 1955. The excavations, carried out by the Department of Antiquities under A. H. S. Megaw, near the modern fishing harbour of Ayios Yeoryios of Peyia, in the District of Paphos, completely cleared this structure which was named Basilica A. They also brought to light another two basilicas, B and C, as well as a the remains of a small bath building, all dating to the 6th century.[3]

All three of these basilicas are of crucial importance for understanding early Christian architecture and decoration in Cyprus, but Basilica A, occupying a prominent position on top of the ridge of the promontory, remains the most important amongst them.[4] This basilica forms part of a larger complex with several subsidiary buildings, including annexes to the north, a narthex to the west, and, further west and on a higher level, a baptistery and a small transept basilica, the only such structure known so far on the island. Basilica A had three aisles separated from each other by 27.8m long colonnades, consisting of eight columns each. Above these there were other, smaller colonnades serving the galleries over the side aisles. Surprisingly, the building, although provided with an atrium, has no narthex. The basilica has three apses and the central one was fitted with a semicircular synthronon. In front of this, in the presbytery, which is decorated with a mosaic pavement, there were remnants of an altar. The presbytery was separated from the rest of the church by means of a chancel screen, considerable fragments of which survive. The nave was paved with a mosaic floor, unfortunately poorly preserved, and had an ambo on its longitudinal axis. Remnants of this were found in the area just beyond the third and fourth column of the colonnade (counting from the east).[5] While the aisles of the basilica were paved with slabs of local schist, the atrium and the baptistery were decorated with mosaic floors. These mosaics are important and well-known.[6] Equally well-known, even though only a few isolated finds have been published, is the fact that this basilica (as well as the other two on Cape Drepanon) had rich architectural decoration and church furniture of Proconnesian marble.[7] What is not generally realized is just how lavishly decorated these buildings were, Basilica A in particular. Only fragments of these marble furnishings survive, but they are enough to demostrate that Basilica A was one of the most opulent basilicas on Cyprus.

The quantity and quality of these marble fittings and objects is indeed staggering for Cyprus where marble was never very abundant, and where marble rarely survives. There is no native marble on Cyprus, so the island always had to rely on expensive, imported material. Unfortunately, since late antiquity, most of this ended up in lime kilns as the inhabitants of Cyprus realized that marble was a source of excellent quality lime. Perhaps because of the geographic isolation of the place, the marble decorating the basilicas at Ayios Yeoryios of Peyia escaped such destruction, although, more recently, a large part of it had an equally unhappy end at the hands of blacksmiths. All the same, Basilica A, together with the Basilica of Campanopetra at Salamis,[8] can claim to give the most complete picture of the decoration of early Christian basilicas on the island. With the exception of a few capitals, columns and some other, larger pieces left on the site, the material is stored in the Paphos District Museum and is presently under study for publication. It includes small-size capitals, panels from the chancel screen, a large number of offering tables (both rectangular and sigma-shaped), large basins, a small sarcophagus-shaped reliquary, and other, less easily identifiable items. Most importantly, it includes many fragments which belong to the ambo where the well-known panel

* The contribution of this article is disproportionate to the immense debt I owe Peter Megaw. As a Cypriot I am grateful to him for dedicating the largest part of his career to the study and promotion of the antiquities of my country, and for saving many of them from certain destruction. As a friend, he has, over the years, given me his unstinting support and encouragement, as well as sound advice and valuable information. Above all, however, by his example, he has shown me how great modesty can be.

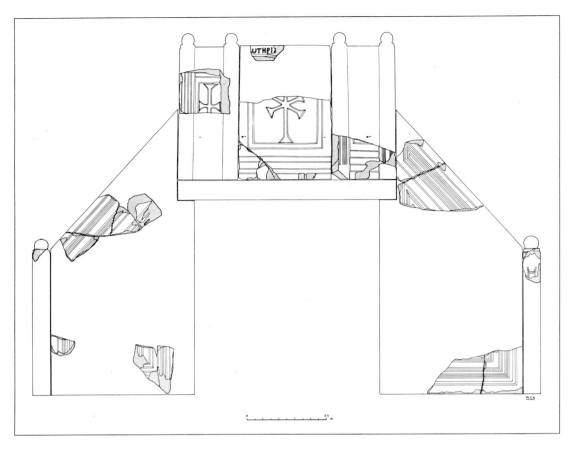

FIG. 5.1*a* (ABOVE) *and b* (BELOW): *Reconstruction of the two sides of the ambo*

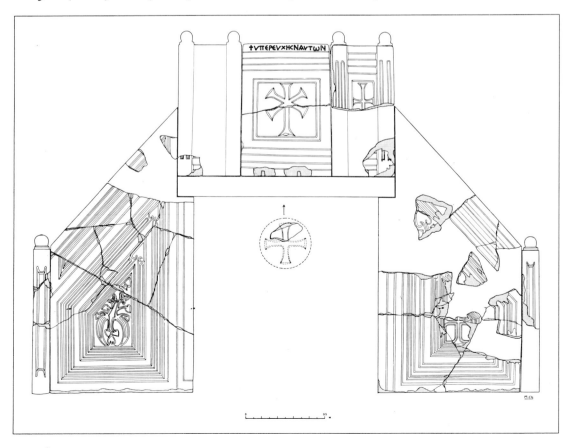

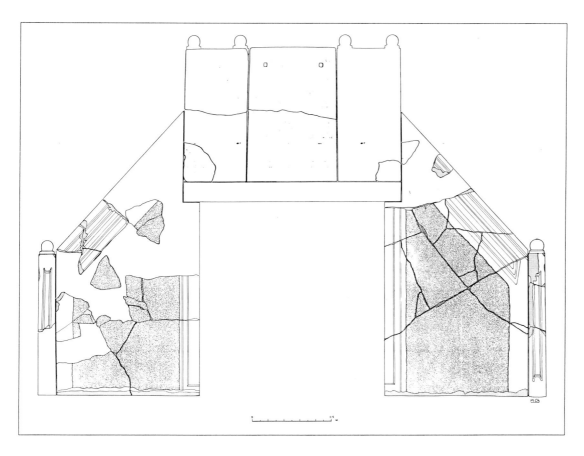

FIG. 5.1*c* (ABOVE) *and d* (BELOW): *Reverse of the fragments used in the reconstruction*

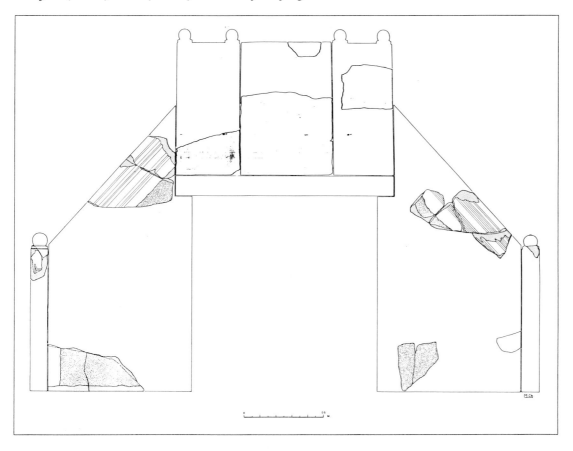

with the inscription ΥΠΕΡ ΕΥΧΗϹ ΝΑΥΤΩΝ comes from.[9] These enable us to reconstruct the whole structure with a fair degree of accuracy. In fact, the fragments are presently being joined together for a planned restoration of the ambo in the Paphos District Museum.[10] It is this ambo and its reconstruction (FIG. 2.1) that form the subject of this short article.

The ambo is monumental and of a type that enjoyed great popularity during the 5th and 6th centuries. Such ambos were made, usually of Proconnesian marble, in workshops in the area of Constantinople and exported widely. They were prefabricated in the sense that their different parts were finished in the workshop but were not fitted together until they reached the church the ambo was destined to serve. From the evidence of the shipwreck at Marzamemi, where the ambo was found as it left the workshop, and where several pieces have unfinished ends, it is clear that some final corrections and adjustments needed to be made during the erection of these ambos.[11] Despite their large size and immense weight, the different parts of these ambos were made in a way that enabled them to hook and fit onto each other, and, with some pinning here and there, the structure could stand without needing masonry support. The ambo from Basilica A belongs to a type, sometimes referred to as the 'bridge type' which, despite several variations, is essentially a rectangular enclosure with two staircases at both ends. One staircase was for ascending the other for descending from the

pulpit. Such ambos were orientated east-west in the nave of the basilica but their exact position there depended on liturgical practices that differed from place to place in the Byzantine world. The staircases were flanked by large decorated parapets of trapezoidal shape, while the pulpit was formed by a platform, usually but not always monolithic,[12] supporting a parapet made of two or more panels. The platform had a circular centre, which was the pulpit proper, and rectangular projections at east and west, for receiving the staicases. The two curved panels in the centre of each side of the pulpit enabled the priest to address his flock on both sides of the ambo.[13]

The example from Ayios Yeoryios had an elaborate parapet, each side of which consisted of three rectangular elements: a central convex panel flanked by two flat ones. The two sides of such ambos were practically identical although it is to be noted that the decoration of the trapezoidal parapets was not neccessarily the same, not only from one side to the other, but also from one panel to the next on the same side. It should also be stressed that the pairs of parapets and panels although appearing similar to each other differ a lot in both dimensions and decorative detail. The ambo from Ayios Yeoryios at Peyia was made of Proconnesian marble and comprised the following elements: a) two pairs of pilasters, each marking the beginning of the steps on either side; b) two pairs of trapezoidal parapets flanking the stairs; c) a monolithic platform; d) four rectangular parapet panels; e) two curved parapet panels; and f) the steps themselves. It is not possible to determine with certainty how the whole thing was fixed to the ground. It would seem, however, that the ambo was not pinned to the floor or, as is more often the case, to a marble socle, since the surviving pilaster and lower parts of the trapezoidal parapets do not have holes on their underside. The lower edges of the latter are all chipped, however, something that may be an indication that they were originally set in some sort of mortar. Masonry fill must have provided considerable support for the two staircases anyway. Unfortunately no evidence survives as to how these were constructed (see below).

Between them the 34 fragments, some composed from many smaller pieces, provide information on practically every different part of the ambo. In the majority of cases there is no doubt as to what component of the ambo they belong to and where this goes in the whole structure. There are a few, however, which certainly come from one of the trapezoidal staircase parapets, but it is impossible to determine which. Their 'floating' position in the reconstruction drawing is thus arbitrary. There are also eight fragments which are so small and damaged that it has proved impossible to assign them to a specific part of the ambo and they are not included on the drawing. We will now examine the available evidence for each different component of the ambo, bearing in mind that all measurements are approximate.

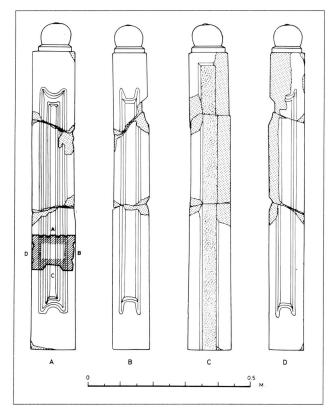

FIG. 5.2. *Pilaster*

A: PILASTERS (FIGS. 5.1–5.2)

One pilaster survives complete, the others are fragmentary but, here as elsewhere, given the design of the ambo, measurements taken from one element can be taken to be valid for the other elements too. The complete pilaster is 104cm high. It has a squarish cross-section, measuring 13.5 x 11.3cm and is surmounted by a knob on a simple, collar-like moulding. The pilaster has a pair of opposite sides decorated with a simple fluting, while a third side has slightly more ornate linear decoration. This is clearly the side along the long axis of the ambo, because the corresponding fourth side is undecorated and has a long roughly finished channel

down its full height. This is the mortice into which the tenon of the trapezoidal parapet of the staircase slotted (see below). These pilasters are often not separately finished but carved as one with the trapezoidal parapets as, for example, at the South Basilica at Aliki[14] and at Hobi.[15] Sometimes, however, they were finished separately as at Ayios Yeoryios, parallels for which are found at the Basilica of Hagios Kyriakos on Delos,[16] the Octagon of Philippi (Ambo A)[17] and the ambo from the wreck at Marzamemi.[18] These examples, however, do not have a mortice and they were simply fitted against the flat vertical edge of the trapezoidal parapet. The parallels for the very simple decoration of the pilasters are too numerous to list.

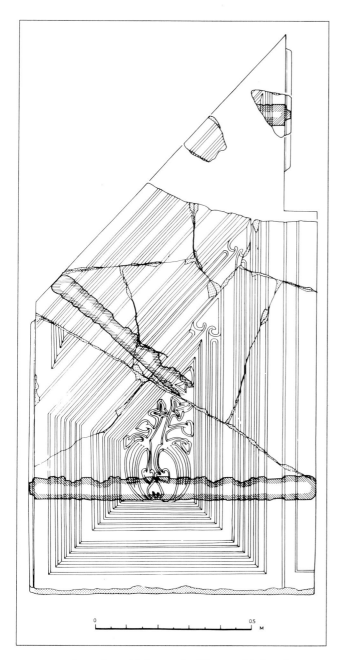
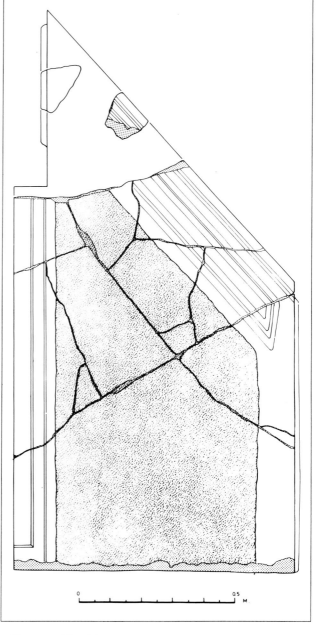

FIG. 5.3*a* (LEFT) *and b* (RIGHT): *Trapezoidal staircase parapet (front and back)*

B: TRAPEZOIDAL STAIRCASE PARAPETS
(FIGS. 5.1, 5.3–4).

These are the large plaques that panelled the steps that led from the floor to the platform. No parapet survives complete, but it is possible to reconstruct their dimensions and aspect with a fair degree of accuracy from the surviving fragments. The approximate width of these parapets was 90cm and their thickness 8cm. The shorter of the two sides was 95cm high and the taller 1.85m. The shorter side had a tenon down its full height, that slotted into the mortice already observed on the pilasters. The edge of the taller side was finished differently. It was rounded for nearly its full height, but a little before the top it stepped inwards and the new short vertical edge was provided with a

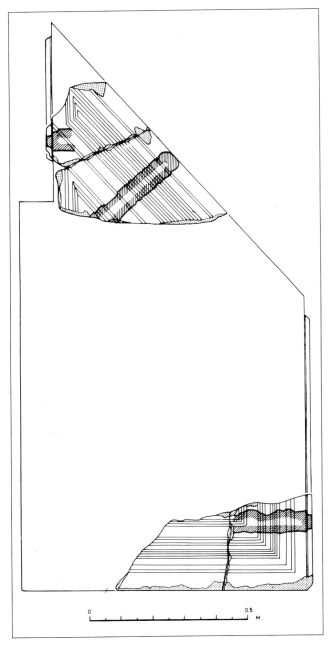

FIG. 5.4: *Trapezoidal staircase parapet fragments*

tenon. It was on this step that the platform sat, while the tenon fitted into a mortice of the rectangular parapet panel above. This device secured the joining together of three different components: the trapezoidal parapet, the platform and the rectangular parapet panel above.[19]

The outside face of these parapets was richly decorated in relief, the mouldings dividing the decoration into three distinct zones: a central trapezoidal panel, a parallelogram at the top, and a separate, vertical space down the taller of the two sides of the panel. As will be seen, each of these three elements played a different role. The main trapezoidal space carried most of the decoration. A variety of mouldings, grooves and fillets define a central panel decorated with a motif. Of the two that survive, one is a strange, stylized vegetal composition, consisting mostly of heart-shaped leaves. A separate heart-shaped leaf is wedged in the apex of the panel. The other surviving central motif consists of a Latin cross the flattened extremities of which merge with the surrounding mouldings. The panel containing the first motif preserves a further decorative detail, not clear on the other fragments. It shows that the heart-shaped leaf wedged in the apex of the central panel is echoed twice, with larger leaves, further up the panel. These are placed along the diagonal towards the apex of the panel at the points where the mouldings meet at an acute angle.

The parallelogram at the top is decorated with mouldings, while high up a simple groove marks its edge which is rounded and smooth. It should be noted that on the reverse of the parapets there is a corresponding parallelogram which stands out from what is a generally unworked surface (see below). This leaves no doubt that this part of the parapet plaque remained free-standing above the steps and was a real, even though low, parapet, its smooth, rounded top acting like the handrail of a balustrade. A similar device is observed in the trapezoidal parapets from the shipwreck at Marzamemi.[20]

The third component of the decoration of these parapets is a separate, vertical band down the taller side of the trapezium. Grooves separate first a plain flat strip and then the edge of the panel, which is again rounded and worked right round the back, looking almost like a separate component of the ambo. As we have seen, this rounded edge did not reach to the top of the panel, where there was, instead, a step with a tenon on the vertical side. Comparison with better preserved examples leaves no doubt that this is the engaged column with the step above it on which the platform of the ambo sat. A notch low down marks a rudimentary base, but unfortunately not a single fragment survives to show how this 'column' ended at the top. This was presumably shaped like a capital but it is impossible to know either its form or its dimensions, save that it would have to be at least 12cm wide. In most ambos this pillar is a separate feature standing in front of the

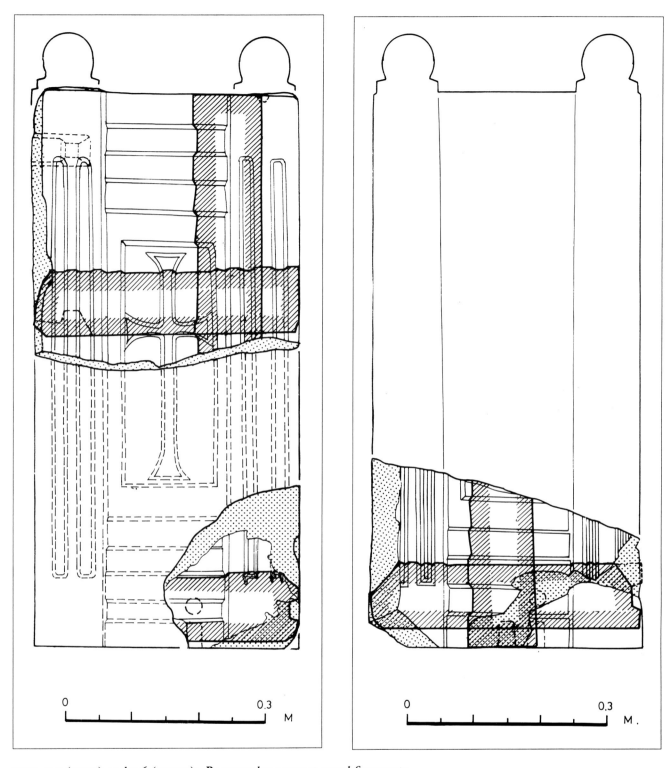

FIGS. 5.5 (LEFT) *and* 5.6 (RIGHT): *Rectangular parapet panel fragments*

tall side of the trapezoidal parapet. In such cases, the vertical edge of the parapet plaque was flat and the flat side of the pillar was put right up to it.[21] In our case, however, the edge is rounded and decorated to look like an attached column. This method of support is less common although widely documented,[22] and is even found in another Cypriot example, from Panayia

Syka now in the Cyprus Museum.[23]

The reverse of these trapezoidal panels was only roughly finished since its largest part would be concealed by the stairs. Except, that is, for this 'column' which needed to appear free-standing, the decorated parallelogram at the top which acted as a low balustrade, and a plain band down the low vertical side of the

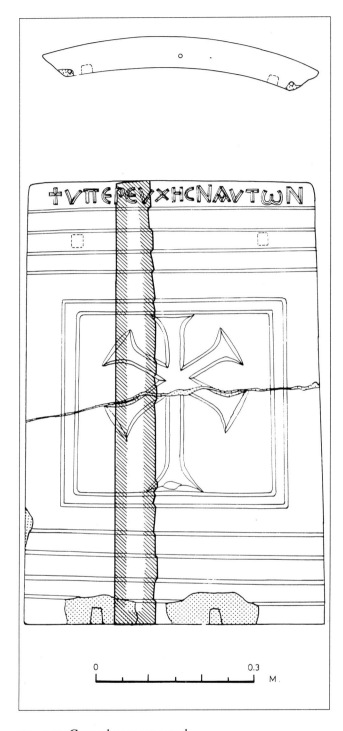

FIG. 5.7: *Curved parapet panel*

trapezium, at the point where it was attached to the pilaster and where the lower steps were. As already mentioned, the unfinished surface at the back of these trapezoidal parapets is indicative of the part concealed by the steps. Here, however, there is a problem since the unfinished surface already begins at a height of *c.* 75cm which is far too high for a first step. Fortunately, we have the ambo from the shipwreck at Marzamemi,[24] those of Basilica A at Philippi,[25] of Hagios Kyriakos on Delos[26] and the South Basilica at Aliki,[27] where there is abundant evidence to show that the first, and

sometimes even the second step started before the pilasters and outside the trapezoidal parapet.

The decoration of these panels is accurate and elegant, and belongs to the standard repertoire for such ambos. Latin crosses decorate the centre of all the trapezoidal panels from the shipwreck of Marzamemi[28] and those from the Basilica Argalon on Mytilene.[29] Two of the panels from Chobi (Georgia) are similarly decorated,[30] and examples from Constantinople are not lacking either.[31] Fairly similar Latin crosses, but set in square frames, also decorate the panels of ambo A of the Basilica of the Octagon of Philippi.[32]

C: PLATFORM (FIG. 5.1)

The solid thick piece (or pieces) of marble forming the platform obviously fell victim to the marble hunters since only one very small fragment of it survives. It can be calculated, however, that it must have been about 1.40m long, and 13cm thick. A common feature of these ambos is to have a circular concave depression in the centre of the underside of the platform decorated (usually) with a six- or eight-branched Christogram.[33] The practical purpose of this cavity was, one assumes, to reduce the weight of this very heavy part of the structure. A small fragment amongst the material from Ayios Yeoryios, preserving the bar of a cross with a flattened end, has a concave face which leaves little doubt that it comes from this part of the ambo. It is too small to permit a reconstruction of the motif, although there does not seem to be enough space for an eight-armed cross.

D: RECTANGULAR PARAPET PANELS (FIGS. 5.1, 5.5–6)

Unfortunately no such parapet panel survives complete. They were 42cm wide, 88cm high (assuming that they were the same height as the adjoining curved panels) and 10cm thick. The fragments of these panels are generally small and a few words should perhaps be said as to why they have been placed where they have in the reconstruction. Three fragments have a mortice on the side which means they must come from near the base of the panel and from the side next to the trapezoidal staircase panel, the tenon in the upper part of which they would receive. The two larger of these fragments also have large holes bored into their bases. These are 4.5cm deep and have a circular cross-section with a diameter of 1.2cm, and show without a doubt that the panels were fixed onto the platform by means of thick metal pins. The largest fragment of all does, at first sight, appear to be a base fragment. It does not, however, have either of these features. Instead, it has a large horizontally bored hole on the back, close to one side. This is 1.6cm deep, with a cross-section of 2.5 x 2.2cm, and since there are corresponding horizontal holes high up on the back of the adjacent curved panels, there can be no doubt that the three parapet panels on each side of the ambo were held together by thick metal clamps.

It is to be noted that the fragments show that the sides of the rectangular panels adjoining a curved panel have all had their front edge chiselled away. This is extremely crudely done, in some cases removing a considerable part of the decoration, something that precludes this being the result of trimming during the mounting of the ambo. It cannot be the work of stone robbers either, and one possible explanation is that some time after it was erected, the ambo collapsed and suffered some damage. During remounting, this disfigurement occurred so as to achieve a better fit between the parapet panels. It was perhaps at this stage that the metal clamps were added too. This is difficult to prove but the mosaic floor of the nave, near where the ambo stood, also shows that it was crudely reworked with very large *tesserae*.

A flat raised surface on either side of the panel is decorated with two vertical grooves with a flat end below and a curved end at the top. This kind of decoration and similar examples elsewhere leave little doubt that these are engaged pilasters, similar to but smaller than the free-standing pilasters examined above. Like them, they were surmounted by small spherical knobs, none of which survives. The only fragment from the top of a panel does in fact have two slightly raised roughened patches at the top which must be the remains of the moulding on which the spherical knob sat. Between these two pilasters, a series of raised and lowered horizontal bands above and below define a central rectangle decorated with a large Latin cross. This has flattened ends, and its vertical limb is considerably longer than the others.

Rectangular parapet panels with small attached pilasters are fairly common. Those from the wreck at Marzamemi are similar in this respect and also in being decorated with elongated Latin crosses.[34] Similar engaged pilasters are seen on the ambo from Cherson, where the rectangular panels are decorated with a cross on a globe, although crosses similar to ours are found on the trapezoidal panels there.[35] Latin crosses on side panels are fairly widespread, and amongst many examples mention can be made of that in the Byzantine Museum in Athens,[36] the ambo of Basilica A at Philippi,[37] that of the Pantanassa at Philippias, where all three components of the parapet are carved out of one piece of marble and all three are decorated with a Latin cross,[38] and the ambo of the Bayazid Basilica in Constantinople, mentioned several times already.[39] Somewhat similar pilasters and crosses are also found on the ambo of Campanopetra at Salamis, where pilasters, rectangular panels and part of a curved panel are carved out of one block of marble.[40]

E: CURVED PARAPET PANELS (FIGS. 5.1, 5.7)

One of the curved parapet panels, and the free-standing pilaster examined earlier, are the only components of the ambo to survive complete. Of the second curved panel only the lower two-thirds and a small fragment from the top survive. Both panels are wider at the bottom than at the top, and much thinner than any other component of the ambo. It would appear in fact that when these panels were clasped to the rectangular panels next to them, they would be tilted slightly backwards —an expedient presumably intended to shift the centre of gravity towards the back and reduce the danger of the parapet panels falling off the platform. The complete panel is 6.2cm thick. It is 88cm high, 57cm wide at the bottom and 54cm wide at the top. The second curved panel is 59cm wide at the bottom and has about the same thickness as its pair. Both panels have two widely spaced vertical holes on their bases, identical to those seen on the bases of the rectangular panels—an indication that they too were pinned to the platform. Rust-coloured staining would indicate that the metal used was iron. The complete example shows that these panels also had a pair of horizontal holes high up at the back. These are 1.5cm deep with a squarish cross-section measuring 2.5 x 2.2cm, and, as we have seen, they were used for joining the curved panels to the rectangular panels next to them by means of metal clamps. The completely preserved panel also has three small holes bored vertically in its flat top. These are about 1cm deep with a diameter of 0.7cm, and are placed one in the centre of the curve but slightly closer to the back face, and one in each of the back corners. Their small dimensions would indicate that something less permanent and light was fitted here. The obtuse angle formed by the three holes would indicate that this was probably a lectern. Lecterns made of thin slabs of marble were fixed in this position on the ambo from the wreck at Marzamemi.[41]

Above and below, the panels are decorated with a series of raised and lowered bands, corresponding to those of the side panels. These define a rectangular space the largest part of which is decorated with a square panel enclosing the Christogram, the vertical bar of which is longer than the others. The raised band at the top of the complete panel bears the inscription +ΥΠΕΡ ΕΥΧΗC ΝΑΥΤΩΝ, indicating that the ambo was put up as a vow by sailors or seamen. A small curved fragment, from the equivalent band on the other panel, preserves the word [C]ΩΤΗΡΙΑ[C], and one assumes that the inscription on this side prayed for the 'salvation' of these same sailors. At least one other example, the curved panel from the ambo of the Basilica Argalon on Mytilene, bears an inscription in a similar place. This reads: ΕΥCΕΒ]ΕCΤΑΤΟΥ ΠΡΕCΒΥΤΕΡΟΥ ΚΕ ΗΓΟΥΜΕΝΟΥ..., but the panel differs in that it is decorated with a cross.[42] Also decorated with a cross, and bearing many similarities in the mouldings and the separate square frame for the cross, are the curved parapet panels from Marzamemi[43] and Rhodes.[44]

The Christogram is not generally used for the decoration of this part of an ambo, but at least one contemprary example can be cited. This is the ambo from Cherson that also bears other similarities to that from Ayios Yeoryios. The Christogram there, although of a slightly different design, is also six-branched and is set in the centre of a square panel, with horizontal mouldings above and below as in our example.[45] A later ambo including in its decoration a rather similar Christogram is that from Hagios Menas at Thessaloniki, where the vertical limb is longer and taller than the others.[46]

F: STEPS

The type of ambo we are examining is tall and for this reason was provided with a minimum of four steps. In our case, as in many others, the number of steps must have been considerably larger. No part of the staircase seems to survive, which must have consisted of the steps themselves and the aggregate of mortar and stone that supported them. It is not known what the steps were made of either. It is interesting to note that amongst the cargo of the wreck at Marzamemi, which is certainly a complete set of marble furniture and decoration needed to decorate a basilica, the steps of the ambo are not included. This, however, may have not been the case everywhere.

It is worth pointing out that amongst the fragments from the site there are two broken rectangular slabs of a striking grey veined marble that could easily be steps. Both slabs are 31 cm. wide which is a comfortable width for a step, but, unfortunately, neither preserves its full length, the maximum surviving extent of which is just under 50 cm. Further indications that these slabs might be steps are: a) both fragments have one of their long edges rounded, and b) both preserve one of their short sides which is covered with considerable remains of mortar. Even if these really are steps, it is impossible to know if they belong to the ambo. The mortar implies that the narrow edges of the steps were set into something, but the back of the trapezoidal panels has nothing but a rough unfinished surface.[47]

* * *

The origins of this type of ambo, despite some doubts expressed in the past, are without doubt Constantinopolitan. The first example that comes to mind is the ambo from Basilica A at Bayazid originally brought forward as a parallel by Megaw.[48] J.-P. Sodini has enumerated more Constantinopolitan examples, including, amongst others, a fragment seemingly from St. John the Baptist at the Hebdomon and several fragments from St. John Stoudios,[49] to which C. Barsanti has added a few more.[50] Outside Constantinople the type had an extraordinarily wide diffusion in Asia Minor, particularly in Phrygia, Bithynia, Caria, Lycia and to a lesser extend Cilicia. It is also commonly found in the Aegean islands. Although widely distributed in mainland Greece, there are relatively few examples. The ambo with two staircases is also found in the Balkans and travelled towards the West at least as far as Ravenna. In the East examples of the ambo have been found as far as the Pontic regions and Crimea.[51] In Cyprus, the example from Ayios Yeoryios of Peyia is the most complete, but not the only one. The evidence, however, with the notable exception of Ayios Yeoryios of Peyia on the west and Soloi on the north, comes mostly from the eastern half of the island. This is, perhaps, not without significance since this is also the part of the island in which the basilicas with the richest *opus sectile* floors are found. All the fragments known so far on the island are made of marble and seem to belong to ambos of the bridge type.[52] These include:

1) A small fragment of the stair parapet and the top of a small column with its capital that supported the platform (showing that, as in our example, column and parapet slab were carved as one) from the Basilica of Hagios Philon, on the Carpas Peninsula.[53]
2) A stair parapet and fragments of a parapet panel, both decorated with a Latin cross, from Aphendrika on the Carpas peninsula.[54]
3) A fragment of the stair parapet with the head of a peacock, and a fragment of a parapet panel from Panayia Syka, also on the Carpas peninsula.[55]
4) Two trapezoidal staircase parapets from Hagios Spyridon at Tremithous, further inland, each bearing an inscription: a) Μέσος πέφυκεν χῶρος ἡγηασμένος and b) Ὁ κλῆ [ρος] ... ΙΩСκέ .. Ε .. Σφη[ρίδων?].[56]
5) Several fragments from Basilica B at Soloi seem to come from trapezoidal stair parapets. One of these was decorated with a bird(?), while another preserves a heart-shaped leaf that brings it close to the example from Ayios Yeoryios.[57]
6) The ambo of the Basilica of Campanopetra at Salamis is the best preserved on the island after that of Ayios Yeoryios. It is also very similar but larger with a double curved panel on each side of the pulpit. These as well as the rectangular panels of the parapet are decorated with a series of mouldings and a large central cross. Extra columns were placed under the platform to support its great weight.[58]

Unfortunately the evidence for an ambo in the Basilica of Hagios Herakleidios at Politiko has not yet been published.[59]

All these fragments seem to come from ambos of the bridge type. One notable exeption is a structure in Basilica B of Soloi on the north of the island. This is a masonry foundation that, according to the excavators, might belong to the type of ambo consisting of a flight of steps leading up to a balcony with a semicircular front. There is also part of a marble base that might belong to such an ambo but this is difficult to determine from the one published photograph.[60]

The above survey shows that the ambo of Basilica A of Ayios Yeoryios at Peyia is in perfect accordance with what occurred in the Byzantine world during the 6th century. The ambo is of a type, widely used, above all in Asia Minor and the Aegean, and although an exact parallel has not been found, all the elements of its decoration can be found on most contemporary ambos elsewhere—even amongst the scant remains of other ambos found on Cyprus. Perhaps, however, the closest ambo of all those examined, both in general appearance and decorative detail, is that from the shipwreck at Marzamemi.[61] This is why I would attribute our ambo to the same period, that is, to the reign of Justinian I (AD 527–565), and more precisely in the second quarter of the 6th century—a date that is supported by the mosaic decoration of the basilica. In a Cypriot context, the importance of this ambo lies in its quite unique good state of preservation, and in the fact that it is not an isolated imported luxury object, but forms part of a building constructed *de novo*, the decoration of which was commissioned as a unified whole. The architectural elements and the fittings are made of Proconnesian marble,[62] quarried on the island of Proconnesos in the Propontis, and there can be little doubt that the workshop that produced them was somewhere in the region of the sea of Marmara, near Constantinople. The large-scale export of such material from the capital to the rest of the Empire has long been accepted, especially for the reign of Justinian I. Because of his policy of founding churches, palaces and other buildings thoughout the entire Empire, the export trade was particularly well organised and efficient. Literary evidence for the export of prefabricated marble church furniture exported from Constantinople is found in the 7th century account of the Miracles of St. Demetrios. There, specific mention is made of a ciborium and an ambo, as well as columns, packed and protected with cloth in the hold of a ship.[63] The shipwreck at Marzamemi, containing over 500 separate pieces of marble, all intended for the decoration and equipment of one basilica,[64] is a splendid example of this 'pre-fabricated' decoration, and we can assume that this is how the material for Basilica A at Ayios Yeoryios arrived in Cyprus in a similar way. It should be stressed, in fact, that, aside for the ambo, there are also many other similarities between the cargo of the Marzamemi shipwreck and the architectural decoration of Basilica A.

For Marzamemi, the ambo, unlike the rest of the cargo, is made of *verde antico*, quarried at Atrax near Larissa. G. Kapitän has therefore suggested that the ship started from Marmara with most of the cargo, but perhaps stopped at a harbour in the Aegean to load the ambo.[65] It must be pointed out, however, that the very similar ambo from the Basilica at Bayazid is made of *pavonazzetto* from the quarries of Dokimion near Synnada in Phrygia. The different material from which the three ambos are made does not, I think, indicate that they were made in three different workshops in different parts of the Empire. Since different marbles were readily available in Constantinople, it is easier to see all three of these ambos as the product of a workshop (or workshops) operating in the region of

the metropolis, in the style that was in vogue at the time. This workshop (or workshops) would normally have used the local Proconnesian marble, but when the occasion arose, perhaps through a commission, it could just as easily use more precious stone quarried elsewhere.

The Constantinopolitan character of the marble decoration of Basilica A at Ayios Yeoryios of Peyia is undeniable. The architecture of the basilica as a whole also shows clear links with Constantinople[66] and, as mentioned earlier, the placing of the ambo on the main axis of the nave reflects Constantinopolitan practice. Centrally located ambos are found elsewhere in Cyprus during the 5th and 6th centuries, as at the Episcopal Basilica of Kourion, the Basilica of Hagia Trias, the Basilica of Campanopetra at Salamis and Hagios Herakleidios at Politiko,[67] and this general period is characterized by a strong orientation of the art and architecture of the island towards the metropolis. This can be observed in large and small basilicas throughout the island, and their floor and wall mosaic decoration. What is perplexing is to find these Constantinopolitan characteristics, but above all the large-scale marble decoration, in an isolated place like Ayios Yeoryios of Peyia, the ancient name of which is not even recorded by history. The site was inhabited during the Hellenistic and Roman periods, and its Early Christian remains show that it was very important. Nothing is known about it, however, except what the excavations have brought to light. Neither the old nor the new excavations, started by University of Thessaloniki in 1992,[68] have thrown any light on the question of the name, although the director, Ch. Bakirtzis, has put forward a tempting theory. According to this, the site on Cape Drepanon was one of the stopovers of the grain ships carrying the *annona civica* from Egypt to Constantinople. To support his theory, he brings forward several convincing arguments, and the ambo and its inscription as evidence of a dedication on behalf of the crew of these ships. There are still many unanswered questions however, like the enormous size of the settlement, and the existance of three basilicas (and there is evidence for more) decorated with imported material. These are unwarranted for what should be a small station with a specific function, and one will have to wait for the progress of the excavations before a final answer can be given to the question of Ayios Yeoryios of Peyia and its basilicas. For the moment, one could also put forward another suggestion. Namely that the site at Cape Drepanon acted as a stopover for pilgrims travelling to and from the Holy Land, as has been proposed for the site of Aperlae in Lycia.[69] In fact, the two towns have many similarities: both lack written history, both are of secondary importance but have an exaggerated number of basilicas (five have been located in Aperlae so far) and both seem to have provided for seafarers.

Archaeological Research Unit, University of Cyprus, Nicosia

NOTES

1. Special abbreviations used for this article include:
    Barsanti 1990: C. Barsanti, 'L'esportazione di marmi dal Proconneso nelle regioni Pontiche durante il IV–VI secolo', *Rivista dell'Istituto Nazionale d'Archeologia e Storia dell'Arte*, Serie III, Anno XII (1989) 91–220.
    Delvoye 1976: Ch. Delvoye, 'L'art paléochrétien de Chypre', *Rapports et Co-rapports. XVe Congrès International d'Études Byzantines* (Athens).
    Fıratlı 1951: N. Fıratlı, 'Découverte de trois églises byzantines à Istanbul', *Cahiers Archéologiques* 5, 163–178.
    Jakobs 1987: P. H. F. Jakobs, *Die frühchristlichen Ambone Griechenlands* (Habelts Dissertationsdrucke–Reihe Klassische Archäologie, Hf. 24) (Bonn).
    Kapitän 1969: G. Kapitän, 'The church wreck off Marzamemi', *Archaeology* 22/2, 122–133.
    Kapitän 1980: G. Kapitän, 'Elementi architettonici per una basilica dal relitto navale del VI secolo di Marzamemi (Siracusa)', in *XXVII Corso di Cultura sull'Arte Ravennate e Bizantina* (71–136).
    Mathews 1971: T. F. Mathews, *The Early Churches of Constantinople. Architecture and liturgy* (London).
    Mathews 1976: T. F. Mathews, *The Byzantine Churches of Istanbul. A photographic survey* (London).
    Megaw 1960: A. H. S. Megaw, 'Early Christian monuments in Cyprus in the light of recent discoveries', in *Akten des XI. Internationalen Byzantinisten-Kongresses* (Munich 1958) 345–51.
    Megaw 1974: A. H. S. Megaw, 'Byzantine architecture and decoration in Cyprus: metropolitan or provincial?', *DOP* 28, 59–88.
    Orlandos 1954: A. K. Orlandos, Ἡ Ξυλόστεγος Παλαιοχριστιανικὴ Βασιλική, ii (Athens).
    Papageorghiou 1985: A. Papageorghiou, 'L'architecture paléochrétienne de Chypre', in *"Cipro e il Mediterraneo orientale". XXXII Corso di Cultura sull'Arte Ravennate e Bizantina. Ravenna, 23–30 marzo 1985* (Ravenna) 299–335.
    Papageorghiou 1986: A. Papageorghiou, 'Foreign influences on the Early Christian Architecture of Cyprus', in V. Karageorghis (ed.), *Cyprus between the Orient and the Occident. Acts of the International Symposium. Nicosia, 8–14 September 1985* (Nicosia) 490–504.
    Roux 1998: G. Roux, *La Basilique de la Campanopetra* (Salamine de Chypre XV) (Paris).
    Sodini and Kolokotsas 1984: J. P. Sodini and K. Kolokotas, *Aliki, II: La basilique double* (*Études Thasiennes* 10) (Paris).
2. Personal communication by A. H. S. Megaw.
3. *Annual Report of the Director, Department of Antiquities* (1949) 16; (1952) 11, 15 figs. 27–28. Other brief contemporary accounts of these excavations include: *ibid.* (1953) 12, 17; (1954) 14, 16; *JHS* 70 (1950) 15, pl. 3b; 73 (1953) 137; 74 (1954) 175, pl. 11c; 75, (1955) 33; *AJA* 55 (1951) 169; *FA* 4 (1951) 545 no. 5183; 7 (1954) 418 no. 5411; 8/9 (1956) 378 no. 5108, 391 no. 5295, 352 no. 7567, fig. 149; *BZ* 47 (1954) 254, 257; 48 (1955) 260, 500; 49 (1956) 519.
4. Megaw 1960, 348–9; A. Khatchatrian, *Les baptistères paléochrétiens* (Paris 1962) 76; A. Papageorghiou, Ἡ Παλαιοχριστιανικὴ καὶ Βυζαντινὴ Τέχνη τῆς Κύπρου (reprint from Ἀπόστολος Βαρνάβας) (Nicosia 1966) 12, fig. 6; Megaw 1974, 71–2; A. H. S. Megaw, 'Interior decoration in Early Christian Cyprus', *Rapports et Co-rapports. XVe Congres International d'Études Byzantines* (Athens 1976) 15–16, 20–21, figs. 19–21, 26, 34–37; Delvoye 1976, 9, 19, 27–8, plans 4–5; D. Pallas, *Les monuments paléochrétiens de Grèce découverts de 1959 à 1973* (Vatican 1977) 275–81; Papageorghiou 1985, 314, fig. 5; Papageorghiou 1986, *passim.*, fig. 7.
5. The position of the altar, the chancel screen and the ambo can just be made out on the plan published in Megaw 1960,

fig. 26; Delvoye 1976, plan 4; and Papageorghiou 1985, fig. 5.
6. S. Pelekanides and P. I. Atzaka, Σύνταγμα τῶν Παλαιοχριστιανικῶν Ψηφιδωτῶν τῆς Ἑλλάδος: I: Νησιωτικὴ Ἑλλάς (Thessaloniki 1974) 150–2, no. 147, pls. 139–141b; W. A. Daszewski and D. Michaelides, *Mosaic Floors in Cyprus* (Ravenna 1988) *passim.*; D. Michaelides, *Cypriot Mosaics*, 2nd edition (Nicosia 1992) 99–107, nos. 56–59, pls. 139–141.
7. Capital with two superimposed rings of flattened acanthus leaves from Basilica A: Megaw 1960, 348, pl. 39a; Delvoye 1976, 36, pl. 3:5; Barsanti 1990, 120, fig. 29. Cushion capital from Basilica C: Megaw 1974, 72, fig. 16; W. E. Betsch, *The history, production and distribution of the late antique capital in Constantinople*, Univ. Pennsylvania Ph. Diss. Fine Arts 1977 (Ann Arbor 1979) cat. 104; Barsanti 1990, 181.
8. Roux 1998.
9. Megaw 1960, 348, pl. 39b; Megaw 1974, 72, fig. 18; Delvoye 1976, 37; Sodini and Kolokotsas 1984, 108 n. 464; Barsanti 1990, 193, fig. 147.
10. It was hoped that the restoration would have been completed by now but unfortunately this has not been possible and so no photographs are yet available. I would like to take this opportunity to thank the Director of the Department of Antiquities, Dr. Demos Christou, and the Ephor of Museums, Dr. Pavlos Flourentzos, for allowing me to continue work on this material, and, above all, Ms Mary Chamberlain, draughtsperson at the Department of Antiquities, for the excellent drawings.
11. Kapitän 1969, 130–2; Kapitän 1980, 105, 115–6.
12. This could sometimes be made of two pieces, and, even more rarely, of three. See examples in Sodini and Kolokotsas 1984, 113.
13. On this type of ambo in general, see Orlandos 1954, 555–562; J. P. Sodini, 'Note sur deux variantes régionales dans les basiliques de Grèce et des Balkans: le tribélon et l'emplacement de l'ambon', *BCH* 99 (1975) 581–88; *idem*, "La sculpture architecturale à l'époque paléochrétienne en Illyricum", in *Actes du Xe Congrès International d'Archéologie Chrétienne. Thessaloniki 28 septembre–4 octobre 1980; I: Rapports (Studi di Antichità Cristiana* 37) (Vatican-Thessaloniki 1984) 290–8; Ch. Delvoye, *Reallexikon für byzantinische Kunst* I, *s.v.* ambo, cols. 129–131; Sodini and Kolokotsas 1984, 94–120; Jakobs 1987, 44–56 (types I and II); Barsanti 1990, 192–7; Kapitän 1980, 98–107.
14. Sodini and Kolokotsas 1984, 28–9, figs. 29–30.
15. L. G. Krushova, 'Mramornye Izdelia Vizantijskogo proischozdenija iz Vostcnogo Pricernomor'ja', *Vizantijskij Vremennik* 40 (1979) 127, 132, figs. 1 and 15; W. Djobadze, 'Remains of a byzantine ambo and church furnishing in Hobi (Georgia)', *AA* (1984) 627ff., figs. 1–6; Sodini and Kolokotsas 1984, 117; Barsanti 1990, 193, fig. 147.
16. A. K. Orlandos, 'Délos chrétienne', *BCH* 69 (1936) 77–8, figs. 7–8; Jakobs 1987, 242, pl. 28.
17. Jakobs 1987, 306, fig. 81.
18. Kapitän 1980, 106–7, figs. 13, 22.
19. The same can be observed on the equivalent part of the ambo of the Basilica of Hagios Kyriakos on Delos (Orlandos (n. 16), 77, figs. 6, 12; Jakobs 1987, 241–3, fig. 28, pl. 6d). A somewhat similar device is observed on one of the staircase parapets of the ambo from the South Basilica at Aliki, although there the system of support of the platform was different, with separate columns bearing most of the weight. See Sodini and Kolokotsas 1984, 95, figs. 93 and 107.
20. Kapitän 1980, 103.
21. For the example from the South Basilica of Aliki, see Sodini and Kolokotsas 1984, 98, figs. 100, 107–8. For parallels, see *ibid.*, 112. In the case of the trapezoidal parapets from the wreck at Marzamemi, it has been observed that they are furnished with 'lateral extensions' which were obviously

meant to fit in corresponding cuttings on the separately carved flanking pillars. The fact that the pillars have no such cuttings, and some other irregularities in the various pieces, must be an indication that the final adjustments for fitting together these pieces were to be done during the erection of the ambo in the church (Kapitän 1969, 130–2; Kapitän 1980, 105).

22. A well-known example is the Bayazid ambo mentioned before (Firatlı 1951, 178, pl. 6a–c; Mathews 1971, 67–73, figs. 56–57; Mathews 1976, fig. 5:2). Others come from Synnada in Phrygia (*MAMA* IV, no. 112, pl. 30),·Amasra (S. Eyice, *CA* 7 (1954) 101, fig. 2), the Katapoliani and the Basilica of the Tris Ekklesies on Paros (A.K. Orlandos, 'Παλαιοχριστιανικοὶ ἄμβωνες Πάρου', *Arch. Byz. Mnem.* 11 (1969) 177–206; Jakobs 1987, 292–4, figs. 65–67, pl. 21a–c, and pp. 294–6, figs. 70–71, pls. 21d–23a respectively) and Basilica B at Philippi (P. Lemerle, *Philippes et la Macédoine Orientale à l'époque chrétienne et byzantine* (Paris 1945) nos. 106–119 and 123–4, pl. 75).

23. A. H. S. Megaw, 'Three vaulted basilicas in Cyprus', *JHS* (1946) 55, fig. 13.

24. Kapitän 1969, fig. on p. 130; Kapitän 1980, 118, fig. 18.

25. Lemerle (n. 22), pls. 10a–b, 25 and 26; Jakobs 1987, 298–300, figs. 73–75, pls. 23c–24d.

26. Orlandos (n. 16), 75–82; Jakobs 1987, 241–3, figs. 27–31, pls. 6b–d, 7a.

27. Sodini and Kolokotsas 1984, 97–8, figs. 107–9.

28. Kapitän 1969, figs. on pp. 130–1; Kapitän 1980, 102–6 and n. 26 for parallels, figs. 19–21.

29. Jakobs 1987, 274–5, pl. 15a.

30. Krushova (n. 15), 127, 132, figs. 1 and 15; Barsanti 1990, 193, fig. 148.

31. See Barsanti 1990, 193–4 for references.

32. Jakobs 1987, 304–7, figs. 81a–b.

33. Six-armed Christogram under platform: Basilica D of Nea Anchialos (G. Soteriou, in Πρακτικὰ τῆς ἐν Ἀθήναις Ἀρχαιολογικῆς Ἑταιρείας (1934) 62, fig. 6; Jakobs 1987, 284–5, pl. 18c); South church of Sebaste in Phrygia (C. Barsanti, *Testimonianze di età macedone in Asia Minore: Le sculture della chiesa nord di Sebaste in Frigia* (Tesi di Dottorato di Ricerca, Università di Roma-La Sapienza (Rome 1987) 98–100, fig. 114); Novae (S. Parnicki-Pudelko, 'Rapports des Fouilles effectuées par l'expédition archéologique de l'Université Adam Mickiewizc à Poznan, Novae-Secteur Ouest', in *AWarzawa* 33 (1982 [1985]) 183ff., figs. 16, 27–28, 33, 36; 35 (1984 [1986]) 131ff., figs. 34–35; 37 (1986 [1987]) 147–9, figs. 16–17).'
    Eight-armed Christogram under platform: Marzamemi wreck (Kapitän 1969, 130 and photograph on p. 131; Kapitän 1980, 110–3, figs. 25–26); Basilica of the Baths on Cos (Orlandos 1954, 557, fig. 523; Jakobs 1987, 262–3, pl. 12b).

34. Kapitän 1969, 130, photograph on p. 131; Kapitän 1980, 116, fig. 29. See n. 40 for parallels.

35. Barsanti 1990, 193, fig. 40.

36. K. Kourouniotes and G.A. Soteriou, Εὑρετήριον τῶν μεσαιωνικῶν μνημείων (EME 1, Athens 1927) 37–8, fig. 34.

37. Jakobs 1987, 298–300, fig. 75.

38. M. Acheimastou–Potamianou, 'Εὕρημα παλαιοχριστιανικοῦ ἄμβωνος εἰς περιοχὴν ναοῦ Παντανάσσης Φιλιππιάδος', *AAA* 8 (1975) 95–103; P. Aupert, 'Chronique des fouilles et découvertes archéologiques en Grèce en 1975', *BCH* 100/2 (1976) 631, fig. 92; Jakobs 1987, 310–2, pl. 29a–c.

39. Firatli 1951, 178, pl. 6a–c; Mathews 1971, 67–73, figs. 56–57; Mathews 1976, fig. 5:2.

40. Roux 1998, 142, figs. 174, 178–9.

41. Kapitän 1969, 130; Kapitän 1980, 117.

42. Jakobs 1987, 274–5, pl. 15c.

43. Kapitän 1980, 114-6, figs. 27-28.

44. A. K. Orlandos, 'Παλαιοχριστιανικὰ λείψανα τῆς Ρόδου', *Arch. Byz. Mnem.* 6 (1948) 50–1, fig. 43; Jakobs 1987, 312–4, pls. 29d, 30a–b.

45. A. L. Jakobson, *Rannesrednevekovyi Hersones* (*MIA* 63) (Moscow-Leningrad 1959) 149–50, figs. 55–56; Sodini and Kolokotsas 1984, 110 n. 541, and 115 n. 555; Barsanti 1990, 192–3, fig. 146.

46. Jakobs 1987, 334–5, pls. 126–127.

47. The trapezoidal slabs from the South Basilica at Aliki have horizontal and vertical slots cut into their sides into which the steps fitted (Sodini and Kolokotsas 1984, figs. 96–97, 109–110), but this seems to be an *unicum*, the normal way of supporting these steps being the use of an aggregate of mortar and stone, remnants of which are sometimes found still adhering to the marble pieces.

48. Megaw 1974, 72. See also Firatli 1951, 178, pl. 6a–c; Mathews 1971, 67–73, figs. 56–57; Mathews 1976, fig. 5:2; Sodini and Kolokotsas 1984, 106–7; Barsanti 1990, 193.

49. Sodini and Kolokotsas 1984, 106–7 and n. 435.

50. Barsanti 1990, 193–4, fig. 149.

51. For a detailed list of the examples from the above regions, see Sodini and Kolokotsas 1984, 107–12. For the Pontic regions in particular, see Barsanti 1989, 192–7, and for Greece, see Jakobs 1987, 44–56.

52. At Hagia Trias, it appears that the ambo was made of local stone, but no further information is available at the moment (Papageorghiou (n. 4), 11).

53. J. du Plat Taylor and A. H. S. Megaw, 'Excavations at Ayios Philon, the ancient Carpasia', *RDAC* (1981) 231, 235, pls. 41.3b and 40.8 respectively.

54. G. A. Soteriou, Βυζαντινὰ μνημεῖα τῆς Κύπρου (Athens 1935) pl. 13.1.

55. Now in the Cyprus Museum: Megaw (n. 23), 55, fig. 13.

56. A. Papageorghiou, 'Ἔρευνα εἰς τὸν ναὸν τοῦ Ἁγίου Σπυρίδωνος ἐν Τρεμετουσιᾷ', Κυπριακαὶ Σπουδαί, 30 (1966) 17–38.

57. J. des Gagniers and Tran Tam Tinh, *Soloi. Dix campagnes de fouilles (1964–1974)* I (Sainte-Foy, 1985) 95–96, nos. 69–70, figs. 176–177. Another two fragments that might belong to an ambo can be seen in the top right corner of fig. 99, but are not mentioned in the text.

58. See G. Roux, *Bible et Terre Sainte* 176 (déc. 1975) 20, and Papageorghiou 1986, 493.

59. Roux 1998, 141–44, figs. 172–82.

60. des Gagniers and Tran Tam Tinh (57), 58–9, figs. 107–109). The incomplete nature of the published evidence was caused by the invasion of the island in 1974. Unfortunately, because of the Turkish occupation of the north of Cyprus, the material from the excavations is still inaccessible. For the type of ambo that might be represented here, see the examples from the Acheiropoietos and the Octagon of Thessaloniki (E. Kourkoutidou Nikolaidou, 'Les ambons paléochrétiens à Thessalonique et Philippes', in *XXXI Corso di Cultura sull'Arte Ravennate e Bizantina. 'La Grecia paleocristiana e bizantina'. Ravenna, 7–14 Aprile 1984* (Ravenna 1984) figs. 1–4. Evidence for what might be a masonry ambo, but of unknown type, also comes from the Acropolis Basilica at Amathous (A. Pralong, 'La Basilique de l'Acropole d'Amathonte (Chypre)', *Rivista di Archeologia Cristiana* n. 1–2, anno 70 (1994) 421).

61. Kapitän 1969; Kapitän 1980.

62. There are, however, some smaller objects, like the offering tables, that are made of a different kind of marble.

63. Ch. Bakirtzis (ed.) and A. Sideri (tr.), Ἁγίου Δημητρίου Θαύματα (Thessaloniki 1997) 328–31, paras. 313–314.

64. Kapitän 1969, 125.

65. 1969, 133.

66. Papageorghiou 1986, 491, 493.

67. Megaw 1974, 72; Papageorghiou 1985, 314; Papageorghiou

1986, 493.

68.   On the new excavations, see Ch. Bakirtzis, 'The role of
       Cyprus in the grain supply of Constantinople in the Early
       Christian period', in V. Karageorghis and D. Michaelides
       (eds.), *Cyprus and the Sea. Proceedings of the International
       Symposium. Nicosia 25–26 September,* 1993 (Nicosia 1995)
       247–53; *idem,* 'Description and metrology of some clay
       vessels from Agios Georgios, Pegeia', in V. Karageorghis and
       D. Michaelides (eds.), *The development of the Cypriot Economy
       from the Prehistoric period to the present day* (Nicosia 1996)
       153–62; *idem,* 'Early Christian rock-cut tombs at Hagios
       Georgios, Peyia, Cyprus', in N. Patterson Ševčenko and C.
       Moss (eds.), *Medieval Cyprus. Studies in Art, Architecture,
       and History in memory of Doula Mouriki* (Princeton 1999)
       35–41.

69.   Aperlae is presently being investigated by a team led by R.
       Hohlfelder and R. L. Vaun. For further information, see the
       University of Colorado at Boulder Public Relations Release
       of 24 July 2000 at: http://www.colorado.edu/NewsServices/.
       An article by R. Hohlfelder will appear in an upcoming issue
       of *The Journal of Nautical Archaeology.*

6

From Constantinople to Lakedaimon: Impressed White Wares

Pamela Armstrong

In 1981 I was invited to join Peter Megaw's team for their excavation season at the castle of Saranda Kolones at Paphos, a privilege eagerly accepted. The excavation provided my first encounter with White Wares, when a few fragments were found amongst the pre-castle remains, and an interest was stimulated in these apparently exotic ceramics.[1]

White Wares formed one of the principal categories in the classification of Byzantine pottery established by David Talbot Rice, based on finds from Constantinople, which was later refined by him in his pioneering book on glazed ceramics.[2] Subsequently two further assemblages of White Wares excavated in the capital were published by Stevenson from the Great Palace, and by Peschlow from Hagia Eirene.[3] White Wares have also been found in large numbers at certain sites outside Constantinople: at Mesembria on the Bulgarian coast of the Black Sea, at Chersonesos in the Crimea, and at Corinth.[4] A general study of White Wares found in southern Russia has shown that they were widespread there, though not in quantity.[5] In 1983 Peter Megaw and Richard Jones published the results of their innovatory scientific analysis of a range of Byzantine and related ceramics, which included a section on glazed White Wares.[6] An interesting result of this work was that the full range of White Wares found at Corinth, of differing style and date, and also the few samples available from Constantinople itself, had a consistent chemical composition, and therefore had almost certainly been produced in one and the same area.[7] Most recently the publication by John Hayes of the ceramics from the excavations at Saraçhane in Constantinople dealt with approximately 20,000 White Ware sherds recovered there, the largest collection of White Wares yet studied.[8] He proposed a new classification based on subdivisions within the white fabric, concluding that they were products of the capital.[9] He was able to identify macroscopically five different fabrics in use at different periods, which taken together with the results of Megaw and Jones, suggests that either one basic clay was prepared in different ways for different products, or minor variations occurred within the clay beds.[10] Early this century kilns were found producing Polychrome Ware, a White Ware with coloured decoration, architectural embellishments for a church and monastic complex near Preslav, in Bulgaria.[11] Hayes suggests that the raw materials might have been imported for this very specific production, while indigenous Bulgarian origins are supported by Mango and Mason.[12] Nikomedia has also tentatively been suggested as a possible place of manufacture for Polychrome tiles, based on a possible reference to 'Nikomedian tiles', but, even if the translation has been correctly rendered, it should be remembered that 'Lakonian' and 'Corinthian' tiles, terms current in both ancient and modern usage, do not indicate origins of manufacture, but shape of tile (and thereby a particular style of architectural construction).[13]

Hayes, working from his large corpus of material, has grouped White Wares in three main categories: Unglazed White Wares, comprising five sub-groups, Glazed White Wares, with another five sub-groups (four are glazed versions of Unglazed White Wares), and Polychrome Ware.[14] The Glazed and Unglazed White Wares are utilitarian in character: lamps, candlesticks, chafing dishes, dishes, bowls, fruit stands and jugs of all sizes. Polychrome Wares are luxury products, comprising revetment tiles and icons, as well as vessels. The elaborate painted decoration gives individual items an intrinsic value which other White Wares lack. In Polychrome Ware the ceramic is really an artist's canvas.[15]

Findspots of both Polychrome and its utilitarian counterparts are shown on FIG. 3.1. This list cannot claim to be exhaustive; many must be still unrecorded.[16] In particular they have been identified at: Otranto in southern Italy;[17] on the islands of Cyprus,[18] Crete,[19] Melos (where they have been found on four different sites),[20] Siphnos,[21] and Aegina;[22] in the Peloponnese at Sparta (Byzantine Lakedaimon),[23] on two sites in the foothills of Mount Parnon,[24] and at Corinth;[25] in central Greece at Athens,[26] Thebes,[27] and the village of Kalapodi in Phokis;[28] in Macedonia at Thessaloniki,[29] at Chrysoupolis and three other sites on the Strymon Delta,[30] and at Anaktoroupolis;[31] at Ganos on the north shore of the Sea of Marmara;[32] along the coast of Bulgaria at Apollonia,[33] Anchialos,[34] Mesembria,[35] and Varna;[36] inland, along the Danube, at Dinogetia'[37] at Djadovo[38] near Nova Zagora, and at Preslav;[39] in the Crimea at Chersonesos[40] and Kertch,[41] and in southern Russia at Tmutarakan,[42] Sarkel,[43] Novgorod,[44] and Kiev;[45] in the Troad, in the city of Nicaea and at two sites nearby,[46] in the city of Nikomedia;[47] and finally in Lycia, at Xanthos[48] on the coast, and inland, in the region of the city of Balboura.[49]

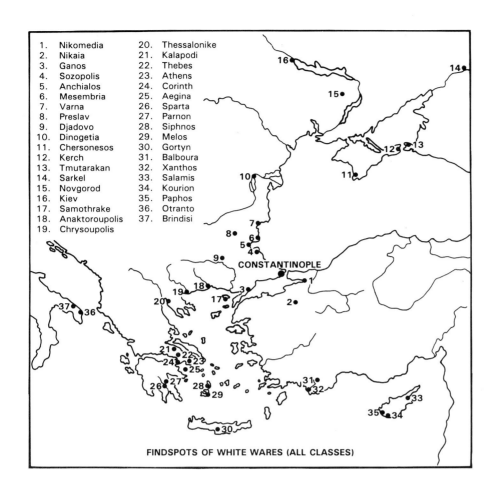

1. Nikomedia
2. Nikaia
3. Ganos
4. Sozopolis
5. Anchialos
6. Mesembria
7. Varna
8. Preslav
9. Djadovo
10. Dinogetia
11. Chersonesos
12. Kerch
13. Tmutarakan
14. Sarkel
15. Novgorod
16. Kiev
17. Samothrake
18. Anaktoroupolis
19. Chrysoupolis
20. Thessalonike
21. Kalapodi
22. Thebes
23. Athens
24. Corinth
25. Aegina
26. Sparta
27. Parnon
28. Siphnos
29. Melos
30. Gortyn
31. Balboura
32. Xanthos
33. Salamis
34. Kourion
35. Paphos
36. Otranto
37. Brindisi

CONSTANTINOPLE

FINDSPOTS OF WHITE WARES (ALL CLASSES)

FIG. 6.1: *Findspots of both Polychrome and its utilitarian counterparts*

The opportunity is taken here to include Sparta, Byzantine Lakedaimon, amongst the known findspots, and to add to the corpus of published pieces found in Constantinople itself. These two separate groups of the same class of Impressed White Ware bowl fragments, belonging to Hayes' Glazed White Ware II category, have been in the public domaine for almost a century, but their existence has remained unnoticed. **1–12** were found in Constantinople and formed part of the 1903 Martin bequest to the Museo Internazionale delle Ceramiche at Faenza in Italy, where they are now on display.[50] Although they do not contribute to knowledge of chronology or classification, their intrinsic interest justifies publication, just as it justified their modern 'trade' in this century. **13–22** were excavated between 1905 and 1909 in the *cavea* of the ancient theatre of Sparta, where houses had been constructed in the Middle Byzantine period.[51] A sample of the excavation finds was donated by the Greek authorities to the Victoria and Albert Museum in London.[52] Excavations at Sparta led to one of the first scientific publications of Byzantine pottery, though no White Wares were included.[53] As evidence for trade between a relatively remote provincial centre and the capital and for the distribution of this pottery type, they deserve attention.

CATALOGUE

The numbers in brackets following catalogue numbers are inventory numbers used by the respective museums. As all the catalogued pieces are bases, form is not referred to in individual entries. Each is illustrated by photograph (PLATES 6.1–6.2); profiles of 1–20 are also drawn (FIGS. 6.2–6.5). Abbreviations: d. = diameter; pres. = preserved; h. = height; fr(r). = fragment(s). Individual catalogue entries are followed by comparanda, where they exist, for the decoration.[54] Measurements are in centimetres.

1-12
Impressed and Glazed White Wares from Constantinople in the Museo Internazionale delle Ceramiche, Faenza (PLATE 6.1, FIGS. 6.2–6.3)
1. (AB 783) BOWL
d. 10.3, pres. h. 3.1. (PLATE 6.1, FIG. 6.2)
Ring foot supporting irregular, thick floor. Frontal bird with stylized plumage looking left enclosed by three (pres.) concentric bands of short diagonal strokes. Olive green glaze streaked with brown pigment inside and to top of footplate outside.
Jakobson 1979, fig. 52, no. 2
2. (AB 784) BOWL
d. 11.4, pres. h. 2.9. (PLATE 6.1, FIG. 6.2)
Ring foot. Frontal bird looking left enclosed by two concentric bands of short diagonal strokes; enclosing band of small impressed rectangles edging smaller circles around middle wall. Yellow-green glaze on inner surface only.

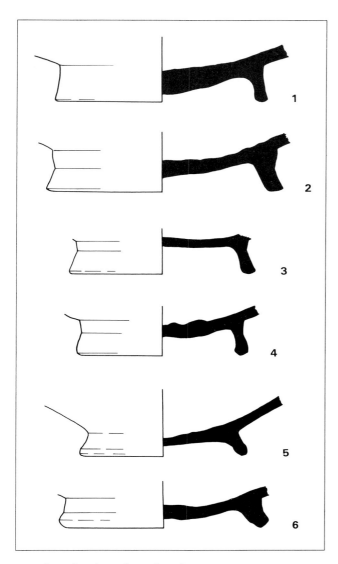

FIG. 6.2: *Sections through* **1-6**

Morgan, 48, fig. 33 no. 103 (= G); Jakobson 1979, fig. 54, no. 5 (with animal in tondo)

3. (AB 785) BOWL
d. 9.1, pres. h. 2.2. (PLATE 6.1, FIG. 6.2)
Ring foot supporting thin floor. Antithetic (probably) bird feeding from tree of life. Orange-yellow glaze on inner surface only.
Morgan, 48, fig. 33 no. 136 (= F); 6 and 7

4. (AB 787) BOWL
d. 8.4, pres. h. 2.4. (PLATE 6.1, FIG. 6.2)
Irregular ring foot. Antithetic poorly outlined birds. Deep yellow glaze speckled with green pigments inside and to top of footplate outside.
Morgan, 48, fig. 33 no. 96 (= D); Jakobson 1978, pl. b

5. (AB 835) BOWL
d. 8.3, pres. h. 3.1. (PLATE 6.1, FIG. 6.2)
Ring foot. Man with spear and dog, shrubbery in background. ?Hunting scene. Orange-yellow glaze on inner surface only.
Morgan, 47, fig. 32 no. 82 (= M)

6. (AB 836) BOWL
d. 10.2, pres. h. 2.5. (PLATE 6.1, FIG. 6.2)
Irregular ring foot supporting irregular floor. Lion within two (pres.) concentric bands of short diagonal strokes. Yellow-green glaze speckled with green pigment on inside and to top of footplate outside.

7. (AB 838) BOWL
d. 6.4, pres. h. 1.6. (PLATE 6.1, FIG. 6.3)
Fine ring foot supporting thick floor. Poorly outlined long-necked bird looking back enclosed by a (pres.) band of small raised squares. Yellow glaze speckled with green pigment on inner surface only.
Jakobson 1978, pl. d; Jakobson 1979, fig. 53, no. 4

8. (AB 884) BOWL
d. 10.4, pres. h. 3.5. (PLATE 6.1, FIG. 6.3)
Ring foot. Poorly formed horse enclosed by band of small raised triangles. Olive green to brown glaze on inner surface only.
Hayes, 19, fig. 6 no. 8

9. (AB 885) BOWL
d. 10.2, pres. h. 4.5. (PLATE 6.1, FIG. 6.3)
Irregular ring foot. Tree of life in tondo surrounded by band of concentric semi-circles. Olive green glaze on inner surface only.

10. (AB 782) BOWL
d. 7.3, pres. h. 2.6. (PLATE 6.1, FIG. 6.3)
Rounded ring foot supporting irregular floor. Circle at centre surrounded by ring of five circular bands of small raised circles. Olive green glaze on inner surface only.
Hayes, 19, fig. 6 no. 10

11. (AB 837) BOWL
d. 8.1, pres. h. 2.7. (PLATE 6.1, FIG. 6.3)
Vertical ring foot. Centre circle surrounded by ring of eight smaller circles alternating with short vertical lines. Yellow-green glaze speckled with green pigment on inner surface only.

12. (AB 789) BOWL
pres. h. 4.2. (PLATE 6.1, FIG. 6.3)
Tall, thin ring foot supporting almost horizontal floor. Frontal bird looking left; small ring at top of each wing. Dark green glaze on inner surface only.

13–22
Impressed and Glazed White Wares from Lakedaimon in the Victoria and Albert Museum, London (PLATE 6.2, FIGS. 6.4-6.5)

13. (C.39–1921) BOWL
d. 9.9, pres. h. 3.1. (PLATE 6.2, FIG. 6.4)
Rounded ring foot with horizontal ledge at junction with wall. Side view of bird with stylized plumage looking right enclosed by ring of concentric triangles. Bright yellow glaze, speckled with yellow-brown pigment on inner surface only. Splashes of thin, clear glaze on under surface.

14. (C.36–1921) BOWL
d. 7.9, pres. h. 3.9. (PLATE 6.2, FIG. 6.4)
Edge of footplate broken. Ring foot, with three external horizontal ledges, supporting thick floor. Profile of bird with stylized plumage looking left. Dark green glaze on inner surface and down to top of footplate on outer surface.
Hayes, 19, fig. 6 nos. 2 and 6; Peschlow, pl. 135 cat. no. 70 (= 5), pl. 135 cat. no. 75 (= 4)

15. (C.42–1921) BOWL
d. 7.2, pres. h. 2.5. (PLATE 6.2, FIG. 6.4)
Ring foot. Frontal bird looking left.
Mottled yellow glaze streaked with many trailing brown pigments inside and on resting surface of footplate.

16. (C.10–1921) BOWL
d. 6.4, pres. h. 1.6. (PLATE 6.2, FIG. 6.4)
Ring foot supporting almost horizontal floor. Floral motif with ten elongated petals radiating from centre. Mottled yellow glaze inside and down to top of footplate outside.
Morgan, 47, fig. 32 no. 140 (= B); Jakobson 1979, fig. 51, no. 9

17. (C.41–1921) BOWL
d. 6.3, pres. h. 2.4. (PLATE 6.2, FIG. 6.5)
Ring foot supporting irregular floor. Four roughly formed quadrants at centre. Mottled yellow glaze streaked by green and yellow brown pigments on inner surface and ouside to top

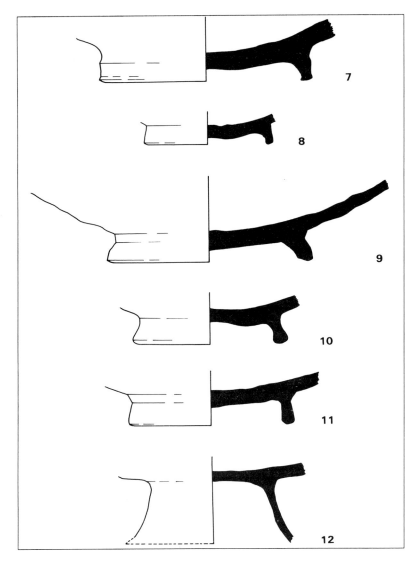

FIG. 6.3 (LEFT): *Sections through* **7-12**

of footplate.
Morgan, 47, fig. 32 no. 120 (= C); Jakobson 1979, fig. 51, no. 11

18. (C.385-1920) BOWL
d. 7.1, pres. h. 2.5. (PLATE 6.2, FIG. 6.5)
Ring foot. Abstract design of circle at centre of radiating lines enclosed by two concentric circles and band of raised rectangles. Deep yellow glaze speckled with brown on inner surface and outside to top of footplate.
Morgan, 47, fig. 32 no. 142 (= G)

19. (C.43-1921) BOWL
d. 10.9, pres. h. 3.9. (PLATE 6.2, FIG. 6.5)
Ring foot supporting irregular floor. Frontal bird looking left enclosed by three pairs of concentric circles. Dark, yellow-green glaze, streaked by green and yellow-brown pigments on inner surface and in band around
lower outer edge of ring foot. Thin clear glaze under floor. Floor marked by foot of another vessel during firing.

20. (C.44-1921) FRUIT STAND?
pres. h. 2.7. (PLATE 6.2, FIG. 6.5)
Ring foot completely broken; two horizontal ledges around junction of foot and body. Indistinct decoration. Olive green glaze streaked by green and yellow-brown pigments on inner surface only.
Peschlow, cat. no. 17, pl. 129. 1

21. (C.40-1921) FRUIT STAND?
pres. h. 1.9. (PLATE 6.2)
Ring foot broken at body. Two bands of four parallel lines cross

at centre of floor and extend up walls; tondo enclosed by band of small circles. Mottled olive green glaze streaked with brown pigments on inner surface only.

22. (C.11-1921) FRUIT STAND?
pres. h. 1.7. (PLATE 6.2)
Ring foot broken at body. Tondo enclosed by two concentric circles separated by short, slightly curved lines. Yellow-green glaze speckled with bright green pigments on inner surface only.
Peschlow, pl. 138 cat. no. 83 (= 1 and 2, chafing dish).

All the pieces were selected for museum collections as good specimens of their kind. It should, however, be remembered that Impressed Wares form a relatively rare category among Glazed White Wares. There are also, in the same class, shapes other than the bowls and dishes presented here.[55] The impressed designs are in relief but were frequently poorly rendered and indistinct. The fabrics are varied in appearance, but all are shades of white. **1–15, 17**, and **19–22** have a grainy fabric, with occasional grey specks. It is generally homogeneous, and quite smooth. In **16** and **18** the clay is pale pink and flecked with small red specks, as a result of overfiring. They correspond to the Glazed White Ware II fabrics described by Hayes.[56] Glazes, fluxed

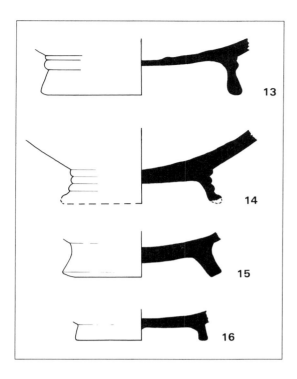

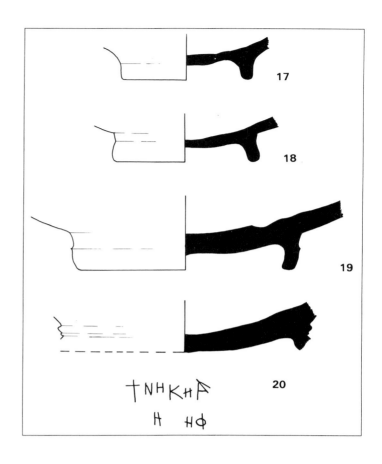

FIG. 6.4 (ABOVE, LEFT): *Sections through 13-16*

FIG. 6.5 (RIGHT): *Sections through 17-20*

by lead, are either yellow (as **15**, **16**, **17**), or shades of yellow ranging from orange-yellow (**3**, **5**, **11**, **22**), or yellow speckled with green (as **4**, **7**) or brown (as **13**, **15**, **18**), through olive-green (**8**, **9**, **10**, **20**, **21**) to plain green (as **14**).[57] The glaze is thickly applied and, though usually lustrous, it frequently has a pock-marked surface (**15**, **16**, **17**, **21**). Glazes sometimes extend on the outer surface to the top of the foot (as **4**, **6**, **14**, **16**). The vessels represented here were all fired upright; frequently the glaze has gathered thickly on the floor so as to obscure the decoration. Marks on the floor of **19**, and glaze on the base of the footplate of **15** indicate that vessels were stacked inside each other in the kiln. **13** and **19** have a second, thin, clear glaze on the underside of the foot and on the ring. They appear to have been glazed twice: first covered completely in a thin transparent glaze, then coated with coloured glaze on the interior and part of the exterior. The ring feet are of irregular form: they may be simple and shallow (as **2–5**, **8**, **10–11**), or they may be tall and thin (as **12**, **20**). **21** and **22** are cleanly broken at the junction of foot and body; they may belong to so-called 'fruit stands' with high pedestals which are susceptible to breaking at this point. The feet may be large and lumpy (**9**), or incurving (**7**), and the floor may be irregular (**6**) or very thick (**1**).

It has never been previously noted that there were two different techniques for producing the impressed decoration. The simple tondo designs of **16** and **17** were probably made by pressing a stamp on to the floor of the bowl, while the more complex decorations found on **9** and **10**, which extend up the walls, could not have been stamped without causing the vessel to collapse.[58] A mould of some sort must have been used to create the decoration where it covers a large area of the interior.[59] To produce the relief decoration, the design was cut into the stamps and moulds. Stamps have been found at Pergamon and another, of unknown provenance, is in the collections of the Ashmolean Museum.[60] Although no Byzantine moulds have been identified, objects which must have had a similar function have been found at the pottery-producing centres of Dvin and Ani in Armenia, and at Nishapur in Iran.[61] While the stamps and moulds were carefully crafted, the quality of relief varies. On the 'tondo-only' impressions the outline of the relief is frequently blurred, as on **4**, **7**, **15**, **16**, **17** and **22**.[62] This may have been caused by clogging of the stamp in repeated use. On bowls with slightly more complex tondo impressions, such as **8**, **11**, **14**, **18** and **21**, the motifs are usually well-defined. Some stamps were incised, producing pseudo-incised impressions on the pots, as on **13** and **14**. Production of such complex stamps may have been time-consuming, but it would have been significantly less so than incising individual bowls. The designs of **3** and **12**, and possibly **5**, are finely-wrought and detailed in a way not particularly suitable for the medium of clay. It is possible that the stamp for these

PLATE **6.1**:
Impressed White Wares
1–12 *from Constantinople*

was formed by being pressed on to a metal original. While birds are common impressed motifs, the bird of **12** has an unusual circle at the top of each wing. Could it originally have been a piece of jewellery, a pendant perhaps, which was used as a mould for a stamp which in turn was used to decorate pots? Likewise, the details of **3** and **5** suggest metal originals. The general appearance of the bowls with 'all-over' decoration is reminiscent of metal, and indeed the closest parallels for the designs are found on Islamic silver ware.[63]

Impressed decorative motifs include birds (**1–4, 7, 12–15**); animals (**6, 8, 10**); mythological (**3–5**) and amuletic (**17**) themes, or are simply abstract (**9, 11, 16, 18, 21, 22**). Within these groupings there is much variation: birds may be fine and detailed, as **3**, or barely recognisable lumps, as **4, 7, 15**; they may be in profile,

as **3, 12, 13**, or in a combination of frontal and profile, as **1, 2, 4, 14, 15**; they may be outlines only, as **4** and **7** or there may be some stylistic attempts to indicate plumage, as **1, 2, 13** and **14**. The iconography seems to make more sense when grouped not by common subjects but by common techniques of rendering the design. For instance, the bird of **14** is more closely related to the abstract **18** than it is to the birds of **3** or **4**. Hunting is a common theme in these reliefs and is portrayed in many aspects: there is a man hunting on **5**; the collar on the bird of **13** indicates that it had been trained to hunt in conjunction with humans; the lion of **6** and the eagles of **1, 2,** and **14** are also hunters.[64] The imagery of eating from the tree of life is conveyed by the iconography of **3**. Possibly the most interesting aspect of the decorations on Impressed White Wares

PLATE 6.2:
Impressed White Wares **13-22** *found at Sparta*

is the parallel cultural influences of the classical and middle eastern traditions. The hunter of **5** is rendered in a classicizing style reminiscent of a warrior, while the tree of life of **9** and the antithetic birds of **3** and **4** find parallels in eastern monumental reliefs.[65]

The chronology of Impressed White Wares has been disputed. The earliest date ever assigned to them was in the sixth century, based on some finds from Hagia Sophia.[66] Jakobson dated the Impressed White Wares from Chersonesos to the second half of the ninth and the tenth centuries.[67] Hayes has effectively demonstrated that while the earliest Glazed White Wares (his GWW I) appeared at Constantinople in appreciable quantities in the seventh century, Impressed and Glazed White Wares, (GWW II) appeared in the ninth century, and were particularly numerous during the tenth.[68] Most of the Saraçhane examples are tenth-century, continuing into the eleventh, but an unfortunate lacuna in the ninth-century deposits obscures understanding of the origins of Impressed Wares during that century. There are indications that some at least of **1–22** belong at the earlier end of the production period of Impressed White Wares. The later phase of GWW I, dated to the eighth century, includes bowls with incised motifs at the centre or bands of cut-out decoration around the rim.[69] The simple style of the bird on **13** calls to mind the incised decorations to be found in GWW I; indeed the stamp itself must have looked just like the centres of some GWW I bowls. The borders of *impressed* triangles on **8** and **13** are reminiscent of the bands of *cut-out* triangles found on GWW I. Perhaps stamping emerged as a production-line method for creating incised-like decorations, and the new technique eventually took on its own character.[70] All the Impressed Wares presented here should be dated to the ninth and tenth centuries.

How do ten fragments of broken bowls from Lakedaimon add to our knowledge, and what do they tell us? They are evidence of contacts and trade between the capital and a remote provincial city. It cannot have been easy to transport bulky ceramics, particularly on the final part of the journey overland between the port and the city.[71] It seems hard to believe that such a task was undertaken because of the aesthetic

merits of the vessels: unlike their Polychrome counterparts, Impressed White Wares were not objects to be
desired for their beauty. Were there people living in
Lakedaimon at this time who wanted familiar products,
who perhaps found it hard to dine without such aids as
chafing dishes, and were used to glazed vessels for food
preparation and serving? One question which poses
itself, and to which there is no obvious answer, is why
glazed pottery was not produced where it was wanted,
rather than transported such a long way. Plain wares
were manufactured locally, but it was not until the end
of the eleventh century that Sparta, like many other
places, became a flourishing glazed ceramic production
centre, utilizing local clays. The answer does not lie in
the glazing technology itself: the glazes of the ninth
and tenth are essentially the same as those applied in
the twelfth and thirteenth centuries.[72] Perhaps there
was some fiscal restriction, or even artistic constraints,
on production outside the capital.

Central and southern Greece experienced large scale
population upheavals throughout the seventh century,
associated with Slav migrations southwards and
subsequent emigration of the indigenous peoples.[73]
This was a gradual process; the 'invaders', nomadic
tribesmen with no coherent civic structure and
probably no concept of territorial invasion, arrived
intermittently. The tenuous nature of their takeover,
combined with more perceptible pressing problems in
the east, meant that Constantinople did not focus its
attention on them for a long time, and imperial
government effectively ceased to administer the Balkan
penisula. The city of Lakedaimon itself became
deserted, its citizens having emigrated to Sicily.[74] The
turning point came during the reign of Nikephoros I
(802–813).[75] He reestablished the *polis* of Lakedaimon
with plantations of Thrakesioi, Armenians and
Kapheroi, all Greek-speaking and Orthodox, from
eastern areas of the empire.[76] Nikephoros also
broached the problem of ineffective government by
creating the administrative theme of Peloponnesos.[77]
The greatest achievement of his non-agressive defeat
of the Slavs was their conversion to christianity.[78] By
the first decade of the tenth century the Slavonic
element in the population had been Hellenized to the
extent that it could not be distinguished.[79] It cannot
be coincidental that White Wares started to reach Lakedaimon at the same time as its 'rehellenization'.
Rehellenization by the use of spoken Greek, and the
preservation of Byzantine political, cultural and
religious practices has already been examined: the use
of Constantinopolitan-produced table wares is a
physical manifestation of the cultural aspect of the
rehellenization of southern Greece.[80]

Finally, stress should be laid upon the contribution
archaeological studies can make to historical understanding. From our map of findspots (FIG. 3.1), even
taking suspected lacunae into consideration, it is clear
that distribution radiates from Constantinople, with
the Black Sea as the primary market, though findspots
are common in other coastal regions and on islands.
Small quantities make their way in or overland to
relatively remote sites. The presence of White Wares,
as demonstrated above, is evidence of Byzantine
authority which may be lacking from other sources. A
specific case study might be the extent of Byzantine
influence in Rus in the tenth century. The evidence of
White Wares in that part of the world added to the
arguments already adduced by Professor Obolensky
would take that particular debate on to another level.[81]
The latter-day Byzantine *koine* must be grateful to Peter
Megaw for his unceasing archaeological labours which
have extended so much our knowledge of the Byzantine
world.

Institute for Archaeology, Oxford

NOTES

1. Residual fragments of White Wares had previously been noted there: A. H. S. Megaw, 'Supplementary Excavations on a castle Site at Paphos, Cyprus, 1970–71' *DOP* 26 (1972) 340.

2. D. Talbot Rice, *Byzantine Glazed Pottery* (Oxford 1930); White Wares form all of his subgroups of class A, as well as B4.

3. R. B. K. Stevenson, 'The Pottery 1936–7' in *The Great Palace of the Byzantine Emperors. First Report* (Oxford 1947) 38–50, pls. 16, 17, 22; U. Peschlow, 'Byzantinische Keramik aus Istanbul. Ein Fundkomplex bei der Irenenkirche', *Ist. Mitt.* 27/28 (1977/78) 363–414.

4. J. Čimbuleva, 'Vases à glaçure en argile blanche de Nessèbre (IXe–XIIe)' in V. Velkov (ed.) *Nessèbre* 2 (Sofia 1980) 202–53; A. L. Jakobson, *Srednevekovi Khersones, XII–XIV vv. (MIA)* 17 (Moscow 1950) 219–21, pls. 36–39; A. L. Jakobson, *Rannesrednevekovi Khersones, (MIA 63)* (Moscow, 1959), 332–57, pls. 1–17; C. H. Morgan, *Corinth XI, The Byzantine Pottery* (Cambridge Mass. 1942) 42–9, 51–7, 64–71, pls. 4–11, 13–18.

5. T. I. Makarova, *Polivnaja posuda iz istorii keramiceskogo importa i proizvodstvo na Drevnej Rusi* (Moscow 1967) *Svod Archeologijeskich Istojnikov* E1–38, 8–34.

6. A. H. S. Megaw and R. E. Jones, 'Byzantine and Allied Pottery: A Contribution by Chemical Analysis to Problems of Origin and Distribution' *BSA* 78 (1983) 235–263; batch D (from Corinth) and batch J (from Constantinople).

7. Megaw and Jones, 242. The area may be large, possibly measured in kilometres.

8. J. W. Hayes, *Excavations at Saraçhane in Istanbul,* Vol. 2, *The Pottery* (Princeton 1992) 12.

9. Hayes, 12.

10. White clay, from an unknown source, was used in small quantities to prepare the bodies of fifteenth-century Iznik tiles: J. Henderson and J. Raby, 'The technology of fifteenth century Turkish tiles: an interim statement on the origins of the Iznik industry' *World Archaeology* 21.1. *Ceramic Technology* (1989), 115–132.

11. K. Mijatev, *Die Keramik von Preslav* (Sofia 1936); I. Akrabova, 'La céramique décorative de Touzlalak', *Fouilles et Recherches, Musée National Bulgare* (Sofia 1947) 101.

12. Hayes, 329, n. 8; R. B. Mason and M. M. Mango, 'Glazed Tiles of Nicomedia in Bithynia, Constantinople and Elsewhere', in C. Mango and G. Dagron (eds), *Constantinople and its Hinterland* (Oxford 1995) 313–358.

13. 'Nikomedian tiles' was proposed by P. Verdier, 'Tiles of Nikomedia' in C. Mango and O. Pritsak (eds), *Okeanos. Essays Presented to Ihor Ševčenko. Harvard Ukrainian Studies* 7 (1983) 633; followed by Mason and Mango, *supra* n.12.

14. Hayes, 12–40.

15. For the decoration of Polychrome Ware see D. Talbot Rice, 'Byzantine Polychrome Pottery, A Survey of Recent Discoveries', *CA* 7 (1954), 69–77; for its use in buildings see A. Pasadaios, Ὁ Κεραμοπλαστικός Διάκοσμος τῶν Βυζαντινῶν Κτηρίων τῆς Κωνσταντινουπόλεως (Athens 1973).

16. Publication of the White Wares from the Saraçhane excavations has stimulated their recognition at other locations: see the acknowledgement in A. di Vita, 'Glazed White Ware I–II di Saraçhane: Nuove Evidenze da Gortina' *Annuario* NS 48–9 (1988–9) 351.

17. H. Patterson, 'Medieval Domestic Pottery' in F. D'Andria and D. Whitehouse (eds.), *Excavations at Otranto* Vol. 2 *The Finds* (Lecce 1992) 163–6, nos. 704–717.

18. Paphos: A. H. S. Megaw, 'Supplementary excavations on a castle site at Paphos, Cyprus, 1970–71', *DOP* 26 (1972) 340; Kourion, from excavations in the 'Episcopal Precinct', publication forthcoming.

19. At Gortyn: A. di Vita, (n.16), 351–5.

20. Kato Komia, Emborio, Perivolia, and Rivari, found during intensive survey: see *An Island Polity. The Archaeology of Exploitation in Melos* (eds. C. Renfrew and M. Wagstaff), = site nos. 21, 43, 92, 95 (in Appendix A). Subsequent fieldwork, with the aim of examining the function of selected sites found during the first survey, identified the hitherto unrecognized Byzantine occupation of these four sites. I am grateful to Richard Catling and Guy Sanders for permission to refer to them in advance of publication.

21. J. K. Brock, 'Siphnos: Hellenistic, Roman and Medieval Pottery', *BSA* 44 (1949) 72, pl. 22, nos. 37 and 39.

22. F. Felten, *Alt-Ägina*, I.2 (Mainz 1975) 75–6, nos. 150–58, PL. 28.

23. As well as **12–22** here, there were other White Wares from the early excavations; their publication, by the present author, is forthcoming.

24. At a place known locally as Soteira (site P284), near the cave monastery of Hagioi Saranda, and at the former location of the village of Chrysapha (site U490), they were found in the course of intensive survey: see P. Armstrong, 'Byzantine and Ottoman Pottery' in William Cavanagh, Joost Crouwel, R. W.V. Catling and Graham Shipley (eds.), *The Laconia Survey*, vol. 2, *BSA supp. vol.* 27, (London 1996) 129, types 10 and 11.

25. Morgan *supra* n.4, 64–71.

26. F. O. Waagé, 'The Roman and Byzantine Pottery', *Hesp.* 2 (1933) 321–2, fig. 17, a & b.

27. A few fragments have been identified from recent excavations, see P. Armstrong, 'Byzantine Thebes: Excavations on the Kadmeia, 1980', *BSA* 88 (1993) 304, nos. 39–41.

28. Excavated from reoccupation levels at a classical temple, see P. Armstrong, 'The Byzantine and Later Pottery' in *Kalapodi* I, ed. R. C. S. Felsch (Berlin, in press), cat. no. 15.

29. From excavations at the Rotunda of Agios Georgios, see Ch. Bakirtzis and D. Papanikola-Bakirtzis, 'De la céramique Byzantine en glaçure à Thessalonique', *Byzantino-Bulgarica* 7 (1981), 421–23; from excavations at the church of Agios Nikolaos Tranos, see D. Evgenidou, 'Η κεραμεική τῆς ἀνασκαφῆς τοῦ Ἁγίου Νικολάου Τρανοῦ τῆς Θεσσαλονίκης' Ἀνθρωπολογικά 3 (1982) 25, nos. 1–7.

30. Found during intensive survey, Delta site nos. 4, 7, and 8; see A. W. Dunn, 'From *polis* to *kastron* in southern Macedonia: Amphipolis, Khrysoupolis, and the Strymon Delta', *Castrum 5. Archéologie de l'habitat fortifié. Archéologie des espaces agraires méditerranéens au Moyen Age* (Madrid/Rome 1998) 399–413.

31. Ch. Bakirtzis, *Deltion, Chr.,* (1976) 325, 326, fig. 3. I am grateful to Archibald Dunn for this reference.

32. P. Armstrong and N. Günsenin, 'Glazed Pottery Production at Ganos', *Anatolia Antiqua* 3 (1995) cat. nos. 80–81.

33. Čimbuleva *supra* n.4, 203, refers to unpublished white wares from Sozopol (= Apollonia).

34. M. Lazarov, 'Arheologičeski razkopki i proucvanija v Burgaski okrag. Rezultati, problemi i zadaci', *Izvestija na balgarskite muzei* 1 (1969) 16, figs, 7, 9.

35. Čimbuleva *supra* n.4, 202–53.

36. Varna = ancient Odessos. Čimbuleva, *supra* n. 4, 203, refers to unpublished white wares from Varna.

37. G. Stefan, I. Barnea, M. Comşa, E. Comşa, *Dinogetia* Vol. 1, *Biblioteca de Arheologie* XIII (Bucharest 1967) 240–3, figs. 146–7.

38. *Djadovo* vol. 1, *Mediaeval Settlement and Necropolis 11th–12th Century*, eds. A. Fol, R. Katincarov, J. Best, N. deVries, K. Shoju, H. Suzuki (Tokyo 1989) 224, fig. 260.

39. K. Mijatev, *Die Keramik von Preslav* (Sofia 1936); I. Gospodinov, 'New Finds at Preslav', *Bulletin of the Bulgarian Archaeological Institute* 15 (1946); I. Akrabova, 'La céramique décorative de Touzlalak', (n.11) 101; S. Vitljanov, 'Kam vaprosa za vizantijskata beloglinena keramika ot Pliska i Preslav' in *Preslav* 3 (1983) 160–7; Christine Vogt and Anne

Bouqillan, 'Technologie des plaques murales décorées de Preslav et de Constantinople (IXᵉ–XIᵉ siècles)', *CA* 44 (1996) 105–116.

40. A. L. Jakobson, *Keramika i keramičeskoe proizvodstvo srednevekovo Tavriki* (Leningrad 1979) 83–93.

41. Makarova *supra* n.5, 78–81, pl. 1, nos. 2–11; pl. 3, no. 4; pl. 4, no.1; pl. 5, nos. 1, 5, 6.

42. Makarova *supra* n.5, pl. 1, nos. 12-19; pl. 2, nos. 2, 3, 6; pl. 5, nos. 3, 7.

43. Makarova *supra* n.5, pl. 1, nos. 2-23; pl. 3, nos. 2, 3, 5; pl. 5, nos. 2, 4, 9; A. Sasanov, 'Les niveaux de la première moitié du XIᵉ siècle à Kerch (Crimée)', *Anatolia Antiqua* 4 (1996), 191–200. There are White Wares, and other finds, from Kertch in the Victoria and Albert Museum.

44. Makarova *supra* n.5, pl. 2, no. 1.

45. Makarova *supra* n.5, pl. 4, no. 2.

46. Many White Wares were found in excavations of the theatre at Nicaea, personal communication from Véronique François; more recently, as a result of intensive survey, they have been found at the sites of Karacakaya Köyü and Hisarcik in the vicinity of Nicaea, see V. François, 'La céramique byzantine en Bithynie' in J. Lefort et alii, *La Bithynie au Moyen Age* (Paris, forthcoming). I am grateful to her for this information, and for permission to refer to it in advance of publication.

47. D. Talbot Rice, 'The Pottery of Byzantium and the Islamic World', in *Studies in Islamic Art and Architecture in Honour of Professor K. A. C. Cresswell* (Cairo 1965) 198.

48. Found during excavation of the cathedral of Xanthos; publication by the present author is in progress.

49. At an otherwise unknown site (Site 29) a few kilometres east of the city, it was found during the course of intensive survey: see P. Armstrong and A. MacDonald, 'The Pottery' in *The Balboura Survey*, ed. J. J. Coulton (Oxford, in press).

50. I am grateful to the Managing Committee of the British School at Rome for a Rome Scholarship, which supported research carried out in Faenza. I am indebted to Dr. Sauro Gelichi for all his advice and help. Professor Gian Carlo Bojani, Director of the Museo Internazionale delle Ceramiche, Faenza, kindly granted permission to publish nos. 1–12, and Giorgio Assirelli and the museum librarian are gratefully thanked for their unfailing kindness and hospitality.

51. See G. Dickins, 'Laconia II. Excavations at Sparta. 1906', *BSA* 12 (1905–6) 394–406, esp. 404, where he records that the houses stood to two storeys; also R. M. Dawkins, *BSA* 15 (1908–9) 3.

52. Given by the Department of Archaeology of the Ministry of Education of the Greek Republic, through Mr. A. M. Woodward. I would like to thank Oliver Watson and Judith Crouch for their help and patience while working at the Victoria and Albert Museum.

53. R. M. Dawkins, J. P. Droop, 'Byzantine Pottery from Sparta', *BSA* 17 (1910–11) 23–28. Further ceramics from the early excavations are in process of publication.

54. The comparanda are found in: Hayes: *supra* n. 8: Jakobson 1978: A. L. Jakobson, 'Srednevekovaja polivnaja keramika kak istoričeskoe javlenie' *Vizantijskij Vremennik* 39 (1978) 148–59; Jakobson 1979: *supra* n.40; Morgan: *supra* n.4; Peschlow: *supra* n.3.

55. Hayes *supra* n.8, 21.

56. Hayes *supra* n.8, 18–19.

57. For the chemical composition of the glazes see: P. Armstrong, H. Hatcher and M. Tite, 'Changes in Byzantine Glazing Technology from the Ninth to the Thirteenth Centuries' in G. Démians d'Archimbaud (ed.), *La Céramique Médiévale en Méditerranée* (Aix-en-Provence, 1997) 225-229.

58. The fabric must have been relatively soft to accept the impressions and so liable to collapse if not handled with suitable caution.

59. See also Hayes *supra* n.8, 12, 'relief moulding'.

60. The Pergamon stamps were identified by Peter Megaw: A. H. S. Megaw, 'A Byzantine Potter's Stamp?', *AAA* 1.2 (1968) 197–200. The Oxford stamp (inventory no. 1980.37), a White Ware, is of grey-white clay and coated with a similar thick glaze, in this case green, as were the vessels it must have been used to decorate.

61. Dvin and Ani: Shelkovnikov, *Sovietskaja Arkheologija* 1 (1958) 214-27, where they were in use in the tenth and eleventh centuries; Nishapur: C. K. Wilkinson, *Nishapur. Pottery of the Early Islamic Period* (New York 1973) 272–6, where they seem to be later, from the eleventh and twelfth centuries.

62. It is difficult, therefore, to produce accurate or meaningful line drawings of the decoration.

63. B. Marschak, *Silberschätze des Orients. Metalkunst des 3.– 13. Jahrhunderts und ihre Kontinuität* (Leipzig 1986): 17— Abb. 94, centre of cup, from the Khazar Khaganate, eighth to ninth centuries; 6, 7, and 8—Abb. 108–9, for tondo enclosed by beaded band, 108 has animal in tondo, from Turkish regions or Sogdiana, date uncertain (proposed eighth century too early); 10—Abb 97, ring of beaded circles on upper body, from Iran 750–75; 8—Abb. 120/121, similar rendering of lion, Hungarian imitation of middle–eastern vessel, late ninth to early tenth centuries.

64. Hunting and its imagery on Byzantine ceramics are discussed in: P. Armstrong, 'Byzantine Glazed Ceramic Tableware in the Collection of the Detroit Institute of Arts', *Bulletin of the Detroit Institute of Arts* 71, 1/2 (1997) 4–15; see also Marie-Louise von Wartburg, 'Bowls and Birds', *infra*.

65. For such classicizing tendencies see C. Mango, *La Civiltà Bizantina dal IX all'XI Secolo* (Bari 1978) 282; for silver plate see Marlia Mundell Mango, 'Imperial Art in the Seventh Century' in *New Constantines: the Rhythm of Imperial Renewal in Byzantium, 4th–13th Centuries*, ed. P. Magdalino (London 1994) 119. Eastern parallels for this type of pottery is given by Jakobson, *supra* n.4, 332–342.

66. F. W. Deichmann, 'Zur datierung der byzantinishen Reliefkeramik', *AA* 1941, cols. 72–81.

67. Jakobson *supra* n.4, 332–42.

68. Hayes, 12–19; *id*; 'A Seventh-Century Pottery Group', in R. M. Harrison, N. Firatlı, 'Excavations at Saraçhane in Istanbul: Fifth Preliminary Report', *DOP* 22 (1968), 203–16.

69. One deposit at Saraçhane (Deposit 36) contained the latest stages of GWW I together with the earliest examples of GWW II; it belongs in the first half of the ninth century: Hayes, 17.

70. Hayes speculates on the function of stamping, since some are indistinct and visually meaningless: Hayes, 21.

71. The port of Byzantine Sparta was in southern Lakonia, in the Helos plain, approached along the channelled course of the river Eurotas.

72. The theory that there was a change in the technological requirements for producing glazes some time in the eleventh century has been tested, and rejected: P. Armstrong *et al*, *supra* n.57, 225-229; see also Guy D. R. Sanders 'Byzantine Polychrome Pottery' *infra*.

73. The principal source is the so-called *Chronicle of Monemvasia*, ed. Ivan Dujčev, *Cronaca di Monemvasia. Introduzione, testo critico, traduzione e note*, (Palermo 1976). The evidence is referred to by A. Bon, *Le Péloponnèse byzantin jusqu'en 1204* (Paris 1951) 31–64. The Greeks took refuge in fortified sites, and on the Aegean islands: see Sinclair Hood, 'Isles of Refuge in the Early Byzantine Period', *BSA* 65 (1970) 37–44; Vasso Pennas, 'The Island of Orovi in the Argolid: Bishopric and Administrative Center' in Nicolas Oikonomides (ed.), *Studies in Byzantine Sigillography*, vol. 4, (Washington 1995) 163–173; those who could afford to go further afield settled in Calabria and Sicily: G. L. Huxley, 'The Second Dark Age of the Peloponnese',

Λακωνικαὶ Σπουδαί 3 (1977) 84–109.

74. For the abandonment of the city see Ch. Bouras, 'City and Village: Urban Design and Architecture', *XVI Internationaler Byzantinistenkongress. Akten, Jahrbuch der Österreichischen Byzantinistik*, 31/1 (1981) 622; for the emigration see the *Chronicle of Monemvasia*, ed. Dujčev, p.12, l.95-6: 'Now at that time the Lakonians left the land of their fathers; they sailed away to the island of Sicily'. That the Lakonians went to Sicily, and did not 'take refuge' at some of the uncomfortable sites closer to home suggests they were prosperous.

75. See P. Niavis, *The Reign of the Byzantine Emperor Nicephorus I* (Athens 1987) 79–91.

76. *Chronicle of Monemvasia*, ed. Dujčev, p.22, l.196-9; P. Charanis, 'Nicephorus I, the Savior of Greece from the Slavs (810 AD)', *Byzantina-Metabyzantina*, i (1946) 75–92. 'Reestablishment' does not necessarily imply that the city was deserted, simply that it was not functioning in a 'civic' manner. Theophanes, while agreeing with these events as related in the *Chronicle*, places then in a rather different context: *The Chronicle of Theophanes Confessor*, eds. Cyril Mango and Roger Scott (Oxford 1997) 667. See also N. Oikonomides, 'St Andrew, Joseph the Hymnographer, and the Slavs of Patras', in J. O. Rosenqvist (ed.) *Λειμών. Studies presented to Lennart Rydén on His Sixty-Fifth Birthday* (Uppsala 1996) 71–78.

77. N. Oikonomides, *Les Listes de Préséance byzantines des IXᵉ et Xᵉ siècles* (Paris 1972) 350, 352; W. Treadgold, *The Byzantine Revival*, 160–1.

78. *Chronicle of Monemvasia*, ed. Dujčev, p.20, l.76-7: 'He (Nikephoros) ordered . . . the barbarians to be made Christian'; he helped his orders to be met by increasing the 'Byzantine' population.

79. The exception that proves the rule is a specific reference to two Slavic tribes in an early tenth-century text, indicating that they stood out sufficiently to be noted: Constantine Porphyrogenitos, *De Administrando Imperio*, ed. G. Moravcsik and R. J. H. Jenkins (Washington 1967), ch. 50, p. 224.

80. J. Herrin, 'Aspects of the Process of Hellenization in the Early Middle Ages' *BSA* 68 (1973) 113–126.

81. The progression of the debate can be found in: A. Poppe, 'The Political Background to the Baptism of Rus', *DOP* 30 (1976) 195–244; D. Obolensky, 'Cherson and the Conversion of Rus', *BMGS* 13 (1989) 244-56; and *idem* 'Byzantium, Kiev and Cherson in the Tenth Century' in *Byzantium and its Neighbours from the Mid–Ninth till the Twelfth Centuries. Papers read at the Byzantinological Symposium, Bechyne, 1990* (Prague 1993) 108–113.

7

The Middle-Byzantine Athenian Church of the Taxiarchs near the Roman Agora

Charalambos Bouras

One of the most important Middle-Byzantine monuments in Athens destroyed last century was the Church of the Taxiarchs alongside the Roman Agora. The church was demolished in 1850 so that a new and larger parish church, completed in 1852, could take its place at a time when Athens, capital of the newly established Greek kingdom, was witnessing rapid population growth. The site of the church in the 'Wheat Market', the commercial district of the town in the later Ottoman period, as well as its position in the immediate vicinity of the west gate of the Roman Agora, established the Taxiarchs, (along with the neighbouring church of Profitis Elias, likewise now demolished), as a building readily accessible to visitors from abroad. This accounts for the relatively large number of illustrations and measured drawings from before 1850 that allow us today to make a satisfactory study of the church's architecture. Up till that time the church was in good condition, although information does exist[1] concerning a fire there during the Revolutionary period.

Firstly, a misunderstanding should be cleared up: in his to date unique catalogue of the medieval monuments of Athens, *Index of Medieval Monuments in Greece*, published in 1929, A. Xyngopoulos[2] classified the present church of the Taxiarchs amongst those Byzantine buildings that had been altered by repairs. This mistaken view was repeated by K. Biris[3] and indirectly by J. Travlos.[4] The ground plan, the dimensions, together with specific information from the General State Archives[5] confirm that the Taxiarchs was completely demolished in order to provide room for the present church.

To glean information about the architecture of the original church of the Taxiarchs, we must refer to documentary evidence gathered prior to its demolition, and search for material remains of the Byzantine church, now included, though not readily noticeable, in the modern church. Depictions of the original church include the following:

1. C. HANSEN, 1833. Perspective pencil drawing of the *propylon* of the Archegetis Athena. In the background the church of the Taxiarchs can be discerned to the south-west. Extensively published.[6]
2. E. PEYTIER, 1833. Two watercolours with perspective views of the church from the north-west. Published.[7]
3. M. G. BINDERSBELL, 1835. Three pencil drawings and watercolours (ground plan and cross sections) and two line drawings in pencil (west and north face). All the drawings have been published.[8] The first three were already well known.[9]
4. J. SKENE, 1838. View of the monument from the north-west. Watercolour.[10] Republished.[11]
5. W. COLE, 1835. View of the monument from the north-west. Watercolour.[12] Republished.[13]
6. A. COUCHAUD, 1842. Line drawing of the ground plan, longitudinal section and elevations of both narrow sides of the monument.[14] The first two were published by A. Xyngopoulos.[15]
7. ANONYMOUS, in the drawing collection of the University of Karlsruhe. Two pencil drawings, at a scale of 1:75, of the west and east face, from 1842–49.[16] Published along with drawings of the neighbouring church of Profitis Elias.[17]
8. T. DUMONCEL, 1845.[18] Perspective illustration of the church from the south-west. Engraving. Repeatedly published.[19]
9. GAILHABAUD (published in 1853 and 1854).[20] Perspective illustration of the church from the south-west (engraving) and two line drawings of the east and west faces of the main church, as if the later narthex had not been added.[21] All were republished by A. Xyngopoulos,[22] where they are mistakenly attributed to an unknown demolished Athenian church. Both line drawings have been republished elsewhere.[23]

These drawings and engravings naturally cannot all be of equal value as architectural evidence. Their unique nature, however, makes them useful when studied together since information can be cross-checked prior to being confirmed or remaining doubtful.

No historical testimonies exist concerning the church of the Taxiarchs.[24] Today, the church also bears the name of the Virgin Gregorousa. No scholarly interest has even been shown in the monument; only references[25] have been made, and an indefinite date of the 11th or 12th century[26] has been silently accepted. The monument underwent at least three building phases: the first saw the erection of the main church, the second the addition of the narthex, and the third probably belongs to the Ottoman period.

In Couchaud's ground plans and sections, a line dividing the original building and the narthex is clearly discernible,[27] while Gailhabaud's idea to draw the face of the main church by itself indicates that he considered the narthex a later addition. The dividing line between the two phases does not appear in Bindesbell's drawing of the north face, although it would appear that structural remains are evident at this particular point[28] and concealed the join. Finally, the bi-lobe window of the church's west cross-arm, visible in the longitudinal section by Couchaud, would be meaningless if the narthex was contemporary with the main church.

The simple bell-tower with its single arch[29] was added to the west arm of the narthex, and is attributed to the third building phase. The outer wall-paintings of the Ottoman period which covered the façade after the filling of its bi-lobe windows with masonry[30] indicate that there was once a shelter here, perhaps a lightly constructed timber porch.

Typologically, the Taxiarchs belongs to the class of domed cross-in-square two-column churches,[31] without a narthex, and with a slightly projecting semi-hexagonal sanctuary apse. Couchaud's ground plan does not indicate how the vaults were constructucted, but Bindesbell's drawing shows that the four corner compartments were covered with cross-vaults; square to the east and elongated to the west. Couchaud's section confirms the existence, at least in the west compartments, of cross-vaults (the arches of the vertical faces), delineated slightly below the springings of the vaults of the cross-arms; this resulted in the elevation of the interior space.[32] The use of cross-vaults, furthermore, allowed the corner compartments to be covered with single sloping roofs of equal height from the ground.[33] The slight reductions of thickness in the side walls at the extremities of the transverse vaults of the cross are a common phenomenon in cross-in-square Middle-Byzantine churches.[34] The use of cross-vaults above corner compartments,[35] while common especially in the 12th century, is also encountered in earlier examples,[36] such as the Theotokos church at Hosios Loukas and Hagia Aikaterini in Plaka, Athens.

As regards the later narthex, the use of cross-vaults on the sides was probably dictated by a wish to integrate the roof surfaces with those of the main church. Other similar examples, however, exist.[37] The existence of two sarcophagi underneath acrosolia at the north and south ends of the narthex[38] emphasizes that the structure was funerary; it was added chiefly to house the tombs of important persons.

The church of the Taxiarchs may be considered a typical Athenian Middle-Byzantine monument as far as architectural forms and decoration are concerned. The marble formal elements (doorframes with decorative cornices, colonnettes with imposts on all the windows, and interior columns with capitals) testify that, despite its small size, this was a carefully built, ornate church. From the surviving depictions, the church does not seem to have had a crepidoma. The façade of the first phase consisted (according to Gailhabaud's drawing) of three entrances between which well-built pillars had been constructed with large blocks, reminiscent of those at the Hagioi Apostoloi in the Athenian Agora.[39] The three entrances are, furthermore, characteristic of other early Athenian churches (the katholikon of the Petraki monastery, Soter of Lykodemos, Kapnikarea, and possibly Hagia Aikaterini in Plaka). From the drawings of the façades by Couchaud, Gailhabaud, and those preserved in the

Karlsruhe archives, it appears that very bulky blocks were used for the lower parts of the walls while the typical cloisonné system is developed further up. Of interest on the long sides were only the cross-arms, similar to those of Hagioi Asomatoi in Theseion.

The three horse-shoe arches at the entrances of the main church are very reminiscent of the side entrances to Kapnikarea[40] and Hagioi Asomatoi in Theseion.[41] They were of poros stone and concentric to others, made of brick.

The dome was a representative example of the 'Athenian dome' with protruding water spouts and marble colonnettes at the corners. It also preserved an archaising element (given that its original model was the dome of the Theotokos church at Hosios Loukas): the horizontal marble string courses at the springing of the windows.[42]

The dog-tooth cornice had been destroyed on the cross-arms, but not along the long sides of the church.[43] On the narrow sides of the building its transformation to dog-tooth frets is once again reminiscent of the Theotokos at Hosios Loukas. In the bi-lobe window of the sanctuary, the dog-tooth fret stopped at the height of the springing of its arch, a feature likewise attested in earlier monuments.[44]

Formal features that appear on the façade of the later narthex are of a later period: on the one hand, the two large windows flanking the doorway (reminiscent of the likewise later exonarthex of the katholikon at Hosios Loukas[45]), and on the other the vivid presence of the horizontal wall crown consisting of a double (?) dog-tooth fret running uninterrupted along the entire width of the façade.[46]

Naturally, the extant drawings of the Church of the Taxiarchs cannot throw any light on constructional questions pertaining to the monument. According to Bindesbell's section plan, the interior was entirely covered with wall-paintings, although according to Couchaud, only fragments had survived. Of the marble templon, two proskynetaria on the pillars which divided the sanctuary from the side-chambers,[47] along with the epistyle,[48] were still in situ.

It would appear that all the building material from the demolished Byzantine church was used in the erection of the modern Church of the Taxiarchs. Certain marble architectural elements from the older church were re-employed in such a manner as to promote them in one way or another. These include the two impost capitals which now crown the columns of the portico, six double-colonnettes, three imposts from double-colonnettes of the bi-lobe windows (now included in the upper zone of the present west side), and finally a plaque of a pseudo-sarcophagus included within the parapet of the gallery of the modern church.

The simple elongated column capitals measure 67cmx49cm in plan and 18cm high. They may be characterised as impost capitals, but from the side they are inscribed along a curve. When they came to be reused, their lower surfaces were unskillfully cut away.

Their narrow sides are decorated with small foliate Greek crosses in shallow relief, a style common to 11th-century Greece. These were certainly not older spolia, but had been fashioned specifically for the Taxiarchs church.[49]

Five of the six solid double-colonnettes of the windows have been included in openings of the façade, and the sixth in the south face. All are perfectly preserved and their capitals (solid with the colonnettes) are decorated on three sides with rosettes surrounded by bands to produce the well-known lyre motif.

The three imposts were placed on top of the three double colonnettes. Their protruding narrow surface is of a typically oblique, trapezoidal shape and is perfectly preserved. The first to the north (PLATE 7.1) is decorated with a foliate cross whose arms are highlighted at the extremities with simple rosettes, while the space above the cross-arms is filled by more rosettes, this time star shaped with eight radials. The middle impost (PLATE 7.2) is adorned with a Greek cross, the end of each of the arms curving inward to produce two five-leaf palmettes, one on each side of the cross. The third impost (PLATE 7.3) is decorated with four complex palmettes symmetrically positioned in two groups. The decoration of all three imposts is in shallow relief, and is stylistically typical of 12th-century sculpture on the Greek mainland with the ground completely covered and a clear interplay of leaf and rinceau motifs.

Undoubtedly the most important of the preserved sculptural members is the plaque of the pseudo-sarcophagus, which may have originally graced one of the arcosolia of the later narthex (PLATE 7.4).[50] Its present dimensions are 65x203cm. The lower zone of the frame surrounding the main depiction has been cut away (given that the plaque had to fit into the parapet of the later gallery); thus originally it would have been some 15cm wider on the narrow side.[51]

The decoration of this plaque, in shallow relief, includes three foliate crosses within square compartments delineated with triple bands. Triple bands also define the entire central motif and are linked to the first group of bands and between each other via circular knots. The lower leaves of the foliate crosses of each compartment are developed into reflected tendril patterns, while the square spaces created above, between the cross arms and the border of each cross, are adorned with small motifs (acanthus-like palmettes for the side crosses, and radial rosettes for the middle one).

The reflected tendril patterns are not all identical. Two independent foliate motifs are depicted on either side of the group of crosses. Each consists of an upright palm leaf (?) and symmetrically arranged semi-palmettes. These two foliate motifs do not entirely match. The surface of the pseudo-sarcophagus is

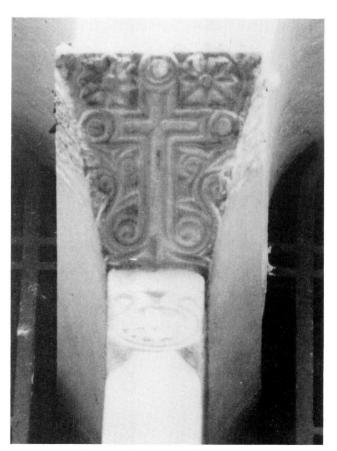

PLATE 7.1: *Athens, Taxiarchs. The first impost.*

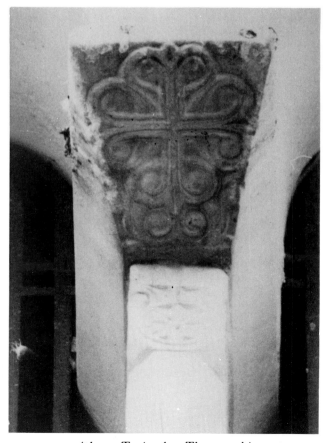

PLATE 7.2: *Athens, Taxiarchs. The second impost.*

PLATE 7.3: *Athens, Taxiarchs. The third impost.*

bordered by a tripartite zone consisting of an astragalus, a concave band and a simple outer frame.

Clearly, this plaque represents a distinguished and original work of decorative sculpture for Middle-Byzantine Greece, and deserves further study, in particular of the decorative motifs.

Firstly, the three crosses are quite common as main motifs on Middle-Byzantine sarcophagi or pseudo-sarcophagi. The central cross is usually differentiated from the other two, no matter what form or style is employed. Of the many that survive,[52] some Athenian examples can be found at the church of the Hagioi Apostoloi in the Agora, the church of the Homologitai, at the Byzantine Museum (Athens) no. 3166,[53] and an unpublished example from the monastery of St. John Kynegos.[54]

Cypress, palm leaf, palm or multi-ribbed leaf motifs are also frequent symmetrical decorative features on sarcophagi,[55] but also on closure panels.[56] They usually surround the crosses and probably have a symbolical meaning. In our plaque, the upright multi-ribbed leaves sprout amongst tendril-like semi-palmettes[57] with pointed tips, and are of a type which most approaches an example from outside Greece.[58]

The astragalus border of the sarcophagus is an Ancient Greek motif that survived or was revived in Middle-Byzantine Greek sculpture. A great number

of examples survive, and the motif is of little use in helping to date the architectural members which it adorns. But it is noteworthy that the form and manner in which our plaque is framed closely resembles the pseudo-sarcophagus of the Hagioi Apostoloi in the Agora, dated to the 12th century.[59]

Acanthus-like palmettes in small banded squares and in a whole range of combinations appear to have been a typical motif for sculptural decoration in the 12th century. Some examples include the doorframe of the Lechoba *katholikon*,[60] the *templon* epistyle of the Soter church at Amphissa,[61] various sculptures in the monastery of Hosios Meletios,[62] doorframes and closure panels in Hagios Nikolaos of Mesaria on Andros,[63] doorframes from ancient Corinth,[64] doorframes from the Athenian Asclepieion[65] and many others. A holy water basin at the monastery of Hosios Meletios, furthermore, bears the motif in the squares above the arms of a foliate cross, just as in our plaque.[66]

The ornate sarcophagus at the Hagioi Apostoloi in the Agora[67] bears even closer resemblances to the Taxiarchs' plaque in the form of the intertwining pointed leaves sprouting at the base of the crosses, the latent inclination towards variety manifested by the small variations of detail in the three crosses, and in particular the general style of the relief which betrays maturity and skill.

It is clear that all the formal elements of the main church date the first phase of the Taxiarchs to the 11th century and perhaps to the first half of that century. The addition of the narthex, on the basis of certain other architectural forms mentioned above, must have been undertaken in the following century. If the marble sarcophagus had been contemporary to the addition of the narthex, then a date of the mid- or second part of the 12th century may be possible. This accords with a trend, attested in Byzantine Greece during the same period, to erect funerary chapels and narthexes. This trend had a social purpose: to raise the power of the local aristocracy by promoting the aristocratic families and their members through donations, building projects and the construction of luxury funerary monuments.

National Technical University of Athens

PLATE 7.4:
*Athens, Taxiarchs.
The pseudo-
sarcophagus.*

NOTES

1. A. Xyngopoulos, *Τα βυζαντινά και τουρκικά μνημεία των Ἀθηνῶν*, (*EME* 1, B', Athens 1928) 92.
2. Ibid., 92-94.
3. K. Biris, *Αἱ ἐκκλησίαι τῶν παλαιῶν Ἀθηνῶν*, (Athens 1940), no.105 and *Αἱ Ἀθῆναι* (Athens 1966) 91.
4. J. Travlos, *Πολεοδομική ἐξέλιξις τῶν Ἀθηνῶν*, (Athens 1960) 211, fig. 140. Topographical diagram of the Wheat Market of Athens in Ottoman times, in which the Taxiarchs is drawn with its present dimensions, namely 13.50 x 20.00m. The original dimensions were 5.65 x 8.30m.
5. Mrs. M. Adamis provided me with information from the archives of the reign of King Otto about a series of documents which refer to the demolition of the Taxiarchs church in 1850 and the erection of the new church in 1854 (see documents 26/6/1850, 24/8/1850, 15/4/1852, 1503 of 15/3/1852 and L.φ3 of March 1852).
6 M. Bendtsen, *Sketches and Measurings*, (Copenhagen, 1993) 217, fig. 62; A. Papanikolaou-Christensen, *Ἀθήνα 1818-1853*, *Ἔργα Δανῶν Καλλιτεχνῶν* (Athens 1985) 104, fig. 126; I. Haugsted, *Τά ἑλληνικά τετράδια τοῦ αρχιτέκτονα Χρ. Hansen*, *Ἀρχαιολογία* (1985) 17, fig. 8.
7 S. Papadopoulos and A. Karakatsani, *Το λεύκωμα Πεϋτιέ*, (Athens 1971) 90-1, pls. 7, 9.
8. M. Bendtsen, (n.6) 304, fig. 84, 85.
9. A. Papanikolaou-Christensen, (n.6) pl. 141.
10. J. Skene, *Μνημεῖα καί τοπία τῆς Ἑλλάδος, 1833-1845*, (Athens 1985) fig. 21.
11. A. Kokkou, *Ἡ μέριμνα γιὰ τις αρχαιότητες στήν Ἑλλάδα*, (Athens 1977) 113, fig. 41.
12. W. Cole, *Select Views of the Remains of Ancient Monuments in Greece*, (London, 1835) no. 4.
13. M. Chatzidakis, *Athènes byzantines*, (Athens 1958) 56, fig. 55.
14. A. Couchaud, *Choix d'Églises byzantines en Grèce*, (Paris 1842) pl. 16.
15. In *EME* 1, B', 92, fig. 103 and 95, fig. 102.
16. S. Sinos, *Die sogenannte Kirche des Hagios Elias zu Athen*, *BZ* 64 (1971) 353.
17. Ibid., 352, note 7, pl. V, fig. 3.
18. T. DuMoncel, *Vues pittoresques des monuments d'Athènes*, (Paris, 1845) pls. 22-3.
19. J. Travlos, (n. 5) 169, fig. 110; K. Biris, *Αἱ ἐκκλησίαι*, (n. 3), 40; Idem. *Αἱ Ἀθῆναι* (n.3) 91; D. D. Kambouroglous, *Μελέται καί ἔρευναι* (Athens 1923) 21.
20. The perspective illustration in *Monuments anciens et modernes*, ii, part 1, *Arch. Eph.* (1853) 864, and the line drawings of the elevations in *L'architecture du Ve au XVIIᵉ siècle*, (Paris 1854) i.
21. In *EME*, 1, B', (Athens 1929), 93, fig. 101 and 87, fig. 91 respectively.
22. Ibid., 87.
23. H. Holtzinger, *Altchristliche und byzantinische Baukunst*, 3, (Leipzig 1909) 169, figs. 269-71, and L. Philippidou, 'Η

χρονολόγησις τῆς Μεταμορφώσεως τοῦ Σωτῆρος Ἀθηνῶν', in *Ἐπιστημονική Ἐπετηρίς Πολυτεχνικῆς Σχολῆς Ἀριστοτελείου Πανεπιστημίου Θεσσαλονίκης*, 5 (1971-2), Supplement, 7, fig. 2. The last publication notes that the Taxiarchs and the unknown church of Gailhabaud are one and the same.
24. D. Kambouroglous, (n.19) 143-4, with information on the erection of the new church.
25. A. Xyngopoulos, (n.1). Couchaud (n.14) 20 provides brief information on the condition of the church.
26. A. Xyngopoulos, (n.1).
27. See A. Couchaud (n.14) 20 states that the later wall of the façade was no different in style from the original face of the church.
28. In the 1840 lithograph and the watercolours of J. Skene and Peytié, the traces of houses that once abutted the church can be discerned. The density of housing in the area, long before the Revolution of 1821, is noticeable in the topographical plan by Verneda. See J. Travlos (n.4) 179, fig. 117.
29. In Bindesbell's drawing, the bell-tower has two arches. This must be a mistake since all the other drawings show one arch. Also, the panorama of Athens by Stademann (Munich 1841) shows the dome and bell-tower of the Taxiarchs, the latter likewise with one arch.
30. A. Xyngopoulos (n.1) 92. The wall-painting depicted the Last Judgement. According to Couchaud (n.14) 20, they were crudely executed.
31. See J. Travlos in *Reallexikon zur byzantinishen Kunst*, col. 382, Athens.
32. The relatively tall columns, 2.70m, permit a cross-vault arrangement. See S. Mamaloukos, 'Παρατηρήσεις στήν διαμόρφωση τῶν γωνιακῶν διαμερισμάτων τῶν δικιονίων σταυροειδῶν ναῶν τῆς Ἑλλάδος', *DChAE*, 14 (1987-8) 194 ff, fig. 5, and note 59, where mention is made of the Taxiarchs.
33. Ibid., 195-7.
34. Asomatoi in Theseion, the *katholikon* of the Kaisariani monastery, Hagios Thomas at Tanagra, the *katholikon* at Lechova, Hagioi Theodoroi annex to the Hosios Meletios monastery.
35. An element known to have originated in Constantinople.
36. See S. Mamaloukos (n.32) and M. Soteriou 'Ο αρχιτεκτονικός τύπος τοῦ καθολικοῦ τῆς Μονῆς Πετράκη καί οἱ σταυροειδεῖς ναοί τῆς Ἑλλάδος', *DChAE*, 2 (1960-1) 114-27.
37. As in the Soter church at Amphissa.
38. Certified by Bindesbell's ground plan and the section by Couchaud. Similar examples can be found at the church of the Homologitai and at Hagioi Apostoloi in the Athenian Agora, the Soter at Amphissa, the Panayia Krina on Chios etc.
39 See A. Frantz, *The Church of the Holy Apostles*, (Princeton

       1971) 36, fig.12, pls. 19b, 25.

40. National Technical University, Βυζαντινά Μνημεῖα, (Athens 1970) pl. 18.

41. E. Stikas, 'Ὁ ναός τῶν Ἁγίων Ἀσωμάτων Θησείου', *DChAE*, 1 (1959) 119, fig. 3.

42. See L. Philippidou (n.23) 8, 9; L. Bouras, Ὁ γλυπτός διάκοσμος τοῦ ναοῦ τῆς Παναγίας στό μοναστήρι τοῦ Ὁσίου Λουκᾶ, (Athens 1980) 25, 26.

43. See the drawing by Bindesbell, north side of the church.

44. See A. H. S. Megaw, 'The chronology of some Middle-Byzantine Churches in Greece', *BSA* 32 (1931–2) 117.

45. See L. Philippidou-Bouras, 'Ὁ ἐξωνάρθηκας τοῦ καθολικοῦ τοῦ Ὁσίου Λουκᾶ Φωκίδος', *DChAE* 6 (1970–2) 13–28. For previously unknown depictions of the demolished exonarthex, see M. Bendtsen (n.8) 395, fig. 135.

46. This is clear in the drawing of the façade in the Karlsruhe collection. On the emphasis of the horizontal on the faces of Greek churches of the 12th century, see Ch. Bouras, 'Βυζαντινές 'ἀναγεννήσεις' καί ἡ ἀρχιτεκτονική τοῦ 11ου καί 12ου αἰῶνος', *DChAE*, 5 (1966-9) 262, 263.

47. Discernible in the drawings by Bindesbell and Couchaud.

48. Discernible in the longitudinal section by Couchaud.

49. In Bindesbell's section plan, one can discern the original position of these two column capitals from their small proportions.

50. In Bindesbell's ground plan and Couchaud's section, the plaque appears to have a length of 2.05m. According to Couchaud (n.15), 20, the sarcophagus was in its original place, and used for child baptisms.

51. The original dimensions would have been 80x203cm.

52. Th. Pazaras, Ἀνάγλυφες σαρκοφάγοι καί ἐπιτάφιες πλάκες τῆς μέσης καί τῆς ὕστερης βυζαντινῆς περιόδου στήν Ἑλλάδα, (Athens 1988).

53. Ibid., on 46 (no. 60), 46 (no. 59), 47 (no. 62) respectively.

54. An intact plaque has been included above the entrance to the *katholikon*.

55. Th. Pazaras (n.52) 103, 104 where examples are provided.

56. As in the 'Peribleptos', near Politika, Euboea (Ch. Bouras, in Ἀρχεῖον Εὐβοϊκῶν Μελετῶν, 28 (1988–9), phot. 5), the *katholikon* of the Phaneromeni on Salamis (unpublished), and the Soter at Galaxidi (unpublished).

57. Perhaps no such other example of similar decoration is known.

58. A. Orlandos, 'Χριστιανικά γλυπτά τοῦ μουσείου Σμύρνης', *Arch. Byz Mnem*, 3 (1937) 138, fig. 11, no. 13. The dating of the sculpture to the 9th or 10th century may be doubtful.

59. A. Frantz, (n.39), 13, 14; L. Bouras, 'Architectural Sculptures of the 12th and early 13th centuries in Greece', *DChAE*, 9 (1977–9) 67, pl. 24, fig. 8.

60. A. Orlandos, 'Οἱ ναοί τῶν Ταρσινῶν καί τῆς Λέχοβας', *Arch. Byz. Mnem.* 1 (1935) 96–8. The doorframe remains unpublished.

61. A. Orlandos, 'Ὁ παρά τήν Ἄμφισσαν ναός τοῦ Σωτῆρος', *Arch. Byz. Mnem.* 1 (1935), 194, fig. 11.

62. A. Orlandos, 'Ἡ μονή τοῦ Ὁσίου Μελετίου καί τά παραλαύρια αὐτῆς', *Arch. Byz. Mnem.*,5 (1939–40) 73, fig. 24, 97, fig. 44.

63. A. Orlandos, 'Βυζαντινά μνημεῖα τῆς Ἄνδρου', *Arch. Byz. Mnem.*, 8 (1955–6) 57, fig. 36, 66, fig. 49.

64. R. L. Scranton, *Mediaeval Architecture*, (=*Corinth* XVI) (1957) nos. 159, 160, 161.

65. A. Xyngopoulos, 'Χριστιανικόν Ἀσκληπιεῖον', *Arch. Eph.* (1915) 63–4, fig. 16.

66. A. Orlandos, (n.62) 103, fig. 51.

67. A. Frantz, (n.39).

8

Peripheral Byzantine Frescoes in Greece: The Problem of their Connections[1]

Karin M. Skawran

When the frescoes of Hosios David in Thessaloniki were discovered, they were quickly recognised as belonging to the main stream of Byzantine art in the twelfth century. But many of those of earlier date that have come to light in more remote parts of mainland Greece and in the Islands, share a simpler style, often categorised as 'monastic', since geography is not always a determining factor. Indeed, the co-existence in the same region, even in a particular church, of both an austere, hieratic style and a more sophisticated, painterly, 'classical' one, is a phenomenon that has been much debated.[2] Clearly the primitive character of some of the Island frescoes is no guarantee that they belong to the earlier phases of Middle Byzantine art. Nor is the simple, formalizing style of the earliest of the three mosaic decorations in Greece, that in Hosios Loukas, simply the result of provincial simplification of a metropolitan idiom. That style illustrates, in the words of the late Doula Mouriki, a common trend in the stylistic development of Byzantine monumental painting during the first half of the eleventh century.[3]

It has become clear that this dichotomy in the art of Byzantium has been too easily explained by postulating a division between a court style and that of the monasteries. Certainly, the best manuscripts of the Stoudios workshop offer poor support for the attribution of a 'monastic' style to monasteries in the capital.[4] Since so little monumental decoration has survived there, we are obliged to turn to early post-Iconoclastic manuscripts to clarify the genesis of Middle Byzantine painting. In the miniatures there is evidence of both a linear, hieratic, and a more sophisticated, painterly style.[5] It now seems permissible to envisage twin currents emanating from the capital: a more painterly, 'classicizing' current, embodying the subtlety of the sanctuary mosaics in Hagia Sophia, and a more austere formalizing current, as is attested by the dome mosaics of Hagia Sophia in Thessaloniki; also that both currents reached the provinces and the islands, though not always with the same impact.

It is true that in the region under discussion, apart from the late twelfth century frescoes in the Monastery of Patmos, where patronage had secured superior artists from the capital,[6] and those of the Episkopi church in Mani,[7] which reflect some acquaintance with the widely distributed Late Komnenian style, that is,

of the late twelfth century, there is only meagre representation of the more sophisticated style.[8] The Episkopi frescoes in Santorini of the High Komnenian period, that is, of the mid-twelfth century, owe little to sophistication, while for the tenth and eleventh centuries, there is little in Northern Greece that quite matches the prevailing austerity of the frescoes on the Aegean islands.

Consequently, it has been suggested that the Greek Island painters were exposed to influences other than those emanating from the capital. Thirty years ago Xyngopoulos suggested that the distinctive style they shared with contemporaries in some other peripheral areas of the Empire, could have been disseminated from Anatolia to the Aegean islands and beyond, along what has been called a *voie monastique*.[9] It is not easy to establish an historical context for such a movement from, let us say, Cappadocia, in the tenth century, to which the earliest of the Island frescoes in question belong, though, as we shall see, relations between monks in Greece and South Italy are attested from an early date. On the other hand, the suggestion that a westward migration of monks took place after the fall of Mantzikert in 1071, has had some acceptance. And some scholars have observed stylistic and iconographical similarities between the provincial frescoes of the Greek islands, and the 'archaic' group of frescoes in Cappadocia, on the one hand, and some in South Italy on the other.[10]

As regards South Italy, recent research has brought to light, notably in the Lives of Saints, evidence of the nature of provincial monasticism, of the relative independence of the monks, and of their travels to and from Greece and Constantinople during the tenth and eleventh centuries.[11] Thus there is evidence of Italian visitors at the Monastery of Hosios Meletios, of which the founder was himself a Cappadocian. This is revealed by the links between the codices copied at his monastery and the output of South Italian scriptoria.[12] It is also known that Elias Spiliotes (860/70–960) lived as a monk in the mountains of Patras before taking up his abode in Calabria[13] and that in the course of his travels, Elias of Sicily (823–903) visited Thessaloniki, the Peloponnese, Epirus and Corfu.[14] The appearance of Hagios Arsenios of Corfu on the medallions depicting Oriental Saints, in the margin of the Bari Exultet Roll, attests the pivotal position of Corfu, on the maritime route not only from Constantinople, but also on that from the Eastern Mediterranean to Southern Italy.[15] Nevertheless, the paramount role of the former is suggested by the direct influence in South Italy, which Guillou has emphasised, of Constantinopolitan models from the Monastery of Stoudios.[16] Furthermore, the two dated wall-paintings that have survived there from before the Norman conquest are both regarded by Hans Belting as belated reflections of Constantinopolitan style around AD 900.[17]

In the light of those conclusions it is time to look again at the basis for the possible indebtedness to Cappadocian migrants of Greek church-painters in peripheral areas, as well as for the concept of an independent link between their work and that of their contemporaries in South Italy. In this process the connections of three characteristic church decorations will be re-examined; one in Naxos, the second in Mani, where a close link with Peloponnesian off-shore Islands is attested by the work of Demetrios of Monemvasia in Kythera,[18] and the third in Corfu.

THE CAVE CHURCH OF THE KALORITISSA IN NAXOS

The painter of this decoration, assigned by Maria Panayotidi to the beginning of the tenth century,[19]

seems to have been indirectly acquainted with stylistic and iconographic tendencies current in the capital at the end of the ninth century; though here also 'archaic' and contemporary elements exist side by side.

The apse composition of the enthroned Virgin (PLATE 8.1) is unusual in including two flanking figures: the Baptist and the Prophet Isaiah, who foretold the Incarnation. In Cappadocia in Direklı Kilise, two flanking prophets are likewise portrayed,[20] and in El Nazar at the end of the tenth century, two Saints.[21] In other respects the apse programme of the Naxos cave is clearly retrospective, perhaps inspired by a local model. For the Apostles undoubtedly derive from the lower zone of a pre-Iconoclastic apse Ascension/ Second Coming, of which we now have an example in Naxos itself in the Drosiani church,[22] where, as in the Kaloritissa fresco, the Virgin among the Apostles is reduced to a nimbed head. The use of the earliest iconography for the Christ Child's hands holding the scroll, on the other hand, can be compared to a similar representation in the sixth century mosaic in the Panagia Kanakaria in Cyprus.[23]

In the treatment of the faces and in the bodily proportions of the Virgin and the Archangels (PLATE 8.2) the artist seemed reluctant to deviate from 'classicizing' prototypes reflecting the bema Virgins of Hagia Sophia in Constantinople and the Church of the Dormition at Nicaea, both of the second half of the

PLATE 8.1: *Naxos, Kaloritissa Cave Church, apse decoration*

PLATE 8.2: *Naxos, Kaloritissa Cave Church, conch of the apse: Archangel*

ninth century, a strong indication of metropolitan influence. As in the surviving frescoes in the Rotunda at Thessaloniki, there is, in the Kaloritissa, an attempt to render the faces of the Archangels plastically. The shaded line along the nose recalls similar treatment in manuscripts, particularly in the psalters assigned to the first years after Iconoclasm.[24] In the features of the Apostles (PLATE 8.3) on the wall below the conch, however, the artist has adopted the more ascetic type of the Macedonian era. The treatment of the clearly defined hairline in the Kaloritissa, (PLATE 8.4) which curves low across the forehead and leaves two rounded corners at either side of the head, recalls the similar treatment of the Apostles in Thessaloniki: in the dome of Hagia Sophia, and in the early tenth century frescoes of the Rotunda,[25] as well as in Ayvalı Kilise in Cappadocia, where independent influence from the capital is possible.[26] The haloes, outlined with a single dark line, find parallels in pre-Iconoclastic practice.[27]

Although the drapery folds are, on the whole, indicated by parallel vertical lines, there is a suggestion of bodily form where these are broken by diagonals, a treatment also observed in the Carpignano Crypts, in the spirited Angel of the Annunciation executed by the Greek painter Theophylaktos.[28] The awkward attempt to indicate bodily volume in the draperies of the Naxos Angel is matched in Theophylaktos's figures, but these have been derived by Hans Belting from the Byzantine miniature style represented by the Kosmas Indikopleustes manuscript of c.880 in the Vatican Library.[29] An intermediate stage of this style has been observed in the frescoes of c.920 at Güllü in Cappadocia, in the Ayvalı church.[30]

Stylistic connections have generally been observed by Panayotidi between the Kaloritissa and Cappadocia,[31] notably the decorations of Çavusin (963–969) and New Tokalı (mid-tenth century). These reflect a blending of 'archaic' and new elements, in which the schematic rendering of the draperies and the crudely organized bodily structure are matched in the Kaloritissa Angels. But the increased slenderness of the Kaloritissa Apostles, recalling the elegant suppleness in those Cappadocian monuments, evokes contemporary manuscripts such as the *Homilies* of St. Gregory of Nazianzos in the Vatican Library and the *Sacra Parallela* of St. John Damascene in the Bibliothèque Nationale, as well as such ivory plaques as that of the Coronation of Romanos II and Eudokia. The Constantinopolitan origins of the frescoes of Çavusin and Tokalı have long been accepted,[32] and the Kaloritissa painter may likewise have received his impulses independently from the capital.

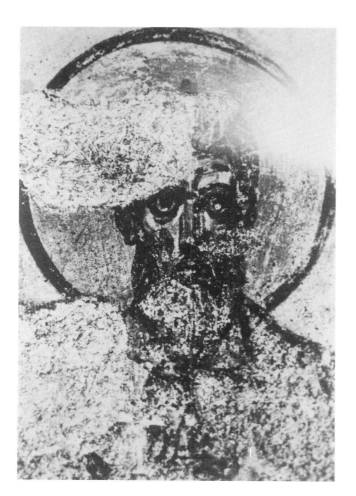

PLATE 8.3 (LEFT): *Naxos, Kaloritissa Cave Church, apse wall: detail of Apostle*

PLATE 8.4 (BELOW): *Naxos, Kaloritissa Cave Church, apse wall: detail of Apostle*

THE CHAPEL OF HAGIOS PANTELEIMON IN MANI

In this vaulted chapel near Ano Boularioi, securely dated to 991/2, the Ascension is depicted in the sanctuary vault, which was the normal place for it in Greek churches of the Middle Byzantine period, as it probably had been already from the ninth century.[33] But the composition in Hagios Panteleimon is atypical on account of the compression of the scene into the very small space available. Only three Apostles appear on each side of the vault, instead of the normal six, the other six being depicted in adjoining areas (PLATE 8.5). John appears deformed and dwarfed (PLATE 8.6). As at Kokar Kilise in Cappadocia, the last Apostle had to be reduced to fit below the wing of the Angel.[34] At Otranto the painter also encountered problems in the distribution of the figures on the available surface. But such awkwardness in handling compositional problems was doubtless common to the provincial painters everywhere.

In the Mani chapel the Orans bust of the patron, St. Panteleimon, appears in the conch of the southern of the twin apses (PLATE 8.7).[35] The prominent portrayal of a patron saint was a common practice before Iconoclasm. Its revival in the Middle Byzantine period was equally widespread; it is indeed attested throughout the supposed *voie monastique*. In Cappadocia, in Hagios Eustathios at Göreme, the patron is figured three times; there are other examples at Platsa and at Kafiona, as well as in the third church decoration examined below, the chapel of Hagios Merkourios in Corfu. Nor are examples lacking in Apulia. Even so, devotion to local patrons is so much a universal phenomenon that it is difficult to attribute it to either radial or circumferential contacts.

The frescoes in Hagios Panteleimon are certainly somewhat uncouth, but this character is not confined to our region, for it occurs in the surviving fragments of the tenth century decorations in Kastoria.[36] Nor is it unknown in early post-Iconoclastic manuscripts: apart from a comparable treatment of the draperies, there are the same disproportionately large heads and hands both in the figures in the *Sacra Parallela* of St. John Damascene in Paris and in the Athonite

PLATE 8.5: *Mani, Hagios Panteleimon, east vault: detail of the Ascension: Luke, Matthew, Andrew*

PLATE 8.6: *Mani, Hagios Panteleimon, east vault: detail of the Ascension: John, Mark, Peter (?)*

manuscript *Dionysiou Codex* 2. Similarly, stylistic analogies have been observed in the 'archaic' group of Cappadocian monuments, especially where the treatment of the features is concerned: in El Nazar (end of the tenth century),[37] the fine lines radiating from the corners of the eyes, and in Kokar Kilise, the prominent curved lines that form the folds of the neck.[38]

These stylistic conventions were also used in the early frescoes in Kastoria and in the mosaics of Hagia Sophia, Thessaloniki. Probably the ultimate source which could have reached Greece and Cappadocia independently, was the Constantinopolitan style represented in the ninth century *Homilies* of Gregory of Nazianzos in Paris.[39]

In Hagios Panteleimon the haloes were decorated with a single row of pearls, as they were in all the contemporary monuments in Greece mentioned above, while in Hagios Stephanos at Kastoria a row of pearls trims all outlines of figures and objects in the Second Coming. In the tenth century, pearl ornamentation was equally popular in Cappadocia,[40] as it was in South Italy.[41] Prototypes for this type of ornamentation are found in such ninth century manuscripts as in the *Sacra Parallela* of St. John Damascene in Paris, which may explain its appearance in fresco in the Temple of Fortuna Virilis in Rome.[42] The stylised trees in Hagios Panteleimon (PLATE 8.5) were a favourite adjunct of the Apostles in the Byzantine post-Iconoclast Ascension tradition, particularly in the tenth century, of which the mosaic in the dome of Hagia Sophia in Thessaloniki is the surviving masterpiece. When they appear in Cappadocia, in Kokar Kilise,[43] as well as in Mani, a common ancestry seems sufficient explanation.

PLATE 8.7: *Mani, Hagios Panteleimon, south conch: St Panteleimon*

THE CHAPEL OF HAGIOS MERKOURIOS IN CORFU

The only securely dated frescoes which continue the 'monastic' tradition as exemplified at Hosios Loukas, adorn the humble chapel of Hagios Merkourios on Corfu of 1074/75,[44] where, as so often, 'archaic' and new elements appear side by side. The twin apses are occupied by patron saints, while the Apocalyptic Vision of Christ occupies the gable end above them (FIG. 8). This composition is rooted in pre-Iconoclastic visions of Christ in Glory, such as that in the apse mosaic of Hosios David in Thessaloniki, and other examples of its revival extend from Sicily and South Italy to Cappadocia.[45] For the rest the decorative programme of Hagios Merkourios consists chiefly of a series of individual figures, full-length or in busts in medallions on the side walls. They conform with the lower registers of the decoration of larger Middle Byzantine churches, which follow examples of early post-Iconoclastic date known to have existed in the capital.

The restricted decoration in Hagios Merkourios, is matched in chapels of small size both in South Italy, in San Vito Vecchio in Gravina in Apulia[46] and in Direklı in Cappadocia.[47] But it can hardly have been confined to peripheral areas. The four scenes that appear among the isolated figures in Hagios Merkourios include an unusual one of St. Mercurius killing Julian the Apostate, a scene which was no local or provincial invention, since it occurs in the *Homilies* of St Gregory Nazianzos.[48]

Stylistically the frescoes of this church strongly resemble the mosaics and frescoes of Hosios Loukas. Faces are treated as a monochrome flat surface on which the details are indicated in quick confident lines (PLATES 8.9 and 8.10). The thick black lines that define the eyebrows continue in a long sweeping movement to define the slender nose. The fold under the eye and the small black shadow below the nose are matched both at Hosios Loukas and in Hagia Sophia at Kiev.[49] Vocotopoulos has drawn attention to the peculiar treatment of the moustaches which do not quite join in the centre, a detail found in the same early post-Iconoclastic contexts in Hagia Sophia in Constantinople and Hagia Sophia in Kiev.[50] When this detail reappears not only in the Corfu chapel, but also in other provincial frescoes, in Santorini (Episkopi), Kythera (Hagia Sophia) and Cappadocia (Old Tokalı), this can hardly establish a mutual interdependence among their painters.

The draperies in Hagios Merkourios are treated in a two-dimensional linear manner, without regard for the bodily structure underneath (PLATE 8.11) and the surface is articulated in a purely decorative manner, matched in the frescoes of Hosios Loukas. The predilection for earth colours in Hagios Merkourios, red, brown and ochre, is also found in the Hosios Loukas frescoes, while the evidence of a green *proplasmos* or underpaint, in the faces of the Corfu Chapel points to an acquaintance with the best tradition in the capital.[51]

CONCLUSION

The unpretentious character of the frescoes of our three churches was to some extent the result of their remote locations. Yet, despite their distance from the capital, those in the Patmos Monastery and in the Samarina church in Messenia, can claim a place in the main stream of Byzantine art. Unlike them most of the frescoes examined above bear a provincial, backward stamp, in iconography or style or both. Initially, however, a retrospective outlook was no speciality of the provinces, for when figural representations were again permissable in the ninth century, those who in Constantinople itself developed fixed iconographic programmes, relied heavily on pre-Iconoclastic models. Consequently, in the early post-Iconoclastic frescoes of the Kaloritissa cave-church, the dependence on Early Christian and 'classical' proto-types which has been observed, was not so much the result of provincial backwardness as of compliance with the Byzantine revival style of their time.

In character with that style is the juxtaposition in the peripheral frescoes of different treatments side by side in a single decoration: the painterly and the linear, so-called 'monastic' style. That a similar juxtaposition survived elsewhere into the eleventh century, notably in the Nea Moni in Chios and in the Panagia ton Chalkeon at Thessaloniki, is a fair indication that both manners had their roots in the capital. Furthermore, when the exclusively linear style employed in the mosaics and frescoes of Hosios Loukas is reflected in the contemporary church decorations of the periphery, this also is attributable to a centrifugal current rather than to independent influences from East or West.

It is, however, equally true to say that the graphic style, so well represented by Hagios Panteleimon in Mani, was the popular language of a provincial society of humble cultural background; as such it lagged behind in adopting the trends current in the larger artistic centres, more exposed to impulses disseminated through hierarchical and secular channels from the capital. But the links which have been noted between frescoes in Mani and the Greek Islands and Hosios Loukas, do suggest a strong intermediary role for the major monastic foundations.

Few outstanding church decorations such as the dome mosaics of Hagia Sophia in Thessaloniki and the frescoes in the Crypt of Hosios Loukas, have survived to mark geographically the centrifugal role of Constantinople in this field. But from the visual material available to us, there are many indications that during the period of Byzantine control the inspiration of the painters in the Aegean islands and elsewhere on

PLATE 8.8 (BELOW): *Corfu, Hagios Merkourios, east end of nave*

PLATE 8.9 (RIGHT): *Corfu, Hagios Merkourios, north apse: Prophet Elisha*

the Southern periphery of the empire, was entirely from the centre, diluted only by provincialism and local factors, including survival of pre-Iconoclastic models, such as those found behind plaster in the Drosiani church on Naxos. What then of the numerous resemblances that have been noted between the frescoes of one fringe area and those of another? The hypothesis of an East-West linkage would stand if this were the only possible source of inspiration in the peripheral areas. But as regards South Italy it has been noted that specialist opinion is united in recognising a consistent and direct dependence of church-painters there on Constantinople itself. A cogent reminder of the direct link via the Egnatia is the funerary chapel built by the governor of Capetanata (Southern Italy) for his family in the Panagia ton Chalkeon in Thessaloniki.

As for the other terminal area, the concept of an independent Cappadocian school has lost much ground of late and, for the formative period, key monuments such as Çavusin and Tokalı have been accepted as directly dependent on Constantinople.[52] Such dependence is not surprising in view of the regularity

of military communications between the capital and central Anatolia. Even after Mantzikert the renewed activity of the Cappadocian painters does not suggest conditions for the westward migration of monks via the Greek Islands.

For the twelfth century the survival of numerous church decorations in Cyprus provides a conspicuous example of the dependence of outlying provinces on the main stream art of Byzantium. By the juxtaposition of the Cypriot frescoes with contemporaries in Macedonia and elsewhere enabled Megaw to recognise 'a basic unity in the development of the Comnenian styles throughout the Empire and wherever the influence of Byzantium extended.'[53] It was only after the seizure of Constantinople in 1204 that the east to west traffic of plundered works of art opened the way for the migration of a sub-Byzantine style, and probably of painters and craftsmen also, to South Italy as well as Venice. But this did not originate in Cappadocia and it did embrace the Franko-Byzantine art of the Holy Land in a movement along the *voie des croisades*.[54]

Emeritus Professor, University of South Africa, Pretoria

PLATE 8.10 (BELOW) and 8.11 (RIGHT):
Corfu, Hagios Merkourios, north apse: Prophet Elijah

NOTES

1. The substance of this contribution was included in a lecture at the British School at Athens in June 1986 on the occasion of the School's centenary.

2. Cormack, R., 'Byzantine Cappadocia: the "Archaic" group of wall paintings', *Journal of the British Archaeological Association*, Ser. iii, XXX (1967) 19ff; Mango, C. 'Lo stile cosidetto "monastico" della pittura bizantina', *Habitat-Strutture-Territoria, Atti del Terzo Convegno Internazionale di Studi sulla Civiltà Rupestre Medioevale nel Mezzogiorno d'Italia, Taranto-Grottaglie* 1975 (Galatina 1978) 45–62; Epstein, A. W., 'The problem of provincialism: Byzantine monasteries in Cappadocia and Monks in Southern Italy'. *Journal of the Warburg and Courtauld Institutes* 42 (1979) 28–46; Mouriki, D. *The mosaics of Nea Moni on Chios* (Athens 1985) 258 ff; Epstein, A. W., 'The fresco decoration of the Column churches, Göreme Valley, Cappadocia. A consideration of their chronology and their models', *CA* 29 (1980) 28.

3. Mouriki, D., *op cit.*, 258; Mango, C., *op cit.*, 61f

4. For example, the *Sacra Parallela* of St John Damascene in the National Library of Paris (Paris Bibl. Nat. gr. 923): e.g. Weitzmann, K., *Die Byzantinische Buchmalerei des IX. und X. Jahrhunderts* (Berlin 1935), pl. IX, fig. 45.

5. Kitzinger, E., *Byzantine art in the period between Justinian and Iconoclasm, Actes du XIe Congrès International des Etudes Byzantines*, IV, 1, Salonica, 1953 (Athens 1955–58) 22ff, esp. 29.

6. Orlandos, A.K., 'Fresques byzantines du monastère de Patmos', *CA* 12 (1962) 285–302.

7. Drandakis, N., *Byzantine wall paintings of Mesa Mani* (in Greek) (Athens 1964) 65–112.

8. Contrast, in mainland Greece, in Hosios Sotiras near Megara such details as the face of Christ in the *Betrayal* and the head of Abraham in the *Sacrifice of Abraham*, which attest acquaintance with the painterly Komnenian style (Skawran, K., *The development of Middle Byzantine fresco painting in Greece* (Pretoria 1982) 89, figs. 322 and 329.

9. Xyngopoulos, A., 'Fresques de style monastique en Grèce', *Actes du IXe Congrès International d'Etudes Byzantines*, Salonica, 1953 (Athens 1955–58) I, 510–516.

10. Millet, G., *L'ancien art serbe; les églises*. (Paris 1919) 45ff. Lazarev, V, *Storia della pittura bizantina* (Turin 1967) 169–170; Xyngopoulos, *op. cit.*, 510 ff; *id. The Monuments of Servia* (in Greek), (Salonika, 1957) 73–74; Mango, *op. cit.*, 47f; Epstein, *op. cit.*, 40. Vocotopoulos, P., 'Fresques du IXe siècle à Corfu', *CA*, XXI (1971) 73–74.

11. Xyngopoulos, *op. cit.*, 512ff; Epstein, *op. cit.*, 44ff; Belting, H., 'Byzantine art among Greeks and Latins in Southern Italy', *DOP* 28 (1974) 1–29.

12. Papadopoulos, C. 'Contribution to the history of monastic life in Greece' (in Greek), II (Athens 1935), 60. Quoted in: Chatzinicolaou, A.M., *et al, Catalogue of the illuminated Byzantine manuscripts of the National Library of Greece*, Vol. I. (Athens 1978), 135–136.

13. *Acta Sanctorum*, Sept III, 857. Quoted in: Chatzinicolaou, A.M., *op. cit.*, n.12.

14. Louillet, G. da Costa, 'Saints de Grèce aux VIIIe, IXe et Xe siècles', *Byzantion* XXXI (1961) 326–330.

15. Avery, M., *The Exultet Rolls of South Italy* (Princeton, 1936), II, 11–13, PL. IX, quoted in Vocotopoulos, *op. cit.*, 177, note 124.

16. Guillou, A., 'Production and profits in the Byzantine province of Italy (10th–11th century): an expanding society', *DOP* XXVI (1974) 100, 104.

17. Belting, H., *op. cit.* n.11 above, 12 f.

18. Megaw, A. H. S., *Archaeological Reports* (1966/67) 19.

19. Panayotidi, M., 'L'église rupestre de la Nativité dans l'isle de Naxos: ses peintures primitives', *CA* 23 (1974) 107–120

20. Lafontaine-Dosogne, J., 'Nouvelles notes cappadociennes',

Byzantion XXXIII (1963) 146; Thierry, *Nouvelles églises rupestres de Cappadoce* (Paris 1963) 190; cf. Panayotidi, *op. cit.*, 110.

21. Restle, M., *Byzantine wallpainting in Asia Minor.* (Recklinghausen 1967), II, pl. 6.

22. Chatzidakis, M., *ADelt.* 22, 2 (1967) 29; Drandakis, 'Pre-Iconoclastic wallpaintings', (in Greek, summary in English) *AAA* 3 (1970) 414–421, 416 f.

23. Megaw, A. H. S. and Hawkins, E. J. W., *The church of the Panagia Kanakariá at Lythrankomi in Cyprus. Its mosaics and frescoes* (Washington, D.C. 1977) 90–91, figs. 85 and 86.

24. Dufrenne, S., *L'illustration des psautiers grecs du Moyen Age* (Paris 1966), I, pls. 1–49, pl. 9 (fol. 65 vo), pl. 3 (fol. 24 vo).

25. Xyngopoulos, A., 'The frescoes of the Ascension in the apse of H Georgios, Salonica' (in Greek), *AE* (1938) 32–53.

26. Restle, M., *op. cit.*, III, pls. 340 and 341.

27. Grabar, A., *La peinture religieuse en Bulgarie* (Paris 1928) 37–38, pl. la; Sacopoulos, M.A., 'La fresque chrétienne la plus ancienne de Chypre', *CA*, 13 (1962) 61–83, fig. 13; Omont, H., *Miniatures des plus anciens manuscrits grecs de la Bibliothèque Nationale du VIe an XIVe siècle* (Paris 1929) pls. VII, XXII, XIV, XXV, XXX, etc., Lazarev, V., *op. cit.*, pls. 98–101.

28. Pace, V., 'Presenze e influence Cipriote nella pittura duecentesca Italiana', *XXXII Corso di cultura sull'arte Ravennate et Bizantina* (1985) pl.

29. Belting, H., *op. cit.*, n.11 above, fig. 15.

30. Restle, M., *op. cit.*, n.21, III, pls. 340 and 341.

31. Panayotidi, M., *op. cit.*, n.19, 116 and note 39.

32. Jerphanion, G. de, *Les églises rupestres de Cappadoce* (Paris 1925–1942), I, 366–373; Lafontaine–Dosogne, J., *op. cit.*, 130; Thierry, N., 'Les églises rupestres de Cappadoce', *Corso di cultura sull'arte Ravennate* (1965) 588–591; Restle, H., *op. cit.*, I, 34–36; Cormack, *op. cit.*, 31–33.

33. Drandakis, N. 'H. Panteleimon, Boularioi' (in Greek) *EEBS* (1969/70) 437–458. The position of the Ascension in Stylianos Zaoutsas' church is not mentioned in the surviving description: (Mango, C. *The Art of the Byzantine Empire* [Englewood Cliffs, New Jersey 1972] 205). The fact that it is recorded after the *Pantocrator* in the dome and the scenes normally found in the South, West and North arms of the nave, suggests that here also it occupied the east vault above the altar.

34. Restle, M., *op cit.*, n.21, III, fig. 479.

35. Drandakis, N., 'Orant saints on the apses in some churches in Mesa Mani (in Greek, summary in English) *AAA* 2 (1971) 232–240.

36. Skawran, K., *op. cit.*, n.8, figs. 25–28, 32 and 33.

37. Restle, M., *op. cit.*, n.21, II, pls. 1 and 5.

38. *Ibid.*, pl. 60a. *Ibid.*, III, pl. 479.

39. Cormack, R., *op. cit.*, 22f.

40. Eg., Restle, M., *op. cit.*, n.21, II, pls. 134–136. Cf. Thierry, *op. cit.*, n.32, pls. 27–34. Restle, M., *op. cit.*, n.21, II, pls. 58–60.

41. Medea, A. de, *Gli affreschi delle cripte eremitiche Pugliese* (Rome 1939) figs. 60–70.

42. La Fontaine, J., *Peintures médiévales dans le temple dit la Fortuna Virile à Rome* (Brussels/Rome 1959). In the tenth century the decoration occurs frequently in ivory panels: Rice, D.T. and Hirmer, M., *Kunst aus Byzanz*, (Munich 1959) figs. 97, 99–101, 105.

43. Restle, M., *op. cit.*, figs. 477 and 479.

44. Vocotopoulos, *op. cit.*, (1971) 152–180.

45. Jerphanion, G. de, *op. cit.*, I, 68–71; Lafontaine-Dosogne, J., 'Theophanies—Visions aux quelles participent les prophètes dans l'art après la restauration des images', *Synthronon* (Paris 1968) 135–143.

46. Medea, A. de, *op. cit.*, 35–43.

47. Restle, M., *op. cit.*, III, plan LXII, pls. 521–522; Jerphanion,

G. de, op. cit., I, 2, 474–476.

48. Omont, *op. cit.*, pl. LIV.

49. Lazarev, V., *Old Russian murals and mosaics from the XI to the XVI century* (London 1966) fig. 19.

50. Examples are listed by Vocotopoulos, *op. cit.*, 168 notes 74-77.

51. Winfield, D., 'Middle and later Byzantine wallpaintings methods. A comparative study' *DOP* 22 (1968) 128.

52. See above n. 31.

53. Megaw, A. H. S., 'Twelfth century frescoes in Cyprus', *Actes du XIIe Congrès International des Etudes Byzantines*, III (Belgrade 1964) 266.

54. See especially Pace, V, *op. cit.*, 259–298.

9
Warrior Saints or Portraits of Members of the Family of Alexios I Komnenos?

Charalambos Bakirtzis

The programme of iconography in the church of the Panaghia Kosmosoteira (1152) is known to have certain distinctive features.[1] These may reflect the wishes of the founder, Isaac Komnenos, who personally oversaw the building of the church. For instance, the concelebrating hierarchs, who are normally depicted in the sanctuary apse, occupy the lower zone of the north and the south walls. A representation of the Holy Communion has recently been discovered not in the sanctuary but in the *prothesis*. The fact that the Annunciation is depicted in the naos underlines its doctrinal and historical, rather than its eucharistic aspect. The distinctive features in the church's iconography also include the four military figures positioned in pairs between the arched windows in the north and south walls, as if they are overseeing the concelebrating hierarchs. Their prominent position, large size and identity all raise questions.

Scholars who have examined the figures have identified them with the warrior saints: Demetrios and Theodore the Recruit on the north wall and Theodore the General and Merkourios on the south wall.[2] They obviously have very individual features and bear only a conventional resemblance to the proposed saints. The uncertainty is reinforced by the absence of inscriptions.

The crowns they wear are by no means uncommon in the iconography of warrior saints. It was in the Komnenian period that warrior saints began to be

PLATE 9.1: *Warrior Saint (Alexios I Komnenos)*

PLATE 9.2: *Warrior Saint (John II Komnenos)*

portrayed with crowns, called *stemmatogyria*. According to Pseudo-Kodinos who was writing in the fourteenth century they were a specific type of headgear worn exclusively by male members of the imperial family with court attire.[3] The Emperor would crown his sons and sons-in-law with *stemmatogyria*: 'a crown of gems and pearls, with four small arcs at the front, at the back and at the sides, if he who is consecrated be a king's son, but at the front alone if he be a son-in-law; the crown is also called a stemmatogyrion'.[4] The gemmed crowns worn by the military figures in the Kosmosoteira have only one arc at the front. The inscribed tinplated bronze marriage crowns in the Byzantine Museum in Athens, are similar in shape and style and have been attributed to Romanos Lekapenos during the first half of the tenth century.[5] Similar crowns are worn by the kings in the miniatures in the Seraglio Octateuch, which, as we know, Isaac himself commissioned from an atelier in Constantinople.[6] It was probably the same atelier as painted the frescoes in the Kosmosoteira.

The doubts about the identity of the figures, together with their size and position in the church makes a different interpretation possible. Three of the four figures share an astonishing likeness with known portraits of members of the family of Alexios I Komnenos. The supposed St Theodore the Recruit (PLATE 9.1), a sumptuously garbed, hardened soldier, has all the facial features of Alexios himself as seen in miniature representations of him in the twelfth century MS Gr. 666 in the Vatican Library.[7] The face and its expression closely conform to Anna Komnene's description of Alexios: 'His brows formed a black arc on either side of his face; beneath were eyes which bestowed upon one a gaze which was at once both stern and yet tranquil.'[8] Opposite him, on the south wall, the figure identified as St Theodore the General (PLATE 9.2) has the erect demeanour of Alexios's eldest son and heir to the throne, John II, as seen in his mosaic portrait in Hagia Sophia, Constantinople; and in a miniature in the Gospel MS Urb. Gr. 2 in the Vatican Library which dates from the twelfth century.[9] John's contemporaries extolled his military exploits: 'he would disappear from Constantinople and like the sun, circle the whole world fighting in the east and in the west'.[10] St Merkourios (PLATE 9.3) next to him can only be Alexios's third born and the founder of the Kosmosoteira, Isaac, as we know him from his mosaic portrait in the narthex of the katholikon of the Chora Monastery in Constantinople.[11] Apart from the skilfully rendered features of a man whom Choniates describes as being in love with kingship (though he

PLATE 9.3: *Warrior Saint (Isaac Komnenos)*

PLATE 9.4: *Warrior Saint (Andronikos Komnenos)*

never attained it),[12] both these latter individuals are wearing the same royal crown. Lastly, the young, beardless soldier (PLATE 9.4) opposite Isaac and next to Alexios on the north wall may be Alexios's third son Andronikos, of whom there is no other portrait known. He died at the age of thirty nine in 1130/1 and is described by Michael Italikos as the 'living statue of Ares'.[13]

We cannot be certain whether there were other representations at the ends of the north and the south wall, on either side of the arched windows. The faint traces of a figure at the east end of the south wall, similar in size and stance to the figures under discussion, may belong to a portrait of another member of Alexios I Komnenos's family.

It was not unusual for the Komnenoi to be portrayed in public buildings, churches, monasteries, palaces and miniatures in manuscripts. Descriptions of, and references to, such imperial portraits still survive.[14] We know for instance, that in the golden chamber of the Great Palace or the Blachernae there was a mosaic of John II mourning his late father amidst scenes from Alexios's victorious battles.[15] Isaac too, mentions in the *Rule of the Kosmosoteira* that there are icons of his parents Alexios and Irene inside in the church.[16]

It comes as no surprise to read Isaac's demands in the *Rule* that the abbots and the monks of the Komosoteira should never depict his likeness either inside or outside the monastery.[17] Even now, two portraits of this Byzantine prince still survive. Whatever truth may be expressed by these lines in the monastery rule, they may have little to do with reality, towards which the Byzantines manifested an indifference in their writings.

Moreover, it was not, apparently unusual for sacred figures to be depicted with the actual facial features of other historical figures. Kurt Weitzmann maintained that the representation of King David in the Sinai monastery has the actual features of the beardless Justinian I, who founded the monastery.[18] He also asserted that the depiction of King Avgarus of Edessa in a tenth century icon in the Sinai monastery is in fact a portrait of Constantine VII Porphyrogenitos.[19] Doula Mouriki claims that the depiction of King Solomon in the mosaic of the Resurrection in the katholikon of the Nea Moni on Chios is an actual likeness of the monastery's founder Constantine IX Monomachos.[20]

So the two alternatives offered in the title of this article, 'Warrior Saints or Portraits of Members of the Family of Alexios I Komnenos?' may be joined by a third: 'Warrior Saints with the Facial Features of Members of the Family of Alexios I Komnenos'.

Ephoreia of Byzantine Antiquities,
Thessaloniki

NOTES

1. Hara Konstantinidi, 'Παρατηρήσεις σὲ παραστάσεις ἱεραρχῶν στὸ καθολικὸ τῆς μονῆς Παναγίας Κοσμοσωτείρας στὴ Βήρα' in Ch. Bakirtzis ed., *First International Symposium for Thracian Studies 'Byzantine Thrace: Image and Character'*, Komotini May 28th–31st 1987, *Byz. Forsch.* XIV (1989), 303-323.

2. Karin M. Skawran, *The Development of Middle Byzatine Fresco Painting in Greece*, University of South Africa, Pretoria, 1982, p165; with bibliography; M. Acheimastou-Potaminianou, Ἑλληνικὴ Τέχνη. Βυζαντινὲς τοιχογραφίες (Athens 1994) 216-8, pl. 28–31.

3. Titos Papamastorakis, 'A visual encomium of Michael VIII Palaeologos: the exterior wall paintings of the Mavriotissa at Kastoria', *DChAE*, 15 (1989–90), 232.

4. J. Verpeaux, *Pseudo-Kodinos, Traité des Offices* (Paris 1966) 272.

5. P. A. Drossoyianni, 'A pair of Byzantine Crowns', *XVI Internationaler Byzantinistenkongress, Wien, 4–9 Oktober 1981, Akten II*, 3, *JÖB* 32/3 (1982) 529–36. This type of crown is described in the Miracula S. Demetrii, §174 (P. Lemerle *Les plus anciens recueils des Miracles de Saint Démétrius*, I (Paris 1979) 165.4: 174).

6. J. C. Anderson, 'The Seraglio Octateuch and the Kokkinobaphos Master', *DOP*, 36 (1982), fig. 1.

7. Io. Spatharakis, *The Portrait in the Byzantine Illuminated Manuscripts* (Leiden 1976) pl. 48; C. Head, *Imperial Byzantine Portraits* (New York 1982) 116–119.

8. B. Leib, *Anne Comnène Alexiade* (Paris, 1937) i.III.

9. Spatharakis, *op. cit.*, pl. 49; Head, *op cit*, 119–121.

10. W. Hörander, *Theodoros Prodromos, Historische Gedichte*, Wiener Byzantinische Studien, XI (Vienna 1974) 246.

11. Paul A. Underwood, *The Kariye Djami* (Bollingen Series LXX & Pantheon Books 1966) ii. pl. 37:a.

12. *Nicetae Choniatae Historia*, ed. I. Bekker (Bonn 1835), 363.10

13. P. Gautier, *Michel Italikos, Lettres et Discours* (Paris 1972) 84.

14. Paul Magdalino and Robert Nelson, 'The Emperor in Byzantine art of the twelfth century', *Byzantinische Forschungen*, VIII (1982), 123–183.

15. Magdalino and Nelson, *op. cit.*, 126–130.

16. L. Petit, 'Typikon du monastère de la Kosmosoteira près d'Aenos (1152)', *Bulletin de l'Institut Archéologique Russe à Constantinople*, 13 (1908), 63:89; G. K. Papazoglou, Τυπικὸν Ἰσαακίου Ἀλεξίου Κομνηνοῦ τῆς Μονῆς Θεοτόκου τῆς Κοσμοσωτείρας (1151/2), Δημοκρίτειο Πανεπιστήμιο Θράκης, Θρακικὴ Βιβλιοθήκη, ἀρ. 3 (Komotini 1994) 122. 1697-8.

17. Petit, *op. cit.*, 59, para. 77; Papazoglou, *op. cit.*, 112. 1526-7.

18. G. Forsyth and K. Weitzmann, *Monastery of St Catherine at Mount Sinai, The Church and Fortress of Justinian* (University of Michigan Press, Ann Arbor, 1973) 15, pl. cxix:b and clxx.

19. K. Weitzmann, 'The Mandylion and Constantine Porphyrogennetos', *CA*, XI (1960), 163–184; reprinted in K. Weitzmann, *Studies in Classical and Biblical Manuscript Iluumination*, ed. H. L. Kessler (Chicago & London 1971) 224-246.

20. Doula Mouriki, Τὰ ψηφιδωτὰ τῆς Νέας Μονῆς Χίου (Athens 1985) 150-1.

10

Byzantine Polychrome Pottery

Guy D. R. Sanders

In his long career Peter Megaw has nurtured an impressive string of aspiring archaeologists and art historians. It is a privilege to have been asked to join some of his tyros and friends in making a contribution to this, his *Festschrift*; my offering can only repay a small portion of the debt I owe for his patience, experience and kindness. My topic is the only one with which, of all Peter's own varied specialist knowledge of things Byzantine, I feel sufficiently comfortable to offer in his honour. It is also dedicated, with great affection, to the memory of Elektra; an artist who would have appreciated the polychrome painted ceramics presented here and a person in whose presence all others seemed monochrome by comparison.

The colourful decoration of White Ware glazed and painted in the Polychrome technique has set it apart from its basically plain green or plain yellow relatives. For this reason it has attracted considerable attention from both art historians and archaeologists who see Polychrome Ware as the apogee of the Byzantine potters' craft of the 9th to 12th centuries. It is un-common enough in the archaeological record to be considered the tableware only of that small section of society with a large alienable income. Its very rarity has caused considerable problems to those attempting a taxonomy and chronology of the ware. The present article draws mainly on the large collection of Polychrome from the American School of Classical Studies' excavations at Corinth.[1] Its intent is not to provide absolute solutions to these various problems of group and date, but to create a framework which will better serve as a point of departure for future research.

The term Polychrome was coined in 1928 by David Talbot Rice to describe a group of glazed and painted pottery recovered in the course of the British Academy's excavations of the Hippodrome in Constantinople that year. Rice characterised his Group IIF Polychrome slightly apart from the other Group II white wares on the basis of its fine sandy white biscuit which, to his eyes, closely resembled the fabrics of Raqqa pottery. He defined Polychrome simply as a ware painted in two or more colours. The excavations produced a broad range of decorative styles in which designs were outlined in brown, black or manganese and in-filled with added colour, particularly a green or a thick white glaze, red and, rarely, what appeared to

be gold leaf. The motifs ranged from the strictly geometric, to vegetal, to figural, while certain kufesque designs, especially on the bichrome black and white decorated wares, recalled an Islamic 'influence but not workmanship.'[2]

Also uncovered during the course of the same 1928 season were a number of glazed Polychrome ceramic revetment plaques of a type known from Patleina in Bulgaria. The Patleina plaques were dated on historical and numismatic grounds to the late 9th or early 10th century. Rice recognised both the Constantinopolitan and Bulgarian plaques as products of the same Byzantine workshops which produced Polychrome pottery.[3] In the Hippodrome excavations however, notwithstanding the fact that in the capital the plaques could be expected to pre-date provincial examples, and so presumably be ninth century, the Polychrome tile fragments were all found in late contexts. Rice considered them be contemporary with the pottery which, from the stratigraphy, he ascribed to the 11th or, at the latest, the 12th century.

In *Byzantine Glazed Pottery*, published a year later, Rice reassigned Polychrome to his new Class IA.[4] He divided Polychrome pottery into two groups; one with black and white glaze decoration, the other using coloured glazes. Further consideration of the Polychrome revetment plaques also resulted in two stylistic divisions; one with decoration analogous to that of the multi-colour pottery, the other with a thicker, warmer overglaze.[5] He redated both pottery and plaques to the 10th and 11th centuries, taking as evidence a ceramic decorative technique described by Theophilos, thought at the time, to have been writing in the mid-10th or early 11th century.[6] After consideration of this philological evidence, he revised his opinion of the Hippodrome stratigraphy which now seemed to support an earlier date than that originally proposed. Rice also felt that 'there seems no reason to dispute the evidence' for the 9th or 10th century date of the Patleina tiles.[7]

British excavations in the Great Palace in Istanbul produced Polychrome only in the contexts grouped to form Stevenson's Stage IV. The majority of the Polychrome pottery belonged to Rice's Black and White class found in the lower layers of each of the contexts making up the Stage and thus stratified below sherds of a more decorative figural style which occurred in upper levels only.[8] Unlike Rice, Stevenson could distinguish between the fabrics of Polychrome and other White Wares only because the former appeared to be harder fired. Stevenson's date for Stage IV, the latter half of the Macedonian dynasty (867–1057), is based partly on coins found therein, including one of John Tzimiskes and his followers (ie. an Anonymous Class A2 follis), and partly on consideration of the Bulgarian finds.[9]

In the publication of a considerable volume of Polychrome material from Corinth, Morgan divided the ware into four groups, only the first three of which have any particular significance. The first and largest group contained Rice's multi-colour variety on which coloured glazes were employed as fillers for a broad range of motifs outlined in matt brown or black glaze. Large areas were left in reserve which in earlier examples was filled with red dots. The forms represented in this group are as diverse as the motifs employed and include a variety of different cup shapes within which a large repertoire of crosses were painted in manganese, and rarely with added red (FIG. 10.1). Morgan dated Group I approximately from the early 9th to late 11th centuries and implied that it flourished in the 10th century before declining. Morgan's Group II corresponded to the figural variety found in the upper levels of Stage IV of the Great Palace excavations and was dated to the 12th century on the basis of its being found in contexts containing coins of Alexius I (1081–1118) and Manuel I (1143–1180). Group III consisted of the Polychrome decorated in black and white noted by both Rice and Stevenson. Morgan dated it by the contexts in which it was found in association with 12th and 13th century Sgraffito and Incised Wares.[10]

Recent work has only partially developed the typology and chronology of Polychrome, but still relies on Morgan's scheme. Finds of Morgan's Group I from Cherson in the Crimea, thought to date to the late 10th century, rank among the finest examples yet discovered.[11] In excavations on the south side of Hagia Eirene in Constantinople, six examples of Polychrome of Morgan's Groups I, II and III, including a unique Polychrome chafing dish, were dated by the excavator to the 10th century.[12]

In his publication of the pottery from Saraçhane, John Hayes proposed a new typology with fundamental differences from Morgan's: Hayes' Class 1 has motifs painted in manganese or black with green and yellow glaze infilling; his Class 2 has motifs in manganese, black or green on a field of red dots and his Class 3 is the equivalent of Morgan's Group III. Using these divisions, Hayes was able to suggest something more about the morphology and chronology of the ware; he rightly observes that the Hagia Eirene deposit is not homogeneous and the date of its contents extends at least until the late 11th century. His Class 1 may begin as early as the second half of the 10th century, Class 2 is found in the late 10th and early 11th century contexts and Class 3 he finds in deposits of the late 11th to early 12th centuries.[13]

The Polychrome pottery from Corinth excavated up to 1938 and published by Morgan, has been reassessed over the past ten years in the light of more recent excavations on the site. This study shows that Morgan's Group I is a large and unwieldy category, containing a range of shapes and decorative styles. It also suggests that Hayes' typology relies on too small a sample to be definitive. The types described below are based on a thorough examination of the hundreds of whole and fragmentary pieces in the Corinth collection. The resulting groups break down satisfactorily by fabric, shape and decoration in a fashion which lends some credence to their integrity.

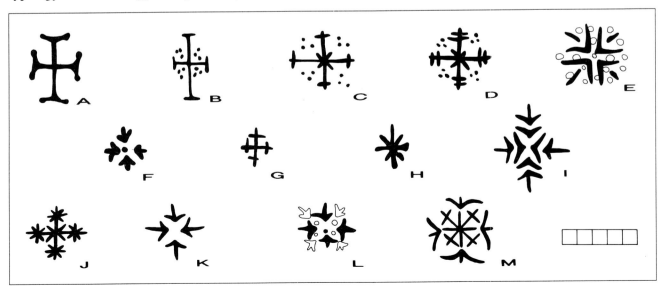

FIG. 10.1: *Designs on the interior of cups.*
A. C–34–1246; as Rice 1930, pl. X, no, 1; C. C–35–494; D. C–36–1237; E. C–38–546; F. C–37–1381; G. C–33–593; H. C–93–6; I. C–37–109; J. C–37–1696; K. C–37–1458; L. C–36–495; M. C–38–277.

FABRICS

The fabrics are described using a system derived from accepted ceramic petrographic practice using predefined replicable standards.[14] Chemical analyses of Byzantine glazed white wares published by Peter Megaw and Richard Jones indicate a possible origin close to Istanbul. The specimens, which were taken from Corinth Lot 1977–34 and included Polychrome, contained large amounts of aluminium oxide but only small quantities of calcium oxide. The composition showed a close correlation with a white clay from Arnavautköy on the European shore of the Bosphoros and used by potters at Anadolu Hisarı on the Asian shore. Work in Oxford indicates that Byzantine White Wares have nothing in common with the white calcareous fabric of Iznik pottery.[15] Recent macro- and micro-examination of the fabric of Polychrome plaques in the collection of the Louvre reveal that the fine white ceramic body contains rare inclusions of bole (a clay rich in iron oxide), argillite, subrounded quartz (up to 800μ in diameter) and iron oxide (from 100μ to, rarely, as much as 1.3mm in diameter).[16] On the basis of a document dated 13.X.1202, describing a church interior decorated with marble revetment and possibly tiles from İzmit, 'ἡ ἔνδυσις τῶν πρὸς δύσιν γαματισμάτων δια τανστρίων(or γανστρίων?) Νικομεδείων σὺν τῷ κοσμήτη', Rice suggested that both the Polychrome pottery and the plaques were produced in the region of Nikomedeia, an inspired conjecture, which in the light of the chemical analyses now seems more plausible, even though the shores of the Bosphoros are more probable.[17]

1. Chalky white to pink fabric with granular break which appears relatively coarse compared with most White Wares, with rare, large, grey or red inclusions prominent. This fabric has well defined firing horizons with a pink core and white edges, or *vice versa*.

White (Munsell 5YR 8/1) to pink (Munsell 5YR 8/4, CEC F5) fabric often with well defined firing horizons. Medium to hard with granular, even break. Rare, medium to very large, sub-rounded, spherical opaque white to grey inclusions; rare, medium to very large, subrounded, spherical red bole. Few large pores visible.

2. Fine, compact, chalky white fabric with considerable range in size, number and quality of inclusions. Some specimens have the full range of inclusions while others have a selection. Only rarely are the inclusions, and then only the black, so populous that they appear remarkable when visually examined without a hand lens.

Medium to hard white fabric with slightly granular, even break. Rare to frequent medium to large, hollow, spherical, rounded or sub-rounded, black inclusions; rare, small to medium, spherical, angular, opaque white (may be tinged orange) inclusions; rare, medium to large, spherical, rounded orange bole; very rare fine to

small, angular, platy gold ?Mica. Rare, large laminar pores.

3. Medium to hard, usually white but occasionally pink, with granular even break. The section appears clean to the eye with rare large laminar voids. Coarser varieties, especially those fired pink in colour have readily apparent red and grey inclusions. Characteristic, and not easily visible against the white clay matrix in which they are embedded, are the relatively numerous opaque white inclusions.

a) Fine. White fabric with granular, even break and few, medium, subrounded spherical opaque white inclusions; rare, medium sub-rounded spherical to tabular red and rare fine, angular, platy sparkling inclusions.

b) Coarse. White to pink (Munsell 5YR 8/4 to 8/3) fabric. Frequent, medium, rounded, spherical opaque white, rare, medium to very large, subrounded spherical red and very rare large to very large, angular spherical grey inclusions; rare fine, angular, platy sparkling inclusions.

DECORATION AND FORM

Type 1 FIG. 10.2, Nos. 1-9, PLATE 10.1.

Pots of this group are generally made in Fabric 1 and only rarely in Fabric 2. The decoration of this group is more or less the equivalent of Hayes' Class 1. The palette is limited to a blue-green which tends to oxidise and decay, manganese and yellow-brown. Only rarely are red or azure used. Designs consist of ordered, clear, bright linear patterns infilled with blue-green and brownish yellow glaze against a white background. Geometric and figural designs, for instance humans, lions and griffons are not unusual. The exterior of dishes and bowls often have a manganese or, rarely, red baseline at the top of the foot and vertical manganese or red lines infilled with blue-green and yellow, but rarely with blue-green alone. Rims of bowls and dishes favour a tongue and panel design infilled with blue-green and brownish yellow. Cups and jugs often have panels of a manganese checkerboard design infilled with alternating boxes of blue-green. This motif also appears on dish rims.[18] This group, which is not obviously among the published finds from the Great Palace, has been found in such quantity in Bulgaria that it has become known locally as Preslav Ware, in the Crimea and at Hagia Eirene and Saraçhane both in Constantinople.[19] The decoration on pottery clearly parallels that of ceramic revetment plaques both in design and colour use, but not always in intricacy. Workshops for making the plaques and the plaques themselves for interior spaces have been found at Tuzlalaka, Patleina and near the Round Church at Preslav.[20] These establishments provide evidence for the existence of itinerant craftsmen; indeed, the workers involved were probably of Constantinopolitan origin and, since they were unable to supply items to order, travelled to make them on site and to

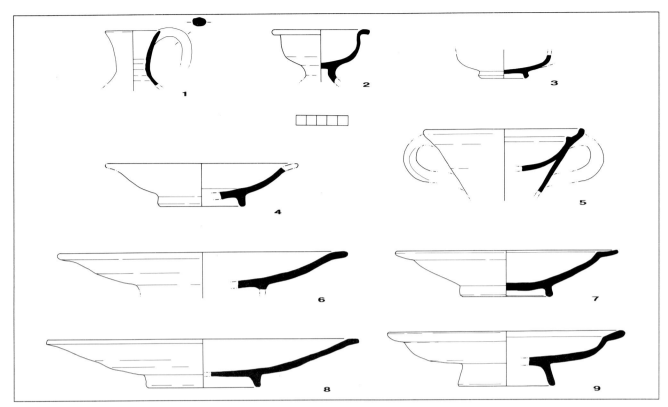

FIG. 10.2: *Type 1. 1. C–38–226; 2. C–37–1543; 3. C–37–109; 4. C–74–28; 5. after Peschlow no. 104; 6. C–63–755; 7. after Peschlow no. 101; 8. C–35–302; 9. after Peschlow no. 103.*

specification.[21] Some may have eventually settled rather than return home. Besides Bulgaria, revetment is also known from the Hippodrome excavations, the Topkapı Sarayi, the Stoudios Monastery (Imrahor Camii) and St Mary Pammakaristos churches in Constantinople,[22] and from Üskübe (ancient Prusias ad Hypium) in Bithynia.[23]

The group is only partly defined by the decoration employed and differentiation from other groups rests partly on shape. Dish shapes generally resemble those of Types 2a and 2b, with a ring base and widely flaring wall, but are generally thicker walled. Cups are both simple, single handled globular varieties with a vertical wall rising to a tapering lip or two handled types with flaring wall rising sharply to a tall vertical rim. The only chafing dish with Polychrome decoration found to date is painted in this style.[24] In addition to the usual shapes, the finds at Corinth include a small pitcher and a stemmed goblet.

Although a single sherd of Type 1 was found in context and published as mid-10th century at Saraçhane, when first read the context was said to contain a significant proportion of early 11th century pottery. The remainder of the Saraçhane material came from contexts dating to the end of the 10th century or later. The form of the Hagia Eirene chafing dish certainly cannot be dated any earlier than the late 10th century. The Corinth finds and contexts indicate that the style was current after about AD 975/1000 and down to about AD 1050/60.[25]

Type 2

This group consists of the simplest decorative techniques, and employs other colours only rarely with the basic colour range of manganese, red, green and yellow on the simplest shapes. It corresponds to part of Morgan's Group I and equates more or less with Hayes' Class 2. The Corinth material of this class can be divided into three subdivisions, 2a, 2b and 2c. These divisions are not clear cut as considerable overlap exists in decoration and forms, especially between 2a and 2b and to a lesser extent between 2b and 2c both in colour use and shapes. This overlap occurs in the use of red as dots for a background filling motif, on pieces in the first two subdivisions particularly. Type 2a can be differentiated from 2b by the use of purple and, rarely blue, as a filler in the decoration of 2b and to a certain extent by the greater variety of shapes represented in the latter. In 2c red is more sparingly used. The decoration and simple shapes of vessels belonging to 2a and 2b set them apart from Types 1, 3a and 3b but the distinction between cups of 2c and the other main groups is unclear. The palette of this group relies heavily upon manganese for outlines, a thick blue–green for filling motifs, a brownish yellow for the rim and other details, red for background detail and occasional lines, and purple or deep blue for highlights. The difficulty in making clear distinctions between the subgroups seems to reflect a chronological evolution over a long period during which time it coexisted with Polychrome of the other types.

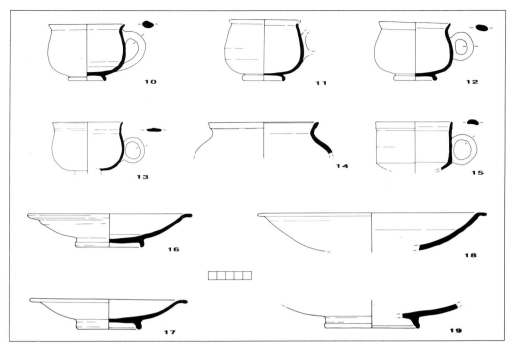

FIG. 10.3 (LEFT): *Type 2a. 10. C–38–193; 11. C–37–743; 12. C–75–15; 13. C—74–85; 14. South Basilica b.724; 15. C–60–53; 16. C–75–20; 17. C–75–19; 18. C–75–16; 19. C–38v31.*

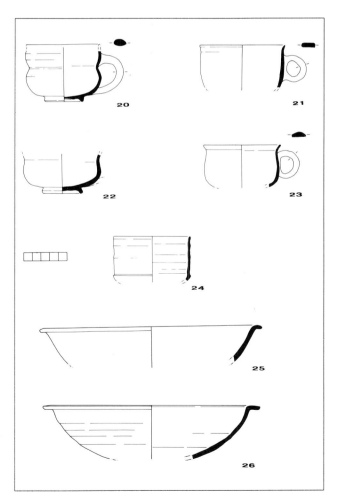

FIG. 10.4: *Type 2b.*
20. C–36–345; 21. C–36–1012; 22. C–34–1246; 23. C–37–1817; 24. C–36v616; 25. C–37–1817; 26. C–67–6.

a) FIG. 10.3, Nos. 10–19, PLATES 10.2, 10.3 and 10.4.

Vessels of Type 2a are made in Fabric 2 and rarely in Fabric 1. It is further characterised by the simplicity of both the shapes and the palette employed. The decoration, which covers almost the entire exterior of the cups and the interior of open shapes, is limited to precisely drawn vegetal motifs, lines and festoons outlined in manganese and infilled with a thick blue-green or warm yellow or yellow-brown on a red slip dotted background. The rims of cups are defined by a manganese line inside and out and painted with a warm yellow or yellowish brown glaze; the handles are invariably striped with manganese and red. Cup interiors are undecorated except in the bottom where a small manganese cross recrossed is painted. The inside and outside is covered with a thin colourless overglaze glaze which tends to oxidize to a lustrous iridescent patina. On dishes and bowls, with a larger area available than cups, the designs are more intricate guilloches and floral designs. Only exceptionally is figural decoration employed; in this case a large yellow donkey or goat fills the entire central portion of the dish. The rims are offset by a horizontal manganese line and have a line of manganese loops actually on the rim. The area between the two lines is filled with blue-green glaze and between the looped line and the lip with yellow–brown. Smaller dishes sometimes have the simpler decoration of cups, such as small ovals or circles of manganese dots. The exterior may be plain or have a thin colourless, yellow or green glaze wash.

Three basic forms are common in this subtype: ovoidal cups, shallow dishes and bowls. The cups have a torus ring base with a squat ovoidal body curving in to a flaring rim with everted lip. The single handle can be a simple oval ring attached to the body above the

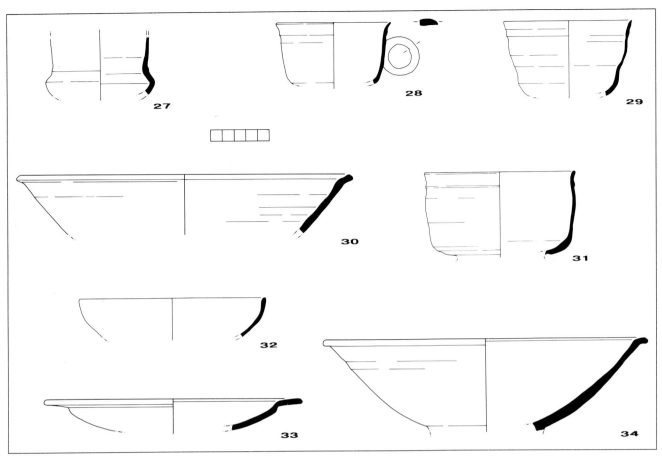

FIG. 10.5: *Type 2c.*
27. C–37–1715; 28. C–34–1468; 29. C–37–148; 30. C–37–734; 31. C–38–530; 32. C–37–890; 33. C–33–627; 34. C–38–373.

maximum diameter or a vertical oval loop attaching at the shoulder and lower body above the foot. Dishes have a low ring foot and a widely flaring convex wall curving up to a horizontal, slightly downturned rim. Only rarely is there a high flaring ring foot. Bowls, which are less well represented than dishes at Corinth are a deeper, almost hemispherical version of the dish. Examples of this type are also documented from Mesembria in Bulgaria and Dinogetia in Romania.[26] Corinth contexts in which the style appears indicate a date in the middle to third quarter of the 11th century.[27]

b) FIG. 10.4, *Nos. 20–26,* PLATES 10.5, 10.6, 10.7 *and* 10.8.

Type 2b is similar to 2a in decoration and fabric (usually Fabric 2, occasionally Fabric 1) but employs purple glaze as a filler in addition to the more usual green and yellow. Dishes and bowls are identical to those of Type 2a but bowls are commoner than dishes. The rim decoration shows a slightly greater variety than 2a with manganese ovals instead of loops on the rim itself or a reversal of the order of coloured infilling. The coloured overglaze is generally thicker than on 2a. The decoration of cups of this group is more varied but

less precise than those of 2a, with a tendency towards geometric patterns such as circles and ovals and guilloche but still on a red dotted background and with a simple cross recrossed inside.

Two red spotted cups stand apart from the remainder, not in shape but in decoration. One shows affinities with Type 2c in the use of added azure glaze, the other with Group 1 with panelled decoration on the rim and vertical manganese lines infilled with green and blue on the handle. Inside both have crosses untypical of the group and have a thick, glossy overglaze. The use of blue seems to be uncommon and is generally a late feature on Constantinopolitan White wares.

The range of cup shapes is considerable. The basic ovoid form of 2a is still present, but with a more vertical wall and less everted rim. A second type, also with a low torus ring base but sometimes with a low, truncated pendant cone inside, has a squat globular body with a tall, vertical convex rim. The handles are the oval loop variety attaching at the rim and to the body above the foot. Rather less usual are cups with a flaring convex body with a tall, straight vertical rim and with a horizontal floor and a straight flaring wall to a tapering lip.

Pottery of this group has been reported from the Crimea and from Constantinople.[28] The contexts of

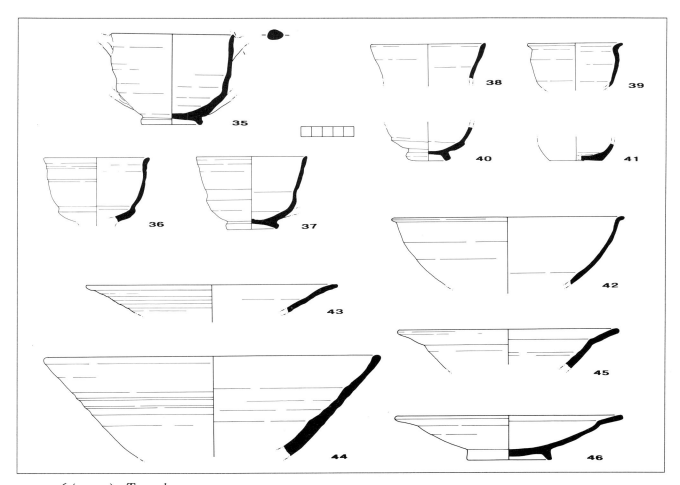

FIG. 10.6 (ABOVE): *Type 3b.*
35. CP.2660; 36. C–37–1806; 37. C–34–545; 38. C–36–1006; 39. C–35–506; 40. C–33–528; 41. C–38–231; 42. C–36–1009 and C–35–463; 43. C–37–33; 44. after Saraáhane II deposit 42.23; 45. after Saraáhane II FIG. *13.23; 46. C–61–119.*

FIG. 10.7 (BELOW): *Type 3a.*
47. C–36–585; 48. C–37–577; 49. C–36–914; 50. C–35–497.

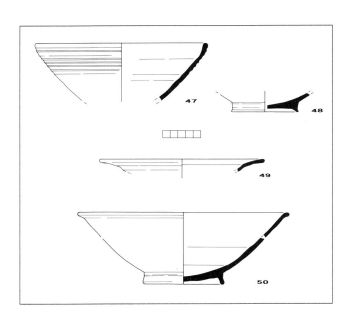

the Saraçhane pieces suggest an early to mid-11th century date, but the Corinth data indicates that it was current in the middle to second half of the 11th century and is certainly no earlier than AD 1000.[29]

c) *FIG.* 10.5, *Nos.* 27-34, PLATES 10.9, 10.10, 10.11, 10.12, 10.13 *and* 10.14.

The fabric of Type 2c is usually Fabric 3 or, occasionally Fabric 2. The decoration of Group 2c strongly favours kufesque vegetable design and, less frequently, even kufesque script. The vegetable consists of rinceaux with seriphs, lobed triangles and antithetic palmettes arranged as script. This latter motif is popular and appears, repeated as a frieze and separated by red dots, high on the interior of bowls and dishes. The main motifs are generally large and clearly drawn in manganese and infilled with clean, bright green and purple, but less often with azure, red or yellow. On dishes this type of decoration often serves as a broad band framing a white background tondo containing figural, often human designs simply executed in manganese and with dipinto legends, for instance the individual wearing a turban found at Corinth in 1937.

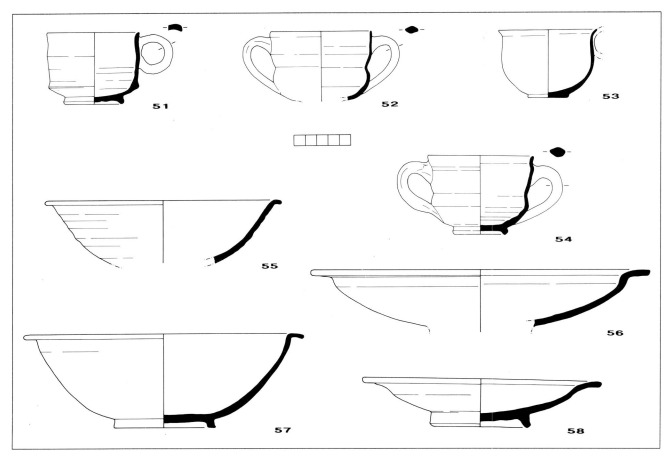

FIG. 10.8: *Plain Glazed White and Red Wares.*
51. C–38–192; 52. C–37–721; 53. C–89–4; 54. C–36–626; 55. C–36–624; 56. C–36–996; 57. C–37–1178; 58. C–37–1988.

One bowl which has large panels of blue and green outlined in manganese and yellow and supported by painted columns, seems to be related to the panelled decoration of Type 3c. The exterior of bowls and dishes bear an added red wash, usually applied in a fairly random fashion, but in one case as a series of reddish brown 'S's'.

Various cup types exist; one large cup has a widely flaring lower body turning sharply up to a vertical convex body with a low raised band below a slightly everted rim. Another has a simple globular form similar to Types 2a and 2b, but with a vertical upper wall and slightly flaring rim offset by a low ridge outside. More usual, however, are two handled cups with a squat, globular body turning up to a tall flaring rim. Both dish types represented at Corinth favour broad rims, the one almost horizontal, the other flaring in a continuous curve from the convex wall. Bowls have straight flaring walls and either a narrow, horizontal, downturned rim or a narrow flaring rim with a rounded lip and concave inside.

The date of 2c is fairly late in the 11th century. Shapes represented at Corinth are closely related to those of Group 3a, below, and to vessels in deposits 42 to 44 at Saraçhane, there dated by Hayes to the middle, second half and end of the 11th century respectively.[30] At Corinth the style is found in contexts with late 11th century coins suggesting an Komnene date[31] therefore supporting the chronology of the Saraçhane finds. Elsewhere this form of decoration is known from Cherson, Kiev, Mesembria and Dinogetia.[32]

Type 3

a) FIG. 10.6, *Nos. 35–46,* PLATES 10.15 *and* 10.16.

Type 3a, exclusively made in Fabric 3 is the equivalent of Rice's black and white class, Morgan's Group III and Hayes' Class 3. The decoration tends to cover the entire interior of open shapes, and both the interior and exterior of semi-closed shapes, such as cups. The thick, opaque white, black and less often turquoise or royal blue glazes are applied in a fashion resembling *cuerda seca* in large, integrated kufesque, floral or abstract designs. A transparent mottled green glaze is sometimes used on the outside of dishes and bowls, and a transparent yellowish brown or dark brown is usually also used on cups. Where carefully decorated the lines of motifs are clean, while sloppier execution tends to result in indistinct lines.

The majority of fragments of this type at Corinth

are from cups; only a few fragments exist from plates or bowls. It is possible to add two new, almost complete profiles to the examples catalogued by Morgan: a cup from an early phase of the excavations before 1932, and a plate found in 1961. Whereas the context in which this particular plate was found seems to support Morgan's 13th century date, a re-examination of other contexts in Group 3 Polychrome found at Corinth and elsewhere give a clear indication that it was made and in use at a considerably earlier date.

Cups are the commonest form represented. These have a low ring base, a slightly bulging lower wall which is pared, a vertical upper wall and a single handle. Larger examples have two handles while flat bases and quatrefoil rims are occasionally found. Plates have a flaring ring foot with a widely flaring wall. Bowls with feet identical to those of dishes have a hemispherical body and outturned rim.

The repeated appearance of Type 3a Polychrome at Corinth with Imitation Lustre, Measles and Sgraffito Wares strongly suggests that the style, which originated in the late 11th century continued to be in use, if not made, into the 12th century. The observation by Hayes that some shapes represented are suggestive of the shapes of other late White Wares,[33] especially of certain plain green and yellow glazed pieces is supported by the Corinth pieces, and they should certainly be regarded as contemporary. At Saraçhane, Type 3a was found in late 11th century deposits and has also been reported from Dinogetia, Hagia Eirene and elsewhere in Istanbul.[34] In the Great Palace excavations, Type 3a Polychrome was found in Stage IV stratified under Type 3b Polychrome and to the exclusion of Groups 1 and 2. This suggests that Type 3a pre-dates 3b while the late date of both styles strongly supports a much later date for the Stage than that suggested by Stevenson and accepted by Hayes.[35] It is worth noting that four fragments of Type 3a tiles were found in the excavations of the monastery of Constantine Lips.[36]

b) FIG. *4.7, Nos. 47-50,* PLATES *8.17 and 8.18.*
By far the smallest group of Polychrome, Type 3b is clearly related to Type 3a in fabric (Fabric 3) in that it has thick opaque glazes resembling *cuerda seca* with large areas infilled with colour. Unlike Type 3a, the motifs do not consist of one large integrated design in black and white, but are broken down into definite zones outlined in black. The palette is rather less conservative than 3a with a greater range of tones. The exterior is often decorated with a patterned or mottled, matt red wash on the exterior. Figural designs are common, with lions in various poses being particularly popular. In the Great Palace excavations, Type 3b was stratified above 3a pieces and were therefore presumed to be later. It is also represented in a late 11th century context at Saraçhane and from Cherson.[37]

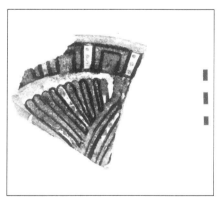

PLATE 10.1: *Type 1. No. 6, C–63–750*

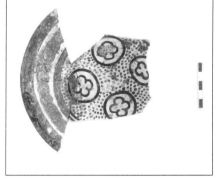

PLATE 10.2: *Type 2a. No. 16, C–75–20*

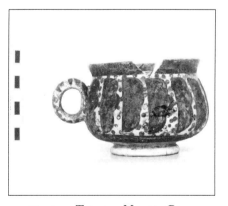

PLATE 10.3: *Type 2a. No. 12, C–75–15*

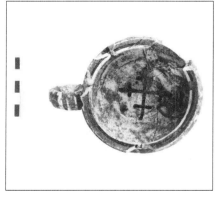

PLATE 10.4: *Type 2a. No. 12, C–75–15*

PLATE 10.5: *Type 2b. No. 21, C–36–1012*

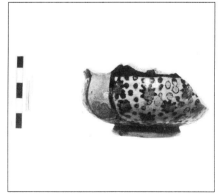

PLATE 10.6: *Type 2b. No. 22, C–34–1246*

PLATE 10.7: *Type 2b. No. 26, C–67–6*   PLATE 10.8: *Type 2b. C–36–636*   PLATE 10.9: *Type 2c.*
                                                                                           No. 31, C–38–530

PLATE 10.10: *Type 2c. C–34–1255*   PLATE 10.11: *Type 2c. C–34–545*   PLATE 10.12: *Type 2c. No. 30, C–37–734*

CHRONOLOGY

The archaeological evidence from Corinth strongly suggests that Polychrome pottery should be considered an 11th to early 12th century phenomenon and that it developed into the familiar Constantinopolitan and regional styles in the later decades of its existence. There is insufficient space here to discuss the Corinth evidence even in outline. It includes numerous contexts in which Polychrome has been found with 11th or early 12th century coins and pottery, and accounts for the general resemblance in shapes between demonstrably late regional styles, such as early Slip Painted Ware and early Green and Brown Painted Ware, especially with Type 2 Polychrome. The shapes of Types 2, 3a and 3b also have close parallels with other Constantinopolitan White wares of the later 11th and early 12th century (see FIG. 10.8). Although this conclusion roughly agrees with Hayes' assessments, it flies in the face of the traditional chronology which dates most Polychrome, particularly the revetment plaques with Type 1 decoration, to the 10th century. Making the case for an 11th century date therefore requires reconsideration of the interpretation of finds published elsewhere rather than internal evidence. Since much of the established opinion relies on only a few apparently solid facts, the most fundamental of which is the published date of about AD 900 for the Patleina and Preslav plaques, the discussion will start with these.

The Patleina plaques have here been assigned to Type 1 on the basis of iconography, decoration and style.

According to Grabar, they were found in a destruction level beneath the floor of the later of two superimposed churches at a monastery in the Tica Pass, founded in the years between the introduction of Christianity to Bulgaria and the donation of a church at the site by Prince Simeon in 907. The monastery suffered three destructions followed by rebuilding, once in each of the 10th, 11th and 12th centuries. Debris from the first of these destructions produced the plaques and contained coins identified by the excavator as issues of John I Tzimiskes (969–76). The historical and archaeological evidence, as interpreted by Grabar, therefore indicated that the church was destroyed in AD 972, along with many others in the region, when John Tzimiskes took the capital, Preslav, some 3 kms distant. Grabar proposed that the plaques therefore adorned Simeon's church of AD 907. This summary of the evidence was accepted by Rice.[38]

The excavation which uncovered the plaques took place between 1909 and 1914 under the direction of Gospodinov who briefly reported on the architecture, including a ceramic workshop for making the plaques, and the small finds. He dated the Polychrome ceramic revetments and pottery to the first Bulgarian Empire 'or, indeed, to the 11th or 12th century'. Zlatarski's brief history of the monastery dates the destruction to the late 10th or early 11th century, after which it was never rebuilt.[39] The excavation and publication were completed soon after Wroth's seriation of anonymous folles, but the coins were evidently read according to

PLATE 10.13: *Type 2c. No. 34,*
C–38–373b

PLATE 10.14: *Type 2c. No. 34,*
C–38–38.73a

PLATE 10.15: *Type 3a. No. 35,*
CP 2660

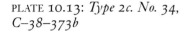

PLATE 10.16: *Type 3a. No. 46,*
C–61–119

PLATE 10.17: *Type 3b. No. 47,*
C–36–585

PLATE 10.18: *Type 3b.*
C–35–482

Sabatier's 1862 classification which attributed almost the entire anonymous follis series, including those found at Patleina, to the reign of John Tzimiskes.[40] The three published coins from this crucial level cited by Grabar all belong to the Anonymous Class A2 series; one can be identified as either variety 14b or 24, another as either variety 39 or 40 and the third as either variety 14b, 24, 33 or 42a.[41] More particularly, these can now be dated on the criteria of size, weight, ornaments, palaeography, iconographic style and their proportions in hoards from 1010/15–1020/25 with the exception of type 42a, which is dated 1020/25–1028.[42] Even if the coins were deposited almost immediately after their minting, they cannot be used as evidence for a destruction by John Tzimiskes. If they date a destruction of the church in which the plaques were used, they attest that this occurred in the second quarter of the 11th century or later. Both Bulgarian accounts and the numismatic evidence refute Grabar's reconstruction of the church's history.

Mijatev, arguing from the Patleina evidence according to Gospodinov and Zlatarski, suggested a date of about 900 for the Preslav plaques and Preslav as the centre of production.[43] This would make the tiles and associated Polychrome pottery, 'Preslav Ware', the local product of a Bulgarian 'golden age' which was terminated by aggressors from the south. Both the date and centre of production have been generally accepted. If Polychrome was indeed a local manufacture, in the light of the contemporary early 10th ceramic industry producing coarse household pottery and the essentially non-monetary exchange economy,[44] it was certainly precocious. Claims of substantiating evidence from other excavations in the area are, sadly, not supported either by publication of their specific contexts nor associated coins. Reasonable doubt can be cast on these claims, not only by the uncritical reliance that most Byzantine archaeologists put on the numismatic evidence, but also by their often indiscriminate use of comparanda.[45]

Excavations at the monastery of Tuzlalaka near Preslav have revealed a small monastic church set within a large and intricate complex. Piles of discards and raw clay, a suitable clay source nearby and two kilns suggest that the Polychrome revetment plaques found in quantity were made on site specifically for use in the monastery. Among the ceramic finds are large quantities of decorated revetment, ceramic architectural members and pottery all belonging to Group 1. The excavator dates these to the end of the 9th or beginning of the 10th century.[46] Since the published evidence for the date is far from conclusive, the style and iconography of the pieces may be of independent assistance.

The simpler decorative border and filling motifs have parallels with those incorporated into the painted decoration of both the Old and New Churches at Tokalı Kilise, dated to the early and mid-10th century respectively. The more intricate geometric and vegetal motifs are more reminiscent of the early to mid-11th century wall mosaics of Hagia Sophia Kiev, Nea Moni and Hosios Loukas, both in style and brilliance. The evidence of the border decoration perhaps suggests a date sometime between about 900 and about 1050 but distinctly favouring the middle or second half of the period.

Figured pieces from Tuzlalaka include images of what is said to be Christ seated on a lyre-backed throne, the Hierarchs, the Panagia Hodegetria, and a nativity scene. Limitations of Byzantine glazing techniques did not easily permit the use of graduated tones to depict form or perspective; ultimately, painterly characteristics were only perfected with the tin glazes of Renaissance Italy. These constraints of the medium limited figural representations to a distinctly linear style.

The Hierarchs are represented iconically, in pairs, in the tympanum of a blind arcade. They are strictly frontal, elongated with organically correct, if stylised drapery. They stand contrapposto with their left leg engaged. Each holds a book, presumably the gospel, in their left hand with their right hand drawn across the body gesturing towards the book. Iconic representations of individual or paired Hierarchs are common from the 11th century, for instance in the southwest chapel of Hosios Loukas where, perhaps significantly, the Panagia Hodegetria is also represented in the same space. The contrapposto stance is rather more typical of later, rather than earlier figures; contrast, for instance, the stance of Saints Irene, Katherine and Barbara from the narthex of Hosios Loukas with that of the late 9th century St. John Chrysostom in Hagia Sophia in Kiev and the early 10th century Emperor Alexander in Hagia Sophia in Constantinople. The facial features and dress of the Hierarchs resemble the linear style, yet with painterly aspects of their 11th century equivalents elsewhere, for instance 11th century manuscript illumination and a niello representation of St. Silvester on a cross in the Dumbarton Oaks Collections. Their heads have the natural proportion and shape of 11th century depictions rather than the stylised, oversized, oval heads of early to mid-10th century monastic figures. Moreover, their expressions are placid, contemplative and naturalistic and find their best parallels in early 11th century equivalents such as in the apse wall figures at Hagia Sophia in Thessaloniki. They are totally unlike the exaggeratedly round-eyed and ascetic expressions of the earlier representations. If these figures are early 10th century, they are painted in a style precocious even by Constantinopolitan standards. Iconographically and stylistically, an early to mid-11th century date is to be preferred. The figure identified as Christ is unusual. He is seated facing frontally and, like the Hierarchs, gestures with his right hand to a book held in his left hand. From the book, gesture and throne one might be excused for thinking, as does Totev, that this is a representation of Christ enthroned. However, the hair is cropped and, if the glaze is not chipped away at this point, apparently balding while the beard is also short; none of these characteristics are typical of representations of Christ in any period. Stranger still is that whereas one would expect a cruciform nimbus radiating from the head of a Christ figure, there is none. The conclusion that this seated figure is a lesser mortal is inescapable. In the context of the writers of the liturgy represented in the tympanum plaques, the larger seated figure placed between the columns may be another, altogether more important author of a sacred work. It may be one of the Evangelists, and if actually represented as an older, balding man, perhaps Mark or Luke.

The lyre-backed throne and its encrustation recall the fine details depicted on gold coins of Constantine IX (1042–55) but it also appears in a cruder form on early 10th century gold coins. Grierson suggests the type was modelled on an icon only completed in the 920s.[47] Presumably the adoption of this particular iconography for an evangelist can be expected to be rather later. In mosaic its closest parallel is not the straight backed throne, supposedly dating to the early 10th century, in the mosaic of Christ enthroned over the Imperial Door of Hagia Sophia in Constantinople. Indeed, it more closely resembles the form of the seat depicted in the mid-11th century Virgin enthroned apse mosaic of Hagia Sofia in Ochrid. In book illumination, it resembles the throne illustrated in a late 11th century edition of *The Heavenly Ladder* of St. John Klimakos.[48] The evidence of the throne type again suggests a range of date between about 920 and 1050, but perhaps inclined rather more towards the later years of the period.

A number of churches in Constantinople were decorated with plaques similar to those from sites around Preslav. A particularly fine example of a Polychrome colonnette, assigned here to Group 2c, was found in the excavation of a small church adjacent to Hagia Eirene. The 11th or first half of the 12th century date ascribed by the excavator has not been universally accepted.[49] Ettinghausen, in discussing the date of the Polychrome revetments in the churches of St. John at the Stoudios Monastery and in the Topkapı Sarayı Basilica, both assigned here to Type 1, is presented with two possibilities for the decoration of the Stoudios church; one late and one early. She rejects the first possibility, that the revetments were erected during a programme of refurbishment of the Stoudios Church by Isaac I Komnenos and his wife Katherine in 1057–1058 in favour of, on what even she admitted was slender evidence, a 10th century date.[50] At the Fenari Isa Camii the tile fragments from the north church principally belonged to the decorative style of Type 1. Mango and Hawkins argued that these tiles were the first at Constantinople for which there was a firm date; to whit that they were applied when the north church was built early in the 10th century (dedicated in AD 907). A strong argument that the tiles probably belonged to a refurbishment of the church can be made from the Type 3 decoration of four of the tile fragments. Type 3 decoration can certainly be placed no earlier than the late 11th century. In the light of the evidence for the date of pottery from Corinth, and the discussion of the Tuzlalaka material above, either a Komnene date, or at earliest, an early 11th century date for these Type 1 architectural revetments seems possible if not probable.

The spectacular Type 1 plaques which are now in the Louvre museum come from Üskübe (ancient Prusia), west of Bolu in Bithynia. A number of these plaques have clear parallels with the decoration of 11th and 12th century objects in other media.[51] One partially preserved piece has a clipeate bust of the Panayia 'the Maker of Victory',[52] ultimately derived from an icon in the Great Palace. This famous icon was carried into battle by the Emperor until the time of Alexios, most notably by Basil II in his victory over Bardas Phokas in 989.[53] The Virgin is represented frontally holding a clipeate bust of Christ. The style is symmetrical with simple linear features. Her expression is tranquil, with heavy lidded, almond-shaped eyes and pronounced, regular, arching eyebrows. The right side of the nose line rises vertically to connect with the right eye-brow. The upper lip of her mouth is defined by a slender bow and the lower lip by a short, horizontal stroke with two thinner strokes to define her chin. Fairly close parallels for the facial features of the Virgin can be found in the crypt figures at Hosios Loukas (11th century) and the figure of Hagia Agape in the church of Hagia Sophia, Kythera (11th to early 12th century).[54]

For many years it was thought that the process of decorating earthenware described by Theophilos referred to Byzantine Polychrome Ware. This association was based partly on the description of the figural style of the decoration and the reference to the use of gold; both are suggestive of Polychrome Ware. The idea was supported by the misconception that Theophilos was a Greek Orthodox monk of Byzantine origins working in the mid-11th or even as early as the mid-10th century;[55] in other words, at the time that Polychrome was thought to have been produced. However, the evidence now seems to indicate strongly that Theophilos can be identified with a central European Benedictine monk and metalworker Roger of Helmarshausen and that the treatise was written in the first half of the 12th century between 1110 and 1140.[56] As such, the passage should reflect the technology of glassmaking and glazing in 12th century central Europe rather than in the eastern Mediterranean one or two hundred years before.

The problems with Hayes' typology and chronology are two-fold. Relatively little of the Saraçhane material belongs to the 11th century, and Polychrome is there too uncommon to differentiate between types properly. More serious is that few of the Saraçhane deposits seem to be uncontaminated and while a few plain glazed or relief fragments may go unnoticed, a fragment of Polychrome stands out and demands attention. Saraçhane deposit 38, 'a homogeneous group, with few survival pieces' consisting of context 1035 which contained one sherd of Group 1 Polychrome, is used as evidence for a possible second quarter of the 10th century date for the style. Elsewhere this same context, 1035, which makes up deposit 38 is described as having been unrecorded during excavation and containing pottery of the early 10th and first half of the 11th century.[57] Its 'homogeneity' is further brought into question by '5+ fragments of Type 54' amphorae in the deposit and the half box of white wares which could not be located for study. The amphorae are considered to be late 10th to early 12th century in date.[58] The possibility that the single fragment of Polychrome is a contamination in the context should be seriously considered. Close examination of the published details of the Saraçhane deposits and contexts which contained Polychrome suggests that none of the Polychrome can be dated with certainty to before the 11th century, even in fairly clean deposits where they may occur as contaminants, for instance those in which where are coins which seem to be obviously intrusive.[59]

The weight of the archaeological evidence supports an 11th to early 12th century date for the three broad types of Polychrome pottery outlined above. The workshops seem to have been staffed by Byzantine Greek craftsmen and were located close to the capital. Revetment tiles decorated using the Polychrome technique were demonstrably also made elsewhere probably by Greek technicians contracted for the task. Since the tiles so closely resemble certain classes of the pottery from the Byzantine capital in decoration, it is entirely reasonable to propose that the churches in and around Patleina were decorated or refurbished after 1000 when the area, including Pliska and both Great and Little Preslav, was reconquered by Basil II. These improvements may well have been instigated under the autocephalous archbishopric at Ochrid, which was established by Basil as an Imperial appointment in 1018 to replace the old Patriarchate. The successors of John, the first Bulgarian-born archbishop were all Greeks from Constantinople, as indeed were a majority of the bishops under them.[60] This Hellenisation of the Slavic church included the adoption of Greek as the official and liturgical language, and may well have had even more far reaching effects. Ceramic revetment, made to measure by itinerant Constantinopolitan craftsmen, could well have been one of the artistic benefits of the reformation.

NOTES

Figures and Plates. All references are to the Corinth Inventory number except those few derived from Rice 1930, Peschlow and Saraçhane II.

1. I am indebted to Mr C. K. Williams II for his encouragement and assistance in the study of the Byzantine pottery from Corinth and am grateful for his permission to publish this material in the collection. Dr. Nancy Bookidis has gone out of her way to make the process of study and writing up as uncomplicated as possible. Thanks are also due to Dr Orestes Zervos for assisting with the finer points of numismatic identification and to Susan Young who made suggestions on how to strengthen aspects of my art historical discussion. Nevertheless, all errors of interpretation and the still weak iconographic elements are entirely mine. Finally I would like to thank Jan Motyka Sanders for editorial help. The present work was written up while on a sabbatical from the British School at Athens on a fellowship generously awarded by the 1984 Foundation.

   Commonly cited works have been abbreviated as follows:

   Corinth XI = C. H. Morgan, *Corinth XI. The Byzantine Pottery* (Cambridge Mass., 1942).

   Durand and Vogt = J. Durand and C. Vogt, 'Plaques de céramiques décorative byzantine d'époque macédonienne,' *Revue du Louvre* 42.4 (1992) 38–44.

   Gospodinov 1914 = J. Gospodinov, 'Razkopki v Patlejna,' *Izvestija* 5 (1914) 31–37.

   Great Palace I = R. B. K. Stevenson, 'The Pottery, 1936-7' in *The Great Palace of the Byzantine Emperors. First Report* (Oxford 1947) 31–68.

   Izvestija = *Izvestija na Arheologiceskija institut* (Bulletin of the Bulgarian Archaeological Institute).

   Mijatev 1936 = K. Mijatev, *Preslavskata keramika* (Sofia 1936).

   Peschlow = 'Byzantinische Keramik aus Istanbul. Ein Fundkomplex bei der Irenenkirche,' *IstMitt* 27/28 (1977–78) 363–414.

   Rice 1930 =D. T. Rice, *Byzantine Glazed Pottery* (Oxford, 1930) 10–19, PLS. III–IX.

   Saraçhane II =J. W. Hayes, *Excavations at Saraçhane in Istanbul II* (Princeton 1992).

   Zalesskaja 1984 =V. N. Zalesskaja, 'Nouvelles découvertes de céramique peinte byzantine du Xe siècle,' *CA* 32 (1984) 49–62.

2. Rice, D. T. 'The Byzantine Pottery,' in S. Casson and D. T. Rice, eds. *Second Report upon the Excavations Carried out in and Near the Hippodrome of Constantinople on Behalf of the British Academy in* 1928 (London 1929) 29–35.

3. Rice 1930, 17, n. 1.

4. Rice 1930, 10–19.

5. Rice 1930, PLS. VIII, IX.

6. Degering, H. 'Theophilus Presbyter qui et Rugerus', *Westfälische Studien...Alois Börner gewidmet*, (Leipzig 1928) 248–62; Rice 1930, 11 n. 1.

7. Rice 1930, 17.

8. *Great Palace I*, pls. 22.1–2, 22.4–5.

9. *Great Palace I*, 46, n. 1 and 2.

10. *Corinth XI*, 64–70, figs. 47–9, 177, pls. XIII–XVII.

11. Zalesskaja 1984, Some of the Cherson dishes were found in a fish salting vat with coins, the latest of which were of Basil II (presumably Anonymous Class A2 Folles 976–1030/35).

12. Peschlow, 405–6.

13. *Saraçhane II*, 13, 35–7.

14. See details outlined in Sanders, G. D. R. 'Excavations at Sparta: the Roman Stoa, 1988–91. Preliminary Report, Part 1 (c) Medieval Pottery.' *BSA* 88 (1993) 253–4. A bibliography of standards can be found in P. Bullock et al. *Handbook for Soil Thin Section Description* (Wolverhampton 1985) 20–38. For practical attempts at standardisation see A.M.Robinson, 'Three Approaches to the Problem of fabric Descriptions,' *Medieval Ceramics* 3 (1979) 3–35 and D. P. S. Peacock, 'Ceramics in Roman and Medieval Archaeology,' in D. P. S. Peacock, ed. *Pottery and Early Commerce* (London 1977) 21–33. Colour: *Munsell Soil Colour Charts* (Baltimore 1975); *CEC Shade Guide* no date; Fédération Européenne des Fabricants de Carreaux Céramiques, Société Anonyme Fiduciaire Suisse, St. Jakobs-Strasse 25, Bale (Suisse). Hardness and size relate to modified Moh's and Wentworth scales can be found in most basic geology textbooks. Percentages of inclusion numbers, inclusion shapes and the percentages of pores are based on J. M. Hodgson, ed., *Soil Survey Field Handbook* (Soil Survey Technical Monograph no. 5 1974); shape of particles as defined by F. J. Pettijohn, *Sedimentary Rocks* (1975) table 3.9.

15. Megaw, A. H. S. and Jones, R. E. 'Byzantine and Allied Pottery: A Contribution by Chemical Analysis to Problems of Origin and Distribution' *BSA* 78 (1983) 256–58.

16. Durand and Vogt, 42.

17. *Acta et diplomata graeca medii aevii*, eds. F. Miklosich and J. Müller (Vienna 1865) vol.iii., 55; Rice 1930, 15.

18. *Saraçhane II*, pl. 8a.1.

19. Bulgaria: Gospodinov 1914, fig. 88; Mijatev 1936, figs. 57–62, pl. XVIII; Akrabova-Žandova, I. 'Rabotilnica za risuvana keramika na jug ot krăglata cărkva v Preslav,' *Izvestija* 20 (1955) 487–509, fig. 20; Ognenova, L. and Georgieva, S. 'Razkopkite na manastira pod Valkachina v Preslav prez 1948-1949 G,' *Izvestija* 20 (1955) 373–417, figs. 23–28; Čangova, J. 'Grasdanska postrojka v mestnosta Selište v Preslav,' *Izvestija* 31 (1969) 211–230, figs. 24.9–10, 25–26; Čangova, J. 'Kăm proučvaneto na preslavskata risuvana keramika,' *Arheologija* (1972.1) 33–39, fig. 9. Crimea: Zalesskaja 1984, figs. 1, 5, 7; Talis, D. L. 'Kharakteristike vizantijskoj keramiki IX-X vv. iz Hersona,' *Trudy Gosudarstvennogo Istoričeskogo Museja* 37 (1960) 125–39; Makarova, T. I. 'Polivnaja posuda, iz istoru keramičeskogo importa i proizvodstva drevnej Rusi,' *Svod arheologičeskih istočnikov* (Moscow 1967) 11–20. Constantinople: Peschlow, nos. 101–105, fig. 16, pls. 140.6, 141.1–6; *Saraçhane II*, pl. 8a.1, 8c.3 and 4, 8e.1-3, 8f, 8g, 8h and 8k.1.

20. Totev, T. 'L'atelier de céramique peinte du monastère royal de Preslav', *CA* 35 (1984) 65–80; Gospodinov 1914, 51–61; Mijatev 1931, figs. 1–52, pls. I–XVII, XIX–XXVIII; Akrabova-Žandova, (see Note 19), figs. 15–19; Ognenova and Georgieva, (see Note 19) figs. 21–22; Čangova 1972, (see Note 19) fig. 24.1–8;

21. Migrant potters are widely attested in recent and modern times; for instance Siphnian potters and the *pitharia* of the Korone district in the Peloponnese and Thrapsano in Crete.

22. *Great Palace I*; Rice 1930, pls. IV, V and IX; Ettinghausen, E. S. 'Byzantine Tiles from the Basilica in the Topkapu Sarayi and Saint John of Studios,' *CA* 7 (1954) 79–86; Rice, D. T. 'Byzantine Polychrome Pottery: a Survey of Recent Discoveries,' *CA* 7 (1954), pl. XXV.2.

23. Durand and Vogt, 38.

24. Peschlow, no. 104, fig. 16, pl. 141, 3 and 4.

25. Peschlow, no. 104. The Corinth data includes *Corinth XI*, no. 369 pl. XVIb found with an Anonymous Class C follis (1042–50), no. 366 pl. XV.h found stratified above an Anonymous Class A1 follis (969–76) and a number of late 10th to mid 11th century coins and C–63–755 from a layer with mid–11th century plain wares.

26. Čimbuleva, J. 'Vases à glaçure en argile blanche de Nessèbre (IXᵉ–XIIᵉ),' in Venedikov, I. et al. *Nessèbre II* (Sofia, 1980) nos. 85–6; Barnea, I. 'Ceramica de Import,' in Gh. Stefan et al. *Dinogetia I*, (Bucharest 1967) figs. 147.18–19, 148.7.

27. For instance *Corinth XI*, no. 333 which came from a level, stratified above two Anonymous Class A1 folles (969–76), in which were two Anonymous Class A2 folles (976–1002); A reservoir excavated in 1975 contained three dishes and a

cup of the style which were found with plain glazed imports and unglazed wares datable to the third quarter of the 11th century.

28. Zaleskaja, V. 'Vizantijskie beloglinjanye raspinye krujki i kilikovidnye čaški po dannym arheologii i piśmennyh istočnikov,' *Sovietskaja Arkeologiji* 1984.4, 217–223, fig. 7; *Saraçhane II*, pl. 8.k.3, 4, 8.l, 8.m.

29. A number of fragments have been found with Anonymous Class A2 folles, equally it is found in mid– to late 11th century contexts dated by both coins and pottery.

30. *Saraçhane II*, 122–128.

31. For instance C–38–530 found with an Anonymous Class F follis (1060–65) and an Anonymous Class J (1080–85) struck over a follis of Nicephorus III is typical of the type of context in which the Group is found.

32. Zaleskaja 1984, figs. 9, 11–15; Megaw, A. H. S. 'Byzantine Pottery (4th–14th century),' in R. J. Charleston, ed. *World Ceramics* (London 1986) fig. 301. Čimbuleva 1980, (see Note 26) nos. 84, 89–90; Barnea, (see Note 26) figs. 148.2, .8–9, .11–12.

33. *Saraçhane II*, 30, 35–37.

34. *Saraçhane II*, deposit 43.22–23, deposit 50.94, pl. 8s, deposits 44.12, 47.6, 50.94. see also pl. 9b from layer 1244 and fig. 13 nos. 21–23 from layers 1081, 934 and 1158/1181; Barnea, (see Note 26) figs. 147.17, 148.1, .6, .13–14; Peschlow, no. 106, fig. 16, pl. 141.7–8; Rice 1930, pl. VI below.

35. *Great Palace I*, pp. 44–46, pl. 17.15–18, 22.1, 2, 4.

36. Mango, C. and Hawkins, E.J.W. 'Additional Notes,' in Macridy, T. *et al.* 'The Monastery of Lips (Fenari Isa Camii) at Istanbul,' *DOP* 18 (1964) 299–315, fig. 53.

37. *Great Palace I*, 45, pl. 22.4, 5; *Saraçhane II*, no. 42.29, pl. 8k.6; Zaleskaja 1984, fig. 10.

38. Grabar, A. *Recherches sur les influences orientales dans l'art balkanique* (Strasbourg 1931) 9–11; Rice 1930, 17.

39. Gospodinov 1914; Zlatarski, V. N. 'Kămă istorijata na otkritija v mestnostata Patlejna stară Bulgarski manastira,' *Izvestija na Arheologičeskoto družestvo* 1.2 (1921–22) 146–162.

40. Wroth, W. *Catalogue of the Imperial Byzantine Coins in the British Museum*, 2 vols. (London 1908) 480–83, pls. LV–LIX; Sabatier, J., *Description générale des monnaies byzantines* 2 vols. (Leipzig 1862).

41. Gospodinov 1914, p. 118, fig. 82. For the identifications see *DOC III*.2, 639, table 24.

42. Ivanisevic, V. 'Interpretation and Dating of the Folles of Basil II and Constantine VIII—the Class A2,' *Zbornik Radova Vizantološkog Instituta* 27–28 (1989) 20–42, see fig. 6 for a typology of secret marks by date.

43. Mijatev 1931, 51–66.

44. For the pottery see, for instance, Čangova, J. 1969 (see Note 19) figs. 8–9. Evidence for the economy is given by Cedrenus who states that Basil II maintained the system of taxation as it had been under Tsar Samuel; that is in kind not in gold. Under Michael IV a change to assessments in coin led to a revolt in 1040–41, see Hendy, M. F. *Studies in the Byzantine Monetary Economy c.*300–1450 (Cambridge 1985) 297.

45. For example Čimbuleva 1980, (see n. 26) 204–212, who dates the incised white wares at Mesembria to the 9th century by analogy to fragments in Stage 2 of the Great Palace excavations. Although one fragment, no. 15, appears to be early, the remainder are best paralleled by pottery in stage IV and are, in fact, late 11th to early 12th century.

46. Totev 1987 (see Note 20); Totev, T. 'Manastirat Tuzlalăka—centăr na risuvana keramika v Preslav prez IX–X v.,' *Arheologija* (1976.1) 11–16; 'Trideset godini arheologičeski razkopi v Preslav,' *Arheologija* (1974.3) 48–61.

47. *DOC III*.2, pl. LVIII.2; *III*.1 p.157.

48. Vatican Library ms. gr. 394, folio 130r, see Lazarev, V. *Storia della pittura bizantina* (Torino 1967) pl. 246.

49. Dirimtekin, F. 'Les fouilles faites en 1946–1947 et en 1958–1960 entre Sainte–Sophie et Sainte–Irène à Istanbul,' *CA* 13 (1962) 181, fig. 24; Megaw 1986, (see Note 32) fig. 306.

50. Ettinghausen 1954, (see Note 22) 87, 'Although the original transept basilica in the court of the Topkapu Sarayi was probably built in the second half of the fifth century, it was renovated later on with a new floor raised above the old one. It is quite likely that the tiles were applied in the course of these renovations. Indeed this assumption is corroborated by other facts: the simple pattern of the second floor would date it approximately to the sixth to the tenth century and of all the coins found from the period after the original foundation of the church, those from the 10th century are more numerous. Meagre as this evidence is, there is a slight edge for the 10th century.'

51. Durand and Vogt, 38–42.

52. Durand and Vogt, pl. 9.

53. *DOP* p. 611, pl. XLVII, 19.1–4.

54. Skawran, K. M. *The Development of Middle Byzantine Fresco Painting in Greece* (Pretoria 1982) fig. 148.

55. Rice 1930, p. 11, note 1; Degering 1928, (see n. 6) 248–62.

56. C. R. Dodwell *Theophilus, De diversibus artibus. Theophilus, The Various Arts*, Translated from the Latin with introductory and notes by C. R. Dodwell (London 1961). For a general discussion of the identification and date of the treatise, see J. G. Hawthorne and C. S. Smith, trans. and eds. *On Diverse Arts. The Treatise of Theophilus* (Chicago 1963) xv–xvii.

57. *Saraçhane II*, 116; Harrison, R. M. 'The Stratigraphy' in R. M. Harrison *et al. Excavations at Saraçhane in Istanbul I* (Princeton NJ 1986) context 1035.

58. *Saraçhane II*, 75, 116–117.

59. For instance, Saraçhane Deposits 38, 40 and 43.

Deposit 38. Layer 1035. Unrecorded layer with pottery originally read as e. 10th century with 1/2 11th century. Coins all early. cf SC I. Later dated by Hayes SC II to 2/4 10th century (note that fig. 7#1 joins between 1035 and topsoil layer 1452. Contents (Polychrome): 1 fragment of Class 1 (Type 1?) 'probably belongs to the assemblage'.

Deposit 40. The pottery, dated by Hayes to the end of the 10th century and was equated to Stage IV of the Great Palace excavations. It should be noted that Stage IV contains a large proportion of mid– to late 11th century pottery. Contents (Polychrome): 40.26 (pl. 8a1) Type 1 from 1285 with 5 other fragments of Class 1 (perhaps Type 1 or 2c?) including *Saraçhane II*, pl. 8c2 and 4.

Deposit 43. Contained much fragmentary pottery. Hayes dismissed a coin of Manuel I as intrusive and the remaining coins as 'not helpful'. The pottery in layer 1272 was initially dated to the mid- (?) 11th century. The layer contained 34 coins, most of which were early. Four coins are indeed apparently helpful to the date of deposition; #847 Alexius I, 3rd coinage (1092-1118), #838 Anonymous Class K (1085–92), #834 Anonymous Class G (c. 1065–c. 1070) and #827 Anonymous Class C (1042?–1050). Contents (Polychrome): 43.21 Type 1; 43.22 Class IIIa Cup; 43.23 Class IIIa bowl (pl. 9a); 2 fragments with a lion of IIIb and eight other fragments.

60. Spinka, M. *A History of Christianity in the Balkans* (Chicago 1933) 91–2.

11

The Chapels in the Byzantine Castle of Sahyun (Qal'at Salah al-Din), Syria

Denys Pringle

THE SITE

Lying 33 km east of Latakia on the western slopes of the Jabal al-Ansariya, Qal'at Sahyun is one of the most spectacular castles in Syria.[1] It is perhaps best known for its formidable defences attributed to the Frankish period of occupation, which lasted from around 1108 until the castle's celebrated bombardment and capture by Salah al-Din (Saladin) in 1188. But the Crusaders made use here, as elsewhere, of a site that had already been fortified by the Byzantines; and after they were expelled from it, the castle remained a family fief of the descendants of 'Amir Nasir al-Din Manguwirish until 1272, when it passed to the Mamluks. The remains of the Byzantine and Muslim periods are extensive, though they have been less intensively studied than those of the Franks.[2]

The early history of the site is obscure. Although it has been identified as *Sigon*, which was held by the Phoenicians at the time of Alexander the Great's arrival in Syria,[3] no Hellenistic or Roman remains have as yet been found there. Sahyun was probably taken by 'Amir Sayf al-Dawla in 948, for in the later tenth century it was in the hands of the Hamdanids of Aleppo.[4] In 975, however, the Byzantine emperor John Tzimiskes, while returning to Antioch from his successful campaign south into Syria and Palestine, captured Sahyun along with the nearby towns of Banyas, Jabala and Barziya (Bourzey).[5]

It is to the Byzantine period that the earliest structural phases of Sahyun may with certainty be attributed.[6] Although it is usually referred to as a castle, the extent of the fortifications suggests that they would have enclosed a civilian settlement of some significance, in addition to the quarters reserved for the military garrison.

The Byzantine castle occupied an elongated promontory, aligned east-west and measuring some 710m in length and 50–150m in width, with deep natural chasms to north and south (FIG. 11.1). On the east it was cut off from gently rising ground by a rock-cut ditch, 140m long, 20–25m wide and (eventually, after later Frankish deepening) 28m deep. Although in the Frankish period the main gate seems to have been on the south, the principal entrance to the Byzantine castle seems to have been on the east. It was set between a pair of rounded towers (later rebuilt to serve as a postern by the Franks), and was reached by a timber bridge, supported on a pinnacle of rock left in the centre of the ditch. Similar rock pinnacles, also apparently Byzantine in origin, occur at Edessa (Urfa), Gargar (Gerger) and Anafa (Nephin).[7]

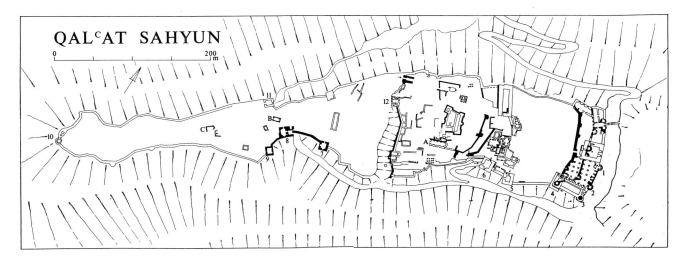

FIG. 11.1: *Sahyun Castle: plan of the Byzantine phase showing the location of chapels A, B and C (drawn by Peter E. Leach, after Deschamps,* Châteaux *(n.2)).*

Behind the ditch were three solid masonry walls. The outer two have been mostly destroyed or obscured by later Frankish and Muslim work, but excavations have shown them to have been some 2m thick and defended by projecting rounded towers. The third wall, which is better preserved, has a somewhat different character, being both thicker (up to 3m) and strengthened by alternating rectangular and cutwater-shaped turrets. Its construction is of rubble concrete with a facing of small blocks, which in places are arranged in a diaper pattern resembling *opus reticulatum* (PLATE 11.1). Although it has been suggested that this masonry may belong to an earlier Byzantine phase of the sixth or early seventh century,[8] it seems more likely that it represents no more than a local example of the decorative treatment of wall facing that is characteristic of Middle Byzantine constructions elsewhere, the principal distinction here being that it is executed entirely in stone rather than in a mixture of stone and brick or tile.[9] It would in any case be very unusual to find *opus reticulatum* in a building as late as the sixth or seventh century, let alone a fortification. Nevertheless, it remains possible, as at Kyrenia Castle,[10] that the wall with the cutwater-shaped turrets and those with the rounded towers belong to different Byzantine phases; but if that were so, unlike Kyrenia where the wall with cutwater bastions is clearly a later addition, at Sahyun it would still not be clear which came first.

Behind its outer ditch and triple walls the Byzantine castle fell into three principal parts. For the first 100m there extended a relatively flat area, apparently largely devoid of buildings, though partially built over in the Ayyubid and Mamluk phases. This was defined on the west by two more walls, cutting across the promontory from north to south. Behind these the ground rises, and at its highest point, set well back from the outer walls and ditch and dominating the entire site, stood the citadel (PLATE 11.3), a trapezoidal structure (24/ 29 by 24m) with rectangular corner-towers and an interior consisting of a series of massive barrel-vaults. Its east wall, being the most exposed to enemy bombardment, was at least 3.5m thick and was strengthened by a cutwater-shaped interval turret. To the west of this the ground falls away, and at a position some 270m from the outer ditch there came another rock-cut ditch, crossed by another timber bridge carried on a rock pinnacle. This led out into a lower ward, which tailed away, following the natural topography and eventually narrowing to a rounded point, at which stood another round tower.

PLATE 11.1: *Sahyun Castle: the inner Byzantine wall, showing masonry resembling* opus reticulatum *(photo. author).*

PLATE 11.2: *Sahyun Castle: chapel A, the east end of the Byzantine chapel (photo. author).*

CHAPEL A

Excavations conducted by Pierre Coupel in 1942 resulted in the discovery of two chapels lying south of the Byzantine citadel. The northern one was built against a wall flanking the south side of the citadel and appears to be contemporary with it, while the southern one, which flanks it in turn, is larger and evidently dates from the Frankish period. Following excavation, M. Coupel undertook the consolidation and partial rebuilding of what remained of both buildings.[11]

The earlier, Byzantine chapel is 8.6m long internally, including the semi-circular apse, and has a somewhat irregular plan on account of having been built against the retaining walls of the citadel (FIG. 11.2, PLATES 11.2 and 11.4). Thus while the south wall is straight and aligned precisely with the arc of the apse, the north wall is dog-legged and of different builds. The nave therefore consists of two juxtaposed barrel-vaults, that towards the west being 3.6m wide and that on the east 3.1m, with the chord of the apse measuring only 2.6m. At the south-west corner, a barrel-vaulted passage, 0.9m wide, ascends towards the west and then to the north, up towards the citadel.

The masonry of the apse and the eastern part of the nave, though much degraded and partially replaced by modern indenting, consists of good ashlar, laid in courses around 20cm high. The rest of the nave is rubble built and is plastered internally. The semi-dome of the apse is also ashlar, as is the wall above it, while the rounded vaults covering the nave are built of split stones, set in mortar and coated with plaster. The springings of the vaults and of the apse's semi-dome are defined by moulded string courses, now almost completely abraided.

The apse appears to have had no window, but there is an internally splayed slit in the wall above it. In its north wall is a rectangular niche; and a larger one is set in the south wall of the nave just in front of it.

Before the construction of the Frankish church against it, the south wall (of which little now remains) appears to have been an external wall. In it, to the west of the niche, are remains of a window and of a door with a rounded relieving arch. A set of elaborately moulded voussoirs that were found in the excavations may possibly have come from the latter; but an abraided stylized capital that was found with them seems for structural reasons more likely to have come from the Frankish chapel (where it may quite possibly have been in reuse).[12] In the north wall of the nave, opposite the window and apparently intended to balance it architecturally, is a rounded-arched semi-circular recess with a rebated edge. Another slit window pierces the surviving northern side of the western nave vault.

The Frankish chapel was built against the Byzantine chapel's south wall and its westward continuation. It seems likely that the latter would thereafter have been used as a side chapel or sacristy, with its south door allowing access into it from the eastern bay of the new building.

The Frankish chapel measures internally 29.85m long and 9 m wide, and consists of a nave of four bays with a semi-circular apse (FIG. 11.2, PLATES 11.5-6). It is built throughout in ashlar with course heights of 21–23cm. The bays were divided by rectangular pilasters with engaged columns facing inward. These no doubt originally carried transverse arches, but it is uncertain whether the bays were barrel-vaulted or groin-vaulted. Judging by the example of other Frankish ecclesiastical buildings surviving in Syria and Lebanon (e.g. Tartus, Amiun, Jubail), the former is perhaps more likely, with a barrel-vault of slightly pointed profile springing off the backs of two rows of blind arches running the

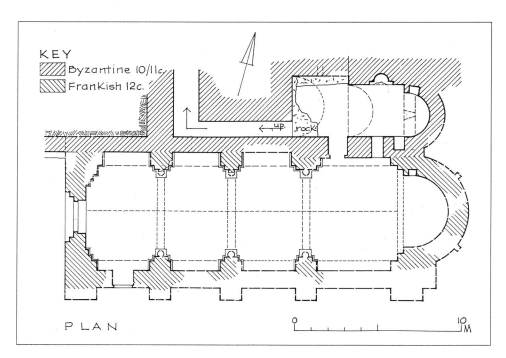

KEY
Byzantine 10/11c.
Frankish 12c.

PLAN

0 .... 10 M

FIG. 11.2: *Sahyun: plan of chapel A (drawn by Peter E. Leach, after Deschamps, Châteaux (n. 2), and author's field notes).*

PLATE 11.3: *Sahyun Castle: the Byzantine citadel from the east, with mosque, hammam and Frankish towers 5 and 6 in the foreground (photo. author).*

PLATE 11.4: *Sahyun Castle: chapel A, the Byzantine chapel from the south (photo. author).*

length of the nave. M. Coupel has unfortunately rebuilt part of the north arcade with a row of semi-circular arches, something for which there appears to have been no evidence and for which he was criticized by Deschamps.[13] In the closely analagous structural arrangement found in the chapel at Crac des Chevaliers, which the Hospitallers built after the earthquake of 1170, the arches are higher and pointed, and the nave vault springs from a cornice moulding running above them.[14]

The main door was in the west wall, and as at Crac there was a subsidiary entrance in the south wall of the west bay. The other openings shown by Coupel in the south wall, however, appear to be spurious.[15]

CHAPEL B

This chapel stands in the lower ward of the castle, some 150 m from the ditch separating it from the upper ward and in the centre of the point where the width of the promontory narrows to 40m (FIG. 11.1, PLATE 11.7). A very brief description of it has been published by Deschamps, together with a photograph; but otherwise it has attracted little scholarly attention.[16]

The chapel is free-standing and orientated N 71° E. Externally it has the form of a rectangular box, measuring 10.8 by 6.4m on plan and some 6.5m in height (PLATE 11.8). Internally it has a rectangular nave and a stilted semi-circular apse (PLATES 11.9–10). The construction is rubble concrete, laid in regular courses and

PLATE 11.5: *Sahyun Castle: chapel A, the Frankish chapel from the west (photo. author).*

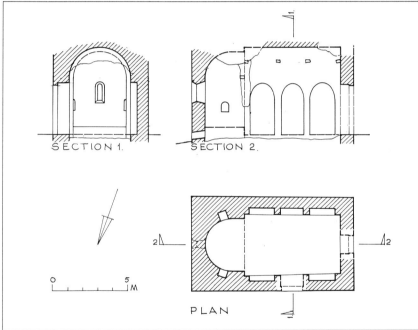

FIG. 11.3: *Sahyun: plan and section of chapel B (drawn by Peter E. Leach from author's field notes).*

plastered internally. The quoins and the door surrounds, however, are built in ashlar, which is well dressed with diagonal tooling and of varying course heights.

The nave is 6.36m long and 3.83m wide at the west end, broadening to 4.14m at the east. It is enclosed by a barrel-vault, which springs from the backs of three blind arches, 40–45cm deep and of rounded somewhat elliptical profile, set in each of the side walls. High in the spandrels above these arches and at either end of the nave may be seen the pockets that formerly took the timber cross-beams that supported the centring during construction of the vault. As there is no indication that any attempt was ever made to block up the holes, it seems likely that the timbers would have been left in place after the centring had been removed and that they have rotted away only since the chapel's aban-

donment. Apart from giving some additional structural support to the vault, they might also have served for the suspension of lamps. On the west a row of at least three (and probably four) ceramic jars built into the wall at the same level possibly served an acoustic purpose.

In the centre of the north and west walls respectively is a tall rounded-arched opening. That on the north is some 1.30m wide and only slightly lower than the arch in which it is set, while that on the west is some 1.22m wide and roughly the same height. Although Deschamps regarded these as a window and a door respectively, it seems more likely that they were both in fact doors.[17] In both cases the jambs and lintels have been robbed, leaving only the semi-circular relieving arch. The fact that each arch has a 4cm internal rebate

PLATE 11.6: *Sahyun Castle: chapel A, the nave of the Frankish chapel looking west (photo. author).*

PLATE 11.7: *Sahyun Castle: the lower ward, looking west towards Byzantine towers 7– 9, chapel B and Frankish tower 11 (photo. author).*

suggests that they were not infilled, but formed lunettes, lighting the interior of the nave.

The apse is narrower than the nave and stilted in plan (3.52m wide, 2.68m deep). A change in the plaster that covers it suggests that its floor level would have been some 52cm higher than that of the nave, though whether the floor was of timber that has subsequently rotted or of material that has been dug away is not entirely certain. As the interior of the building has evidently been cleared of rubble at some stage, it may be that the raised apse floor was inadvertently removed in the same operation. Below the floor level and just above the present ground surface, the east wall of the apse is pierced by a rough aperture, 50cm high and 25cm wide, which slopes downward towards the exterior. The likeliest explanation for this is that it was

a drain, placed behind the altar; alternatively, if the floor was of timber, it could possibly have served to ventilate the space below it, in which a tomb or relics might possibly have been located.

The apse was lit by a rounded-arched double-splayed window, 1.74m above the floor level. At its narrowest point, this was some 1.2m high and 0.4m wide. In the north and south walls of the apse, flanking the position of the altar and 0.82m above the floor level, are two rounded-arched niches (51cm wide, 50cm deep, and 70cm high). A beam slot at the spring of the semi–dome may also have served to carry the centring during construction; like those of the nave, it was probably left *in situ* when the centring was dismantled and was perhaps used subsequently to support lamps or a timber icon screen.

PLATE 11.8: *Sahyun Castle: chapel B, from NW (photo. author).*

The whole interior was thickly plastered; but little trace may now be seen of the remains of paintings noticed by Deschamps.[18]

CHAPEL C

Deschamps also identified the apse and walling of another chapel, located some 75m west of chapel B. The published plan suggests that it would have been comparable in size to chapel B, but no description is given.[19]

DISCUSSION

At first sight, all three chapels appear to be associated with the Byzantine phase of occupation of Sahyun (975–*c*.1108). This is suggested both by their masonry, which is generally similar to that of the fortifications of the same period, and by the fact that chapel A is physically attached to one of the lower walls of the citadel and has a later Frankish chapel built against it. More precise dating either of the chapels or of the fortifications themselves is unfortunately not possible in the present state of knowledge.

In terms of their architecture, the Sahyun chapels are generally similar to the simpler type of church building constructed in Syria and Palestine between the time of the Islamic conquest and the arrival of the Crusaders: small single-celled structures with a barrel-vaulted nave and a semi-circular apse.[20] Examples from other Middle Byzantine fortresses in northern Syria, however, are elusive, though this is mainly due to the lack of excavations. The identification of a chapel at Qal'at Barza (Barziya, Bourzey) is doubtful,[21] and none has been identified at Qal'at Mhalba (Balatonos), Harim (Harrenc) or elsewhere.

In Cyprus, the church in the Byzantine castle of St Hilarion appears to be eleventh century and to have belonged to the monastery that preceded the fortifica-tion of the site.[22] In Kyrenia the chapel is twelfth century and placed outside the main part of the castle.[23] Both of these structures, however, were domed and had a narthex, something altogether more elaborate than the modest structures at Sahyun.

Closer analogies are to be found further north, in Cilicia.[24] In the Land Castle at Korykos there are three chapels, two of which (along with most of the castle itself) are assigned by Robert Edwards to the early twelfth-century Byzantine phase, and one to the Armenian phase of the late twelfth century onwards.[25] Somewhat curiously, although the Byzantine chapel U at Korykos has the same structural arrangement of blind arcading supporting the barrel-vault of the nave as occurs in chapel B (and the Frankish chapel) at Sahyun, the Sahyun chapels appear to have little else in common with Edwards' characterization of the Byzantine castle chapels of Cilicia, but a great deal in common with the Armenian ones.[26] In the case of Sahyun chapel B (and to a lesser extent chapel A) the similarities include a barrel-vaulted nave and semi-circular apse enclosed by a rectangular external wall; a splayed apse window (though at Sahyun it has a double rather than a single splay); joist holes left at the level of the vault springing; two doors of which one is on the west (though in Cilician examples the second is more often on the south than on the north); doors with semi-circular relieving arches (though in chapel K at Anavarza, the tympana were filled in and there were segmental rear-arches behind the lintels),[27] and round-headed niches set in the north and south walls of the apse. The only significant differences, apart from the masonry, are the lack of a cornice moulding at the spring of the apse's semi-dome (though this does exist in chapel A and is in any case not ubiquitous in Cilicia), and the blind arcading of the nave walls, which is unrecorded in the Armenian chapels of Cilicia. In the castle at Çardak, which was at various times in

Byzantine and Armenian hands, Edwards also noted in the chapel, which he identifies as Armenian, four ceramic acoustic pipes placed in either side of the nave vault some 22cm above the springing, such as we have in the west wall of chapel B at Sahyun.[28]

The explanation for the apparently close similarity between the Sahyun chapels, in particular chapel B, and the Armenian rather than the Byzantine castle chapels of Cilicia, is not immediately obvious; indeed, considering our lack of knowledge about Middle Byzantine churches in northern Syria in general, it may be hazardous even to attempt one at this stage. There is certainly no reason to doubt the validity of Edwards' characterization of Byzantine and Armenian chapels for Cilicia, based as it is on minute examination of a large number of examples. Even if chapel B at Sahyun were to date from the very end of the eleventh century, however, it would still pre-date most of the Cilician chapels that Edwards considers. This raises the possibility that the models adopted by the Armenian builders in Cilicia in the late eleventh and twelfth centuries might have been local, or perhaps even North Syrian, rather than derived from Armenia proper, as Edwards suggests.[29] Such an idea, however, would appear to be negated by the wealth of comparable examples known from Armenia itself.[30]

An altogether more plausible explanation is that chapel B was itself built by Armenians, for their own use. In such a case its date of construction could be placed after the Frankish occupation of Sahyun around 1108, for the presence of Armenians in the Principality of Antioch in the twelfth century is well attested.[31] In 511 AH/AD 1117–18, for example, the Muslim occupants of the castle of Marqab, overlooking Banyas (Valania), were replaced by a mixed garrison of Franks and Armenians.[32] In 1118, the Rubenid Prince Levon, brother of T'oros I, led a contingent of troops to assist Roger of Antioch in capturing 'Azaz, near Aleppo;[33] and, the following year, 500 Armenian horsemen fought with Prince Roger in the disastrous battle of the *Ager Sanguinis*, in which he lost his life.[34] In such circumstances it seems very possible that the lower ward of Sahyun might have contained an Armenian garrison, with perhaps even a civilian settlement, during the early twelfth century, and that chapel B was their church. Until the structural elements of Sahyun can be more precisley dated and the archaeological context of the chapel better understood, however, it will be difficult to tell for certain.

School of History and Archaology
Cardiff University, Wales.

PLATE 11.9 (ABOVE): *Sahyun Castle: chapel B, the apse (photo. author).*

PLATE 11.10 (BELOW): *Sahyun Castle: chapel B, the nave looking west (photo. author).*

NOTES

1. My visit to Sahyun on 27 April 1984 was made possible by a travel grant awarded by the British School of Archaeology in Jerusalem.

2. Among the many published accounts of the castle may be noted: E.G. Rey, *Étude sur les monuments de l'architecture militaire des croisés en Syrie* (Paris 1871) 105–13, figs. 31–5, pl. XII; M. Van Berchem and E. Fatio, *Voyage en Syrie*, *Mémoires de l'Institut français d'archéologie orientale du Caire*, XXXVII–XXXVIII (Cairo 1913–15)267–83, pls. LIX–LXII; P. Jacquot, *L'État des Alaouïtes: terre d'art, de souvenirs et de mystère: guide* (Beirut 1929) 203–14; P. Deschamps, 'Au temps des croisades: le château de Saone', *Gazette des beaux-arts*, 6s., 4 (1930) 329–364; id., 'Les entrées des châteaux des croisés et leurs défenses', *Syria*, 12 (1931) 369–87, pls. LXXVII–LXXXVI; C. Cahen, 'Note sur les seigneurs de Saone et de Zerdana', *Syria*, 12 (1931) 154–9; *Syrie—Palestine—Iraq—Transjordanie, Les Guides bleus*, ed. M. Monmarché (Paris 1932) 270–74, fig.; P. Deschamps, 'Le château de Saone et ses premiers seigneurs', *Syria*, 16 (1935) 73–88, pl. XIX; C. Cahen, *La Syrie du Nord à l'époque des croisades et la principauté franque d'Antioche*, Institut française de Damas, Bibliothèque orientale, I (Paris 1940) 168–9; R. C. Smail, *Crusading Warfare (1097–1193)* (Cambridge, 1956) 236–43, plan 6, pl. VI–VIII; P. Deschamps, *Terre Sainte romane*, Zodiaque: la nuit des temps, XXI (La Pierre-qui-Vire, 1964) 31–43, pls. 1–12; W. Müller-Wiener, *Castles of the Crusaders* (London, 1966) 44–5, pls. 12–21; G. Saadé, *Château de Saladin* (Qalaat Salah-ed-Din) (Latakia 1966); id. (J. Sa'ada), 'Tarîkh Qal'at Salâh al-Dîn', *Annales archéologiques arabes syriennes*, 17 (1967), Arabic section, 59–78; T. S. R. Boase, *Castles and Churches of the Crusading Kingdom* (Oxford 1967) 48–51; G. Saadé, 'Histoire du château de Saladin', *Studi medievali*, 3s., 9.2 (1968) 980–1016; P. Deschamps, *Les Châteaux des croisés en Terre Sainte*, III. *La défense du comté de Tripoli et de la principauté d'Antioche*, Bibliothèque archéologique et historique, XC (Paris 1973) 217–47, 7 plans, pls. VIII–XXX; T. E. Lawrence, *Crusader Castles*, new edn. with notes and introduction by D. Pringle (Oxford 1988) xxix–xxx, xxxvii, 42–9, 126–30, figs. 22–28; J. Riley-Smith (ed.), *The Atlas of the Crusades* (London 1991) 56–7; H. Kennedy, *Crusader Castles* (Cambridge 1994) 84–96, colour pl. 3, pls. 35-42, figs. 13–14; D. W. Morray, 'Sahyûn', *Encyclopaedia of Islam*, new edition, VIII (Leiden 1995) 850–51.

3. R. Dussaud, *Topographie historique de la Syrie antique et médiévale*, Bibliothèque archéologique et historique, IV (Paris 1927) 149.

4. G. Saadé, *Château de Saladin* (n.2).

5. Matthew of Edessa, 'Chronique', *Recueil des Historiens des Croisades, Documents arméniens*, I (Paris 1869) 18; trans. A. E. Dostourian, *Armenia and the Crusades, Tenth to Twelfth Centuries: The Chronicle of Matthew of Edessa* (Lanham Maryland 1993) 32; Deschamps, *Châteaux* (n.2) 219; S. Runciman, *A History of the Crusades*, 3 vols. (Cambridge 1951–54), I, 32.

6. A. W. Lawrence, 'A Skeletal History of Byzantine Fortification', *BSA*, 78 (1983) 171–227 (at 218–19).

7. T. E. Lawrence, *Crusader Castles* (n.2) 39, 129, figs. 11a–11b, 21 ; Cahen, *La Syrie du Nord* (n.2) 126; Deschamps, *Châteaux* (n.2) 233 n.1, 300, pls. LXI–LXIII. See also P. Leriche, 'Les défenses orientales de Tell Arqa au moyen âge', *Syria*, 60 (1983) 111–32.

8. C. Foss and D. Winfield, *Byzantine Fortifications: An Introduction* (Pretoria 1986) 180, n.155; cf. Deschamps, *Châteaux* (n.2) 242, pl. XXIVb.

9. On the masonry of Middle Byzantine fortifications, see Foss and Winfield (n.8) 142–5, 162–4. Diaper patterning in tile is found on tenth-century churches of the Peloponnese and Epirus, and as late as the twelfth century in Mani and

elsewhere in Greece; see H. Megaw, 'Byzantine Architecture in Mani', *BSA*, 33 (1933) 137-62, pls.17–21 (at 147–8, pls. 19d, 21b).

10. A. H. S. Megaw, *A Brief History and Description of Kyrenia Castle* (Nicosia n.d.); id., 'The Arts in Cyprus, B. Military Architecture', in H. W. Hazard (ed.), *The Art and Architecture of the Crusader States, A History of the Crusades*, ed. K. M. Setton, IV (Madison, Wisconsin 1977) 196–207 (at 199–203).

11. P. Deschamps, 'Les travaux de M. Pierre Coupel au château de Sahyoun (Syrie)', *CRAI* (1945) 263–8; id., *Châteaux* (n.2) 218–19, 243, 247, pls. XXVII, XXX, plans 1–3, and unnumbered; Müller–Wiener (n. 2), plan 2.13; Saadé, *Château de Saladin* (n.2), no. 34.

12. Deschamps, *Châteaux* (n.2) 243, pl. XXVIIa-b.

13. Deschamps, 'Les travaux de M. Pierre Coupel' (n.11) 268.

14. Deschamps, *Terre Sainte romane* (n.2) 93–4, fig., pls. 38–39.

15. Deschamps, *Châteaux* (n.2), plan 2.

16. Jacquot, *L'État des Alaouïtes* (n.2) 213; Deschamps, 'Les travaux de M. Pierre Coupel' (n. 11) 268; id., *Châteaux* (n.2), 244–5, pl. XXXa–b, un-numbered plan; Müller-Wiener (n.2), plan 2.16; Saadé, *Château de Saladin* (n.2), no. 26; *Syrie—Palestine—Iraq— Transjordanie, Les Guides bleus* (n.2) 274.

17. Deschamps, *Châteaux* (n.2) 244–5.

18. Deschamps, *Châteaux* (n.2) 245.

19. Deschamps, *Châteaux* (n.2) 245, un-numbered plan.

20. D. Pringle, 'Church-building in Palestine before the Crusades', in J. Folda (ed.), *Crusader Art in the Twelfth Century*, BAR, S152 (Oxford 1982) 5–46 (at 8, figs. 1.2–1.4).

21. Deschamps, *Châteaux* (n.2) 348; cf. 156.

22. A. H. S. Megaw, *A Brief History & Description of St. Hilarion Castle*, 7th ed. (Nicosia 1963) 4–5, pl.

23. A. H. S. Megaw, *A Brief History and Description of Kyrenia Castle* (Nicosia n.d.) 4, pl.

24. R. W. Edwards, 'Ecclesiastical architecture in the fortifications of Armenian Cilicia [I]', *DOP*, 36 (1982) 155–76, 41 figs.; id., 'Ecclesiastical architecture in the fortifications of Armenian Cilicia: second report', *DOP*, 37 (1983) 123–46, 91 figs.

25. Edwards, 'Ecclesiastical architecture [I]' (n.24) 173–5, figs. 38–41; id., *The Fortifications of Armenian Cilicia*, Dumbarton Oaks Studies, XXIII (Washington D.C. 1987) 161–7.

26. Cf. Edwards, 'Ecclesiastical architecture [I]' (n.24) 156, 164–5, 173, fig. 13.

27. Edwards, 'Ecclesiastical architecture [II]' (n.24) 132–4, figs. 38–46. The date appears to be 12th century: cf. Edwards, *Fortifications* (n.25) 65–72.

28. Edwards, 'Ecclesiastical architecture [I]' (n.24) 166–7, figs. 13, 18–19; id., *Fortifications* (n.25) 111–13.

29. 'Ecclesiastical architecture [I]' (n.24) 164.

30. See, for example, J.-M. Thierry and P. Donabédian, *Les Arts arméniens* (Paris 1987), with references.

31. Cahen, *La Syrie du Nord* (n.2) 337–8; Smail, *Crusading Warfare* (n.2) 46–8.

32. Deschamps, *Châteaux* (n.2) 259–60.

33. Matthew of Edessa, trans. Dostourian (n.5) 222–3; Edwards, *Fortifications* (n.25) 6.

34. Matthew of Edessa, trans. Dostourian (n.5) 223–4; Cahen, *La Syrie du Nord* (n.2) 284–6; Runciman, *History of the Crusades* (n.5), II, 150.

12

Bowls and Birds: Some Middle Byzantine Glazed Bowls from Swiss Private Collections

M.-L. von Wartburg

A considerable body of Middle Byzantine pottery was rescued from the wreck of Pelagonnisos near Alonessos by the Greek Archaeological Service. This discovery as well as the publication of several comparable groups of pottery from museums and private collections markedly increased our knowledge of certain types of Middle Byzantine glazed pottery.[1] This holds true for the repertoire of vessel shapes as well as for the techniques and motifs of decoration. A comparative assessment of these criteria had to be based for a long time on C. H. Morgan's *The Byzantine Pottery from Corinth* (1942), the only extensive publication of such material.[2] With a few exceptions, Middle Byzantine glazed vessels published after 1942 (mainly variants of 'Sgraffito Ware' plus a few examples of 'Painted Ware'[3]) come from the cargoes of wrecks, which were in most cases looted during illicit operations. These vessels are often in a rare state of preservation, almost all complete or near-complete. But as a rule we lack the information about find spots and find conditions which might provide important clues for the dating of these vessels.

Still, it seems useful to publish as many as possible of these objects widely scattered in private collections. They will help us to form a better idea of the scope and variety of the repertoire of this class of pottery.[4] Such a publication can of course never provide a substitute for a sufficient range of reliably dated vessels. This is the more regrettable, as Morgan's dating of the Corinth groups did not result primarily from stratigraphical observations, but from stylistical comparisons. V. H. Elbern observed already in 1972 (when describing new acquisitions of the Berlin Museums) that the Corinth groups ought to be seen 'weniger im Nacheinander, als in einem Nebeneinander'.[5] This state of affairs makes it advisable to refrain for the time being from too sophisticated chronological subdivisions, and to be content with a general mid-12th to early 13th century date for these types of pottery.[6]

The vessels from Swiss private collections to be published here fit into this general chronological context. They form a fairly homogeneous group of 'Fine Sgraffito' ware, as defined by J. W. Hayes. Two of the 14 vessels listed in the Catalogue below belong to the widely distributed type of bowl with central medallion and concentric bands. The other 12 pieces represent the so-called 'free style' type and show fairly large-sized animal figures.[7] All bowls are made of reddish-brown clay, covered by an off-white slip and a translucent lead glaze with a yellowish or sometimes greenish hue.[8] The decoration, engraved with a fine point into the dark clay body, is confined to the inside. The surface of the bowls is often severely damaged, covered by lime deposits and petrified small marine animals after having rested on the bottom of the sea for centuries. This makes it sometimes difficult to recognize clearly the incised motifs.[9]

VESSEL SHAPES

The vessels listed in the catalogue represent four different shapes. (Measurements in cm: height = h., rim diameter = r.d., base diameter = b.d.).

Shape 1 (FIGS. 12.1 and 12.2):
Deep bowl with wide flaring wall, plain rim with round or pointed lip and rather low ring base. Variant 1A (FIG. 12.1): continuously curving or fairly straight wall which ends in a slightly incurved rim. Variant 1B (FIG. 12.2.M): outer wall with a marked angle in the upper third of the vessel, while the inside is continously curved. Variant 1C (FIG. 12.2.13, 2.O): vertical (sometimes slightly inturned) rim on a straight wall.[10] Measurements: h. *c*.8.5–9.5, r.d. *c*.24.5–26.5, b.d. 10.5–11.5.

Shape 2 (FIG. 12.3):
Small plate with almost straight sloping wall and low ring base. Plain, flat-topped, sometime slightly inturned rim. Bottom inside sometimes slightly convex.[11] Measurements: h. *c*.3.5–5.0, r.d. *c*.20.0–23.0, b.d. *c*.8.0–11.0.

Shape 3 (FIG. 12.4.F):
Shallow body with upright rim and low or very low (sometimes hardly discernible) ring base.[12] Measurements: h. *c*.4.0–5.0, r.d. *c*.20.0–24.0, b.d. *c*.10.0–14.0.

Shape 4 (FIG. 12.4.B):
Small, deep bowl with very low ring base. Almost straight, sloping walls with plain rim.[13] The shape obviously represents a common Islamic type.[14] Measurements: h. *c*.6.5–8.5, r.d. 18.0–21.0, b.d. 8.0–9.0.

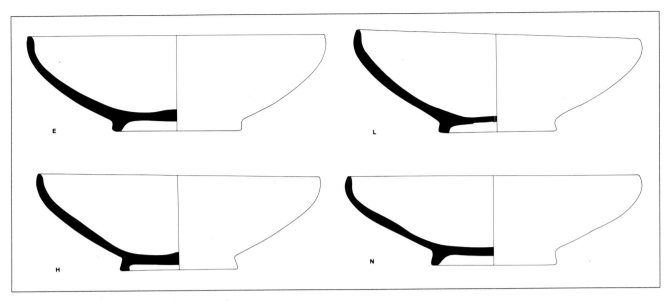

FIG. **12.1**: *Examples of vessel shape 1A. 1:3*

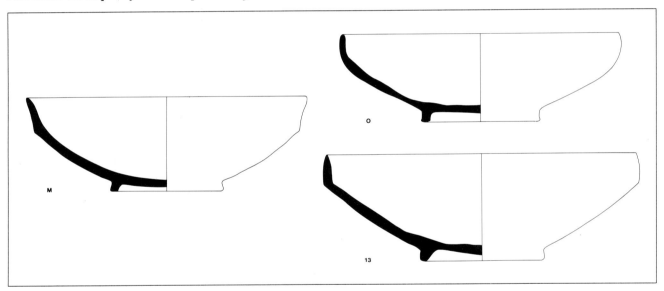

FIG. **12.2**: *Examples of vessel shape 1B (M) and 1C (O, 13). 1:3*

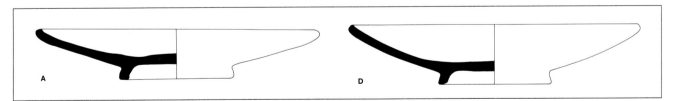

FIG. **12.3**: *Examples of vessel shape 2. 1:3*

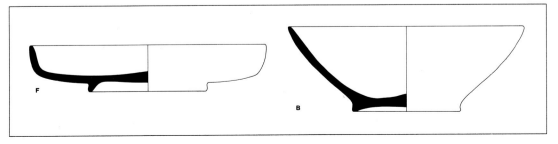

FIG. **12.4**: *Examples of vessel shape 3 (F) and 4 (B). 1:3*

CATALOGUE

A. PLATE with bird, pigeon (?).
FIGS. 12.3.A, 12.5.A, PLATE 12.1.A.
Shape: 2, h. 3.9–3.5, r.d. 20.2, b.d. 8.2.
Ware: bright reddish brown clay, partly of a lighter shade; slip off-white, at some points flaked off; traces of light yellow-green glaze on inside bottom. Surface scratched; outside and inside patches of marine incrustation.
Decoration: bird facing right, encircled by a band of 13 widely spaced chevrons arranged anti-clockwise. Flattened crown, protruding forehead; eye marked by a circle, above it an eye-stripe (?); pointed, slightly curved bill. Body plumage suggested by scale pattern, head and tail separated from it by double lines; wing and tail obliquely hatched; legs given rather schematically. Proportions of body and tail are not well balanced. The drawing is rather sloppy and somehow impressionistic; it is thus impossible to define exactly the bird species.

B. SMALL DEEP BOWL with bird, finch species (?)
FIGS. 12.4.B, 12.5.B; PLATE 12.1.B.
Shape: 4, h. 7.5, r.d. 19.8, b.d. 9.0. Base ring very low, bottom relatively thick.
Ware: bright reddish brown clay, in parts brown; slip nearly completely washed off. Faint traces of a light greenish glaze still visible. Remains of (partly removed) marine incrustation.
Decoration: small short-legged bird, walking to the right, encircled by five chevrons. Bird outlined in bold contours; wing and tail obliquely hatched; legs sketched crudely. The schematically executed drawing makes it impossible to define exactly the bird species. Encircling the bird are concentric bands filled with delicate geometric patterns; the bold circle lines are drawn with the help of dividers (prick hole visible at the bottom of the bowl).

C. DISH, body of bird with mammal-like head.
FIG. 12.6.C.
Shape: 3, r.d. *c*.18.0.
Ware: orange-brown clay; whitish-buff slip; glaze gone; marked marine incrustations.
Decoration: bird standing to the right, with its head turned and inclined to the left; eye marked by a double circle. Body plumage suggested by scale pattern, head and tail separated from it by double lines; wing and tail obliquely hatched; strong talons. Bird framed with parallel arranged scrolling tendrils.

D. PLATE, pigeon.
FIGS. 12.3.D, 12.7.D, PLATE 12.2.D.
Shape: 2, h. 4.5, r.d. 20.2, b.d. 8.0.
Ware: reddish brown clay, in parts brown; slip at some points flaked off; faint traces of the original light yellow glaze under a secondary glaze coating. Marked marine incrustations on the outside, a few incrustations inside.
Decoration: bird walking to the right, framed by two symmetrically arranged, stylized scrolling tendrils. Oval head with pointed, slightly curved bill; round eye. Body plumage suggested by scale pattern; head, wing and tail separated from it by double lines; wing, tail and feathering of legs obliquely hatched. The position of the legs with their strong talons suggests a perspective view.

E. DEEP BOWL, pigeon.
FIGS. 12.1.E, 12.7.E.
Shape: 1A, h. 8.7, r.d. 26.4, b.d. 11.4.
Ware: reddish brown clay; whitish slip; yellowish mat glaze with some greenish hues, fine cracks. Rim slightly damaged.
Decoration: bird standing to the left on a scrolling tendril; a similar tendril reaches upward from its tail end. Body plumage suggested by scale pattern; head separated from it by a double line; wing, tail end and feathering of legs obliquely hatched. Legs rather schematically drawn, the right one put slightly forward.

F. DISH, pigeon (bunting, finch ?).
FIGS. 12.4.F, 12.7.F.

Shape: 3, h. 4.0, r.d. 20.0, b.d. 10.0.
Ware: reddish brown clay; whitish-buff slip which covers the outside only for a few centimetres below the rim; glaze washed off; marked marine incrustations.
Decoration: squat bird standing to the right, framed with two symmetrically arranged scrolling tendrils. Body plumage suggested by scale pattern; wing and tail separated from it by a double line; wing, tail end and feathering of legs obliquely hatched. Strong legs with marked talons. Drawing slightly clumsy.

G. DEEP BOWL, rail (partridge species ?).
FIG. 12.8.G.
Shape: 1A. r.d. *c*.25.0
Ware: reddish brown clay; only traces left of yellow glaze with olive hue, grey spots and fine cracks; marked marine incrustations on rim and outside.
Decoration: bird walking to the right: squat body, fairly long bill; long legs and talons. Body plumage suggested by scale pattern; wing and tail obliquely hatched. Bird encircled by widely spaced chevrons; one of these he seems to keep in his bill.

H. DEEP BOWL, falcon or goshawk.
FIGS. 12.1.H, 12.9.H, PLATE 12.2.H.
Shape: 1A, h. 9.0–8.3, r.d. 24.8, b.d. 10.4.
Ware: reddish brown clay, in parts darker with a greyish hue; slip off-white, partly washed off; inside grey spots; only a small opaque dot of yellowish glaze preserved. Marked marine incrustations, especially on the upper parts of the outside.
Decoration: bird standing very erect to the right, head turned to the left; framed by two scrolling tendrils with feathered leaves. Bird drawn with simple precise contours; body plumage suggested by stippling; wing and tail obliquely hatched. Head separated from body by a double line; hooked bill; eye marked by a circle, with an eye-stripe leading off from the pupil. Strong talons, rather sketchily executed. The bird keeps one of the symmetrically arranged scrolling tendrils with his bill, the other one with his left leg. The animated vivacity of the composition lends a kind of stately elegance to the slim figure of the bird.

J. DEEP BOWL, goshawk or sparrow-hawk.
FIG. 12.9.J.
Shape: 1A, r.d. *c*.25.0–26.5.
Ware: reddish brown clay; slip off-white, partly washed off; inside grey spots; remains of yellow glaze with olive hue at the inside bottom, dark grey spots and fine cracks.
Decoration: bird walking to the right, head turned to the left; framed by two stylized, symmetrically arranged scrolling tendrils with feathered leaves. Bird of prey-type head, with hooked bill and large round eye. Body plumage suggested by scale pattern; wing, tail and feathering of legs obliquely hatched. Strong legs with marked talons. The bird keeps one of the scrolling tendrils with his bill, and seems to rest his left leg on the other one.

K. DEEP BOWL, falcon or goshawk.
FIG. 12.9.K.
Shape: 1A, r.d. *c*.26.0
Ware: bright red clay; slip buff-white; yellowish glaze with grey spots and fine cracks. Rim partially damaged.
Decoration: bird of prey in profile, standing to the right, encircled by a band of 17 widely spaced chevrons; on both sides of the bird a lancet-shaped, hatched leaf. Throat and body plumage suggested by short strokes; crown, wing, tail and feathering of legs obliquely hatched; wing and tail separated from the body by double lines. Strong legs with heavy talons.

L. DEEP BOWL, fish.
FIGS. 12.1.L, 12.10.L, PLATE 12.3.L.
Shape: 1A, h. 9.5–8.3, r.d. 25.0, b.d. 10.5.
Ware: reddish brown clay, in parts light brown; slip off-white; glaze completely washed off; inside surface shows grey spots. Traces of marine incrustations, especially outside around the rim.

Decoration: fish swimming to the left, framed above and below by scrolling tendrils with feathered leaves, almost symmetrically arranged. Double-lined body contours; head separated from scale-patterned body by double lines. Mouth and pupil marked by deep incisions. Tail fin obliquely hatched, body fins represented by groups of 3–5 strokes.

Compare: near-identical vessel, *Malcove Collection*, 181, no. 252; Hayes 1992, 44 (pl. 11 b), 46 (fig. 17.1, pl. 9 j).

M. DEEP BOWL, fish.

FIGS. 12.2.M, 12.10.M.

Shape: 1B, h. *c*.9.0, r.d. *c*.26.0, b.d. *c*.10.5.

Ware: reddish brown clay; yellowish glaze almost completely washed off; inside and outside marked marine incrustations.

Decoration: fish swimming to the right, framed above and below by almost symmetrically arranged scrolling tendrils with stylized feathered leaves. Body and fins horizontally hatched; head separated from body by double lines; eye marked by a double circle.

Compare e.g.: *Corinth XI*, pls. 42 i, 42 j; *Lindos IV*, 2, eds. L. Wriedt Sorensen, P. Pentz (Copenhagen 1992), figs. 74, 86 no. 12245. For vessels depicting several fish cf.: Brouscari, 504 figs. 1, 18; Ioannidaki-Dostoglou, 169 figs. 30–31.

N. DEEP BOWL, ornamental decor.

FIG. 12.1.N, PLATE 12.4.N.

Shape: 1A, h. 8.2, r.d. 25.6, b.d. 10.8.

Ware: reddish brown clay; slip off-white, in parts washed off, missing completely on rim; translucent yellowish glaze, preserved almost everywhere only as thin opaque coat with fine cracks; grey spots on the inside bottom.

Decoration: central medallion (Diam 5.7) surrounded by two concentric bands at a distance of 1.2 viz. 5.1 cms (the inner 0.9 cms, the outer 1.0–1.1 cms wide). The contour lines of these bands, drawn with the help of dividers (prick hole visible), are slightly off-centre. The medallion (divided by a centre band) is partly filled with scale pattern, the concentric bands with curved and degenerated spiral motifs. Filling motifs delicately and elegantly drawn.

O. DEEP BOWL, ornamental decor.

FIG. 12.2.O, PLATE 12.4.O.

Shape: 1C, h. 8.4, r.d. 25.4, b.d. 10.9.

Ware: reddish brown clay; slip off-white, on the inside partly flaked off, isolated dots on the outside; opaque glaze with a

greenish hue (yellowish around the rim) and marked cracks; grey spots on the inside bottom.

Decoration: central medallion (Diam 5.8) surrounded by two concentric bands at a distance of 1.2 viz. 5.0cms (the inner 0.8cms, the outer 1.2cms wide). The contour lines of these bands are drawn with the help of dividers. The medallion (divided by a centre band) is partly filled with curved and spiral motifs, the concentric bands with running spirals.

Compare e.g. (for N and O): *Corinth XI*, 130–31, fig. 105; Hayes 1992, 139 no. 8, pl. 10 b; Armstrong 1989, 8 no. 31; M.-L. von Wartburg, *AA* (1998) 154–155.

ORNITHOLOGICAL ANALYSIS OF THE BIRDS REPRESENTED

The pictorial motifs denote an especially interesting aspect of the bowls described in the Catalogue: most of them show birds. This seems hardly just chance. It is true, of course, that ornamental motifs generally form the most widespread decorative pattern of 'Fine Sgraffito' ware. But amongst the 'free-style' variants of decoration, birds—and, to a lesser degree, fish—seem to be the most popular motif. Even the small group of bowls discussed here represent a rich variety of bird species, drawn with a wealth of detail in a surprisingly naturalistic manner.[15] Thus a comparative iconographic study, which first analyses the drawings from an ornithological point of view and then puts them into a wider context, seems both desirable and rewarding.

The discussion of each of the six motif groups is preceded by a list of the relevant vessels. The bowls from Swiss private collections are designated by the capital letters used in the catalogue (A–K), comparative pieces published elsewhere by Arabic numerals (1–30). A synopsis according to vessel shapes appears at the end (Appendix).

FIG. **12.5** (LEFT): *Indefinable birds. 1:3 (no. 1 after Malcove Collection)*

FIG. **12.6** (BELOW): *Bird with mammal-like head. 1:3*

1. *Indefinable birds* (FIG. 12.5, PLATE 12.1)
Catalogue: **A, B.**
Comparisons: 1 (FIG. 12.5) = *Malcove Collection*, 183, no. 254: combining traits of bird of prey and dove. 2 = *Islamische Keramik, Hetjens-Museum*, Ausstellungs-Katalog (Düsseldorf 1973), 76, no. 89: birds with raven-like heads, but bodies which are definitely too elongated for that species.

The two catalogue pieces show sloppily drawn, badly proportioned birds with rather schematic feet; they can not be classified definitely. The framing chevron motif (**A, B** and 1) is fairly common and also occurs on vessels of the other groups (e.g. **G, K,** 7). Comparable, rather awkwardly drawn birds are far too numerous to be listed here.[16] The two examples chosen for comparison represent a special type: birds which combine elements of rather different species in the same figure. Thus despite their accurate drawing they cannot be clearly defined.

2. *Bird with mammal-like head* (FIG. 12.6)
Catalogue: **C**
Comparisons: 3 = Brouscari, 504, fig. 2; 4 = *Corinth XI*, pl. 42g, no. 1226.[17]

A fair number of close parallels demonstrate that this is not an isolated eccentric motif, created accidentally. The comparable pieces show near-identical details, e.g.

the drawing of the eyes. Their overall composition—the animal surrounded by two branches with leaves—is also closely related.

Griffins and harpies as well as sphinxes and centaurs, suggestive of oriental influence, form part of the general pictorial repertoire of Byzantine art.[18] Fantastic figures as those discussed here seem, on the other hand, to be less common. Body and posture obviously resemble birds of prey; but the mammal-like head, turned back, escapes definition. The head of a quadruped on bowl no. 281 from Pelagonnisos seems to provide the closest parallel.[19] Heads of similar shape also occur on small figures (cheetahs?) within medallions on vessels from Pelagonnisos and Corinth, as well on a plate in Berlin.[20]

3. *Pigeons (Columbidae)* (FIG. 12.7, PLATE 12.2.D)
Catalogue: **D, E, F.**
Comparisons: 5 = Brouscari, 506, fig. 3; 6 (FIG. 12.7) = *Byzantium*, 57, no. 20, fig. 21; 7 (FIG. 12.7) = *Byzantium*, 57, no. 21, FIG. 20.

A number of traits suggest that the birds drawn on these six vessels may be attributed to the *Columbidae* family:[21] small head with a short fine bill; short stout legs with marked hind talon; plumage differentiated clearly in a way typical for the species—including details such as tail feathers shaded by straight lines; scale pattern on breast and flank; neck band indicated by double lines (typical for the Collared Turtle-Dove). These diagnostic elements appear, perfectly executed, on vessels **D, E** and 5. The birds on vessels 6 and 7 represent doves as well, despite their slightly longer tail feathers. The bird drawn on vessel **F**, on the other hand, differs from the other representations of this group and cannot be classified definitely. The rather stout body and especially the form of the bill are reminiscent of some species of the bunting or finch family.

If we compare the overall pictorial composition on these vessels, we notice that all birds, except for **E**, turn to the right. Bowls **D, F,** 5 and 6 represent surprisingly close parallels: birds and framing scroll motifs are the same. The decorations of **D** and 5 especially are identical to the minutest detail, although the vessel shapes are different (see Appendix). The birds incised on the bottom of the deep bowls **E** and 7 (shape 1A) are framed by a pair of scrolling tendrils, respectively a sequence of chevrons. This fairly large group of bowls shows clearly that not only the same species of bird, but also the same combinations of bird and decorative framing pattern occur on different vessel-types.

4. *Rails* (partridge species ?) (FIG. 12.8)
Catalogue: **G.**
Comparisons: 8 (FIG. 12.8) = *Malcove Collection*, 182 no. 253. Similar in principle, but less careful: 9 = M. Georgopoulou-Meladini, *A. Delt.* 28 (1973), Chr., 314, pl. 270d; 10 = *Corinth XI*, fig. 104b, no. 1103; 11 = ibid., pl. 43d, no. 1211; 12 (?) = K. Κορρέ–Ζωγράφου,

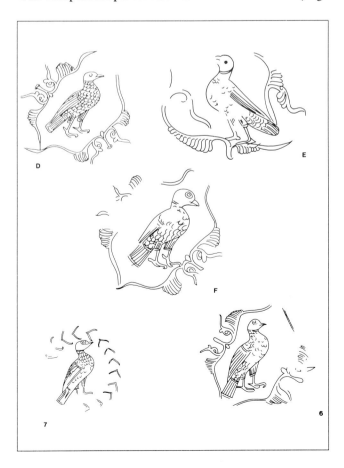

FIG. 12.7: *Pigeons. 1:3 (no. 6 and 7 after Byzantium)*

FIG. 12.8 (ABOVE): *Rails (or partridge species?). 1:3 (no. 8 after Malcove Collection)*

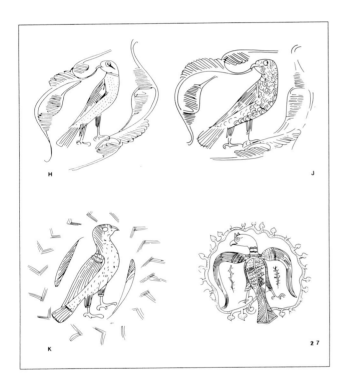

FIG. 12.9 (ABOVE): *Raptorial birds. 1:3 (no. 27 after BPA)*

FIG. 12.10 (ABOVE): *Fish. 1:3*

Τά Κεραμεικά τού Ελληνικού χώρου (Athens 1995), 36-7, no. 52.

The rather few specimens known so far seem to suggest that this species of bird was favoured less as a decoration motif for bowls. The thick-set body with short wings and tail, the long legs, and especially the bill typical for water rails are to be distinguished clearly on G and 8, to some degree also on 9. The thick-set body is prominent also in the decoration of 10, 11 and 12, but these more sloppily executed figures can be defined only in a general way as a species of wild fowl. The secondary decorative elements—delicately feathered leaves on 8, chevrons on the other bowls—are arranged in a similar way around the birds.

5. *Wading birds* (Curlew, Bustard, Crane) (FIG. 12.11, PLATE 10.3.14)

Birds of these species thus far occur rarely on fine sgraffito vessels; they are not represented on the bowls described in the catalogue.

Published pieces: 13 (FIGS. 12.2, 12.11) = Elbern, 46, fig. 9; 14 (FIG. 12.11, PLATE 12.3) = BM 1967.12-7.3, also P. Hetherington, *Byzantium, Stadt des Goldes, Welt des Glaubens* (Lucerne 1982) 60, fig. 2; 15 = *Corinth XI*, pl. 47k, no. 1380.[22]

Plumage, attitude of the body and form of the bill of the birds shown on the fine sgraffito vessels 13–15 seem to point primarily to a crane or an ibis. Other representations of wading birds are known only from vessels of related wares, *inter alia* the 'Incised Sgraffito' fragment no. 1558 from Corinth.[23] A harpy riding an ostrich appears on a 'measles-technique' bowl, which V. H. Elbern compares to our fragment 13.[24] A number of other fragments show that clearly definable birds occur fairly often in this specific class of vessels.

6. *Birds of prey* (*Falconidae, Accipitridae*) (FIG. 12.9, 12.12, PLATE 12.2.H).

Catalogue: H, J, K.

Comparisons for H, J: 16 = Brouscari, 508, fig. 7 (nearly identical with H); 17 = *Corinth XI*, pl. 42c, no. 1109; 18 = *The World of Ceramics, Masterpieces from the Cleveland Museum*, ed. J. Neils (Cleveland 1982), 34, no. 36; 19 = Talbot Rice, 218, fig. 6; 20 = *Corinth XI*, pl. 42b, no. 1107 (scroll different).

Comparisons for K: 21 = Brouscari, 508, fig. 6 (very similar); 22 = Museum Antalya; 23 = Elbern, 43, fig. 4; 24 = R.H. Randall, 'The Walters Art Gallery Acquires Byzantine Wares', *Archaeology* 21 (1968), 300.

Special representations: 25 = Talbot Rice, 211, 218, figs. 7 and C; 26 = *Corinth XI*, 174 fig. 157A; 27 (FIG. 6.9) = Ioannidaki-Dostoglou, 170, fig. 26 (NA 16/1410).

Birds with their prey: examples known thus far come from the Pelagonnisos wreck: 28 (FIG. 12.12) = *BPA*, 232, fig. 273 (NA 14/137): hare looking to the right; 29 (FIG. 12.12) = *BPA*, 233, fig. 277 (NA 20): hare looking backwards; 30 (FIG. 12.12) = *BPA*, 232, fig. 274 (NA 15/1415): roe deer or gazelle.

The large number of comparable pieces demonstrates that representations of birds of prey were fairly common in Byzantine pottery. The generally slender bodies of the birds as well as certain details, such as the feathering of the leg which does not reach to the talons, suggest that they represent not large-sized eagles (true *Aquilae*), but *falconidae* (such as *falco peregrinus*—Peregrine Falcon, *falco columbarius*—Merlin Falcon, *falco biarmicus*—Lanner Falcon, *falco cherurg*—Saker Falcon) and *accipitridae* (*accipiter gentilis*—Goshawk, *acccipiter nisus*—Sparrow–Hawk, eventually also *milvus milvus* or *milvus migrans*—Red or Black Kite). The plumage in which breast and flank (indicated by hatching or scale patterns) are clearly differentiated from wing and tail, is typical for those species. Significant are, furthermore, the shape of head and bill, the robust talons, the conspicuously long tail, and (especially with falcons) the long pointed wings.

The vessels discussed here represent the birds primarily in two attitudes: either facing to the right with the head turned back, or in true profile. To the first group belong the compositions of the bowls **H, J,** 16 (and most probably also 17) which are almost identical, except for a different rendering of the plumage on bowls **J** and 17. The delicately pro-portioned scrolling tendrils which frame the birds lend the slightly stiff looking animals a certain elegance and vivacity. Bowls 18, 19 and 20 of the same group differ in the motifs surrounding the bird. On bowl 18 the very skilfully drawn falcon is encircled by a concentric band and two stylized leaves; bowls 19 and 20 show pairs of branches arranged fairly arbitrarily (not symmetrically as usual).

The forward looking birds of the second group appear, if compared with the vessels just described, on the whole rather less impressive. Their erect bearing and plumage are almost identical on bowls **K,** 21 and 22; bowls **K** and 22 also show a corresponding secondary decoration of two lancet-shaped leaves and encircling chevrons. 21 represents not only a shape unusual in the 'free style' pottery, but also a rather particular tendril composition.[25] An almost complete correspondence of decoration despite different shapes is to be noted with regard to 23 and 24 (23 = shape 4, 24 = shape 3); even details of the drawing, such as the attitude of the bird with slightly raised wings, the long tail with a plumage pattern reminiscent of the goshawk (*accipiter gentilis*), and the legs resting on bunches of leaves, are very similar.

Not all bird motifs conform, however, with these two versions. Bowls 25–27 offer variants of bird

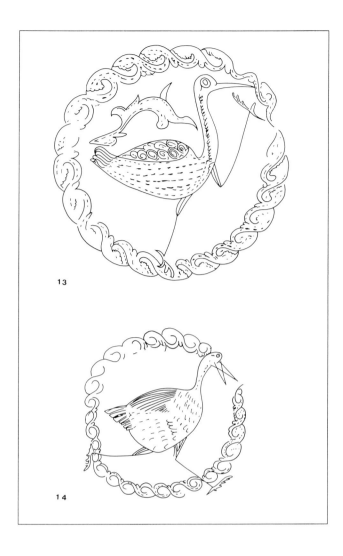

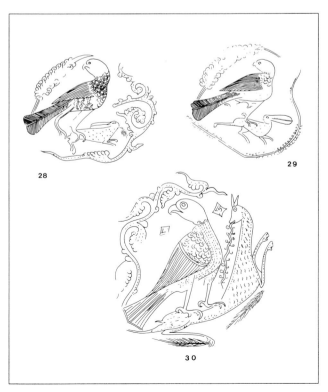

FIG. **12.11** (LEFT, TOP):*Wading birds. (no. 13 after Elbern, 14. after Hetherington)*

FIG. **12.12** (LEFT, BELOW): *Birds of prey. (nos. 28–30 after BPA)*

representation which seem unique thus far in the 'Fine Sgraffito' ware. For the bird walking to the right with its head put forward (25), no really comparable parallel seems to exist. This might be explained by the fact that birds of prey—except for the Wasp- or Honey-Buzzard (*Pernis apivorus apivorus*)—are rarely ever seen to walk on the ground. The conception and expressive quality of the bird represented on bowl 26 also seems unique. The magnificent looking animal, walking to the left, is drawn with firm double contours and with an attempt at a perspective view. The clearly contured head with its sturdy bill and the large outspread wings (which end in stylized floral motifs) are especially impressive. Bowl 27 (FIG. 12.9), on the other hand, presents a definitely heraldic character: the bird with outspread wings in frontal view, the turned head in profile. It seems surprising that comparable representations are very rare in Fine Sgraffito ware, because traditionally they were used widely as a motif.[26]

Animals attacking their prey represent no doubt one of the most spectacular pictorial motifs of 'Fine Sgraffito' technique. For a long time only two complete

examples of the 'animal combat' motif were known, at Berlin (from Miletus) and at Dumbarton Oaks.[27] The wreck of Pelagonnisos now has yielded a large and impressive group of comparable pieces. Three of the five examples published thus far (28–30, FIG. 12.12) show birds bringing down their quarry.[28] The drawing is of high quality: bird and captured prey are depicted in a convincing way; characteristic features, proportions, and movements of the animals are rendered skilfully. The encircling scroll ornaments are also drawn competently and lend a kind of playful elegance to the lively and dramatic scene. The attitude of the birds with the head bent back is very similar to the single birds on vessels H, J and 18. This close similarity may point, on the one hand, to a common centre of production;[29] it is of basic importance, on the other hand, for an integration of the bird vessels discussed here into a wider iconographic and cultural context.

BIRDS AND HUNTING

An analysis of this context must concentrate on the three bowls showing birds of prey with their quarry in a basically identical composition (28–30, FIG. 12.12). Representations of hunting birds, overpowering their prey with their strong claws, undoubtedly denote a widely diffused pictorial motif with a tradition stretching back over long centuries.[30] The animals depicted as prey are primarily hares (as on bowls 28 and 29), wildfowl, or water-birds (often bustard, rail, duck, or crane).[31] Larger game such as roe deer or gazelle (as on bowl 30) appear rarely.[32] These scenes are undoubtedly drawn from life, from the observation of actual hunting with falcons: they reflect the typical way in which different species of birds of the chase act during a hunt. Goshawk, sparrow hawk, or Lanner

FIG. 12.13 (LEFT, ABOVE): *Cypriot plate with falconer (13th century). (after Παπανικόλα-Μπακιρτζῆ, see n. 56)*

FIG. 12.14 (BELOW): *Falconry scene on ivory casket. Capella Palatina, Palermo, early 13th century. (after Federico, see n. 57)*

falcon were trained primarily on winged game or hares; for the hunting of bigger game rapacious birds living in open country were preferred, such as the Greenland falcon (*falco rusticolus*) or the Saker falcon (*falco cherrurg*).[33]

To this day art historians interpret pictorial motifs of this type—whether they occur in Western, Byzantine, or Islamic art—in very different ways. Byzantine scholars often are prone to see in it a kind of religious symbolism.[34] Islamic scholars, confronted with a large number of objects depicting the various aspects of hunting (see e.g. FIG 12.14), are more inclined

to consider them as a reflection of actual falconry—a reflection, however, which can be taken also as a symbolic *chiffre* for the iconography of the 'Royal Hunt'.[35]

If this pictorial tradition indeed derives, as we believe, from the realities of falconry, its origins and basic requirements can only be fully understood if we review briefly the history of the art of hunting with birds. As the literary and especially the pictorial evidence is fairly extensive, we have to confine ourselves in the present context to a summary of some salient points.[36]

PLATE 12.1 (ABOVE): *Indefinable birds (A* [LEFT] *and B* [RIGHT]*)*

PLATE 12.2 (ABOVE): *Pigeon (D* [LEFT]*) and raptorial bird (H* [RIGHT]*)*

1. The art of falconry was doubtless practised in Arabia before the advent of Islam, but gained special importance only with the establishment of the Caliphate.[37] There is reason to assume that this process was influenced by contacts with Persia and Byzantium.[38] One has to admit, however, that it is difficult to verify the Byzantine influence in detail,[39] as the evidence for falconry in Byzantium exhibits an almost complete gap of several centuries, from about the early sixth to tenth century. It should be noted in this context, however, that Arab expertise also influenced to a large extent Frederick II's treatise on falconry and ornithology *De arte venandi cum avibus*, written around 1241–1250.[40]

2. Pictorial representations of a falconer with his bird or of whole scenes of falconry are of prime importance in our context. The basic lines of their iconographic development in the Mediterranean and adjacent countries may be summed up as follows. A very informative group of mosaics date from a relatively short period, the late 5th and the early 6th centuries.[41]

PLATE **12.3**: *Wading bird (14* [ABOVE, LEFT]*) and fish (L* [ABOVE, RIGHT]*) (14 by courtesy of the Trustees of the British Museum)*

PLATE **12.4**: *Ornamental decor (N* [ABOVE, LEFT] *and O* [ABOVE, RIGHT]*)*

From the mid 6th to the later 10th century, however, equivalent representations are very rare.[42] The end of the 10th century marks a significant change: the number of relevant examples increases perceptibly; the geographical range of their origin widens; the objects bearing such pictorial motifs become more varied. These tendencies steadily grow stronger towards the 12th and early 13th century, the period of the pottery discussed here.[43] The famous *codex Fredericus II De arte venandi cum avibus* (Cod. Vaticanus Palatinus lat. 1071), the so-called 'Manfred version', represents without doubt a landmark in the developement of the iconography of falconry. Yet this richly illuminated work still poses many problems—*inter alia*, the question of its possible sources and of the date of its illustrations.[44]

3. Modern research has suggested that falconry remained the jealously guarded prerogative of certain privileged groups of society.[45] Considering what we know about the realities of social life, such a strict division seems hardly tenable.[46] But the arts do indeed reflect the growing importance of falconry as a status symbol of the nobility since the 6th/7th centuries. This phenomenon is strikingly documented, *inter alia*, by a group of Hispano-Arab and Fatimid ivories of the 10th to 12th centuries. They combine, often on the same object, court ceremonies, feasts, and hunting scenes in stately and imaginative opulence.[47] Several of these ivory objects show very clearly that the 'predator and prey'-motif (which sometimes appears in several variants on the same object) forms an integral element of hunting scenes with mounted falconers.[48]

Falconry motifs on pottery, however, represent a different situation. The object itself as well as long established traditions of style and decoration tend to fashion a terse imagery, which often emphasizes or employs only a partial aspect of a hunting scene.[49] This fragmentation of the iconographic repertoire of falconry and the application of separate pictorial elements to individual bowls is demonstrated especially well on Fatimid and stylistically related vessels from North Africa and Sicily—e.g. by a comparison of two vessels from Egypt whose realistic style is hardly to be surpassed. One of these vessels depicts a falconer on horseback, carrying his bird on his left gloved fist;[50] the other shows a falcon capturing a water bird, probably a crane.[51] Other examples of the fragmentation of falconry scenes are provided by the mounted falconer on a fragment from Palermo,[52] by a North African (?) waster depicting a falcon chasing a hare,[53] or by a North African 'bacino' built into the church of San Pietro a Gardo di Pisa, which shows a predator killing a gazelle.[54]

The 'predator and prey'-motif conceived as an integral element of falconry may give a clue also to the interpretation of the Fine Sgrafitto vessels discussed in this paper (28–30, FIG. 12.12). The single animals depicted on several vessels represent birds of the chase or their preferred preys; they are thus very likely related to the imagery of falconry. It has to be admitted that no Fine Sgrafitto vessel definitely showing a falconer has been published so far. But at least a 13th century plate (FIG. 12.13) made in Frankish Cyprus, at Paphos,[55] demonstrates that the representation of falconers on ceramic vessels is not confined to the Islamic world. Form and expression of the naïvely realistic decoration do not relate to any known pictorial tradition.[56] Significant details decisive for the interpretation of the drawing, such as the jesses fixed at the bird's talons, are depicted free from stereotypical iconographic formulae.[57] The Paphos plate originates from a cultural milieu corresponding in many respects to that of the Fine Sgrafitto bowls, which were also imported into Cyprus.[58] Thus it may be assumed that the lack of falconers' images in the Byzantine pottery of the 12th–13th century represents only an accidental gap in our evidence. Possibly it is not even a real gap. The warrior armed with shield and maze on a Sgrafitto bowl from the Athenian Agora (P 9396) is accompanied by a falcon which may well represent his own hunting bird. This would be even more likely if the warrior were indeed to be identified with Digenis Akritas, whose hunting passion is well attested. The interpretation of the scene 'The Horseman and the Angel' on a Fine Sgrafito bowl found in Corinth in 1966, on the other hand, is still ambiguous. But the hare and the two falcons (one of them just behind the rider's outstretched left arm) may well suggest a connection with falconry.[59]

This brief attempt to analyse a specific group of pottery within a wider cultural context must remain tentative in several respects. For the time being it raises more questions than it answers. Only a study with a far wider scope, chronologically as well as regionally, will be able to demonstrate how intensely the same motif groups were used in widely different contexts, in Islamic lands as well as in the eastern and western world of Christianity.

Zurich, May 1997

APPENDIX:

Shapes	1A	1B	1C	2	3	4	ui
Motif groups:							
indef.	1		A		B		2
Mammal-like					C 3		4
Pigeons	E 7		D	F 5 6			
Rails	G 8				10		9 11 12
Wading birds			13 14				15
Birds of prey	H J K 19 25		16		18 20 24 27 28 29 30	23	17 21* 22 26*
Fish	L	M					
Geom	N		O				

* special shapes

Groups with similar foliage decor
1: A, B, G, K, 1, 7, 9, 10, 11, 12, 22
2: D, F, 2, 5, 6
3: C, E, H, J, 16, 17
4: L, M
5: 13, 14, 27
6: 23, 24

2 and 3 combined: 3, 19, 20
2 and 4 combined: 25
Others: N, O, 4, 8, 15, 18, 21, 26, 28, 29, 30

REFERENCES:

Armstrong 1989 = P. Armstrong 'Some Byzantine and Later Settlements in Eastern Phokis', *BSA* 84 (1989) 1–47.
Armstrong 1991 = P. Armstrong, 'A Group of Byzantine Bowls from Skopelos', *OJA* 10 (1992) 335–347.
BPA = *Byzantine and Post-Byzantine Art*, Athens, July 26th 1985 –January 6th 1986 (Athens 1985).
Brouscari = E. Brouscari, 'Collection Paul Canellopoulos (XVIII), Vases Byzantins', *BCH* 112 (1988) 503–517.
Byzantium = Byzantium. *The Light in the Age of Darkness, Catalogue Ariadne Galleries* (New York 1988).
Corinth XI = C. H. Morgan, *Corinth xi: The Byzantine Pottery*, (Princeton 1942).
Déroche, Spieser = V. Déroche, J.–M. Spieser (eds.), *Recherches sur la céramique byzantine*, (*BCH Supp.* XVIII 1989).
Elbern = V. H. Elbern, 'Mittelbyzantinische Sgraffito–Keramik: Neuerwerbungen für die Frühchristlich–Byzantinische Sammlung', *Berl. Mus.*, N.F. 22 (1972) 41–51.
Hayes 1992 = J. W. Hayes, *Excavations at Saraçhane in Istanbul. Vol.2: The Pottery* (Princeton 1992).
Ioannidaki-Dostoglou = E. Ioannidaki-Dostoglou, 'Les vases de l'épave byzantine de Pélagonnèse-Halonnèse', in Déroche, Spieser, 157–171.
Kritzas = Π. Χ. Κριτζάς, Τὸ βυζαντινόν ναυάγιον Πελαγοννήσου-Ἀλοννήσου, *AAA* 4 (1971) 176–185.
Malcove Collection = *The Malcove Collection*, ed. S. D. Campbell, (Toronto 1985).
Talbot Rice = D. Talbot Rice, 'Late Byzantine Pottery at Dumbarton Oaks', *DOP* 20 (1966) 205–219.

NOTES

1. For Pelagonnisos-Alonessos see: Kritzas, 176–182; Ioannidaki-Dostoglou, 157–171, nos. 1–15; *BPA*, 229–242, nos. 263–264, 269–297. These three publications comprise 37 vessels of a total of 1490 predominantly ceramic finds (Kritzas, 178).
2. *Corinth XI*.
3. The painted wares include: 'Slip painted' and 'Black and Green painted' (also in combination with sgraffito decoration). The term 'Sgraffito' is used here in its general sense, including the so-called 'incised', 'gouged', and *champlevé* techniques. Unfortunately, a generally accepted terminology for these pottery types does not exist yet—as shown, e.g., by a comparison of the nomenclature of Morgan (*Corinth xi*, 64–95, 115–162), Hayes (Hayes 1992, chapter six, 44-48) and Armstrong (Armstrong 1989, 43).
4. For wares from wrecks comparable to the Pelagonnisos finds see primarily Talbot Rice, 218, nos. 3–4; R. H. Randall, 'The Walters Art Gallery acquires Byzantine Wares', *Archaeology* 21 (1968) 300; Elbern, 41–51; *The World of Ceramics, Masterpieces from the Cleveland Museum*, ed. J. Neils (Cleveland 1982) 34–35; *Malcove Collection*, 181–184, nos. 252–255; Brouscari, 503–517; *Byzantium*, 57, nos. 20–22; Κ. Κορρέ-Ζωγράφου, Τά Κεραμεικά τού Ελληνικού χώρου (Athens 1995), 37 fig. 52. For find groups comparable to the wrecks of Kastellorizo (G. Philotheou, M. Michailidou) (*ADelt* 41 (1986) Meletes, 271–330) and Skopelos (Armstrong 1991, 335–347) see: I. Loucas, 'Les plats byzantins ... glaçure inédits d'une collections privée de Bruxelles', in Déroche, Spieser, 177–183; *Malcove Collection*, 185, no. 256; *Splendeur de Byzance. Catalogue* (Bruxelles 1982) 237–38, nos. C11, C12; *Byzance. L'art byzantin dans les collections publiques françaises, Catalogue* (Paris, 1992), 394 no. 303; Κορρέ-Ζωγράφου (above), 7, 37 fig. 50. The large number of complete vessels, which raises the question of the origin of these widely exported wares even more pointedly (see n. 27), is definitely a great help in defining more precisely the fragments found in excavations or surveys.
5. Elbern, 47, also 49 and 50. New finds from the Sanctuary of Aphrodite in Palaipaphos (Cyprus) point to similar

conclusions (see M.-L. Wartburg, *RDAC* 1997, 184–194). For critical reservations see also G. D. R. Sanders, 'Excavations at Sparta: the Roman Stoa, 1988–91. 'Medieval pottery', *BSA* 88 (1993) 251–52, 258.

6. See Hayes (1992, 44–48, also Introduction, 3–4) who is in the comfortable but rare position to deal with stratified material (church in ruins certainly before 1204: R.M. Harrison, *Excavations at Saraçhane in Istanbul*, London 1986, I. 113). Yet despite all critical differentiations he interprets the chronology of his groups in close relation to the publications of Stevenson, Morgan and Megaw (who regards the earthquake at Paphos in 1222 as a key date). Even if finds from a specific shipwreck cannot be given an absolute chronological datum, the fact that different wares were transported in the same vessel clearly indicates a roughly identical time range for pottery groups which are ascribed until now—on stylistic and qualitative arguments—to different phases. For example, the hitherto published material from Pelagonnisos (see n. 1) seems at least to call in question Morgan's detailed sequence of 'Sgraffitto Wares' (*Corinth XI*, chap. 6, 115–159); for a further example see Armstrong 1991, 339–340.

7. Their similarity to published groups of the Pelagonnisos material (cf. n. 1) is obvious. See also Hayes 1992, 44–46.

8. Typical for a somewhat coarser fabric are the inclusions of grey grit and lime. The exterior is rarely covered completely; normally slip and glaze end at some distance from the rim.

9. The drawings of the vessels published here show only the clearly discernible incised lines

10. See e.g. for 1A: *Corinth XI*, fig. 103J; Brouscari, fig. 18.1; Ioannidaki-Dostoglou, figs. 17, 21; Armstrong 1991, figs. 2.3, 4.7–9, 5.10; Hayes 1992, fig. 81, no. 51.14; 1B: Ioannidaki-Dostoglou, fig. 3; 1C: *Corinth XI*, 99, fig. 75C; Elbern, 45, Skizze D; Brouscari, fig. 18.7; *Byzance* (n. 4), 394 no. 303; Hayes 1992, fig. 82, nos. 51.16–17; the finds from Kastellorizo provide a whole series of this type (n. 4): Philotheou-Michailidou and Loucas).

11. e.g. *Corinth XI*, figs. 75B, 103G, 128C, 215; Ioannidaki-Dostoglou, figs. 15, 19, 31; Brouscari, fig. 19.8; Hayes 1992, no. 51.8.

12. e.g. *Corinth XI*, figs. 103A–B, 121A–B, 128A–B; Ioannidaki-Dostoglou, figs. 5, 9, 25, 27, 29; Brouscari, 516, fig. 19.5; Hayes 1992, figs. 17.1 (no. 51.86) and 81, nos. 51.5–7.

13. e.g. *Corinth XI*, figs. 95D, 103K, 111H, 121F, 128F; Elbern, 43, Skizze B; Ioannidaki-Dostoglou, figs. 7, 11; Brouscari, fig. 18.9; Hayes 1992, fig. 81, no. 51.15.

14. e.g. V. Porter-O. Watson, 'Tell Minis Wares', in J. Allen-C. Roberts (eds.), *Syria and Iran* (Oxford 1987): 180 bowls; Hayes 1992, fig. 81, no. 51.3.

15. How far these decorations are based on manuscript illustrations is a question which can hardly be answered decisively. But the miniatures of birds in the *codex Vindobonensis* or the Vatican codex may give a good idea of eventual models. See Z. Kádár, *Survivals of Greek Zoological Illuminations in Byzantine Manuscripts* (Budapest 1978) 77, Cod. Vindob. med. gr. 1. fols. 464r–485v (pls. 119–128); Cod. Vat. Chis. F. VII, 159, fols. 228v–2321v (pls. 129–137). Of special interest in our context are e.g. the superbly observed members of the families *falconidae* (p. 84, pls. 119.1a–b, 129.3a–b) and *rallidae* (p. 85, pl. 133.27, 128.6, 136.10), or the bustards (p. 85, pls. 128.2, 136.3).

16. But see for some examples of these types Morgan, *Corinth XI*, 122 FIG. 97, 138 fig. 112); A. Frantz, 'Middle Byzantine pottery in Athens', *Hesp.* 7 (1938) 444, 445, 452; or Philotheou-Michailidou (n. 4), fig. 15, pl. 66.

17. To this type belongs most probably also fragment no. 1106 from Corinth (e.g. *Corinth XI*, 133 fig. 108).

18. Some examples of such monsters on pottery may be listed here. Griffins: *Corinth XI*, 123 no. 1018, pl. 41h; A.L. Jakobson, *MIA* 17 (1950) pl. 26 no. 103; W. de Bock,

'Poteries vernissées du Caucase et de la Crimée', in *Mémoires de la Société Nationale des Antiquaires de France* 56 (1897), 216–219, nos. 11 and 12; A. Bank, *Byzantine Art in the Collections of Soviet Museums* (New York, 1978), 314 no. 228. –Harpies: Elbern, 43, Inv.Nr. 32/66, fig. 3; *Corinth XI*, 94 fig. 70.–Centaur: G. Duthuit, F. Volbach, *Art Byzantin* (Paris 1933) 67, pl. 67B (leopard, centaur); *Corinth XI*, 118 fig. 92; ibid., 155 fig. 132. See also J. Notopoulos, 'Akritan iconography on Byzantine pottery', *Hesp.* 33 (1964), 118.

19. *BPA*, 235 fig. 281.

20. *Corinth XI*, 339 fig. 225B; Elbern, 42 fig. 1; *BPA*, 235 fig. 279.

21. See also D. Buckton (ed.) *Byzantium* (London 1994) 170, no. 188b. Amongst representations of birds, pigeons seem to be one of the most common subjects; this is confirmed by a large number of fragmentary pieces which cannot be listed here.

22. For a further example, see Ἔκθεση Χριστιανικῆς Ἀρχαιολογικῆς Ἑταιρείας (1884–1984), Athens 1994, 70–71, no. 128. Other comparable pieces are mentioned by Elbern, 48, with notes 26–27.

23. *Corinth XI*, 155, pl. 51h, no. 1558.

24. Elbern, 48–49 and *Corinth XI*, 94 fig. 70, no. 668.

25. For a similar shape *Corinth xi*, pl. 44b and p. 311, fig. 209; also Notopoulos (n. 18), 117, pl. 22.7; Buckton (n. 21); for the composition see Buckton, no. 188a. Shape and decoration of the rim may suggest a possible link with 'laqabi' or 'Tell Minis' ware.

26. For a rare example on 'Fine Sgraffito' ware see R.M. Dawkins, J. P. Droop, 'Byzantine pottery from Sparta', *BSA* 17 (1910–1911) 26 no. 31, pl. 16.31. Examples on 'Glazed White Ware' are fairly numerous, see e.g.: O. Wulff, *Die Altchristlichen und Mittelalterlichen Byzantinischen und Italienischen Bildwerke*, III. (Berlin 1911) 103 nos. 2019–2023, pl. 18; R. B. K. Stevenson, *The Great Palace of the Byzantine Emperors, First Report, The Pottery* 1936–7 (Oxford 1947), pl. 17.5–7; U. Peschlow, 'Byzantinische Keramik aus Istanbul', *Ist. Mitt.* 27/28 (1977/78) pl. 127 no. 7, pl. 136 no. 75; Hayes 1992, pl. 4c. For an example in 'Polychrome Ware' (peacock, 10th c.) see *Byzance* (n. 4), 388 fig. 296B. For a Cypriot vessel in Sgraffito technique (Paphos, 13th c.) see Δ. Παπανικόλα-Μπακιρτζῆ, Μεσαιωνικὴ εφγαλμένη Κεραμικὴ τῆς Κύπρου (Thessaloniki 1996), 76 no. 25. The motif was also very prominent on Islamic and related wares, e.g.: A. Lane, *Early Islamic Pottery* (London 1953), pl. 47C (Lakabi, 12th c.); K. von Folsach (ed.), *Islamic Art. The David Collection* (Copenhagen 1990), 105 fig. 133 (Lakabi, 12th c.); G. Curatola (ed.), *Eredità dell'Islam. Arte islamica in Italia* (Milan 1993) 173 no.71 (Ifriqiyya, 11th c.); G. Berti, 'Ceramiche islamiche del Mediterraneo occidentale usate come "bacini" (secoli XI–XIII)', in S. Scuto (ed.), *L'età di Federico II nella Sicilia Centro–Meridionale, Atti,* (Gela 1990) 105, 329 fig. 3a.

27. Both show a griffin attacking a gazelle or roe deer with a floral spray in their mouth, which seems to be a typical feature. See O. Wulff, W. F. Volbach, *Die altchristlichen und mittelalterlichen byzantinischen und italienischen Bildwerke*, III. Ergänzungsband (Berlin 1923) 49–50 J.6662, and *Handbook of the Byzantine Collection Dumbarton Oaks* (Washington 1967), 88 no. 306.

28. The two other pieces depict a cheetah (or panther) and a griffin grasping a roe deer (Kritzas, 179, fig. 9; 181, fig. 11). In the closely related 'Incised ware' the motif of the cheetah pouncing on a roe deer seems to be more common, see: *Corinth XI*, 154, 335–338, illustrated nos. 1698, 1699, 1702, 1705, 1714; for combinations with a hare see nos. 1701, 1728, 1731.

29. The question of origins is still debated. See especially: A. H. S. Megaw, R. E. Jones 'Byzantine and allied pottery: a contribution by chemical analysis to problems of origin and

distribution' *BSA* 78 (1983), 261; Armstrong 1989, 43; Hayes 1992, 44 especially n. 13.

Whether coarser variations of the clay composition indicate a different production centre for vessels decorated in the same style seems at least questionable.

30. See e.g. J. Sourdel-Thomine, B. Spuler *Die Kunst des Islam, Propyläen Kunstgeschichte*, (Berlin 1973) IV., 264; G. C. Miles 'Byzantium and the Arabs: relations in Crete and the Aegean Area' *DOP* 18 (1964), 29. For early examples on coins see, M. R. Alföldi, *Antike Numismatik* (2nd edn., Mainz 1982), Teil I. 91, fig. 133 (Acragas, around 400 BC); ead., Teil II. 96, pl. 7 (Istros, 4th c.); for a Sassanian representation, K. Erdmann, 'Silberschale mit einem Adler über einem Huftier' in *Stiftung zur Förderung der Hamburgischen Kunstsammlungen, Erwerbungen* 1963, 32–34.

31. Examples of the composition 'bird and hare' appear on pottery as well as on mosaics, reliefs and ivories. Pottery: E. J. Grube, *Islamic Pottery of the 8th to the 15th century in the Keir Collection* (London 1976) 120–122 no. 77 (North Africa, 10th–11th c.), 152 no. 99 (Syria, 12th c.).—Mosaics: I. Florent–Goudouneix 'Il pavimento della Basilica' in *San Marco. I mosaici, Le iscrizioni, La Pala d'oro* (Milan 1991), 222–3 (floor in *opus tesselatum*, showing three different versions, 12th c.); M. Andaloro (ed.), *Federico e la Sicilia dalla terra alla corona, arti figurative e arti suntuarie* (Palermo 1995), 15 fig. 16 ('Sala di Ruggero', Palazzo Reale, Palermo, 12th or 13th c.?).—Reliefs: D. Talbot Rice, *Byzantine Art* (Harmondsworth 1968), 48 figs. 8–10 (examples from Achthamar, 915-21; Athens, 12th c.; Trebizond, 13th c.); *BPA*, 24 no. 6 (Mistra, 11th–12th c.); *Federico* (above), 15 fig. 17 (Castello, Barletta, 12th c.?); Buckton (n. 21) 140 n. 151.—Ivories: E. Kühnel, *Die Islamischen Elfenbeinskulpturen, VIII–XIII. Jahrhundert* (Berlin 1971), 80 no. 132 (Sicily?, around 1200), 73 no. 103 (Egypt, 12th c.), 74 no. 104 (Egypt, 11th–12th c.), pl. 101–2 some additional fragments; *Splendeur* (n. 4), 116 no. 25 (Byzantine, 12th c.).

Examples of the composition 'bird and bird' on pottery: Grube (above), 138, 142–143 no. 89 (Egypt, 11th–12th c.), 248 no. 216 (Syria, 13th c.), E. Kühnel, *Islamische Kleinkunst* (2nd edn., Braunschweig 1963), 99 fig. 54a (Mesopotamia, 12th c.);—on reliefs: Miles (n. 30), 29 figs. 76 (Thebes, 12th c.), 77 (Rayy, 12th c);—on ivories: Kühnel 1971 (above), 45 no. 38 (Cordoba, 11th c.); R. H. Pinder-Wilson, C. N. L. Brooke, 'The reliquary of St. Petroc and the ivories of Norman Sicily', *Archaeologia* 104 (1973), 284 pl. 56a (Sicily, 12th c.).

32. Examples of the composition 'bird and roe deer or gazelle' on pottery: Eredità (n. 26), 177 no. 77 (Ifriqiyya, early 11th c.); —in wallpainting: Sourdel-Thomine, Spuler (n. 30), 221 pl. XXII (Samarra, between 836–39 AD);—on rock crystal flask: ibid., 264 pl. 197 (Fatimid, late 10th early 11th c.);—on relief: *Museum für Spätantike und Byzantinische Kunst, Staatliche Museen zu Berlin* (Mainz 1992) 237 no. 141 (Constantinople 12th c.); —on ivories: Kühnel 1971 (n. 31), 44 no. 37 (Cordoba, 11th c.), 63 no. 82 (South Italy, 11th c.), 56 no. 62 (South Italy, 11th c.), 73 no. 102 (Egypt, 12th c.); for some smaller fragments see also pl. 101–2. Several variants of birds attacking different mammals or birds are depicted around 1140 on the ceiling of the Capella Palatina at Palermo (U. Monneret de Villard, *Le pitture Musulmane al Soffitto della Capella Palatina in Palermo* [Rome 1950] fig. 10 and passim).

33. The training of rapacious birds for the hunting of a specific prey was an essential part of falconry from the very beginning. See e.g. D. Möller, F. Vir, (eds.), *Al-Gitrif ibn Qudama al-Gassani, Die Beizvögel. Ein arabisches Falknereibuch des 8. Jahrhunderts* (Hildesheim 1988); C. A. Wood, F. M. Fyfe (eds.), *The Art of Falconry, being the De Arte Venandi cum Avibus of Frederick II of Hohenstaufen* (2nd edn., London 1955), Introduction 39, also 507–556; H.

Brüll, G. Trommer (eds.), *Die Beizjagd. Ein Leitfaden für die Falknerprüfung und für die Praxis* (4th edn., Berlin 1997).

34. e.g. *Splendeur* (n. 4), 86. See also H. Peters, 'Falke, Falkenjagd, Falkner und Falkenbuch' in: *Reallexikon zur Deutschen Kunstgeschichte* (Stuttgart 1968) 1301–1305.

35. e.g. Grube (n. 31), 142–143, 152; Sourdel-Thomine, Spuler (n. 30) 264.

36. Some relevant aspects of the subject will be discussed in greater detail in a subsequent publication.

37. See F. Vir, 'La fauconnerie dans l'Islam médiéval d'après les manuscrits arabes, du 8ème au 14ème siècle' in *La chasse au moyen âge. Actes du Colloque de Nice*, 22–24 juin 1979 (Paris 1980) 189–195; also introduction to *Al–Gitrif* (n. 33) 9–54.

38. Contacts with Byzantium are evidenced in Al–Gitrif's treatise on hawking (see n. 33), chapter 1 (67–71) or 2 (73, 76), and Introduction 11, 15, 26, 29, 32–33, 38–39, 41-42, 48-49. See further D. Möller, *Studien zur mittelalterlichen arabischen Falknerliteratur* (Berlin 1965), 11, 29, 34, 43.

39. Clear evidence for an early practice of hawking in Byzantium, rarely noticed so far, is found in Phaedra's servant carrying a falcon, as described in Procopius of Gaza, Ἔκφρασις Εἰκόνος, written between 495–530 (ed. P. Friedländer, in *Studi e Testi* 89, Vatican 1939, c. 26 l. 276–278; see also p. 113). It can hardly be mere coincidence that the figure described by Procopius finds its exact counterpart in the falconer represented on the Hippolytos mosaic at Madaba (H. Buschhausen, in *Byzantinische Mosaiken aus Jordanien*, [Wien 1986] 143, 150–154, pl. 9). The literary evidence for hawking increases perceptibly from the 11th century onwards (cf. H. Hunger, *Die hochsprachliche profane Literatur der Byzantiner* [Munich 1978] II. 268–269); it is to be noted, however, that the famous Hierakosophion attributed to Demetrios Pepagomenos dates from the 15th and not from the 13th century: A. Diller, *Byzantion* 48, 1978, 35–42.

40. See Wood, Fyfe (n. 33), Introduction 37, 42, 47, 49; B. van den Abeele, *La fauconnerie au moyen âge. Connaissance, affaitage et médecine des oiseaux de chasse d'après le traités latins* (1994), 26-29; also J. Fried, 'Kaiser Friedrich II. als Jäger oder Ein zweites Falkenbuch Kaiser Friedrichs II.?', *Nachrichten der Akademie der Wissenschaften in Göttingen*, I. Philologisch-Historische Klasse 4 (1996), 121, 131. Fried— in contrast to van den Abeele and others—thinks it unlikely that al-Gitrif was known at Frederick's court, ibid., 139 n. 115 and 116.

41. Mosaic from Argos: G. Akerström-Hougen, 'The calendar and hunting mosaics of the Villa of the Falconer in Argos. A study in Early Byzantine iconography', *Acta Instituti Atheniensis Regni Sueciae* 23 (Stockholm 1974); ca. 500 AD. Mosaic at Madaba: Buschhausen (n. 39); before 530 (according to Friedländer, n. 39, 95; Buschhausen dates it to the time of Justinian). North African mosaics (5th–6th century): M. Blanchard-Lemée et al., *Sols de l' Afrique Romaine* (Paris 1995), 182; for the special case of Kélibia, where falconry and bird-catching with limesticks are shown among various hunting scenes, see also M. Ennaïfer, 'Etat de la recherche dans le domaine de la mosaïque en Tunisie', in J.-P. Darmon, A. Rebourg (eds.), *La Mosaïque Gréco-Romaine IV* (Paris 1994), 238–239. The assumption that the Vandals brought hawking to North Africa is hardly tenable; the literary evidence quoted by K. Lindner (*Reallexikon der Germanischen Altertumskunde*, 1976, 167) does not support it. The *sermo* 'De tempore barbarico (II)' (PL Suppl. 3, 287–298) was not composed by Augustinus, but by his contemporary Quodvultdeus; 'avibus canibusque' (l.c. 291) clearly does not refer to hawking. The passage in 'Sermo ad fratres in eremo, XXXVIII' which mentions hawking (PL 40, 1305–1306), was written by a Belgian monk in the 13th century (J. Machielsen, *Clavis patristica pseudepigraphorum medii aevi*, IA, Turnhout 1990, 252 nr. 1165).

42. Textiles, which played a particularly important part in the

process of imagery transmission (Miles, n. 30, 29–30 and O. Grabar, *The Formation of Islamic Art* [Yale 1987] 166, 176), are of a certain relevance for this period. For Coptic examples (6th–8th c.): Peters (n. 34) 1276; for representations on silk from other regions: R. Ettinghausen, O. Grabar, *The Art and Architecture of Islam: 650–1250* (3rd edn., London 1991), 243, fig. 261 (Iran, 10th c. ?); R. Ghirshman, *Iran. Parther und Sasaniden*, Universum der Kunst (Munich 1962) 236-7, 368, fig. 288 (Iran, 10th–11th c. ?); it can hardly be excluded that the fragment in Berlin (J. Beckwith, *Early Christian and Byzantine Art*, 2nd edn. [Harmondsworth 1979] 175, fig. 146; Constantinople ?, late 8th or 9th century) represents falconers as well. For the general problem of provenance and chronology of these relevant textile examples see L. von Wilckens, *Die textilen Künste von der Spätantike bis um* 1500 (Munich 1991) 40–57. Whether the two metal plaques with mounted falconers from Staré Mesto, 9th c. (Z. Vana, *Die Welt der Alten Slawen* [Prag 1983] 154) and Persia, 10th c. (G.C. Miles, *AmNumSocMusN*. 11, 1964, 283; K. Lindner, *Beiträge zu Vogelfang und Falknerei im Altertum* [Berlin 1973] 151) can be dated definitely to these centuries is still open to discussion. A probable further 10th century example is represented by an Iranian wall painting with a mounted falconer (*BMMA* 37, 1942, 116, 118, fig. 45; also Ettinghausen, Grabar, above, 250).

43. Even a number of examples of painting and sculpture selected at random illustrate this change clearly: Illuminations in Pseudo-Oppian's *Cynegetica*, 11th c., Venedig, Bibl. Marciana, cod. gr.Z.479, fol. 2v. and 54v. (Kádár, n. 15, 91–93, 106, 108, pls. 138.3, 139.1; Lindner, n. 42, figs. 42, 43, 62). For a discussion of possible sources of the relevant illustrations see K. Weitzmann, *Greek Mythology in Byzantine Art* (Princeton 1951), 93–151; J. C. Anderson, 'Cod. Vat. Gr. 463 and an eleventh–century Byzantine painting center', *DOP* 32 (1978), 194–196; Kádár (n. 15), 119–121; also Lindner, n. 42, 88–90; arguing from the point of view of the history of falconry.—Painting of mounted falconers on the ceiling of the Capella Palatina at Palermo, around 1140 (Monneret de Villard, n. 32, 41–2, figs. 11–12, 247–8).—Fresco with mounted falconer in the 'Casillas de Berlanga (Soria), ermita de San Baudilio', 1125?, (J. Sureda, *La pintura romanica en España* [Madrid 1985] 319–327; see also M. Núñez Rodríguez, 'Scénes de chasse dans la peinture de l'Espagne chrétienne', in *La chasse*, n. 37, 535–548).—Drawing in ink of a falconer on horseback, Fostat, before 1200 ? (E. J. Grube, in B. W. Robinson (ed.), *Islamic Painting and the Arts of the Book. The Keir Collection* [London 1976] 26, 60–61, pl. 9).—Relief of a hunting scene with an inscription which explicitly mentions a falcon (NISUS), San Zeno, Verona, first half of 12th century (A. von Hülsen-Esch, *Romanische Skulptur in Oberitalien als Reflex der kommunalen Entwicklung im 12. Jahrhundert* [Berlin 1994] 131, 219, fig. 83).

44. D. Walz, in *Das Falkenbuch Friedrichs II* (Graz 1994) 11, postulates a date between 1258–1266. The study of W.F. Volbach, 'Le miniature del codice Vatic. Pal. lat. 1071 De arte venandi cum avibus', *Rendiconti, Atti della Pontifica Accademia Romana di Archeologia* 15 (1939) 145–175, represents—in my opinion—still the most convincing treatment of the problem. In contrast to Volbach, Willemsen assumes in his commentary to *Fredericus II, De arte venandi cum avibus*. Ms. Pal. Lat.1071, Biblioteca Apostolica Vaticana (Graz 1969), 13, 20–22, that the personal influence of the emperor makes itself strongly felt in the miniatures illustrating the text. Fried (n. 40), 150–154, seems basically to share Willemsen's opinion.

45. e.g. D. Evans, 'The Nobility of Knight and Falcon' in H. Bill, R. Harvey (eds.), *The Ideals and Practice of Medieval Knighthood* (London 1990), II. 79–99; R. S. Oggins, 'Falconry and medieval social status', *Mediaevalia* 12 (1989),

43-55; H. Bresc, 'La chasse en Sicile (XIIᵉ–XVᵉ siècles)', in *La chasse* (n. 37), 203–205, 207.

46. e.g. Bresc (n. 45) 208; for the Arab regions Vir (n. 37) 195.

47. See Kühnel 1971 (n. 31), above all 38 no. 31, 39 no. 32, 40 no. 33, 41 no. 35, 68 no. 88; for an interpretation of the formal and iconographic vocabularies see also Grabar (n. 42), 166–169, or Ettinghausen, Grabar (n. 42), 145–155, 202–204. Evidence for falconry as a status symbol is also presented by objects which depict well known members of the nobility carrying a falcon (among them also women), see Peters (n. 34), 1323–1325, 1345. He mentions, *inter alios*, king Harold and count Guy on the Bayeux Tapestry of around 1066–1077 (fig. 5), countess Adelheid of Holland on a seal used in 1201 (fig. 9), or count Ludwig of Frohburg on an onyx of around 1240 (fig. 12).

48. See Kühnel 1971 (n. 31), nos. 32, 35, 88. The same holds true for a number of painted ivories from Norman Sicily (12th–13th centuries), see Pinder-Wilson, Brooke (n. 31) 279–80. For examples in other media compare, e.g., the Fermo (Umbria) chasuble of St. Thomas Becket, dated to 1116 AD, produced in Almeria (see Wilckens, n. 42, 186 and F. Gabrieli, U. Scerrato, *Gli Arabi in Italia*, Milano 1979, 480-81, figs. 522–23) or the relief of a hunting scene at the West portal of San Zeno, Verona (see n. 43).

49. Persian lustre ware is an interesting case in this respect, as the vessels can be decorated with single motifs, with a series of motifs, or with the representation of complete scenes. See *inter alia* pls. 37–42, in O. Watson, *Persian Lustre Ware* (London 1985), or E. J. Grube (ed.), *Cobalt and Lustre* (Oxford 1994), nos. 227–229, 231, 233, the so-called 'mina'i' pottery.

50. Victoria and Albert Museum, 12th century, see Lane (n. 26), 22, fig. 26B. For a similar piece in the Freer Gallery of Art, see Watson (n. 49), 30, fig. 3. Of interest in this context is also a tile with a mounted falconer from Alaeddin's Palace, Konya, second half of 12th century (G. Öney, 'Mounted Hunting Scenes in Anatolian Seljuks', *Anadolou* 11, 1967, 151, fig. 21).

51. Grube (n. 31), 142, no. 89 (11th–12th century).

52. Eredità (n. 26), 194 no. 82 (12th century).

53. Grube (n. 31), 120 no.77 (10th–11th century).

54. Eredità (n. 26), 177 no. 77 (early 11th century).

55. I owe my introduction to the pottery of Paphos to Peter Megaw whom I met there for the first time in 1973. I am very grateful for all I learnt from him about glazed pottery during the subsequent years.

56. Παπανικόλα-Μπακιρτζῆ (n. 26), 87, pl. 4.

57. For an example of a realistically represented falconry scene, obviously based on observation, see the Fatimid ivory plaque in Florence (*Eredità*, n. 26, 156 no. 63 upper right). Even more impressive in its strong naturalistic character is the representation of hunters training their falcons with the help of the long jess to kill a gazelle (fig. 14; ivory casket from the Capella Palatina, Palermo, early 13th century?: *Federico*, n. 31, 170 no. 36).

58. The assumption that this type of pottery is of Cypriot origin, see A. J. Boas, 'The import of western ceramics to the Latin Kingdom of Jerusalem', *IEJ* 44 (1994), 102–22, where he calls the ware 'Mid-twelfth-century Byzantine Sgrafitto', is hardly tenable. Cf. also n. 27.

59. Agora: Frantz (n. 16), 465, fig. 30. See also Notopoulos (n. 18), 108–133. Corinth: W. Biers, 'The Horseman and the Angel,' *Archaeology* 30 (1977) 333–337, fig. 333; in contrast to many representations on Islamic 12th/13th century bowls, unambiguous hawking utensils, like the falconer's glove, the lure and/or the jesses on the birds talons, are not shown.

13

Zeuxippus Ware: Some Minor Observations

Demetra Papanikola-Bakirtzis

In 1968, an article by A. H. S. Megaw drew attention to a group of high-quality ceramics with particularly fine and sophisticated decoration.'[1] He named it *Zeuxippus Ware*, because the first examples that came to notice were by the Baths of Zeuxippus in Constantinople.[2] In the article, he described the ware's characteristic features and divided it into two classes. Class I comprised items with simple engraved decoration; class II, wares whose decoration was enriched with touches of brown.

Twenty years later, he returned to the same subject in 'Zeuxippus Ware Again', a paper read at the symposium on Byzantine ceramics organised in Athens by the French Archaeological School. Megaw here presented further information about this splendid 'pottery family', as he called it, and amended some of his previous claims, chiefly with regard to dating, distribution and origin.[3]

The present article in a volume dedicated to the author of 'Zeuxippus Ware' ventures some minor observations and comments on the subject.

SOME MORE ZEUXIPPUS WARE FROM KATO PAPHOS ON CYPRUS

As we know, the excavations in the Saranda Kolones castle in Kato Paphos, Cyprus, have yielded a considerable quantity of Zeuxippus Ware. In both his articles, Megaw discussed these fmds at length, and linked them with the level related to the earthquake which destroyed the Paphos castle in 1222.[4]

Another site at Kato Paphos which has also produced Zeuxippus Ware is Chrysopolitissa. The excavation of the large seven-aisled basilica there located medieval levels rich in glazed pottery, including some fine examples of Zeuxippus.[5]

PLATE PM 2577/3. ht. 4.5, diam. 19.5ra (PLATE 13.1*a*)
Dark-fired red body. Low, flaring, sharp-edged foot. Flaring rim with upturned lip. Interior-central gouged disc within concentric gouged circles; alternate fine-point ovals and pendent triangles in rim border; touches of yellow-brown on motifs; colourless glaze. Exterior: irregular tongues of slip; scars left by tripod-stilt.

PLATE PM 2577/4. ht. 5, diam. 20.5 (PLATE 13.1*b*)
Red body, blackened at rim. Low-flaring, sharp-edged foot. Flaring form with sharp lip. Interior: within a medallion edged with gouged grooves, three fine-point circles containing trefoils between pendent triangles roughly overpainted with brown.

Exterior: irregular tongues of slip. Colourless glaze over interior and upper part of exterior. Scars left by tripod-stilt.

BOWL 2577/30. ht. 7.5, diam. 18 (PLATE 13.1*c*)
Purple–fired red body. Low, flaring foot. Almost hemispherical body. Interior: within a central medallion bordered by a double groove, three ovals with phi motifs and pendent triangles in between. From the edge of the medallion radiate triangles, in which sprout florets, with palmette-shaped motifs in between. Touches of brown on motifs. Exterior: irregular tongues of slip. Green glaze on interior and upper part of exterior. Scars left on the well by tripod-stilt. On the interior of the foot traces of tripod-stilt of vessel stacked above.

JUG PM 2577/29. Ht. pres. 16, diam. base 7 (PLATE 13.1*d*)
Red body. Flat base, globular body. Decoration: large and small circles, beautifully drawn, all over the body. Shiny green glaze extending to foot.

These four examples have been selected from the Zeuxippus finds at Chrysopolitissa because each one in its own way enriches our knowledge about this group of ceramic ware. The first two add two complete plates to the known items of Zeuxippus Ware. Their engraved decoration is highlighted with touches of brown, hence they belong to class II.[7] Their discovery at Chrysopolitissa swells the number of Zeuxippus items at Kato Paphos and confirms that the presence of so many pieces from this group at Paphos in the early thirteenth century can be due only to systematic trade, which at that time was almost exclusively in the hands of the commercial cities of Italy.[8]

The third item from Chrysopolitissa, No 2577/30, has engraved decoration with radial floral motifs resembling the decoration of a plate from Constantinople and a central medallion with a phi similar to that on a bowl fragment, again from Constantinople.[9] The engraved decoration on all three vessels is touched with brown, and consequently they belong to class II. However, although the two vessels from Constantinople have the colourless glaze typical of this class, the glaze of bowl 2577/30 from Chrysopolitissa is atypical for class II, being green, rather than colourless. It could be placed in a sub-division of class II—II B, for instance—whose identifying features would be sgraffito decoration touched with brown splashes, and with green glaze.[10]

As far as the jug, No PM 2577/29, is concerned, its decorative technique places it not among the sgraffito but the slip-painted ware, a treatment often found on the exterior of bowls, usually under colourless glaze.[11]

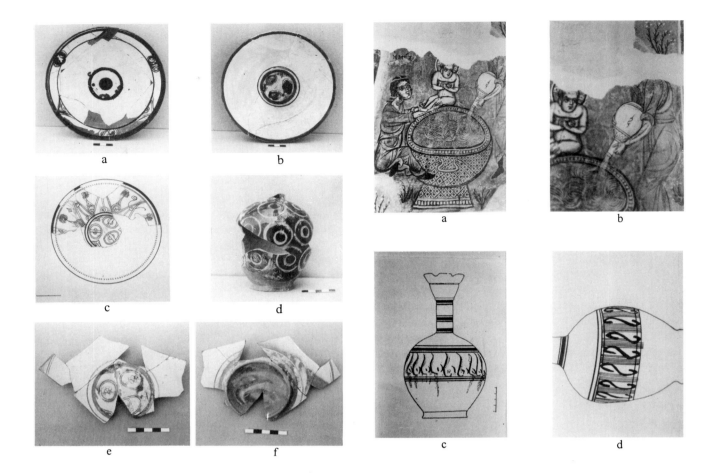

PLATE 13.1: *Zeuxippus Ware from Chrysopolitissa*
a: PM 2577/3, b: PM 2577/4, c: PM 2577/30, d:
PM 2577/29, e and f: Fragment of a plate from Kitros

PLATE 13.2 *a and b: Wall-painting of the Bathing of*
Christ. Panayia Amasgou, Cyprus; c: Zeuxippus jug from
Cherson; d: S-shaped motifs on a Zeuxippus jug from
Saranda Kolones (from 'Zeuxippus Again')

The Chrysopolitissa jug has a counterpart in a yellow-glazed item from Saranda Kolones published by Megaw.[12] A third, similar, piece excavated at Cherson was published recently in the catalogue of an exhibition of finds from that Crimean city.[13]

ZEUXIPPUS WARE FROM BYZANTINE KITROS IN PIERIA, NORTHERN GREECE

In recent years the extensive excavations which have been conducted in Pieria, near ancient Pydna and south of Makriyalos, have brought to light the ruins of Byzantine Kitros. So far, the town's episcopal church and part of the fortifying wall have been uncovered. Not far from this latter site, on plot No 568, are the remains of a private building, probably a house.[14] The ceramic material has yielded part of an item (BK 4508/6) with features typical of Zeuxippus Ware: the foot and centre of a plate of typical dense red clay. The interior is decorated with a central medallion with three circles containing palmettes, with pendent triangles in between; the exterior with slip cut by gouged grooves and lines. Both interior and exterior are covered with colourless glaze (FIG. 13, PLATE 13.1*e*, *f*).[15]

This is no rare fragment, nor does it add a great deal to what we know of Zeuxippus typology. Its significance lies in the fact that this is one more site to which we now know that Zeuxippus Ware had spread. It is important to note that there was not a great deal of Zeuxippus Ware in Thessaloniki, judging by the few examples which rescue digs have found there.[16]

Fragment BK 4508/6 is particularly important, however, because it was found in the same level and indeed right next to the place where a hoard of forty-five aspers was discovered. The hoard is believed to have been secreted in 1219 and has been linked with the burial of a large number of caches in Northern Greece during the turbulent period between 1204 and 1261. Notable years of trouble were 1208, when Theodore I Laskaris was crowned; 1224, when the ruler of Epirus, Theodore Komnenos Doukas, overthrew the Latin kingdom of Thessaloniki; and 1226, when the Empire of Nicaea annexed the despotate of Thessaloniki.[17]

This numismatic evidence confirms Megaw's argument in his latest article that class II Zeuxippus Ware, to which the Kitros plate belongs, continued to circulate after the Frankish conquest.[18]

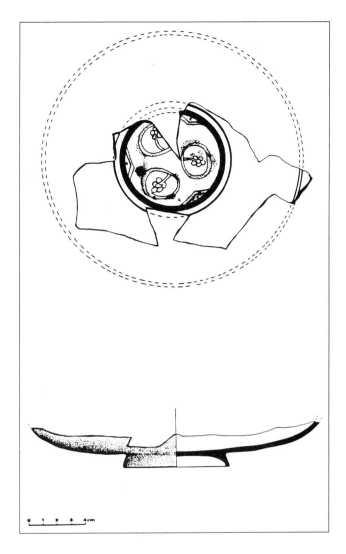

FIG. 13.1: *Zeuxippus Ware: the foot and centre of a plate of typical dense red clay.*

ZEUXIPPUS WARE IN A WALL-PAINTING?

A wall-painting of the Nativity in the Church of the Panayia Amasgou near the village of Monagri, Cyprus, includes an interesting representation of the Bathing of the Christ Child (PLATE 13.2*a, b*).[19] Seated on the ground, the midwife holding the Infant is about to give him his first bath. In front of her is the bath itself and facing her is Salome, minus the upper part of her body and her head.

Although the representation has some special features —notably with regard to the moment depicted, which is not the actual bathing of the Child, but just before— I do not intend to discuss anything other than the container from which Salome is pouring water into the bath. It is a narrow-necked vessel, resembling a handleless jug, and its whitish colour and simple form suggest that it is made of slip-covered clay. Its decoration consists of a metope of S-shaped motifs around the shoulder and a similar, though larger, 'calligraphical' S in the centre of the body.

Vessels which have a similar shape to the jug in the fresco, have been found in excavations at Cherson and the Saranda Kolones castle (PLATE 13.2*c, d*).[20] According to Megaw, they are Zeuxippus Ware and have similar decoration to this one in that they have a metope-type band around the shoulders, though they lack the large S on the body. Their decoration, engraved with a fine and a broad point, and their colourless glaze on whitish slip create the same decorative and chromatic effect as the jug in the wall-painting in the Panayia Amasgou. These similarities are so strong that one simply cannot resist venturing the bold, but very engaging hypothesis that the painter of the fresco had in mind a specific Zeuxippus jug, whose luxurious quality he felt was appropriate to the Holy Child's first bath.

The theory is reinforced by the fact that the artist depicts all the objects in the scene not conventionally but realistically, one particularly striking example being the copper basin and its characteristic handle. Moreover, Andreas and Judith Stylianou have dated the fresco to the late twelfth century and Susan Boyd has dated it to the first quarter of the thirteenth,[21] which exactly coincides with Megaw's dating of the Saranda Kolones jugs.[22]

Lately, examples of Zeuxippus Ware are being located on new sites with ever increasing frequency.[23] At the same time, there is growing speculation as to whether or not the ware was produced in more than one centre, and the question of imitations and derivatives is also being discussed.[24] Clay analysis projects are currently under way in an effort to resolve these problems.[25]

The growing interest in Zeuxippus Ware undoubtedly makes it one of the most keenly discussed groups of Byzantine pottery and fully justifies the close attention which Megaw drew to it thirty or so years ago.

Museum of Byzantine Culture, Thessaloniki

NOTES

1   A. H. S. Megaw, 'Zeuxippus Ware', *BSA*, 63 (1968), 67–88 (hereafter 'Zeuxippus').

2   In the *Preliminary Report upon the Excavation carried out in the Hippodrome of Constantinople in 1927 on Behalf of the British Academy* (London 1928), D. Talbot Rice classifies the pottery which came to be known as Zeuxippus Ware as 'Group C, Shiny Olive Incised Ware'.

3   A. H. S. Megaw, 'Zeuxippus Ware Again', in V. Déroche and J.-M. Spieser, ed., *Recherches sur la céramique byzantine*, *BCH, Suppl.* XVIII (1989), 259–266 (hereafter 'Zeuxippus Again').

4   'Zeuxippus', 85–6; 'Zeuxippus Again', 264.

5   The Chrysopolitissa excavations were conducted by the Cypriot Department of Antiquities under the supervision of A. Papageorgiou, whom I should like to thank for so kindly making finds available for publication.

6   Dimensions are given in centimetres. Index numbers preceded by the letters PM refer to items in the District Museum of Paphos.

7   'Zeuxippus', 71–2.

8   'Zeuxippus', 87; 'Zeuxippus Again', 266. For the spread of Zeuxippus Ware in the East Mediterranean, see also D. R. Pringle, 'Some More Proto-maiolica from Athlit (Pilgrims' Castle) and a Discussion of its Distribution in the Levant', *Levant*, 14 (1982), 111; id., 'Thirteenth-century Pottery from the Monastery of St Mary of Carmel', *Levant* 16 (1984), 104 No 57, fig. 8; id., 'Medieval Pottery from Caesarea: The Crusader Period', *Levant* 17 (1985), 190 Nos 59, 60, fig. 11.

9   'Zeuxippus', 77, pl. 17a; 74, No 15, 16d.

10 Megaw, 'Zeuxippus', 72 n.23, discusses a possible subdivision of Class II with examples touched up with a colour other than yellow-brown, but he does not discuss examples covered with glaze other than colourless, such as the green glaze of our PM 2577/30. The centre of a Zeuxippus bowl in the Benaki Museum, Athens, has the same features as our bowl from Chryssopolitissa, namely sgraffito decoration with brown splashes and green glaze; see D. Papanikola-Bakirtzis, R. Mavrikiou and C. Bakirtzis, *Byzantine Glazed Pottery in the Benaki Museum* (Athens 1999) 114, cat. no. 244.

11 'Zeuxippus', pl. 15d, 15e; 'Zeuxippus Again', 264, fig. 5d.

12 'Zeuxippus Again', 264, fig. 5c.

13 *Byzantine Cherson* Exhibition catalogue, I. S. Chichurov, ed., (Moscow 1991), No 248.

14 E. Marki, in *A. Delt.*, 42 (1987), Chr., 411.

15 I should like to thank Ms E. Marki for making this find available for publication.

16 C. Bakirtzis and D. Papanikola-Bakirtzis, 'De la céramique en glaçure à Thessalonique', *Byzantinobulgarica*, 7 (1981), 429, fig. 11. The presence of Zeuxippus Ware in mainland Greece is generally limited, see *Byzantine Ceramics, The Art of Sgraffito*, ed. D. Papanikola-Bakirtzis (Thessaloniki 1999) 22.

17 Y. Touratsoglou, '"Θησαυρός" άσπρων τραχέων/1983 από την Άρτα', *A. Delt.*, 36 (1981) Mel., 216, 219.

18 'Zeuxippus Again', 261, 264, 266.

19 S. Boyd, 'The Panagia Amasgou, Monagri, Cyprus', *DOP*, 28 (1974), 293–4, figs. 19, 20, colour fig. B; A. and J. Stylianou, *The Painted Churches of Cyprus* (London 1985), 241, fig. 137.

20 A. L. Jakobson, *Keramika i Keramicheskoe proizvodstvo srednevekovoj Tavriki* (Leningrad 1979), 125, fig. 78:4; 'Zeuxippus', 264, figs. 5b, 5e.

21 Boyd, *op. cit.*, (n.19), 322; Stylianou, *The Painted Churches*, 241.

22 'Zeuxippus Again', 264.

23 J.-M. Speiser, *Die Byzantinische Keramik aus der Stadtgrabung von Pergamon* (Berlin/New York 1996) 51; G.

Berti-S. Gelichi, 'Zeuxippus Ware' in Italy, *Materials Analysis of Byzantine Pottery*, ed. H. Maguire (Washington, D.C. 1997) 85–104; E. J. Stern, Excavations of the Courthouse Site at "Akko: The Pottery of the Crusader and Ottoman Periods, *Atiqot* XXXI (1997) 52–55; V. François, 'Sur la circulation des céramiques byzantines en Méditerranée orientale et occidentale' in *VIᵉ Congrès International sur la Céramique Médiévale en Méditerranée* (Aix-en-Provence, 1997) 233–234; H. Amouric, F. Richez, L. Vallauri, *Vingt mille pots sous les mers* (Aix-en-Provence 1999) 20–21.

24 J.-M. Spieser, 'La céramique byzantine médiévale', *Hommes et richesses dans l'Empire byzantin, VII–XV Siècles*, eds. V. Kravari, J. Lefort, C. Morrisson, Réalites byzantines, 3 (Paris 1991) 251, 257–258; P. Armstrong, 'Zeuxippus Derivatives from Sparta', *Philakon. Lakonian Studies in Honour of Hector Catling*, ed. J. Motyka Sanders (Athens 1992) 1–9; G. D. R. Sanders, 'Excvations at Sparta: The Roman Stoa, 1988–91, Preliminary Report, Part Ic, Medieval Pottery', *BSA* 88 (1993) 257–258.

25 A. Boas, 'The Import of Western ceramics to the Latin Kingdom of Jerusalem, *IEJ* 44 (1994) 104–107; S. Y. Waksman-J.-M. Spieser, 'Byzantine Ceramics Excavated in Pergamon: Archaeologial Classification and Characterization of the Local and Imported Production by PIXE and INAA Elemental Analysis, Minerology, and Petrography', *Materials Analysis of Byzantine Pottery*, n.23, 105–134; P. Armstrong, H. Hatcher, 'Byzantine and Allied Pottery, Phase 2: Past Work on Materials Analysis and Future Prospects, ibid., 1–8; A. H. S. Megaw, P. Armstrong, H. Hatcher, 'Zeuxippus Ware: An Analytical Approach to the Question of Provenance', *Pré-actes du VIIᵉ Congrès International sur la Céramique Médiévale en Méditerranée* (Thessaloniki 1999) 13–14. A project focusing on Zeuxippus Ware is undertaken in France by V. François (CNRS, Aix-en-Provence) and Y. Waksman (CNRS, Lyon).

14
Un but de pèlerinage: Notre-Dame de Nicosie

Jean Richard

L'usage d'assigner au pécheur repentant, après confession de ses fautes et absolution, l'accomplissement d'un pèlerinage à titre de pénitence, est fort ancien dans l'Eglise. Les 'pénitenciels' du haut Moyen-Age, et ce jusqu'au XIIIᵉ siècle, ont codifié cet usage, en précisant que pour certains péchés 'énormes', le pénitent pouvait être astreint à se rendre aux sanctuaires les plus vénérés—les plus lointains aussi—: Rome, Compostelle et notamment le Saint-Sépulcre.[1]

On sait comment cette coutume fut à l'origine de la définition de l'indulgence de croisade, telle qu'elle s'ébauchait au temps de Grégoire VII et d'Alexandre II, avant que le pape Urbain II lui donnât son acception définitive, en ajoutant au pèlerinage l'accomplissement d'une oeuvre pie: participation à la défense de l'Espagne chrétienne, à la libération du Saint-Sépulcre. Ces services rendus à la Chrétienté relevaient celui qui s'y consacrait d'une des obligations du pénitent: l'interdiction de porter les armes; mais elle laissait subsister les autres exigences morales qui incombaient à un pécheur repentant.[2]

Pour beaucoup de croisés, la participation à *l'iter Hierosolymitanum* restait un pèlerinage expiatoire. On voit même un trouvère, à propos de la prise de croix de saint Louis, s'étonner de ce que le roi s'assujettisse à l'obligation de partir en croisade alors qu'il n'avait pas commis de faute qui l'y contraigne![3]

La Papauté, dans le cours du XIIᵉ siècle, s'était inquiétée des conséquences de la confusion entre le pèlerinage et la croisade, l'un et l'autre offrant à un pécheur les mêmes perspectives de rémission des péchés par l'accomplissement de la pénitence suprême, celle qui pouvait se substituer à toutes celles que les confesseurs imposaient à leurs pénitents. Alors que la Terre Sainte avait un besoin urgent de secours, on voyait des princes, et non des moindres, se rendre au Saint–Sépulcre, visiter les Lieux-Saints et repartir sans avoir fourni d'assistance aux Chrétiens d'Orient. C'est ce qui amena Alexandre III à promulguer le 29 juillet 1169 la bulle *Inter omnia* qui subordonnait l'obtention de la rémission de la pénitence à un séjour de deux ans en Terre Sainte, le pénitent devant se mettre au service des princes chrétiens d'Orient.[4]

On ne peut affirmer qu'Alexandre III parvint de la sorte à multiplier les vocations de croisés. Mais la doctrine qu'il avait élaborée (elle n'abolissait pas pour autant la faculté d'obtenir l'indulgence attachée au pèlerinage du Saint–Sépulcre en dehors du service des princes latins) devait faire son chemin dans la définition des privilèges spirituels liés au voeu de croisade.[5]

Or une nouvelle extension de l'application de l'obligation de pèlerinage à la rémission des fautes s'est fait jour au plus tard dans le cours du XIIIᵉ siècle—: c'est l'usage adopté par les cours de justice d'astreindre un coupable—meurtrier, rebelle, par exemple—à effectuer un pèlerinage en compensation du pardon de sa faute. Ce pardon apparaissait comme un acte de miséricorde, ou comme un moyen de ramener la paix entre deux lignages; mais celui qui en bénéficiait se voyait imposer l'obligation d'aller visiter un ou plusieurs sanctuaires, en y priant pour l'âme de sa victime. Cette forme d'expiation se révèle très proche de ce qu'était la pénitence imposée au pécheur par son confesseur.[6]

Sans doute un grand nombre de croisés, au XIIIe siècle, sont-ils partis pour la Terre Sainte après avoir été condamnés par leurs juges à accomplir ce voyage en contrepartie du pardon qui leur avait été octroyé.[7] Mais avec la chute des dernières places de Terre Sainte, une formule de substitution intervint: au lieu de se rendre dans le royaume de Jérusalem, le coupable pardonné devait se rendre dans celui de Chypre.[8] Celui-ci, en effet, avait pris la place des terres latines de Syrie comme point de départ d'une croisade qui devait rester au programme de la Chrétienté jusque dans les dernières décennies du XIVᵉ siècle: Chypre même joua effectivement ce rôle jusqu'à la fin du règne de Pierre Iᵉʳ.[9]

Le nom de Chypre apparaît donc de façon courante dans les sentences rendues, en particulier, par les justices des villes de Rhénanie, de Flandre et des Pays-Bas, sous la forme 'à Chypre', parfois 'au royaume de Chypre', exceptionnellement 'à Famagouste', cette ville étant sans doute considérée comme le port de débarquement. C'est en tout cas de l'évêque Baudouin de Famagouste qu'émane le plus ancien des certificats que nous possédions, témoignant de l'accomplissement du pèlerinage. La plupart de ceux-ci paraissent avoir été délivrés par les rois de Chypre, et c'est au nom de ceux-ci qu'ont été rédigés les faux certificats que fournissait une officine de Venise, que démasquèrent à la fin du XVe siècle les magistrats de Maestricht.[10]

La particularité de ces pèlerinages expiatoires à Chypre tient à ce qu'ils ne comportent pas l'indication d'une visite à un sanctuaire, mais la mention d'un séjour à effectuer dans l'île, pendant un délai d'un ou de deux ans (exceptionnellement plus). La 'paix de Saint-Jacques' de Liège, en 1487, précise que 'la résidence et stuc de unne an entier se doit entendre que on doit demeurer résidemment en l'ysle de Cipre, en la cité de Nicosie ou autre bonne ville oudit ysle'[11]. La raison d'être de ce séjour, pour une durée équivalant à celle que stipulait la bulle *Inter omnia* (deux ans pour une rémission complète, un an pour une rémission de la moitié de la pénitence), correspond évidemment à cette durée pendant laquelle le pénitent devait rester disponible pour toute campagne contre les Infidèles décidée par le roi.[12] Dans la réalité, les certificats se bornent à témoigner de la bonne conduite du pèlerin. Mais progressivement, les villes acceptent le rachat de l'obligation de pèlerinage et le nom de Chypre apparaît avec beaucoup d'autres dans des tarifs stipulant le montant de ce rachat.[13] Dans d'autres cas, le pèlerinage forcé prend l'allure d'un bannissement, en particulier lorsqu'il s'agit du châtiment d'une révolte.[14]

Le pèlerinage de Chypre n'en diffère pas moins des autres par l'absence de référence au sanctuaire qui doit faire l'objet d'une pieuse visite—visite, rappelons-le, normalement enrichie d'indulgences, sans doute applicables à la victime de l'acte de violence qu'il s'agit d'expier. Ainsi trouve-t-on dans les tarifs les noms de Notre-Dame de Sardenay, célèbre sanctuaire marial proche de Damas, de Saint-Antoine de Rhodes, de Sainte-Sophie ou Sainte-Anastasie de Constantinople, de Sainte-Catherine du Mont-Sinaï, voire de Saint-Thomas dans l'Inde.[15]

Toutefois un certain nombre de mentions font apparaître de façon inattendue le nom de 'Notre-Dame de Nicosie', qui a fait problème pour les historiens.[16] Les attestations concernant ce sanctuaire sont peu nombreuses au regard du grand nombre de celles qui concernent Chypre sans autre indication. Toutefois les juges de Gand, ceux de Delft, l'Audience de Flandre, ont infligé des pèlerinages expiatoires dont le but est bien cette église de Nicosie dont le nom reste un peu énigmatique. Et on est conduit à penser que lorsque la notion d'un séjour à Chypre comme mise à la disposition de la royauté chypriote de combattants éventuels pour la croisade s'est effacée, dans les dernières années du XIVe siècle sans doute (c'est alors que 'le Turc' prend la place du 'sultan' comme adversaire habituel des croisés), on a été amené à envisager le 'voyage' de Chypre de la même manière que les autres pèlerinages: la visite à un sanctuaire vénéré. Et que c'est alors—la première attestation est de 1370[17]— que le pèlerinage à l'église Notre-Dame est apparu comme un substitut du séjour dans l'île.

Ce qui a conduit des historiens à supposer qu'il pouvait s'agir d'une simple méprise, c'est qu'aucun récit de voyageur n'a fait état d'une visite à une église de Nicosie dédiée à Notre-Dame. Les lieux que l'un ou l'autre a fréquentés pour des motifs de dévotion sont d'ailleurs peu nombreux. La colonne de la flagellation de saint Paul à Paphos, l'église Notre-Dame de la Cave proche de Famagouste (particulièrement vénérée par les marins), le lieu de la naissance de sainte Catherine,

également voisin de Famagouste[18], le monastère de Stavrovouni ('Saint-Paul d'Antioche et la Croix-en-Chypre') auquel s'attachait le souvenir de la croix du bon larron, et surtout le tombeau de saint Jean de Montfort, dans l'église des Cisterciens de Beaulieu[19] sont à peu près les seuls buts de pèlerinage que mentionnent ceux des voyageurs qui nous disent avoir profité de leur escale en Chypre pour de pieuses visites.

Il est évident que la liste n'est pas exhaustive, Leontios Makhairas a énuméré une longue série de saints chypriotes avec le nom des lieux où on les vénérait, et nous savons que Grecs et Latins communiaient dans les mêmes vénérations. En ce qui concerne la dévotion mariale, on peut évoquer le témoignage d'Etienne de Lusignan, qui relève l'existence d'un certain nombre d'icônes miraculeuses: celle de Notre-Dame de Paphos, qu'on disait avoir été peinte par saint Luc,[20] celles de Phaneromeni, des Carmes, des Frères Prêcheurs—celle-ci dite 'Chastillonette' (Castiliotissa)—, de Tripimeni, 'et en outre à Nicossie l'image de saint Luc qui guarissoit les demoniacles'.[21]

Cette dernière mention nous amène à nous interroger sur l'identité de cette dernière image, dont la vénération pourrait remonter très haut et avoir connu une vogue considérable. Il pourrait en effet s'agir de l'image conservée à Nicosie dans l'église de Notre-Dame de Tortose, laquelle avait, au temps d'Etienne de Lusignan, cessé d'être l'église d'une communauté de religieuses bénédictines—la disparition de cette dernière pouvant être intervenue, comme dans d'autres cas de monastères de moniales,[22] au cours du XVe siècle.

L'histoire de Notre-Dame de Tortose a été obscurcie par une double erreur: Mas-Latrie a rendu par 'Notre-Dame des Trois Rois' l'inscription figurant sur la tombe d'Echive de Dampierre, conservée à l'entrée de l'église arménienne[23]; or la pierre tombale, datée de 1340, donnait à Echive le titre d'abbesse de la Crois d'Antioche et de Notre-Dame ds Trs'; une autre dalle de la même église portait l'épitaphe d'une sous-prieure de 'Nostre Dame de Tourtoze', morte en 1318. L'identification de cette église à celle de Notre-Dame de Tortose est donc assurée[24]. C'est donc par erreur que Camille Enlart a décrit l'église en question sous le nom de Notre-Dame de Tyr[25], ce qui a entraîné la dénomination d'une des rues actuelles de Nicosie (en fait, la localisation de Notre-Dame de Tyr reste inconnue).

Pour Notre-Dame de Tortose, c'était une communauté de religieuses venues d'Antioche où, sous le nom de *Sancta Crux de Carpita*, elles avaient bénéficié d'un indult du pape Alexandre IV (6 mars 1257), conférant des indulgences à ceux qui visiteraient leur église, 'en raison de la dévotion qu'elles portaient aux saints François, Antoine, et à sainte Claire'. Cette maison religieuse avait selon cet indult, été réformée par des Franciscains; son genre de vie s'était vraisemblablement aligné sur celui des Ordres mendiants, dont les religieuses avaient cherché à imiter la recherche de la pauvreté. Nous savons par le témoignage d'Amadi et par une bulle de Clément V qu'elles portaient un habit de drap 'vergé', blanc rayé d'une bande noire, avec des manches étroites, sans chemise, et qu'elles avaient pour coiffure un chaperon—vêtement qui rappelle un peu l'habit primitif des Carmes qui leur valait le surnom de 'Barrés'. Elles avaient à leur tête une prieure. Leur fondation est attribuée à *quidam vir sanctus*, ce qui paraît la rattacher à ce mouvement érémitique qui avait implanté plusieurs communautés masculines dans la Montagne Noire, près d'Antioche. Mais les *Carpitane*, réfugiées à Chypre sans doute depuis 1268, firent demander au pape Clément V par Ayton de Curch (l'historien Hayton) de prendre l'habit bénédictin (la coule et le voile noirs), d'avoir à leur tête une abbesse et non plus une prieure, et de changer le nom de leur maison en ajoutant au vocable de la Croix d'Antioche celui de Notre-Dame de Tortose (8 février 1308). Amadi ajoute que de nombreuses indulgences furent accordées aux bienfaiteurs du couvent, ce qui ne pouvait qu'y attirer les pèlerins, en quête précisément d'indulgences.[26]

Ces indulgences étaient sans doute attachées à la vénération d'une 'image de Notre-Dame qui avait été apportée de Tortose par les soins de soeur Echive de Bouillon, qui fut abbesse de ce dit monastère'.[27] Ce passage d'Amadi nous permet de rattacher cette vénération à celle dont était l'objet l'église de Tortose.[28] Un récit de voyage de 1285–1291 nous apprend qu' 'à 24 milles de Tripoli se trouve la cité d'Antarados, qu'on appelle vulgairement Tortose. Dans cette cité se trouve une petite chapelle, sise au milieu de la cathédrale ... On dit qu'elle a été construite par les apôtres Pierre et Jean en l'honneur de la sainte Vierge Marie. Elle est jusqu'à ce jour l'objet d'une grande vénération, et bien des miracles y interviennent par son intercession'.[29] Joinville s'y est rendu en pèlerinage, et il nous a laissé son témoignage: il y a vénéré ' le premier autel qui fut érigé sur la terre en l'honneur de la Mère de Dieu'; il rapporte aussi qu'on y amenait les hommes qui avaient le diable au corps pour obtenir leur guérison.[30]

Ceci nous ramène précisément au texte de Lusignan parlant d'une icône qui guérissait les 'démoniaques'. Joinville ne cite pas cette icône; mais le texte d'Amadi relatif au transfert de celle-ci confirme une autre tradition selon laquelle une image très ancienne, attribuée à saint Luc, était associée à l'autel érigé en l'honneur de la Vierge. C'est cette icône qu'aux alentours de 1291 la future abbesse Echive de Bouillon avait enlevée de Tortose et transportée à Nicosie.

Si notre hypothèse est exacte, 'Notre-Dame de Nicosie', proposée à la vénération des pèlerins, ne serait autre que l'antique image miraculeuse qui, à Tortose, attirait un "grand pèlerinage" dès les XIIe et XIIIe siècles. Que sa notoriété ait été suffisante pour qu'on l'eût inscrite parmi les buts assignés aux 'pèlerins forcés' des XIVe et XVe siècles n'aurait rien de surprenant.

12 rue Pelletier de Chambure, Dijon

NOTES

1. C. Vogel, 'Le pèlerinage pénitentiel', *Pellegrinaggi e culto dei santi in Europa fino alla prima crociata* (IV° Convegno del centro di studi sulla spiritualità medioevale, 1961, Todi 1963) 39–94.

2. J. Richard, 'Urbain II, la prédication de la croisade et la définition de l'indulgence', in Hehl, Seibert et Staab (eds.), *Deus qui mutat tempora, Festschrift Alfons Becker* (Sigmaringen 1987) 129–135.

3. D'après une chanson sur la prise de croix du roi, éditée par W. Meyer dans *Nachrichten der Kgl. Gesellschaft der Wissenschaften zu Göttingen*, 1907.

4. *Qui ad defensionem Terrae idoneus et ad hoc obsequium expeditus, suscepta poenitentia, biennio ibi ad defensionem terrae permanserit, et sudoris certaminis ad preceptum regis et majorum terrae pro amore Christi portaverit, remissionem injunctae poenitentiae se laetetur adeptum*—Alexandre III reprenait une disposition du Décret de Gratien, reprise par Alain de Lille, et visant spécialement les coupables d'incendies volontaires: *Poenitencia ei detur ut Hierosolymis aut in Hispania in servicio Dei per annum integrum permaneat*: Alain de Lille, *Liber poenitentialis*, ed. J. Longère (Analecta mediaevalia Namurcensia, 18, Louvain et Lille 1965) 64.

5. M. Purcell, *Papal Crusading Policy, 1244–1291* (Leiden 1975) 36–51, 99–103.

6. E. van Cauwenbergh, *Les pèlerinages expiatoires et judiciaires dans le droit communal de la Belgique au Moyen-Age* (Recueil de travaux publiés par les conférences d'histoire et de philologie, fasc. 48, Louvain 1922); J. van Herwaarden, *Opgelegde bedevarten* (Assen 1978).

7. M. Purcell (n.5) 116–117.

8. Un exemple de novembre 1296: le Parlement condamne les coupables d'un guet-apens dont a été victime le chambellan de Tancarville à divers pèlerinages (Saint-Thibault en Auxois, Notre-Dame de Boulogne, Notre-Dame de Chartres, Saint-Nicolas de Bari). Celui qui lui avait crevé un oeil devra se rendre à Chypre: E. Boutaric, *Arrêts du Parlement*, I, n°2992.

9. P. W. Edbury, *The Kingdom of Cyprus and the Crusades, 1191-1374* (Cambridge 1991).

10. E. van Cauwenbergh (n.6) 217–218; H. H. E. Wouters, *Grensland en Bruggehoofd* (Assen, 1970), 54–76 et appendice.

11. E. van Cauwenbergh (n.6) 67–68, 163; J. van Herwaarden (n.6) 54–73, etc.

12. Des Gantois, les Borluut, envoient deux pèlerins à Chypre pour y servir un an; le sire de la Gruthuse, en 1372, y envoie dix de ses valets.

13. Nombreux tarifs édités par les deux auteurs sus-mentionnés. A Bruxelles, on fixe le montant du rachat d'une demie année de séjour à Chypre pour 50 florins; à Louvain, en 1484 *een bedevert in Cypres* est racheté pour 50 patars; *een bedevert in Cypre ende jaar ende dach daer in te bliven* (séjour d'un an et un jour) 100 patars.

14. Ainsi des Gantois sont envoyés à Chypre avec l'ordre d'y rester jusqu'à leur rappel (E. van Cauwenbergh (n.6) 67–68), des Brugeois se voient assigner un séjour de trois ans à Chypre, d'un an à Venise ou à Naples.

15. Cf. les tarifs d'Alost ou de Termonde.

16. Cf. la réflexion de Hubertus Wouters (n.10) 54, à propos d'une mention de *tons Vrouwen te Nycossien in Sypers*, de 1401: J. van Herwaarden (n.6) 213, 135, 359.

17. Ibid., 631.

18. Cité par Georges Lengherand, lequel ajoute que ceux qui visitaient ce lieu pouvaient porter comme insigne de leur pèlerinage la roue, comme ceux qui étaient allés au tombeau de la sainte, au Sinaï, mais avec une différence dans la représentation, et décrit un certain nombre d'autres pèlerinages à accomplir dans l'île (*Voyage de Georges Lengherand, mayeur de Mons...*, éd. Marquis de Godefroy-Menilglaise (Mons 1861) 109 et suiv.).

19. J. Richard, 'The Cistercians in Cyprus' in M. Gervers (ed.)

The Second Crusade and the Cistercians, (New-York 1991) 199–203.

20. Lengherand signale qu'on vénérait chez les Dominicains la relique de la main de saint Luc.

21. Etienne de Lusignan, *Description de toute l'isle de Cypre* (Paris 1580) 64 v°.

22. Notre-Dame de Tyr (devenue un couvent de Bénédictins) Saint-Théodore, etc.

23. L. de Mas-Latrie, *L'île de Chypre. Sa situation présente, ses souvenirs du Moyen Age* (Paris 1879) 361.

24. T. J. Chamberlayne, *Lacrimae Nicossienses* (Paris 1893) 49–112 et 172. Cet auteur regardait N.-D. de Tortose comme l'église des Chartreuses à la suite de témoignages de voyageurs postérieurs à 1571; mais il a ensuite rectifié cette identification. La tradition, recueillie par G. Hill, *History of Cyprus*, vol 2, 3, n.6, rapporte que l'église dite *Tartugha*, d'abord convertie en magasin par les conquérants turcs, fut ensuite attribuée par ceux-ci à la communauté arménienne de Nicosie.

25. C. Enlart, *L'art gothique et de la Renaissance en Chypre* (Paris 1899), i, 142–156. Cf. J. Richard, 'Les comptes du collecteur de la Chambre apostolique dans le royaume de Chypre (1357–1363)' *Epeteris*, du Centre de Recherche Scientifique de Chypre, 13–16, (1984–1987) 39 et 47.

26. *Chroniques d'Amadi et de Strambaldi*, ed. L. de Mas-Latrie, I (Paris 1891), 292; Registres d'Alexandre IV, n°1777; *Regestum Clementis papae V*, n°2436. Sur le mouvement érémitique du XIIe siècle auquel se rattachaient la fondation de Jubin près d'Antioche, plus tard devenue cistercienne, Machanath et Carraria, cf. B. Z. Kedar, 'Gerard of Nazareth, a neglected 12th century writer in the Latin East: a contribution to the intellectual and monastic history of the Crusader states, *DOP*, 37 (1983) 5–77; A Jotischky, *The perfection of solitude. Hermits and Monks in the Crusader States* (Philadelphia 1995). Le nom de *Carpita* paraît être celui du lieu, sans doute très proche d'Antioche, où s'était établi ce monastère.

27. Amadi, loc. cit.

28. P. Deschamps, *Terre Sainte Romane* (La Pierre-qui-Vire 1964) 231–236 et planches; C. Enlart, *Les monuments des Croisés dans le royaume de Jérusalem* (Paris 1927–28), 2 vols. et 2 albums, ii, 395–426.

29. W. Neumann (ed.), *Philippi descriptio Terrae Sanctae* (Genève, 1880) 174. Cf. aussi Paulin Paris, *Guillaume de Tyr et ses continuateurs*, 411, 491. Burchard de Mont-Sion y a dit la messe, et Raymond, fils de Bohémond IV d'Antioche, y fut tué par des Assassins pendant qu'il y était en prière. Les auteur musulmans témoignent de la vénération des chrétiens envers l'église de Tortose quand ils rapportent le saccage de cette église par Saladin: *Recueil des historiens des croisades, Historiens Orientaux*, 3, 109.

30. *Vie de saint Louis*, ed. N. de Wailly (Paris 1874) § 118.

15

A Medieval Tombstone in the Paphos Museum

H. W. Catling

I am delighted by the invitation to contribute to this volume in honour of Peter Megaw, for whom I have great veneration as well as great affection. By chance, I spent much of my first day in Cyprus with him, in August 1950. I came to take part in the first season of the Ashmolean Museum's excavation at Myrtou, *Pigadhes*, under the direction of Joan du Plat Taylor. I had travelled from Venice on the *Campidoglio* at the same time as a houseguest to-be of Peter and Elektra Megaw; in meeting his guest at Limassol he had undertaken to take me under his wing and bring me to Nicosia. I then observed, without understanding, the fragment of a day in the life of the Director of Antiquities, Cyprus, a day of a kind with which I should later be very familiar. We went first to Limassol Castle, where Peter inspected progress on the building's conversion for use as a District Museum. We then went to Episkopi for lunch at the beautiful American Excavation House (now a local museum) with George McFadden, working at Kourion for Pennsylvania University, where the affairs of the American Expedition were discussed. Next came a visit to Kolossi Castle, where Peter consulted with Colonel Joe Last, at that time in charge of a conservation programme on the castle. Finally came a late afternoon drive to Nicosia. A year later I was back in Cyprus for two years *en famille* as a Travelling Scholar of the Worshipful Company of Goldsmiths; this had been made possible because Peter had agreed to act as supervisor of my postgraduate work on Bronze Age Cyprus to satisfy the Company's requirements. He, and Porphyrios Dikaios, Curator of the Cyprus Museum, gave me the run of the Department's records and the Museum's collections with a freedom and generosity I was too green to understand or appreciate. I remained in touch with Peter during an 18-month period working in Oxford, and early in 1955 I returned to Cyprus as a contract officer on Peter's staff in the Department of Antiquities, a role in which I continued until August 1959. Later still, I was to follow him, at one remove, as Director of the British School at Athens, an appointment he had filled with the greatest distinction from 1963–1968. Peter and Elektra continued to divide their time between Athens and Paphos during most of my Athens years, and we remained in close and regular touch. I continually benefited from his wise counsel, based on a lifetime's experience of Greece and Cyprus; while he never interfered, he never refused a request for help. From 1986 until after my retirement in 1989, Peter represented the Managing Committee in the annual selection process in Athens for the awards of the School's Centenary Bursaries, where his knowledge and experience made him a very shrewd elector. How much I owe to Peter over the years I cannot say, but the debt is immense; he has been an inspiring but self-effacing role-model, though I am acutely conscious of how far I have fallen short of his example.

The full extent of Peter Megaw's contribution to the preservation and understanding of Cyprus' cultural inheritance has not yet received adequate acknowledgement. During his Directorship of the Department of Antiquities, from 1936–1960, there was no area of the Island's past with which he failed to concern himself. He took close interest in the Department's excavations directed by Porphyrios Dikaios, and later, by younger colleagues; his encouragement and practical assistance did much to speed the publication of their work. But transcending his other achievements, has been his work of conservation and interpretation of the standing monuments of Early Christian, Byzantine, Lusignan and Venetian Cyprus. The list of monuments saved by his efforts from destruction or irreparable ruin is astonishing, as are his many successes in liquidating unsightly modern accretions which diminished the ancient buildings; nowhere was this work more effective than in Famagusta. All this is a reminder of the incomparable richness of Cyprus in the ecclesiastical, military and civil architecture of the Frankish East, from the cathedrals and churches of Nicosia and Famagusta, the exquisite Premonstratensian monastery of Bellapais, the harbour fortress of Kyrenia, the mountain castles of St. Hilarion, Buffavento and Kantara, town houses such as the so-called Musée Lapidaire in Nicosia, every one of which has benefited from Peter's care, skill and learning.

The subject of my paper has been chosen partly as a reminder of Peter's huge contribution to Frankish Cyprus in general, partly because of his devotion to Paphos and partly through my interest in the class of medieval monuments here discussed which goes back to my childhood; I hope it will be of interest to the honorand.

ACKNOWLEDGEMENTS

I am indebted to the late Frank Greenhill for a shared enthusiasm for the incised tombstones of Cyprus; my debt to his published work will be obvious. In the Paphos Museum I was generously assisted by Mr. Takis Herodotou. I am grateful to the Curator of the Cyprus Museums, Dr. Pavlos Flourentzos, for allowing me to publish the object described here and for the gift of the photograph reproduced as PLATE 15. Elizabeth Catling made the sketch, FIG. 15.

A MEDIEVAL TOMBSTONE IN THE PAPHOS MUSEUM

Cyprus is exceptionally rich in incised figural tombstones, on which the effigy of the deceased is engraved directly onto the cover-slab of a grave or tomb-chest. This class of monument was developed in western Europe,[1] where it was particularly widespread and popular from the 13th to 17th centuries. There was a fairly close relationship between incised slabs and monumental brasses.[2] On the latter the design was incised on latten plates, which were then attached to the actual tombstone. No brass has yet been reported in Cyprus. The use of incised slabs in Cyprus was introduced by the Lusignans and their followers; few are earlier than 1300. Such memorials were particularly popular during the 14th and earlier 15th centuries.

The medieval tombstones of Cyprus have attracted intermittent scholarly interest. One of the first to be published is the monument to Sir Brochard de Charpignie (*c.*1300) now in the Musée de Cluny, Paris, said to have been found in Larnaka in 1852.[3] An extended account, illustrated by the drawings of W. Williams, Chief Engineer of Cyprus, was published in 1894 by Major Tanquerville J. Chamberlayne.[4] Other references are to be found in the work of C. Enlart[5] and G. Jeffery.[6] R. Gunnis[7] has numerous references to the tombstones, in which he took a particular interest, having, it seems, been responsible for removing a large part of the important series in the Omariegh Mosque, Nicosia (the former Church of the Augustinians) to temporary storage in the Bedestan. Most recently, this material has been treated, though not exhaustively, by F. A. Greenhill,[8] whose indifferent health prevented him visiting Cyprus. Greenhill published a list of 197 tombstones and fragments, thirteen of which he illustrated, all but one based on heelball rubbings of the stones made for him by two friends in Cyprus between 1955–59.

The incised tombstones of Cyprus have had a chequered history since before the capture of the island by the Ottoman Turks in 1571: many must have perished in the destruction of churches wrought by the Venetian military engineers when Nicosia was fortified *de novo* in the 1560s, notable among them the church of the Monastery of St. Dominic, the mausoleum for many members of the ruling family. Relatively large though the surviving corpus of tombstones and fragments certainly is,[9] it can only represent a small fraction of what originally existed. Though the great majority of stones was undoubtedly located in the churches of Nicosia and Famagusta, examples are known from the other towns and, indeed, from churches in some of the villages.[10] Although some stones remain *in situ* (more or less) in the buildings for which they were designed (e.g. in the former Cathedral Church of St. Sophia, Nicosia, now the Selemiye Mosque; the Arab Achmet Mosque, Nicosia, built over the remains of an unidentified Latin church, in the Armenian Church, Nicosia, previously the Benedictine Abbey of Our Lady of Tyre; and in Famagusta, in the former Latin Cathedral Church of St. Nicholas, now the Lala Mustapha Mosque), many more have been removed, for one reason or another, for storage and/or exhibition in secular surroundings. During the 1950s, many of the stones removed earlier from the Church of the Augustinians (*supra*) to the Bedestan were transferred to the Medieval Museum established in the Topkhané, (also known as Kasteliotissa), which formed a part of the old palace of the Lusignan kings, in the vicinity of the Paphos Gate. Stones from St. Sophia were also brought to the Topkhané. Others remained in the Bedestan (Church of St. Nicholas). In 1984, during a visit to the grounds of the 18th century house of the Dragoman Hadjigeorgakis Kornessios in Nicosia, then under restoration, I noticed fragments of many tombstones lying loose; I imagine by this time they have been reinstated in more permanent fashion.

Under Peter Megaw's supervision, a register of tombstones and fragments was compiled in the Department of Antiquities, to record both those remaining *in situ*, those in one way or another relocated, and the *disiecta membra*. A large number of the stones was photographed; prints from these negatives are part of the photographic archive of the Cyprus Museum. In what follows, a number prefixed by 'T' refers to this list. Greenhill makes use of the T series of numbers in his list of Cyprus slabs.[11] It must be emphasized, however, that the handlist, at least in the form in which I had access to it, was not exhaustive.

The purpose of this paper is to draw attention to the fragment of a tombstone that came to light relatively recently in Paphos, where it is now displayed in the medieval gallery of the Paphos Museum (PLATE 15, FIG. 15). It was acquired in 1969 with other lapidary items, found by chance in Kato Paphos from time to time, from Eleni Lazarou, of Omirou Street, Paphos.[12] It has no close provenance, but its source is likely to have been one of the Latin churches of Kato Paphos.[13] The tombstone may be described as follows:-

Inventory no. Paphos museum 4/69
Fragment of blue limestone slab
Extant ht. .83m, extant w .42 m, thickness .21m
Extant ht of effigy .655m, extant w .40 m

The slab is broken all round. There is minor bruising

of the worked surface, leaving a few incised details blurred. It preserves the head, shoulders, part of the chest and left upper arm of a man wearing a hawberk of mail or scale armour.[14] The workmanship is rough and summary, the engraving, especially in the body outline, hesitant and erratic. As will be seen, the figure is unusual in several ways. Though the engraver made an attempt to show the rows of mail/scales in horizontal lines, the arrangement quickly became chaotic. The figure is frontal. The hair is cut short, leaving the ears fully exposed. There is either a small bald patch on the crown of the head, or a tonsure. There is a fringe on the upper forehead. The brow is shown by a curved line above each eye; there are Cypriot parallels for this device (e.g. T.43, an unknown girl of *c*.1370 = Greenhill pl. 140, but in many cases the brow lines are straight—e.g. T.93, Sir Joseph Vizas (1402) = Greenhill pl. 69a). The eyes are open; on many Cypriot effigies the eyes are closed, by means of a straight line for the top contour of the eye, a curved line for the lower—e.g. T.102, Sir Heude de Vis (*c*.1360) = Greenhill pl. 68a. Also unusual on our effigy is a curved line under each eye suggesting the lower limit of the eye socket, giving

some structure to the face. This feature is sometimes suggested by a brief horizontal stroke under each eye, e.g. no T number Marie, daughter of Sir Gautier de Bessan (1322) = Greenhill pl. 139a. The thin nose is prominent, and bulbed in normal fashion. There is damage to the mouth and the exact form is uncertain. The ears are prominent. In most Cypriot effigies the ears are concealed, either by head coverings or long hair. The head is set on a high, slender neck. The rest of the body is encased in armour, to which we shall return. Enough remains of the effigy for it to be certain that the hands were not at breast level joined in prayer, as is so frequently the case. Were we to understand the figure as recumbent, the hands might have been crossed at the wrists, resting on the abdomen, in a manner Greenhill notes as typical of some Italian military figures, e.g. Pietro Barrili (1320), in the Church of St. Lorenzo, Naples = Greenhill pl. 45c. But the open eyes suggest our figure is standing, in one of the postures in which armoured figures were from time to time portrayed —with sword in right hand, left resting on the top of a low-slung shield e.g. Heinrich *der Ungehorsame*, son of Landgraf Heinrich I of Hesse

FIG. 15.1: *Sketch of tombstone, Paphos Museum (ht. of effigy preserved 0.65m)*

PLATE 15.1: *Incised medieval tombstone, Paphos Museum (ht. of original 0.83m; photo. Dept. of Antiquities, Cyprus)*

(1298) in the Elisabethkirche, Marburg = Greenhill pl. 60c; and in a variant, a lance is held vertically by the right hand, the shield as before e.g. Sir Clelon de Sauz (1270), Fontaine-les-Dijon, France = Greenhill pl. 52a. In Cyprus, T.289 Sir Arnat Visconti (1397) = Greenhill pl. 68c, stands on two wyverns, heater–shaped shield held by the left hand (invisible behind it), sword in the right hand level with the left, both well below the waist.

Our figure comes from a part of Cyprus which, for all its medieval importance[15] has preserved fewer remains of the centuries of Lusignan and Venetian rule than any other. Symptomatic of this is the contrast between, on the one hand, the completely preserved Latin cathedrals of Famagusta and Nicosia, and the remaining fragment of the Latin cathedral of Paphos and, on the other, between the splendidly preserved castle of Kyrenia and the excavated remains of the late 12th century castle of Saranda Kolones at Paphos.[16] Also typical of this imbalance is the absence of medieval funerary monuments in Paphos. Jeffery[17] refers to 'a small and early gravestone' loose in the yard of the Church of the Panayia Theoskepasti, whose inscription refers to 'Bernart le fis de Sire George Lescrivam des Alemans', who died in 1247. He also cites[18] a second loose stone, undated, in the church of Ayios Yeoryios inscribed for Harior(?) Bedouin and his father. In neither case is there a reference to an effigy. Our fragment could be the first figural medieval tombstone recovered from Paphos.

The armour is unusual. It appears to consist of a hawberk, with plain, narrow collar fitting closely at the base of the neck; the hawberk is composed of either chain mail or scales (*infra*). At mid–shoulder level there appears to be a narrow, horizontal fillet, picked out by a zig-zag pattern. In addition, some kind of narrow horizontal band appears on the upper arm, just below the shoulder. Though military effigies on tombstones in the West wearing a mail hawberk are normally also shown wearing a surcoat over the hawberk (cf. for instance, the two figures (*c.*1270) on a slab at Jerpoint Abbey, Eire, = Greenhill pl. 44c), there are examples with no surcoat, e.g. Alars de Cimai, (*c.*1210), Vireux-Molhain, Ardennes, France, = Greenhill pl. 45b. From Cyprus, Brochard de Charpignie (*c.*1300) (*supra*) wears a hawberk, but no surcoat, though he has a puzzling item covering the hawberk at breast-level. Many similarly armed figures are shown with mail head-covering, *(coif-de-mailles)*, either in place on the head (as in Brochard de Charpignie, *supra*, or Sir Eudes de Frolois (1309), Abbaye de Fontenay, Côte d'Or, France = Greenhill, pl. 50a), or thrown back from the head resting in folds on the upper shoulder (as in Sir Robert d'Urville (*c.*1325), Gouvix, Calvados, France = Greenhill pl. 52c). In other representations, the *coif* is missing, but the hawberk has a high, integral collar, as Pierre de Pedoy (1334), Gouzangrez, Val d'Oise, France = Greenhill pl. 54c.

The shoulder-fillet, with zig-zag ornament, remains puzzling. Perhaps it is no more than it appears to be, a decorative border to relieve the monotony of the mail/scale surface of the hawberk. I do not know a parallel. Suppose we associate the fillet with the band on the upper arm, could we relate the two to the manner in which the top of the surcoat is represented? (e.g. Sir Nicoles des Armoises (1303), Château 'Les Rosiers', Séchault, Ardennes, France = Greenhill pl. 49b). That is to say, the 'fillet' is the border at the top of the surcoat, while the band on the arm is the lower edge of the left arm-hole of the surcoat. This would assume that the engraver made a serious blunder in which he somehow conflated the convention for showing the entire hawberk with the convention for showing the surcoat over the hawberk. There is a further possibility. We have here *two* pieces of protective armour, both of mail/scale. One is an undergarment, in the form of a sleeved vest, on the shoulders and arms of which was mail/scale of which we merely see the part covering the body from neck to mid-shoulder and the arm; the second a surcoat to which mail/scale has been attached. With neither of these suggestions am I particularly impressed. I set them out, however, to show that it is not necessary to dismiss the Paphos figure as nonsensical.

Even now we are not at the end of the unusual features of the Paphos slab. Normally in Cyprus one would expect such a figure to stand or lie beneath a canopy;[19] there is room to the left for the shaft; there is room overhead for part of the pediment. Frequently in Cyprus there was a conflation of marginal inscription and canopy, so that the text starts at the foot of the dexter shaft, extends round the outline of the pediment, and, if necessary, completes itself down the sinister shaft (e.g. no T number Sir Pierre Leiaune (1343), Arab Achmet Mosque, Nicosia = Greenhill pl. 67b). The latter practice is not, of course, unvarying and the text may appear as the (elsewhere) more normal marginal inscription e.g. Sir Arnat Visconti (1397). Here however, and on other Cypriot examples, there has not been space on the slab for both the inscription and the shafts. The shafts were therefore sacrificed, and the canopy begins at the level of the capitals. This device is also seen on the slab for Sir Joseph Vizas (1402) *supra*.

The unusual features of our slab may be summarised:

i. The open eyes suggest the figure is standing.

ii. He has short hair, against Greenhill's observation[20] '(sc Military) figures are usually shown bareheaded, with long flowing hair down to about 1370, after which it begins to be worn shorter, being cut to ear length by about 1400.'

iii. The hair itself, cut very short and straight, the bald patch/tonsure, and the fringe, stands apart from other hair-styles in Cyprus.

iv. His hands are not folded in the standard position of prayer.

v. His armour is difficult to interpret. I am not aware of a parallel in Cyprus.

vi. Though there is space on what remains of the slab, there is no trace of coat-of-arms, inscription, or canopy.

Among the surviving corpus of figural tombstones in Cyprus there is certainly much variety in the quality of engraving, from the excellence of Sir Arnat Visconti (1397), and the fragment of Sir Hodra Prevan (c.1400), once in St. Sophia and more recently in the Bedestan store, via the clumsy proportions of Sir Jospeh Vizas (1402) *supra*, to the extremely crude figure of a woman who perhaps died in childbirth, uncertain date, now in the Limassol Museum = Greenhill pl. 139b. Undoubtedly, close study of the material would suggest workshop groupings, or, at least, groupings where engravers were clearly following the same patterns. For instance:-

Sir Pierre Leiaune (1343), Arab Achmet Mosque, Nicosia takes with him, almost certainly, the fragment of

Sir Raoul de Blanche Garde (c.1340) St. Sophia, Nicosia. There are differences in detail, but unimportant.

A more substantial group, whose dates, both actual and suggested, cover half a century, is represented by a normally canopied figure in armour, frontal, recumbent, feet well separated, hands joined in prayer on the breast, long haired, eyes closed, surcoat over mixed armour, the base garment of which may be a mail/scale hawberk, sheathed sword lain on the body, hilt on the abdomen, point between the heels, partly covered by blazoned heater-shaped shield, of which eight examples, arranged in chronological order are:

T.31 Sir John Tenouri (1341) formerly in the Church of the Augustinians, Nicosia.

T.52 Unidentified (canopy, head and shoulders) (c.1350) Nicosia.

T.35 Sir Thomas Prevost (c.1360) formerly in the Church of the Augustinians.

T.21 Sir Philipe de Milmars (c.1360) formerly in the Church of the Augustinians.

T.102 Sir Heude de Vis (c.1360) formerly in the Church of the Augustinians = Greenhill pl. 68a

T.259 Sir Thomas de Montholif (1363) St. Sophia, Nicosia.

T.69 Sir John Antiaum (c.1385) formerly in the Church of the Augustinians.

T.95 Sir Aigue de ?Bessan (c.1390) ?formerly in the Church of the Augustinians.

It will be noticed that all these are from Nicosia; more than half of them come from the same church. The Paphos slab stands apart from both these groups, whose workshops are likely to have been located in Nicosia. Different again is Sir Brochard de Charpignie (c.1300), *supra*, said to have been found in Larnaka. Unfortunately, there are no available illustrations of the one or two military figures surviving in Famagusta, of which one, for Salvo, son of ?Giovanni Bramini, is in the Cathedral of St. Nicholas.[21] Another is mentioned by Jeffery[22] who describes it as a, '... figure of a knight in plate armour, holding his shield on which are the Prevost arms...'. It seems in general, characteristic of Famagusta that some of its effigies were executed at a much smaller scale than those of Nicosia.[23] Though there are suggestive pointers in that direction, the evidence is at present inadequate to argue strongly for distinct regional styles among the medieval tombstones of Cyprus.

In his discussion of the representation of war-gear on incised tombstones, Greenhill[24] refers to the depiction of what he took to be scale armour on the memorials of Cyprus. He says:-

In Cyprus ... during the first half of the fourteenth century, scales were evidently a normal alternative to mail, and several ... portray complete panoplies of scale-work. Sir Balien Lambert ... wears hawberk, hose and gloves of scale, with schynbalds of plate or leather and linen surcoat.

Greenhill continues by describing the plate and/or leather accessories which are worn by other Cypriot examples with their scale hawberks and linen surcoats. A casual glance at a figure like that of Sir Heude de Vis (c.1361), part of whose hawberk is visible, certainly suggests scale-plates rather than chain mail. I am inclined to believe, however, that this is as likely to be an engraver's shorthand-method for representing mail as carefully observed real-life armour composed of scales. Here it is noteworthy that the very different style of engraving employed on the monument for Brochard de Charpignie (c.1300) shows unquestionable chain mail, using an engraving convention similar to that employed on western tombstones e.g. Richard de Jaucourt (1340), Saint-Seine-l'Abbaye, Côte d'Or, France = Greenhill pl. 55b. The chain mail used in the aventail worn by Sir Arnat Visconti (1397), St. Sophia *supra*, is engraved in the same unmistakeable fashion but, again, the Visconti monument comes from a very different workshop tradition from those depicting the supposed scale armour. I believe the evidence provided by the new Paphos monument goes far to endorse the view that many Cypriot tomb engravers depicted chain mail in such a fashion as to mislead us into interpreting what we see as scale armour.

I have left until last the date at which this tombstone was engraved. Its many unusual features make this additionally difficult. Almost the only criterion must be the type of armour; as Greenhill's observation about the length of hair worn by military men in Cyprus seems inappropriate. The figure cannot possibly be as late as 1400, the date by which knights' hair is supposed to have retired above their ears. I interpret the engraving as a representation of chain mail, whether one or two garments are intended. The figure is almost certainly standing. Greenhill[25] notes this as a feature of the tombstones of England, France and Flanders up to *c*.1280, whereafter ' ... the figure is usually shown with hands joined in prayer ...'. (He adds, however, that free-standing military figures are the norm in Germany and Scandinavia until well into the sixteenth century.) The period of transition from mail armour to plate armour begins, certainly in France and the Low Countries *c*.1320; perhaps our figure was engraved no later than this date. I see little hope of selecting an upper limit. I propose, with reservations, that the stone be dated to 1300 plus or minus 20 years. If such a date is anywhere near correct the man commemorated should have been born well after the earthquake at Paphos which destroyed the Frankish Castle, the excavation and interpretation of which has been one of Peter Megaw's major contributions to the archaeology of medieval Cyprus.

Langford

ADDENDUM

This paper was submitted in 1994. I have subsequently wondered whether I am wrong to see the figure as a representation of the deceased. Might it have been, instead, an ancillary figure—an archangel, say, or a military saint—in a much larger composition. There is a kind of parallel, described but not illustrated by Greenhill, II, 72—'Christ throned in glory, with B. V. M. to dexter and St. John to sinister, both standing, and a knight of the Lusignan family in heraldic surcoat kneeling on either flank, placed in an arcade of five bays. Apparently on of the long sides of a royal tomb-chest.' There is a heelball rubbing of this stone in the Greenhill Collection in the Society of Antiquaries. The original should still be in the Topkhané (Kasteliotissa), Nicosia.

I remain exercised concerning the conventions used by engravers in Cyprus to represent scale of mail armour. While mail is undoubtedly shown on some slabs, there are others where scale seems more likely. Unfortunately, our Paphos stone is ambivalent.

NOTES

1.   F. A. Greenhill, *Incised Effigial Slabs*, 2 vols (London 1976) hereafter 'Greenhill'.
2.   For example, M. Norris, *Monumental Brasses: The Craft* (London 1978). See now S. Badham and M. Norris, *Early Incised Slabs and Brasses from the London Marblers* (London [Soc. Of Antiquaries] 1999).
3.   W. F. Creeny, *Illustrations of Incised Slabs on the Continent of Europe* (London 1891) 19, hereafter 'Creeny'. Creeny dated the stone to '*c*.1270'; the date was revised by Greenhill, vol II, 113.
4.   *Lacrimae Nicossienses*, Paris.
5.   *L'Art Gothique et la Renaissance en Chypre* (Paris 1899).
6.   *A Description of the Historic Monuments of Cyprus* (Nicosia 1918) hereafter 'Jeffery'.
7.   *Historic Cyprus* (London 1936; second edition 1947).
8.   Greenhill, especially vol I, 41–44.
9.   Greenhill, vol II, 1 had note of 737 incised slabs in England.
10. For example, the tombstone of Simone, wife of Sir Renier de Gibelet (1302), in the Latin S chapel attached to the Church of the Panayia Angeloktisti at Kiti = Greenhill, pl. 138c.
11. Greenhill, vol II, 69–81.
12. The circumstances are referred to in Minute Paper 1/3/69.
13. Sadly little of medieval Paphos remains above ground. A fragment survives of the Latin Cathedral in the northeast sector of the town. The plan of the church of the Franciscans has been recovered by excavation, immediately adjacent to, and north of, the great basilican church of Chrysopolitissa in the southeast sector of the town. Churches of the Augustinians, of St. Peter and of St. Nicholas are known to have existed, but have yet to be identified on the ground.
14. For an account of medieval armour depicted in incised slabs see Greenhill, vol I, 129–189.
15. F. G. Maier and V. Karageorghis, *Paphos: History and Archaeology* (Nicosia 1984) 300–324.
16. A. H. S. Megaw, 'Progress in Early Christian and Medieval Archaeology', *Archaeology in Cyprus 1960–1985*, ed. V. Karageorghis (Nicosia 1985) 292–298.
17. Jeffery, 404.
18. Jeffery, 404.
19. Greenhill, vol I, 42–43.
20. Greenhill, vol II, 71.
21. Greenhill, vol II, 73.
22. Jeffery, 152.
23. Personal observation – H. W. C.
24. Greenhill, vol I, 156–157.
25. Greenhill, vol I, 133–134.

16

Notes sur quelques monuments de Famagouste
à la fin du Moyen Age

Catherine Otten-Froux

Si l'île de Chypre à l'époque médiévale a toujours suscité de nombreux travaux depuis l'ouvrage de Louis de Mas Latrie,[1] l'étude de l'urbanisme et plus précisément de la topographie des villes chypriotes a été très peu abordée. Cependant à l'imitation des études d'histoire urbaine qui se sont développées pour l'Europe occidentale, Nicosie d'une part,[2] et surtout la ville et le port de Famagouste ont attiré l'attention des historiens ces dernières années. C'est à cette dernière ville que je souhaite m'attacher. L'observation des monuments encore existants et surtout l'étude des documents d'archives ont permis de préciser un certain nombre de points, qui firent l'objet de publications récentes.[3] La base de toute recherche dans ce domaine reste cependant l'ouvrage pionnier de Camille Enlart,[4] bien que surtout consacré à l'histoire de l'art et à la description des monuments de Chypre. Ce travail est repris et complété par endroit par George Jeffery.[5] Malheureusement aucune fouille systématique n'a jamais été menée dans la ville et même les travaux considérables de déblaiement entrepris dans la zone des remparts et particulièrement autour de la porte de Limassol, et les consolidations effectuées peu avant la deuxième guerre mondiale par le Département des Antiquités, n'ont pas suffi à éclaircir les zones d'ombres qui subsistent concernant l'identification de certaines églises encore en ruines.[6]

Les XIVe et XVe siècles constituent une période intéressante car la ville a connu d'abord un essor formidable en relation avec la perte de la Terre Sainte par les Francs, l'île de Chypre devenant un refuge pour les populations de Syrie-Palestine et la dernière plaque tournante aux mains des Chrétiens pour les échanges commerciaux avec l'Orient musulman.[7] Très rapidement le port de Famagouste est devenu le principal port de l'île, supplantant Limassol; la ville et ses habitants ont fait l'admiration des voyageurs, et attiré des convoitises. A cette période de prospérité, succède un long déclin lorsqu'après la guerre de 1373–1374 entre Gênes et les forces royales de Pierre II, la ville doit être confiée aux Génois comme gage des paiements du roi, ainsi que le stipule le traité d'octobre 1374. Gênes va alors administrer Famagouste pendant 9 ans, avant d'en recevoir la pleine possession à la suite du traité de février 1383, et d'en faire, jusqu'en 1464, une colonie complètement autonome des possessions des Lusignan, un véritable état dans l'état.[8] Par chance ces deux siècles ont laissé de nombreuses sources, publiées et inédites, qu'il s'agisse des chroniques,[9] des récits de voyageurs,[10] des actes notariés.[11] ou des registres de l'administration génoise de la ville et notamment de la Trésorerie, la *Massaria*.[12] Les mentions d'institutions religieuses y sont fréquentes. Effectivement les églises étaient nombreuses à Famagouste. Certaines ont pu être identifiées par C. Enlart. Depuis presqu'aucun progrès n'a été réalisé en la matière en raison du manque de données archéologiques et de l'absence d'indication topographique fiable dans les sources plus récemment publiées. Mon but ici n'est pas de donner une description complète de la ville pendant la période génoise, plus modestement je souhaiterais formuler quelques remarques et hypothèses concernant certaines églises peu connues, la localisation ou l'identification de tel ou tel bâtiment religieux, en utilisant les sources génoises inédites du XVe siècles. Une des difficultés réside d'ailleurs dans l'existence probable de plusieurs églises dédiées à un même saint, en particulier ceux vénérés à la fois dans l'Eglise romaine et dans les Eglises orientales, par exemple saint Antoine.[13]

L'ÉGLISE SAINTE-CATHERINE

Les documents génois nous renseignent sur une église dédiée à sainte Catherine, à laquelle est attaché un hôpital. Elle apparaît dans un document du 11 mai 1452, lorsque le notaire Antonio Foglieta rédige l'inventaire de ce qui se trouve dans la sacristie, l'église et l'hôpital. Le notaire ignore le nom du fondateur dont les armoiries sont visibles sur des objets, à côté de celles de la famille de Camilla.[14] Grâce à d'autres documents, nous savons que l'église a été construite à la fin du XIVe siècle par Joseph Zaphet, un marchand bien connu de Famagouste, qui s'est enrichi dans le commerce entre l'Orient et l'Occident, trafiquant notamment avec des marchands de Barcelone,[15] et qui s'est installé en 1364 à Montpellier, où il devient bourgeois de la ville;[16] il rédige son testament le 8 octobre 1381 et institue comme exécuteurs testamentaires Eliano et Enrico de Camilla, génois, qui donnent procuration le 20 février 1383 à Luchino Cigalla et Giuliano de Castro pour repérer, faire réparer et louer les maisons qu'avait autrefois Joseph Zaphet dans l'île.[17] Le soin de l'église Sainte-Catherine et de son hôpital a été confié aux chanoines de l'église cathédrale de Gênes, qui en 1466 doivent choisir un administrateur parmi les héritiers d'Enrico ou d'Eliano de Camilla conformément au testament de Joseph Zaphet.[18] En 1452, les possessions de l'église sont alors les suivantes d'après l'inventaire dressé par Antonio Foglieta:[19]

dans la sacristie une grande caisse où sont les choses suivantes: trois calices d'argent avec leurs patènes dorées dans leur étui de cuir, un encensoir[20] d'argent avec son étui en cuir, un petit récipient (*bacile*)[21] en argent avec les armes de la famille de Camilla et d'autres dont on dit qu'elles sont celles du donateur qui a auparavant construit cette église, deux burettes en argent pour l'autel. De même quatre corporaux. De même deux petites nappes (*mandili*) tissés de soie et d'or. De même deux nappes de soie legères et vertes, telles quelles. De même un parement de velours cramoisi travaillé d'or à la byzantine (*bisantiati ex auro*) pour le maître autel. De même *frexium* ?[22]... [lacune dans le manuscrit] pour le dit autel avec quatre figures de saints et avec les armes de Camilla et du patron de l'église. De même deux parements pour les autels secondaires, pour la moitié rouge travaillé à la byzantine, et l'autre moitié de velours bleu. De même trois parements verts, un pour le maître autel et les deux autres pour les autels secondaires. De même un *puniale*[23] à la byzantine de velours rouge et or avec son *frexium* d'or. De même une chasuble de velours rouge travaillé d'or à la byzantine avec aube (*camixia*), étole et manipule à la byzantine comme ci-dessus, et un cordon de soie rouge. De même deux tuniques (*tunice*) de velours rouge travaillé d'or à la byzantine, c'est-à-dire pour le diacre et le sous-diacre. De même une chasuble de bocassin blanc avec une croix rouge. De même une chasuble de toile bleue avec une croix blanche. De même une chasuble de soie avec des figures (*affigurate* = damassé?) presque toute déchirée. De même une chasuble de bocassin blanc avec une croix bleue. De même deux aubes de toiles munies de leurs étoles, manipules et autres. De même, une étole de soie rouge et bleue, et un *orraitum*.[24] De même trois surplis (*cote*) de toile blanche. De même hors de la caisse deux grands candelabres de bronze pour des torches. De même un grand chandelier de fer. De même une croix de fer avec sa *grimpa*[25] qui est normalement au sommet de l'église.

Dans l'église, il y a deux tentures en coton blanc et bleu pour le maître autel, de part et d'autre, avec leurs tringles de fer. De même trois parements de coton bleu avec des croix blanches pour les autels. De même neuf nappes légères et grandes pour les autels, telles quelles. De même une autre nappe assez grande. De même un lutrin de bois pour chanter. De même quatre bancs. De même deux petites cloches. De même trois candelabres de bronze pour le maître autel. De même quatre petits chandeliers de fer. De même un petit récipient de bronze. De même une croix de bois doré pour l'autel. De même quatre tapis troués, tels quels. De même un grand missel de l'ordre des Prêcheurs. De même un autre petit missel romain. De même deux bréviaires. De même un livre appelé collectaire, dans lequel sont les prières des Saints. De même un psautier. De même un grand livre appelé graduel. De même un petit livre de papier, de peu d'épaisseur et de peu de valeur contenant la bénédiction nuptiale. De même deux vieux cahiers, tels quels. De même un livre appelé graduel. De même un petit missel,

tel quel. De même un psautier presque tout déchiré, tel quel. De même un breviaire, tel quel. De même un grand lectionnaire qui commence par '*In illo tempore stabat Iohannes*' écrit en lettres noires.[26] De même un grand antiphonaire. De même un tissu sur la croix qui est au milieu de l'église.

Dans la salle de l'hôpital, il y a une caisse ou grand '*sospitale*'. De même onze petits morceaux de vieille toile déchirée de valeur à peu près nulle, qui étaient, dit-on, des draps. De même trois paires de draps de toile tels quels. De même quinze écuelles ou '*sananirii*' d'étain. De même onze bols (*gradereti*) d'étain. De même 3 récipients de bois (*tagerii lignei*) De même trois chaudrons, un grand et deux petits. De même un sceau (*rexentale*) pour puiser l'eau. De même deux sceaux de bois pour l'eau. De même un coffre ferré. De même une petite table avec ses trétaux. De même deux vieilles caisses assez grandes. De même un coffre ferré sans couvercle, tel quel. De même quatre paires de draps neufs de toile de chanvre de trois pièces chacun.[27] De même trois paires de draps neufs de lin de trois pièces. De même 8 matelas. De même huit bonnes couvertures et deux vieilles. De même sept coussins pleins de laine. De même, huit pressoirs, et un autre tel quel. De même dix bancs. De même deux grandes jarres (*ydria*) ou *pitarrea*. De même deux grandes perches (*trabes seu bordonarii*).

L'hôpital semble de dimension modeste, puisque l'on ne compte que huit matelas. On ignore malheureusement la raison de la réalisation de cet inventaire, de même que la localisation de cette église à Famagouste.

Parmi les églises citées dans les documents génois du XVe siècle, plusieurs reçoivent régulièrement tous les deux mois des gratifications de la part des autorités génoises de Famagouste au moment de la distribution des soldes et des aumônes; elles sont répertoriées dans les registres de la *Massaria* à partir de 1391. Les listes varient peu; on retrouve à chaque fois Saint-François, Saint Dominique, Saint-Augustin, Sainte-Marie du Carmel, Sainte-Claire, Sainte-Marie-de-Tyr, Sainte-Marie-de-Tortose, l'hôpital Saint-Etienne; en 1391 il faudrait rajouter Sainte-Marie-Madeleine et Saint-Lazare, qui disparaissent par la suite, en 1442 et 1443 Saint-Jean,[28] et en 1445, Sainte-Marie de Bethléem.[29] A cette liste il faut ajouter d'autres bâtiments religieux comme Sainte-Marie de Mistachiel, qui donne son nom à un quartier,[30] Sainte-Barbara qui doit être démolie en 1461,[31] Saint-Jacques-des-Grecs cité comme repère pour la localisation d'une maison,[32] une chapelle dédiée à Saint-Lazare dont les revenus vont à l'église cathédrale Saint-Nicolas[33], Saint-Cosme-et-Damien[34] une église des Saints-Apôtres,[35] Saint-André, proche de Sainte-Marie de Tyr,[36] une église du Saint-Sauveur, proche de Saint-Nicolas,[37] Saint-Ciprien,[38] Saint-Siméon, qui est une église grecque,[39] Saint Luc,[40] Saint Serge.[41] On connaît une *contrata sancti Suzomani*.[42] L'église Saint-Georges des Grecs est attestée en 1438 et 1439, quand elle reçoit les revenus d'une vigne de Nicolo Asar, soit une végète de vin.[43]

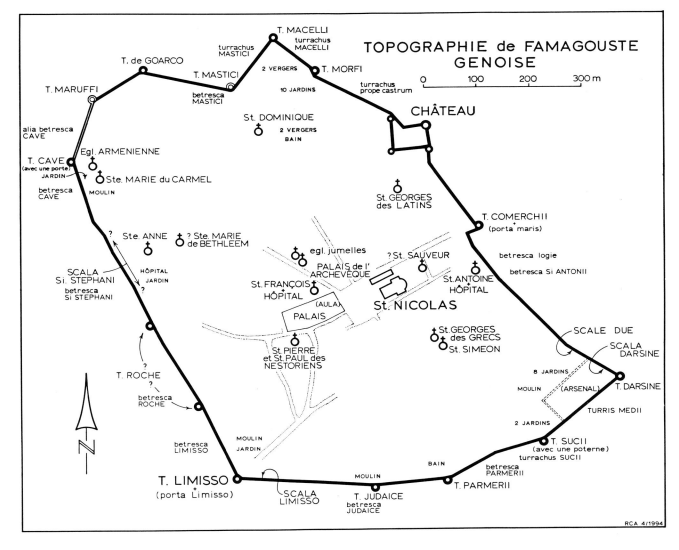

FIG. 16: *Plan de Famagouste génoise*

L'ÉGLISE SAINT-PIERRE-ET-SAINT-PAUL ET L'ÉGLISE DES DOMINICAINS

L'église Saint-Pierre-et-Saint-Paul est citée à plusieurs reprises; c'est une église nestorienne qui possède des maisons dans la ville; le 7 avril 1456, Timothée, archevêque de Tarse, loue *a livello* pour 29 ans à Antonio Cigalla pour sa fille, une maison appartenant à l'église Saint-Pierre-et-Saint-Paul pour 40 besants annuels.[44] L'église des Nestoriens, sans précision du vocable, est également citée dans un acte du 4 novembre 1439.[45] Les documents génois ne fournissent aucun élément quant à sa localisation. S'agit-il bien du bâtiment qui est maintenant connu sous ce vocable d'après l'identification de C. Enlart,[46] et que nous avons indiqué comme tel sur notre plan? T. Mogabgab indiquait avoir vu des traces d'inscriptions en syriaque à l'intérieur lors de travaux de nettoyage et acceptait cette identification.[47] Mais l'église connue sous le nom de Ayios Yeorghios Exorinos contient également des inscriptions en syriaque et a aussi été attribuée aux Nestoriens.[48] Y a-t-il deux églises nestoriennes? Une des deux est-elle une église jacobite dont nous savons qu'il existait une communauté à Famagouste?[49] Par ailleurs, il faut se rappeler qu'en 1300 il y avait déjà une église Saint-Pierre-et-Saint-Paul dont le prêtre était un certain Dimitri;[50] était-elle alors déjà une église d'une communauté orientale? Les documents génois ne permettent pas de répondre à cette interrogation, ils ne fournissent que la preuve du passage de l'évêque de Tarse Timothée et l'existence d'une église nestorienne dédiée à Saint-Pierre et Saint-Paul.

En tout cas l'hypothèse récemment émise par P. W. Edbury de l'identification de l'édifice actuellement connu sous le vocable de Saint-Pierre-et-Saint-Paul avec l'église des Dominicains ne peut être retenue pour plusieurs raisons.[51] La première est l'existence d'inscriptions en syriaque trouvées par T. Mogabgab, dont nous venons de parler. La seconde raison repose sur les indications topographiques trouvées dans la documentation génoise. Dans certains cas les localisations sont données par rapport aux tours des remparts de la ville, c'est pourquoi il faut ici faire une parenthèse et en dire quelques mots. Nous avons indiqué sur notre plan (FIG. 16) les noms des tours tels qu'ils apparaissent dans les registres de la *Massaria* du milieu du XVe siècle, à l'occasion de l'enregistrement du versement des soldes aux hommes postés sur les remparts. L'ordre d'énumération est toujours le même en commençant par la tour de l'Arsenal situé dans l'angle sud-est de la ville. Les travaux menés avant la seconde guerre mondiale par le Département des Antiquités ayant montré que dans les tours examinées qui remontent à la période vénitienne, des structures plus anciennes étaient toujours présentes[52] nous nous sommes trouvés confortés dans notre reconstitution qui suit le tracé actuel des murs et respecte les tours actuelles à l'exception du bastion Martinengo bien entendu, dont nous connaissons la construction par les Vénitiens. En ce qui concerne le mur nord, l'actuel bastion San Luca, à l'ouest, près de l'église des Arméniens, devait correspondre à la tour Cava,[53] la tour Maruffi a disparu lors de la construction du bastion Martinengo, la tour de Goarco correspond à l'actuel bastion del Mozzo, la tour du Mastic a disparu, mais elle est encore citée et située à la place que nous lui avons donnée, sur le plan publié par Frigerio,[54] la tour

PLATE 16.1*a*: *Linteau du portail sud de l'église dite des Hospitalliers.*

Macelli correspond à l'actuelle tour Diamante, la tour Morfi à la tour Signoria.[55] La zone de la ville entre la tour du Mastic et la tour Morfi devait être peu peuplée; il en est ainsi sur les gravures du XVIe siècle où l'on voit les soldats y manoeuvrer; dans les documents génois on y dénombre 10 jardins, 2 vergers. Par ailleurs il y a également une place appelée *platea Morfi*. J'émettrai l'hypothèse que le nom de la tour ainsi que de la place vient de la présence d'un palais ayant appartenu au comte de Morphou.[56] C'est à partir de cette place que l'on peut situer Saint-Dominique.[57] Dans les descriptions des possessions de la commune de Gênes, on signale attenant à cette place les bains Saint-Dominique.[58] C'est pourquoi je placerai l'église des frères prêcheurs dans cette zone, c'est-à-dire au bout de la rue qui part de la place entre la cathédrale et le palais royal, ce qui est en accord avec le texte de la chronique d'Amadi signalant les remaniements d'Amaury[59] et avec les indications du plan de Gibellino. Pourquoi ne pas supposer qu'il s'agit de l'église appelée Ayia Photou et que Enlart identifiait avec Sainte Claire?[60] Toutefois la petite taille de l'église pourrait se révéler un obstacle à cette identification. Lorsque des travaux ont été fait à cet endroit en 1937–1939, T. Mogabgab laissait entendre qu'il pensait que ce bâtiment avait servi plutôt à une communauté d'hommes, malheureusement il n'apporta jamais les preuves de sa supposition.[61] Quant à l'église des Clarisses, elle est en construction en 1333,[62] et donne son nom à un quartier cité pour la localisation d'une maison en 1390.[63]

SAINT-ETIENNE ET SAINT-ANTOINE

Il existe aussi une église Saint-Etienne avec un hôpital;[64] il est impossible de la situer avec exactitude, mais sachant qu'une portion du rempart ouest porte le nom de saint Etienne (*scala et betrescha Sancti Stephani* entre *turris Roche* et *turris Cave*), on peut supposer que l'établissement religieux se trouvait au milieu de la partie ouest de la ville, à proximité des remparts (cf. le plan). Giovanni Raù dans son testament rédigé en 1333 lui lègue 150 besants blancs et rappelle que son père faisait partie de cette fraternité.[65] Nicolas Martoni y assiste à l'office.[66] Cet hôpital est souvent cité dans les documents du XVe siècle. Il reçoit régulièrement une gratification de la part du gouvernement génois de Famagouste, son nom apparaît sur toute les listes de paiement d'aumônes dans les registres de la *Massaria*.[67] En janvier 1440, Giorgio Mesant est *gubernator* de cet hôpital,[68] alors qu'en 1441, le prêtre Ventura Misach et frère Antoine, prieur de Sainte Marie du Carmel sont gouverneurs de l'église Saint Etienne.[69] L'église Saint-Etienne possède des biens, notamment une petite maison qui est louée en novembre 1453.[70] L'hôpital est encore cité en 1454.[71]

Il faut aussi se pencher sur le cas de Saint-Antoine. Il existait très probablement plusieurs bâtiments religieux dédié à ce saint populaire aussi bien en

Orient qu'en Occident. La première église des Templiers était dédiée à ce saint.[72] Il existait aussi un monastère copte à Famagouste dont l'église était dédiée à saint Antoine.[73] Enfin un hôpital Saint-Antoine situé près de la mer et dont il reste encore quelques ruines était bien connu des voyageurs et recevait des legs testamentaires. M. Balard et P. Edbury ont rassemblé les renseignements le concernant.[74] En janvier 1440, frère *Iohannes de Candia* est prieur du monastère de Saint-Antoine à Famagouste.[75]

L'EGLISE DES HOSPITALLIERS

Une dernière église va maintenant retenir notre attention: une des deux 'églises jumelles', celle connue sous le nom d'église des Hospitalliers. Dans une des rues qui débouchent sur la place entre la cathédrale Saint-Nicolas et le palais, et proche de cette place, se trouvent deux églises voisines, de petite taille, attribuées par C. Enlart aux Hospitalliers et aux Templiers (voir plan).

Il existait au XVe siècle à Famagouste une église de l'ordre de Saint-Jean-de-Jérusalem. A. Luttrell relève que le 13 août 1406, frère Antonio Zeni a reçu une licence pour partir de Rhodes et être chapelain dans l'église Saint-Jean de Famagouste.[76] Comme nous l'avons dit plus haut, en 1442 et en 1443, l'église Saint-Jean reçoit de modestes gratifications (20 besants par *paga*) de la part de l'administration génoise de Famagouste; au même moment des réparations y sont faites, financées par la commune.[77] En 1443, un religieux dominicain se dit *gubernator ecclesie Sancti Iohannis*.[78] En 1456, quatre livres de l'église Saint-Jean sont déposés dans la chambre du capitaine Lamba Doria.[79] Malheureusement aucune indication topographique ne permet de localiser cet édifice, ni même de dire s'il s'agit bien d'un seul et même bâtiment ni s'il appartient aux Hospitalliers—quel crédit peut-on apporter à l'identification d'Enlart de l'église des Hospitalliers? C'est le point que je voudrais maintenant examiner.

L'identification de C. Enlart repose avant tout sur un écu du linteau du portail sud:

> Le portail sud est couronné d'un cordon saillant à moulures gothiques, d'autres moulures de même style ornent la voussure et descendent sur les pieds-droits; le linteau de marbre porte en saillie à son centre un écu à la croix de Malte. Le portail de l'ouest, fort mutilé, avait une ordonnance analogue.[80]

La description de Jeffery, dans son ouvrage publié en 1918, est la suivante:

> The south door formerly possessed a lintel formed out of the half of a marble column cut lengthwise, and carved on its inner surface with three shields. The coats of arms in the centre has been erased, the shield on the left contains the plain cross of the Hospital, whilst that on the right is charged with the bearings of a knight commander of the Order, in chief the cross, in point party per fesse wavy. This marble lintel was removed from the doorway in 1900 and now reposes in the medieval museum of Famagusta.[81]

S'il s'agit bien du même linteau que celui vu par Enlart, pourquoi Enlart ne signale-t-il qu'un seul écu? Par ailleurs les portails tels qu'ils apparaissent aujourd'hui, ne correspondent exactement à aucune de ces descriptions. Le portail sud comporte bien un linteau avec au centre un écusson portant une croix patée, mais ce linteau n'est pas en marbre, il a été exécuté dans la même pierre calcaire jaune que celle utilisée pour la construction de la plupart des monuments de la ville (cf. PLATE 16.1). Le portail ouest pour sa part présente un linteau en marbre blanc portant trois écussons d'une très belle exécution, apparemment postérieurs au premier (PLATE 16.2);[82] ce sont ceux décrits par Jeffery.

PLATE 16.1*b* (detail): *Linteau du portail sud de l'église dite des Hospitalliers.*

PLATE 16.2: *Linteau du portail ouest de l'église dite des Hospitalliers.*

PLATE 16.3 (ABOVE) and 16.4 (BELOW): *Monument épigraphiques génois d'après E. Skrzinska – E. Rossi, Iscrizioni genovesi in Crimea ed in Costantinopoli. cf. note 84.*

L'écu de gauche porte une croix, celui du milieu est martelé et illisible déjà du temps de Jeffery, contrairement à l'affirmation de W. Rudt de Collenberg qui y voit des traces des armes de Lusignan ancien,[83] le troisième écusson n'a pas été identifié.

Jeffery, suivant Enlart, reconnaît dans l'écusson de gauche la croix de l'ordre de l'Hôpital de Saint-Jean-de-Jérusalem. Or la croix est un motif commun en héraldique et elle n'est pas l'apanage du seul ordre de Saint-Jean de Jerusalem, surtout sur un relief en pierre

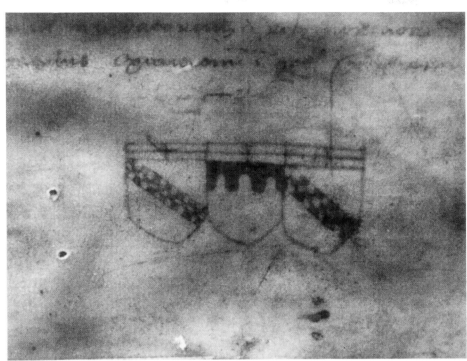

PLATE 16.5: *Couverture du registre 'Diversorum Negotiorum' de la curia du capitaine de Famagouste (A. S. G., San Giorgio, sala 34, 590/1290 (autorisation N.15/99 - Proto 2672.V/9.99)*

où les émaux sont absents. La croix est également l'emblème de Gênes, qui a possédé Famagouste pendant près d'un siècle. Si l'on admet que le premier écu peut trouver une autre lecture que celle jusqu'alors proposée, et que le second est méconnaissable, l'explication du linteau et peut-être l'identification de l'église repose sur le troisième écu qu'il faut identifier. Cet écu est blasonné : 'coupé enté, au chef une croix'. Si l'on regarde certains monuments épigraphiques armoriés retrouvés à Péra ainsi qu'à Amastri, on constate que l'on retrouve le même écu; il est attribué à la famille génoise Campofregoso.[84] (voir PLATES. 16.3 et 16.4) Effectivement, en consultant des armoriaux génois,[85] ou l'ouvrage de Rietstap,[86] les armes de la famille Fregoso ou Campofregoso sont les suivantes: 'coupé enté de sable sur argent'. Deux points font cependant problème. Notre écu porte au chef une croix, que nous identifions comme la croix de Gênes; les écus de Pera ne l'ont pas, et sur ces derniers, la partie en relief est au chef, la partie évidée en pointe; c'est l'inverse sur notre écu. En ce qui concerne la présence de la croix de Gênes au chef, c'est un privilège qui était généralement accordé à certains individus pour services rendus à la Commune ou bien à certains commandants de navire ou d'escadres lors d'expéditions militaires au service de la commune de Gênes.[87] Privilège individuel à l'origine, certaines familles ont cependant eu le droit de porter perpétuellement au chef la croix de Gênes sur leurs armoiries comme la famille Cibo; ce n'est pas le cas de la famille Campofregoso. Cependant nous sommes confortés dans notre attribution des armoiries à la famille Campofregoso par un dessin à la plume sur la couverture en parchemin d'un registre de la Curia de Famagouste, intitulé *Diversorum Negotiorum*, daté

de 1438–1439, conservé à l'*Archivio di Stato* de Gênes (voir PLATE 16.5).[88] Ce dessin très pâle, représente trois écus; ils portent tous trois au chef la croix de Gênes. Les deux écussons extérieurs sont ceux de la famille Cibo, qui porte habituellement au chef la croix de Gênes. C'est effectivement Andrea Cibo qui est capitaine et podestat de Famagouste en 1438–1439. Quant à l'écusson central, il correspond bien aux armes de la famille Campofregoso, tel qu'on le trouve dans les armoriaux. Il n'y a pas de membre de la famille Campofregoso occupant alors un poste officiel à Famagouste, par contre c'est Pietro di Campofregoso qui est doge à Gênes à cette date-là, ce qui explique la place centrale de ses armoiries sur le dessin du parchemin. Il ne faut pas confondre le doge de Gênes avec son homonyme l'amiral Pietro di Campofregoso, chef de la flotte et de l'armée qui a conduit victorieusement la guerre de 1373–1374 contre les forces royales chypriotes.

Comment expliquer l'inversion des parties en creux et en relief de l'écusson du linteau par rapport à ceux de Péra ou Amastri? S'agit-il d'une particularité coloniale propre à Chypre? Ne s'agirait-il pas plutôt d'une particularité attachée à un personnage bien précis, une brisure peut-être. Nous possédons dans un ouvrage du XVIIIe siècle de Piaggio, un dessin du monument funéraire de l'amiral Pietro di Campofregoso, mort en 1404, monument qui a depuis disparu.[89] Sur ce dessin, les armes du défunt sont représentées cinq fois. Dans tous les cas, les couleurs sont l'inverse des couleurs habituelles de la famille Fregoso, l'argent est au chef. La croix de Gênes n'apparaît pas sur les armes du monument funéraire. Cependant il est vraisemblable que dans une colonie, la croix de Gênes figure sur les armes de l'amiral victorieux pour rappeler son appartenance. C'est pourquoi au vu de ces particularités, je proposerais d'attribuer l'écu que nous étudions à l'amiral Pietro di Campofregoso. L'hypothèse pour lire les écus du linteau du portail occidental de l'église dite des Hospitalliers serait alors la suivante: à droite les armes de Gênes, à gauche les armes de l'amiral Pietro di Campofregoso, au centre l'écu martelé pourrait être celui des rois de Chypre, comme suggéré par Rudt de Collenberg; le linteau aurait été sculpté entre 1374 et 1383, lorsque la ville de Famagouste avait été confiée à Gênes en gage des paiements du roi; lorsque la ville devint possession génoise à la suite du traité de février 1383, on aurait supprimé les armes royales.

La soi-disant 'église des Hospitalliers' serait-elle donc une église des Génois, ou plus précisément une église que les Génois se seraient appropriés après 1374, car on admettra sans problème avec C. Enlart que la construction du bâtiment puisse être antérieure? Même si l'hypothèse de lecture du linteau se révélait exacte, et elle restera toujours une hypothèse en raison de l'état de l'écusson central, cela ne nous permet pas de dire qu'à coup sûr cette petite église était l'église des Génois. Certes l'église se trouve en face de fondations de bâtiments généralement attribués aux communautés marchandes italiennes (*loggia* des Génois), mais cette attribution est également hypothétique. Enfin ce linteau a 'voyagé'. S'agit-il bien de celui vu par Enlart? Probablement pas car Enlart ne parle que d'un écu au centre du linteau. Jeffery décrit bien ce linteau mais il n'était déjà plus en place en 1918. On sait que l'église a été restaurée en 1938 pour abriter la section de Famagouste des Francs-maçons, c'est à cette occasion que le linteau a été mis en place au portail ouest.[90] Ce linteau ne proviendrait-il pas d'un autre bâtiment? C'est une possibilité à envisager quand on se souvient des dommages qu'ont subi les monuments de Famagouste au XIXe siècle. On peut simplement dire que les Génois au lendemain de leur victoire de 1374 ont voulu tout de suite laisser leur empreinte sur un monument, mais quel monument?

Nous avons voulu mettre en valeur l'importance de la documentation écrite génoise pour la connaissance de Famagouste médiévale, à la fois pour l'existence de certaines églises, pour la continuité de l'utilisation de certaines autres et pour leur localisation. Les traces matérielles de la présence de Gênes ont toujours été considérées comme peu importantes; grâce à l'identification du linteau du portail ouest de l'église dite des 'Hospitalliers', nous avons peut-être ajouté un monument de plus à la liste.

Université Marc Bloch de Strasbourg

NOTES

1. L. de Mas Latrie, *Histoire de l'île de Chypre sous le règne des princes de la maison de Lusignan*, 3 vols (Paris 1852–61). Sur l'histoire de Chypre en général, l'ouvrage classique de G. Hill, *History of Cyprus*, 4 vols (Cambridge 1948) est maintenant remplacé au moins pour la partie médiévale par les t. 4 et 5 de Th. Papadopoullos (ed.) Ἱστορία τῆς Κύπρου (Nicosia 1995-1996) où l'on trouvera la bibliographie plus récente. On consultera aussi P. W. Edbury, *The Kingdom of Cyprus and the Crusades, 1191–1374* (Cambridge 1991).

2. G. Grivaud, 'Nicosie remodelée (1567). Contribution à la topographie de la ville médiévale', Ἐπετηρὶς τοῦ Κέντρου Ἐπιστημονικῶν Ἐρευνῶν, 19 (1992) 281–306.

3. M. Balard, 'Famagouste au début du XIVe siècle', in J. Heers (ed.), *Fortifications, portes de villes, places publiques, dans le monde méditerranéen*, (Cultures et civilisations médiévales, 4, Paris, sans date) 279–300; idem, 'Il paesaggio urbano di Famagosta negli anni 1300', *La Storia dei Genovesi*, 5 (Genoa 1985) 277–291; B. Arbel, 'Traffici marittimi e sviluppo urbano a Cipro (sec. XIII–XVI)', in E. Poleggi (ed.), *Città portuali del Mediterraneo; storia e archeologia*, (Genoa 1989) 89-94; M. Balard, 'Villes portuaires et fondouks génois en mer Egée et en Méditerranée orientale (XIVe–XVe siècles)', ibid. 75–84; idem, le chapitre 6 Οι Γενουᾶτες στὸ μεσαιωνικὸ βασίλειο τῆς Κύπρου in Ἱστορία τῆς Κύπρου (n.1), iiii, p. 258-332; P. W. Edbury, 'Famagusta in 1300', in N. Coureas, J. Riley-Smith (eds.) *Cyprus and the Crusades* (Nicosia 1995) 337–353; B. Imhaus, 'Remarques sur une maison renaissance à Famagouste', *Thesaurismata*, 27 (1997) 225–229. Sur les fortifications, G. Perbellini, 'Le fortificazioni di Cipro dal X al XVI secolo', *Castellum*, 17 (Rome 1973) 7–58; A. H. S. Megaw, 'The arts in Cyprus. Military Architecture', in K. M. Setton (ed.)*The History of the Crusades*, iiii, (Madison 1977) 197–198. Sur le port, F. Frigerio, 'Un plan manuscrit inédit du XVIe siècle du port de Famagouste', Πρακτικὰ τοῦ δευτέρου διεθνοῦς Κυπριολογιχοῦ Συνεδρίου, (Nicosia 1986) ii, 297–302; R. Gertwagen, 'Maritime activity concerning the ports and harbours of Cyprus from the late 12th to the 16th centuries (1191–1571)', in N. Coureas, J. Riley-Smith (eds.) *Cyprus and the Crusades* 511–538.

4. C. Enlart, *L'art gothique et la Renaissance en Chypre*, 2 vols (Paris 1899).

5. G. Jeffery, *A description of the Historic Monuments of Cyprus* (Nicosia 1918, réimpression London 1983). Le livre de R. Gunnis, *Historic Cyprus* (London 1936) est de peu d'utilité pour notre propos.

6. T. Mogabgab, 'Excavations in Famagusta, 1935', *RDAC* (1935) 20-22; idem, 'Excavations and Improvements in Famagusta', *RDAC* (1936) 103–105; idem, 'An unidentified Church in Famagusta', *RDAC* (1936) 89–96; idem, 'Shorter reports. Repair of Ancient Monuments, 1937–39' *RDAC* (1937–1939 paru en 1951) notamment p.174–178; idem, 'Excavations and Researches in Famagusta, 1937–1939', ibid. 181–190.

7. D. Jacoby, 'The rise of a new emporium in the eastern Mediterranean: Famagusta in the late thirteenth century', Μελέται καὶ Ὑπομνήματα, 1 (Nicosia 1984) 145–179; M. Balard, 'L'activité commerciale en Chypre dans les années 1300', in P. W. Edbury (ed.), *Crusade and Settlement*, (Cardiff 1985) 251–263; C. Otten-Froux, 'Les relations économiques entre Chypre et le royaume arménien de Cilicie d'après les actes notariés (1270–1320)' in *L'Arménie et Byzance* (Paris 1996) 156–179; P.W. Edbury, 'The Genoese community in Famagusta around the year 1300: a historical vignette', in L. Balletto (ed.) *Oriente e Occidente tra medioevo ed età moderna, Studi in onore di Geo Pistarino* (Genoa 1997) i, 235–244.

8. Les traités ont été publiés par C. Sperone, *Real grandezza della Serenissima Repubblica di Genova* (Genoa 1669) (trad.

italienne de l'ouvrage de L. de Gongora) et en plus, pour le traité de 1374, dans *Liber Iurium Reipublicae Genuensis*, 2, *Historiae Patriae Monumenta* (Turin 1857) 9, col. 806–815.

9. Leontios Makhairas, *Recital concerning the Sweet Land of Cyprus entitled 'Chronicle'*, ed. R. M. Dawkins, 2 vols. (Oxford 1932); R. de Mas Latrie (ed.), *Chroniques d'Amadi et de Strambaldi*, 2 vols (Paris 1891–1893); Florio Bustron, *Chronique de l'île de Chypre*, ed. R. de Mas Latrie, (Collection de documents inédits sur l'histoire de France, Mélanges historiques, 5; Paris 1886); *The Chronicle of George Bustronios*, trad. R. M. Dawkins, (Melbourne 1964).

10. On trouvera facilement les principaux textes rassemblés dans C. Cobham, *Excerpta Cypria, Material for an History of Cyprus*, (Cambridge 1908, réed. Nicosia 1969); T. Mogabgab, *Supplementary Excerpts on Cyprus, or further materials for a History of Cyprus*, 3 fascicules, (Nicosia 1941–1945); G. Grivaud, *Excerpta Cypria Nova, vol. 1, Voyageurs occidentaux à Chypre au XVe siècle*, (Centre de Recherche Scientifique, Sources et Etudes de l'Histoire de Chypre, 15, Nicosia 1990).

11. Dans la collection *Notai genovesi in Oltremare, Atti rogati a Cipro da Lamberto di Sambuceto (11 ottobre 1296–23 giugno 1299)*, ed. M. Balard, (Genoa,1983); *Atti rogati a Cipro da Lamberto di Sambuceto (3 luglio 1300–3 agosto 1301)*, ed. V. Polonio, (Genoa 1982); *Atti rogati a Cipro da Lamberto di Sambuceto (6 luglio–27 ottobre 1301)*, ed. R. Pavoni, (Genoa 1982); *Atti rogati a Cipro da Lamberto di Sambuceto, (gennaio–agosto 1302)*, ed. R. Pavoni, (Genoa 1987); *Atti rogati a Cipro da Lamberto di Sambuceto (31 marzo 1304–19 luglio 1305; 4 gennaio–12 luglio 1307) e Giovanni de Rocha (3 agosto 1308–14 marzo 1310)*, ed. M. Balard (Genoa 1984); à cela il faut ajouter: 'Actes passés à Famagouste de 1299 à 1301 par devant le notaire génois Lamberto di Sambuceto', ed. C. Desimoni, *Archives de l'Orient Latin*, 2, (1884) 3–120, et *Revue de l'Orient Latin*, 1 (1893) 58–139, 275–312, 321–353; *Nicola de Boateriis, notaio in Famagosta e Venezia (1355–1365)*, ed. A. Lombardo, (Venice 1973). Il existe des actes de notaires génois encore inédits, par exemple, pour le XIVᵉ siècle, ceux de Lazarino de Erzeniis (cf. communication de L. Balletto au 3ᵉ Congrès International d'Etudes Chypriotes, Nicosia 1996) de Giovanni Bardi (cf. S. Mangiante, 'Un consiglio di guerra dei Genovesi a Cipro nel 1383', *Atti della Società Ligure di Storia Patria*, 77, (1963) 255–262; E. Ashtor-B. Z. Kedar, 'Una guerra fra Genova e i Mamlucchi negli anni 1380', *Archivio Storico Italiano*, 133, (1975) 3–44; C. Otten-Froux, 'Le retour manqué de Jacques I en Chypre', *Les Lusignans et l'Outre Mer*, (Poitiers 1993) 228–240), et surtout Antonio Foglieta pour le XVᵉ siècle (édition préparée par nos soins à paraître; cf. L. Balletto, 'Note sull'isola di Cipro nel secolo XV', *La Storia dei Genovesi*, 12 (Genoa 1994) 119–144; L. Balletto, *'Piemontesi del Quattrocento nel Vicino Oriente'* (Alessandria 1992) passim). Sur la documentation génoise, voir G. Pistarino, 'Fonti documentarie genovesi per la storia medievale di Cipro', *Saggi e Documenti*, 6 (Civico Istituto Colombiano, Studi e Testi, 8) (Genoa 1985) 337–375.

12. Il existe une vingtaine de registres encore inédits conservés à l'*Archivio di Stato* de Gênes (abrégé ci-après *A.S.G.*); quelques extraits des registres pour les années 1391, 1407, 1435, 1437, 1442, 1443, ont été publiés par N. Iorga, 'Notes et extraits pour servir à l'histoire des croisades au XVᵉ siècle', *Revue de l'Orient Latin*, 4 (1896) 99–118.

13. Sur les différents sanctuaires dédiés à saint Antoine, voir infra.

14. A. S. G., *Notai*, n° 843, acte n°7: parmi le mobilier de la sacristie, on trouve *bacile unum parvum argenteum cum armis de Camilla et quadam alia, que, ut dicitur, est olim patroni qui prius construit dictam ecclesiam*.

15. Arxiu Catedral de Barcelona (ACB), *Extravagants, Llibre de Deu e deig de Berenguer Morey (del viatge a Xipre amb la nau de Joan Lombarda, Romeu d'Olzinelles i Arnau Roure i anys despres 1357–1376, f. 8r° (compte de 1358).

16. J. Combes, 'Un marchand de Chypre bourgeois de Montpellier', *Etudes médiévales offertes à M. le doyen Augustin Fliche*, (Montpellier 1952) 33–39.

17. A. S. G., *Notai*, (Giovanni Bardi), n° 381, f.140 r°–v°.

18. A. S. G., *Notai*, (Andrea de Cario), filza 21, acte 129 du 16 mai 1466.

19. A. S. G., *Notai*, n° 843, acte 7; le document est inédit, j'en donne ici une traduction en attendant la parution de l'édition complète des actes du notaire.

20. *turribulum*: ce mot peut aussi désigner un ciboire en forme de tourelle.

21. Il s'agit peut–être du plateau qui sert au lavement des mains du prêtre.

22. *fressium* désigne une frange; il s'agit probablement d'une bordure en tissu brodé, garnie de franges.

23. La signification du mot *puniale* est incertaine; il s'agit peut–être d'une chape (*pluviale*) ornée d'une bande de tissu avec des franges.

24. La signification est incertaine; *orarium* désigne une étole, ou bien une voilette ou un châle.

25. Il s'agit probablement d'un système de fixation.

26. *Jean 1*, 35; c'est le début de l'évangile de la vigile de saint André (29 novembre). Je remercie M. Marcel Metzger, de la Faculté de Théologie Catholique de l'Université de Strasbourg pour ses conseils concernant ces objets liturgiques.

27. *Item paria quatuor linteaminum tele canapis novorum de telis tribus pro singulo*: il faut comprendre que chaque drap était formé de l'assemblage de trois pièces de toile de dimension standard, connue du rédacteur du document.

28. Pour 1391, A. S. G., *San Giorgio*, sala 34, 590/1268, f. 96; pour 1442, ibid., 590/1273, f. 340; pour 1443, ibid., f. 285.

29. A. S. G., *San Giorgio*, sala 34, 590/1276, f. 64 v°.

30. Le notaire Antonio Foglieta instrumente un acte *in contrata Sancte Marie de Mistacheli*, A. S. G., *Notai*, n° 843, acte 22.

31. A. S. G., *San Giorgio*, sala 34, 590/1286.

32. A. S. G., *Notai*, n° 843, acte 153.

33. A. S. G., *San Giorgio*, sala 34, 590/1292, f. 19; Saint Lazare apparaissait déjà dans la liste des églises recevant une aumône en 1390 (A. S. G., *San Giorgio*, sala 34, 590/1268, f. 96).

34. A. S. G., *San Giorgio*, sala 34, 590/1268, f. 75.

35. *Ibid.*, 590/1268, f. 75.

36. Le jardin du tailleur Giovanni *Verdonus* touche *ab uno latere ecclesie Sancte Andree ab alio latere ecclesie Sancte Marie de Sur ab alio via publica* (A. S. G., *San Giorgio*, sala 34, 590/1276, f. 542).

37. Une boutique est située *in contracta Sancti Salvatoris per contra ecclesia Sancti Nicolai* (*Massaria* de 1456, A. S. G., *San Giorgio*, sala 34, 590/1280, f. 144 v°).

38. Par exemple, A. S. G., San Giorgio, sala 34 590/1279, f. 91.

39. A. S. G., *San Giorgio*, sala 34, 590/1268, f.136 v°; en 1440, *papa Nicola Conomo, kalogero* est *procurator et gubernator ecclesie Sancti Simeonis*, (A. S. G., *San Giorgio*, sala 34, 590/1292, f.22v°). Jean Richard a rappelé que les moines du Sinaï avaient des droits sur Notre-Dame de la Cava, église située en dehors de Famagouste et lieu de pélerinage célèbre. Vers 1328, ces moines ont bâti à Famagouste une église dédiée à saint Simeon et un prieuré où résident quelques uns d'entre eux (J. Richard, 'Un monastère grec de Palestine et son domaine chypriote', Πρακτικὰ τοῦ δευτέρου διεθνοῦς Κυπριολογικοῦ Συνεδρίου, (Nicosia 1986) ii., 66).

40. *Contracta Sancti Luce* citée en 1454 (A. S. G., *Notai*, n° 843, acte du 23 septembre 1454, sans numéro).

41. *Contracta Sancti Sarchis*, cité dans un acte du 9 juillet 1457 (A. S. G., *Notai* n° 843, acte 198).

42. A. S. G., *Notai*, n° 843, actes 9 et 11.

43. A. S. G., *San Giorgio*, sala 34, 590/1290, f. 39 et 126 v°.

44. A. S. G., *Notai*, n° 843, acte 138. En cas d'absence de l'archevêque c'est le prêtre Ventura Misac qui recevra les loyers. L'archevêque de Tarse Timothée est effectivement

45. A. S. G., *San Giorgio*, sala 34, 590/ 1290, f. 51.

46. C. Enlart, *L'art gothique*, (n.4) i., 301–311. Voir aussi M. Balard, 'Il paesaggio urbano', (n.2) 282; T. S. R. Boase, 'The arts in Cyprus,. The ecclesiastical Art', ch. 5 de K. M. Setton, (ed.) *A History of the Crusades*, iiii (Wisconsin 1977) 177–178.

47. T. Mogabgab, 'Excavations and Researches in Famagusta, 1937-1939', *RDAC* (1937-1939, paru en 1951), 188–189.

48. C. Enlart, *L'art gothique*, (n.4) 259–260 et 356–365; G. Jeffery, *Historic Monuments*, (n.5) 144–147; T. Mogabgab, *RDAC* (1937–1939), 185.

49. Voir par exemple Jacques de Vérone, cité dans C. Cobham, *Excerpta Cypria*, (n.10) 17.

50. *Atti rogati a Cipro da Lamberto di Sambuceto (6 luglio–27 ottobre 1301)*, ed. R. Pavoni (Genua 1982) doc. 71 et 72.

51. P. W. Edbury, 'Famagusta in 1300', *Cyprus and the Crusades*, (n.2) 343.

52. *RDAC* (1935), 2, 20-22; *RDAC* (1936), 103-104; *RDAC* (1937–1939), 174 et 181–185.

53. La *turris Cave* ainsi que la *porta Cave* se trouvaient à proximité de l'église des Arméniens, dont l'identification ne semble pas faire de doute (cf. C. Enlart, *L'Art gothique*, (n.4) 365–368; G. Jeffery, *Historic Monuments*, (n.5) 143–144); c'est ce qui ressort de la localisation d'un jardin *positus ad Cavam, cui coheret ab uno latere ecclesie Erminorum et ab alio latere apud portam Cave* (A. S. G., *San Giorgio*, sala 34, 590/ 1268 f. 144 v°)

54. F. Frigerio, 'Un plan manuscrit inédit (n.3) 297–302; cette tour se retrouve sur un autre plan du XVIᵉ siècle conservé à Venise à la Bibliothèque Correr (cartella piante n°28). C'est d'après ce dernier plan que nous avons pu tracer les murs de l'Arsenal. Je remercie Richard Anderson pour l'exécution du plan de Famagouste génoise et spécialement pour sa patience face aux changements répétés que je lui ai demandés.

55. Les tours sont énumérées dans par exemple A. S. G., *San Giorgio*, sala 34, 590/1276 ou 1279 ou 1280; on trouvera la liste des tours dans l'article de M. Balard,'Villes portuaires et fondouks génois', (n.3) 83 note 13, et dans idem, 'Οι Γενουᾶτες' (n.3) 266.

56. Il existe un jardin *positum retro palatium de Morfi* (A. S. G., *San Giorgio*, sala 34, 590/1268, f. 144.

57. Des jardins sont situés *in contrata de Morfi apud Sanctum Dominichum* ou encore *apud ecclesia Sancti Dominici* (A. S. G., *San Giorgio*, sala 34, 590/1268, f. 143 v°).

58. A. S. G., *San Giorgio*, sala 34, 590/1279, f. 85 v°.

59. Amadi, *Chronique*, (n.9) 327: '*Fecce mutar la piaza che era avanti la corte del re et metteria drio a li Predicatori*'.

60. C. Enlart, *L'art gothique*, (n.4) 377–379.

61. T. Mogabgab, *RDAC* (1937–1939), p. 186.

62. Cf. le testament du pisan Giovanni, fils de feu Federico de Rau qui laisse 100 besants blancs *monialibus et monasterio monalium Sancte Clare de Famagusta pro fabrica eiusdem ecclesie* (C. Otten-Froux, 'Documents inédits sur les Pisans en Romanie', in *Les Italiens à Byzance*, (Paris 1987), 184).

63. A. S. G., *San Giorgio*, sala 34, 590/1268, f. 369r°.

64. C. Enlart, *L'art gothique*, (n. 4) i, 266–267; P.W. Edbury, 'Famagusta in 1300',(n.3) 342; M. Balard, 'Οι Γενουᾶτες' (n.3) 274.

65. C. Otten-Froux, 'Documents inédits', 185.

66. C. Cobham, *Excerpta Cypria*, (n.10) 23; texte latin: 'Nicolas de Marthono notarii, Liber peregrinationis ad Loca Sancta', ed. L. Le Grand, *Revue de l'Orient Latin*, 3 (1895), 628.

67. Par exemple A. S. G., *San Giorgio*, sala 34, 590/ 1276, f. 285. Il reçoit 12 besants par *paga*.

68. A. S. G., *San Giorgio*, 590/1292, f. 5v°.

69. Ibid, f. 119.

70. A. S. G., *Notai*, n° 843, acte 61.

71. Ibid., acte 77.

72. Florio Bustron, *Chronique*, (n.9) 170.

73. '*Ego scripsi hoc de legenda Sancti Anthonii quam inveni in arabico apud monachos Egipcios qui morantur Famaguste in ecclesia beati Anthonii, que est in eminencioni loco civitatis illius*' cf. F. Halkin, 'La légende de Saint Antoine traduite de l'arabe par Alphonse Bonhomme, o.p.', *Annalecta Bollandiana*, 40 (1942), 200; F. Halkin, 'Un monastère copte à Famagouste au XIVᵉ siècle', *Le Muséon, Revue d'Etudes orientales*, 59 (1946), 511–514.

74. M. Balard, 'Il paesaggio urbano', (n.3) 283; P. W. Edbury, 'Famagusta in 1300', (n.3) 339–340; sur les ruines, voir aussi C. Enlart, *L'art gothique*, (n. 4) 368–371; G. Jeffery, *Historic Monuments*, (n. 5) 156.

75. A. S. G., *San Giorgio*, sala 34, 590/1292, f.7 v°.

76. A. Luttrell, 'The Hospitallers in Cyprus after 1386', in *Cyprus and the Crusades* (Nicosia 1995) 131.

77. Respectivement : A.S.G., *San Giorgio*, sala 34, 590/1273, f. 340, et 590/ 1276, f. 285 et 64 v°.

78. Il s'agit de *frater Gabriel Spinula ordinis predicatorum, gubernator ecclesie sancti Iohannis* (A.S.G., *San Giorgio*, sala 34, 590/1276, f. 285 v°).

79. A. S. G., *San Giorgio*, sala 34, 590/1281, f. 3v°.

80. C. Enlart, *Art gothique*, (n. 4) i, 375–376.

81. G. Jeffery, *Historic Monuments*, (n.5) 132.

82. Je remercie Brunehilde Imhaus pour la photographie de ce linteau.

83. W.-H. Rudt de Collenberg, 'L'héraldique de Chypre', *Cahiers d'Héraldique*, 3 (Paris 1977) FIG. 29.

84. Ces monuments ont été publiés E. Skrzinska – E. Rossi, 'Iscrizioni genovesi in Crimea ed in Costantinopoli', *Atti della Società Ligure di Storia Patria*, 56 (1928), et E. Dalleggio d'Alessio, 'Le pietre sepolcrali di Arab Giami', *Atti della Società Ligure di Storia Patria*, 69 (1942).

85. A. Della Cella, *Le famiglie di Genova e delle Riviere*, manuscrit du XVIIIᵉ siècle, 3 vols., Bibliothèque Universitaire de Gênes.

86. J. B. Rietstap, *Armorial général précédé d'un dictionaire des termes du blason*, (réed. Lyon 1950) ii, 708.

87. J. F. Bernabo di Negro, *L'araldica di Genova. Origini e significati di una realtà storica e sociale*, (Liguria 1983) 131–138.

88. A. S. G., *San Giorgio*, sala 34, 590/ 1290.

89. D. Piaggio, *Monumenta Genuensia o Epitaphia, sepulcra et inscriptiones cum stemmatibus, marmorea et lapidea existentia in ecclesiis genuensibus*, 7 volumes manuscrits, Civica Biblioteca Berio, Genova.

90. D'après une note manuscrite inédite de T. Mogabgab.

17

The Prehistory of the Cyprus
Department of Antiquities

Charlotte Rouché

The subject of this article is, of course, very relevant to the purpose of the present volume; but it is also perhaps of a more general historical interest. It shows, firstly, the rather accidental origins of the Department, which would not have come into being without the efforts of a series of energetic and generous private individuals. It shows wide differences of view between comfortable gentlemen administrators in London and the officials of the Cyprus government, confronted with far more pressing problems than those of preserving antiquities. And, of perhaps more significance for the future, it also shows the growing influence within British policy of what had been an essentially foreign phenomenon—the use of cultural policy as part of a wider political agenda.

Cyprus came under British administration in 1878; it was annexed in 1914, and only became a Crown Colony in 1924. But the protection of its antiquities had been an issue since the nineteenth century, when the island was energetically pillaged for antiquities, particularly by the notorious General Luigi di Cesnola.[1] The first Antiquities Law was introduced under the Ottomans in 1874, in an attempt to retain some of the material which had been pouring out of the island, and a Museum was opened in 1883. A fuller Antiquities Law was introduced in 1905, which provided not only for the control of excavated material, but also for the identification and protection of ancient monuments. Although some such monuments were defined, however, there was no proper follow-through: in 1934 Sir George Hill could write: 'It is to be remarked that at present no notices are to be seen on any such sites, or on any monuments, pointing out that they are scheduled, explaining what that word implies, and reminding readers that the defacement and spoliation of them is an offence against the law that no decent citizen or visitor should dream of committing.'[2]

Despite the wide scope of this law, however, the history of the previous decades meant that the focus of attention was principally on protecting excavated material; the body set up to deal with the administration of the law was called the Museum Committee, and the development of the Nicosia Museum, still in temporary accommodation, was their main achievement. Work was begun on a new Museum in 1908, built from public money and private subscriptions in memory of Queen Victoria, and it opened in 1909. The curator, Menelaos

Markides, appointed in 1912, served for almost 20 years, despite being hampered by ill-health; he retired in 1931, to be replaced by Porphyrios Dikaios.[3]

The law had also given the High Commissioner the right, but not the obligation, to appoint a Curator of Antiquities. Since 1903 George Jeffery had served in this capacity; he had retired in 1913, but been brought back into public service during the First World War, and remained Curator until his death in 1935:

> In charge for something like thirty years, as Curator, of the Ancient Monuments of Cyprus was George Jeffery, the distinguished English architect responsible for designing the Anglican Cathedral and Close of Jerusalem. Jeffery dedicated the greater part of his long life to the care—a thankless task until the High Commissionership of Sir Hamilton Goold-Adams[4]—of Cyprus's rich but neglected monuments of the Middle Ages. For his labours he received £80 a year until Goold-Adams raised this insulting honorarium to a figure more consistent with the Curator's qualifications and the importance of his charge. His annual budget for conservation was equally contemptible.[5]

Sir Ronald Storrs wrote, judiciously, 'Owing to his own disposition (and that of some of his critics) less than justice has been done to his painfully acquired habit of making one pound serve where others would have expended ten'.[6] The fundamental problem was lack of resources. From the beginning the preservation of antiquities was heavily dependent on private donations, and the Museum Committee established in 1905 was to be elected by donors to the Museum.[7] This problem was compounded by a concentration on the conservation of excavated material, rather than on the maintenance of buildings. In his book on Cyprus, quoted above, Sir Harry Luke gave a spirited defence of the achievements of the British administration in most spheres; but he commented: 'But where the Cyprus Administration of those days was wanting was in the cultural and aesthetic spheres. . . . I cannot refrain from recalling its failure adequately to protect the island's magnificent mediaeval remains'; he continues with some depressing examples.[8] Similarly, H. D. Purcell describes how Bellapaïs was used as a rifle range by British troops, and, until 1891, buildings at Famagusta were used as quarries for Port Said.[9]

After the First World War, and the end of Turkish

sovereignty, the British Administration of Cyprus was busy with political problems, and did little more about the archaeological heritage of the island; but the island's sites shared in the general steady increase in archaeological activity in the Mediterranean. Some concern for the antiquities of the island is indicated by the fact that T. E. Lawrence was apparently offered the post of Director of Antiquities in Cyprus; he refused 'because he thought that he would be called upon for social duties'.[10] In 1927 the Antiquities Law, which allowed archaeologists to retain one-third of their discoveries but forbade export of any antiquities, was modified, to allow the authorised export of excavated material. This was followed by several archaeological campaigns in Cyprus, the most distinguished of which was probably the Swedish excavation of Vouni. These undertakings, however, tended to be focussed on the Cypriot and Graeco-Roman past.

Interest in the Byzantine and mediaeval monuments of Cyprus was more slow to develop. Sir Ronald Storrs, governor from 1926 to 1932, 'arranged a separate Byzantine section in the Museum, to balance a small mediaeval collection in an old Venetian *fondaco*'.[11] In 1931 the Archbishop of Cyprus invited Professor George Soteriou, Curator of the Byzantine Museum at Athens, to come and study the Byzantine monuments of Cyprus.[12] But the principal agent of change in British attitudes was Harold Buxton, son of Sir Thomas Fowell Buxton (a prosperous brewer), and brother of Noel Buxton, who was made a Labour peer in 1930.[13] He had been a military chaplain in the First War, serving in France and with the Russian army in the Caucasus; he was appointed British Chaplain in Nicosia in 1927, and Archdeacon of Cyprus in 1928. In March 1931 he walked up to the church at Asinou, of which he had learnt from a publication by Jeffery.[14] Buxton was deeply impressed, and arranged for it to be photographed by the Mangoian brothers; it is presumably no coincidence that the church was declared an ancient monument in April 1932. When Buxton received the photographs he sent prints to Eric Maclagan and Professor Norman Baynes.[15] Because of the large number of inscriptions, Baynes looked for an epigrapher to consult; he knew Georgina Buckler of Oxford, who had recently published a study on Anna Comnena,[16] and her husband, the American ex-diplomat and scholar William Buckler, who was an established expert on Greek inscriptions. He therefore sent the photographs to the Bucklers, who both became very interested; Georgina Buckler was able to identify the donor named in one of the inscriptions. Her thesis on Anna Comnena had been written under the supervision of Professor Dawkins, editor of the *Chronicle of Makhairas*, so that she was well aware of the history and culture of medieval Cyprus.

On February 25 1932 William Buckler lectured to the Society of Antiquaries on 'the frescoes found by Archdeacon Buxton in the disused church of the Panagia at Asinou',[17] using Buxton's photographs as slides, and an account provided by Buxton; the lecture was advertised as being by them both. In order to deliver his lecture Buckler stayed in London with his friend Dr. George Hill, the distinguished numismatist and Director of the British Museum (1931–36); he dined before the lecture at the Athenaeum with Hill and Sir Charles Peers. Archaeology was not the only interest which brought them all together. Charles Peers, FBA, had trained as an architect, and become a distinguished antiquary and architectural historian, the surveyor of Westminster Abbey (he was knighted in 1931); he was also the heir to an estate at Chislehampton, in Oxfordshire. In 1930 he and a group of friends launched the Chislehampton Housing Society Ltd., to build decent and attractive housing for the working classes.[18] Thanks to his learned connections, the vice presidents included John Buchan, President of the Oxfordshire branch of the Council for the Preservation of Rural England, and George Hill; the Executive Committee included Georgina Buckler. The Bucklers, George Hill and Sir Charles Peers were therefore meeting regularly on this account also.

The lecture on Asinou stimulated some interest, and Buckler decided to follow it up. In March, Buxton and Buckler were corresponding about giving Buxton's photographs to the Courtauld Institute 'as Miss Welsford asked'. Buxton was also looking for a photographer to take colour photographs (one had been recommended to him by Crowfoot, the excavator of Jerash) and an artist to make drawings. 'I should like to know, first, whether there exists now in England any Society (or Byzantine Museum?) as a 'centre' for the collection (or purchase?) of such reproductions? Do you think the S. Kens. Museum would purchase them?'.[19]

In mid-March the Bucklers were on holiday in the south of France, where they lunched with William Buckler's old friend Edith Wharton at Hyères. She wrote to them on Easter Sunday (27 March):

> Berenson was full of regret when he found you had so lately been here. He wants so much to see you again, & when I told him about the little church on the slopes of Troodos, and cousin Anna's horse-tamer' (a reference to the text of one of the three donor inscriptions in the church) 'he was neither to hold nor to bind. He implores me to tell Willie that for the last four or five years all his studies & travels have been centred on Early Christian origins, & that he can't rest till he has: 1. Willie's lecture. 2. Photos of the frescoes (*or* how to get them). 3. The Horse-Tamer & chapel builder's inscription.[20]

Bernard Berenson also wrote while he was at Hyères, in more measured terms:

> Dear Buckler, Edith has shown me the photos of the frescoes in a chapel somewhere in Cyprus. She asks to write about them. I do not want a copy of the inscription but

would like the names of the donors and the data for a date. Furthermore, I should be grateful for a set of the photographs. They would be of real use at I Tatti, not only for my own work but for other students as well. So far as I can judge from these photos the originals must be of a good average and on the whole remarkably well preserved. The Panagia between Michael and Gabriel is so much heavier that I wonder whether it has been repainted.

Pity the apostles above the Hodogetria have not been entirely photographed, & the figures in the embrasure of the arch.

The first impression of these compositions is that they are in fresco. I know little of about the same date. There are fragments at Mistra, & others in a small church to the north west of the Lycabettos near Athens. At Trebizond there must have been some of the same period, reproduced in Texier I seem to remember.

At home I could give you references to Millet & to Orlandos.

The Hodogetria is almost identical—no, not as a composition but in style—with a lunette over the door to S. Angelo in Fornis between Casino & Caserta.

The *contrapposto* of the Madonna above the St. George is unexpected at so early a date. It would suggest vicinity to the mosaics at Kahri Jamia at Constantinople, dated 1302 or 1303.

The letter ends with an offer to send Buckler a copy of Berenson's own *Studies in Medieval Painting*—'It opens with the only article I have ever done on a Byz. subject'.[21]

In May, Archdeacon Buxton was in Oxford, and lunched with the Bucklers, whose interest in Cyprus was steadily increasing. 'Miss (Joan) du Plat Taylor came down to talk about Cyprus; lunched and had tea'.[22] This interest culminated when on September 10, 1932, a day which 'was to introduce into my life a new and permanent interest',[23] William Buckler set off to visit Cyprus. He took within him his son-in-law, Major Vivian Seymer, who was a practising architect. They sailed from Trieste, on 13 September, meeting on the boat Dorothy Garrod, 'on her way to a cave in Palestine', and, most appropriately, Rupert Gunnis, then aide-de-camp to the governor, Sir Ronald Storrs. Gunnis had become much involved with the antiquities of Cyprus, serving for some time on the Museum Committee as Inspector of Antiquities; he stayed on to live in Cyprus after Storrs left (at the end of 1932), and was to publish an archaeological guide to the island.[24]. He proceeded to give considerable help and advice to guide the travellers round Cyprus; this had the consequence that they did not in fact meet Jeffery, who was on bad terms with Gunnis.[25]

They landed at Larnaca on 18th September, and went straight to Nicosia, where they met and were shown round by Mr. Dikaios. From Nicosia they undertook a series of trips—to Antiphonitissa, to Bellapaïs and Hilarion and, on 21 September, to 'the main object of our whole trip', Asinou. With their guide, George Savvidis, they walked up from Nikitari [PLATE 17.1],

and 'worked on, photographing and copying inscriptions so many hours that we only had time to trudge back in the semi-darkness to our deserted car and then sleep in it, in the warm Cyprus air. Next day we devoted ourselves again to the Asinou frescoes from 8.30 to 5, and then went back to our Nicosia Hotel'. After visiting several other sites, they returned on 26 September to Asinou with 'the Nicosia photographer Mangoian'; and at the end of the day Buckler and the photographer returned to Nicosia, leaving Vivian Seymer and Stavidis to camp at Asinou and continue their work. They stayed on in Nicosia, visiting a host of sites until 3 October, when they travelled down to Ktima—Buckler was laid low for a day by food-poisoning from a meal at Episkopi, but was well enough to sail on 5th October to Brindisi. The principal result of their visit was a publication of the church at Asinou, with a description of his visit by Harold Buxton, a description of the church building, with elegant drawings, by Vivian Seymer, a description of the frescoes by William Buckler and a historical note by Georgina Buckler; this remains the fullest publication in English of the church at present.[26] William Buckler also published an short account of the sixteenth century frescoes at Galata.[27]

By late October Archdeacon Buxton was again in England: he lunched with the Bucklers in London on

PLATE 17.1: *The walk to Asinou, 21 September 1932.*

27 October, and came to stay with them in Oxford on 5th–7th November. And it was apparently in October that the Colonial Office first opened a file on The Antiquities of Cyprus. On 19 October 1932 Sir George Hill spoke on the telephone to Clauson of the Colonial Office, who minuted: 'The combined influence of the governorship of Sir R. Storrs, the advanced age of Mr. Jeffery and the lack of money has had a very detrimental effect on the structural state of many ancient monuments.'[28] A few days later Mrs. Royall Tyler and her son (the future Director of Dumbarton Oaks) were in Oxford, and called to see William Buckler's photographs of Cyprus—the first slight link in a chain which would lead to the extensive programmes of research and conservation carried on by the Dumbarton Oaks Center on churches in Cyprus, including Asinou.

On November 16 1932 William Buckler and Vivian Seymer attended a meeting at the British Museum of the Joint Archaeological Committee for organizing the control of antiquities in the Near and Middle East, a body made up of representatives of the various learned societies interested in the archaeology of the area, including the British Academy; the chairman was Professor Frederick Kenyon, and Sir George Hill was the honorary secretary. They presented the following report.

THE CARE OF CYPRUS MONUMENTS

The conservation of mediaeval monuments in Cyprus is far from satisfactory
(1) Because of the age and the apathy of the present Curator (his salary is £250 per annum; his age, about 75).

The following buildings, seen in September 1932 (all 'Ancient Monuments' under the Curator's charge) are suffering from neglect:
    The Bedestan in Nicosia (15th C.)
    Bellapais Abbey, E. end (14th C.)
    The chapel royal at Pyrga (14th C.)
    St. George 'of the Greeks' Church, Famagusta
    Hilarion Monastery and Castle
    Lambousa Church (14th C.)
(N.B. Bellapais and Hilarion are the two largest and most picturesque relics of the Lusignan Kingdom: 13th-15th C.)

(2) Because many Orthodox churches, even though disused or in ruin, are not under the effective control of the Curator; e.g., the churches of Antiphonitissa and of Asinou, both of them 'Ancient Monuments', cannot be touched without the Archbishop's approval.

The following frescoed churches, now unused except perhaps for an annual *panegyris*, are totally unprotected:
    The 'Panagia', Asinou (1106)
    Upper Church, Moudoulas (1272)
    St. Demetrianos, Dali (1316)
    The Archangelos, Pedoulas (1479)
    Two churches, Galata (1502 and 1511)

(N.B. These churches contain frescoes which in quality, antiquity and preservation are unique examples of Byzantine art.)

(3) Because the funds now available are inadequate. For *urgent* repair or protective work special grants could doubtless be obtained, if a well known authority declared such work to be necessary.

The desiderata seem to be
a) to retire the present Curator—or to limit him to the care of Evcaf buildings; e.g. the Nicosia mosque—and to appoint a new Curator.
(b) to place under government control all disused or ruinous churches.
(c) to obtain from some expert a report as to the cost of the work urgently needed, and to devise means for defraying that cost, when known.
                                    W.H.B.
                                    16th Nov: 1932[29]

In the discussion Buckler and Seymer pointed out that there was an unsatisfactory division of responsibilities between Jeffery, responsible for standing monuments, and Gunnis, who, as Inspector of Antiquities, was responsible for material found below ground—with his principal concern being to control the sale of such antiquities. There was discussion of the need to send someone out to report on the situation; it was suggested that Sir Charles Peers might go, and Buckler and Hill were invited to prepare a memorandum to this effect. The meeting was also attended by A. J. Dawe of the Colonial Office, who had already expressed sympathy on this issue: 'My own view is that the condition of the antiquities in Cyprus is a scandal of which we ought to be ashamed, and that in spite of financial stringency we ought seriously to consider whether something cannot be done'. He went on to ensure that the business be brought to the attention of the new Governor, Sir Reginald Stubbs, who had not yet left to take up his new post: 'I imagine that these matters could be disposed of at the Athenaeum at lunchtime'.[30]

After the meeting, Buckler and Seymer lunched with Archdeacon Harold Buxton and his brother, Noel Buxton. On the same day, Buckler also wrote to the Archbishop of Canterbury, proposing that Harold Buxton be considered as the next Bishop of Gibraltar. In answering, Cosmo Gordon Lang said that he had already been considering Buxton, who in fact was consecrated Bishop in 1933.[31] Buckler was also approaching his friends and acquaintances on this issue. John Buchan wrote in general support: he pointed out that it would be easier to raise charitable funds 'if an Archaeological Institute were started, as Hill of the British Museum suggests'.[32] Buckler was of course an American citizen, with no official position in the British establishment, but with a large number of contacts; it seems likely that one route he used was his membership of the small but influential Society of Dilettanti, who held their bicentennary dinner on 4

December 1932.

On 6 December the Joint Archaeological Committee forwarded their memorandum to the Colonial Office, setting out, and deploring the current situation, and suggesting that a senior official—'no-one of less standing than the Senior Inspector of Ancient Monuments under H. M. Office of Works—should be invited to report on the condition of the antiquities of Cyprus ... The British Government is alone amongst those having interests in that part of the world in doing nothing for the antiquities which it should protect'— the first use of an argument which was to recur several times in the future.[33] But there was some hope for improvement under Reginald Stubbs, son of a former Bishop of Oxford, who wrote to Hill 'I was, as you may guess, brought up in an atmosphere of historical study, and I almost adopted archaeology as a profession; and one of the chief reasons why I have accepted the government of Cyprus is to have an opportunity for the historical studies which I have had to neglect for a good many years.'[34]

On 6 January 1933 George Hill wrote to thank Buckler for putting him up for membership of the Dilettanti. In the letter he discusses Cyprus business: Peers and Hill were awaiting an invitation from the authorities to visit Cyprus: 'I feel, myself, very doubtful whether it will come: not for me, anyhow'. The same letter also discusses how to raise money for the Chislehampton project: Hill subsequently provided a generous loan of £2,000 at 3% interest.[35] Hill wrote again, however, later the same day, after a telephone call from Charles Peers; he reports that 'the Office of Works are quite keen that (Sir Charles Peers) should go (to Cyprus), because they want him to go on to Jerusalem and look at the mosque'. He also suggests that in principle, the project should be paid for from the public funds, if the report is to carry due weight; ' but 'there could, of course, be no objection to economising by having a volunteer as assistant architect and chauffeur! ... Clauson thinks Stubbs will get the money out of the Cyprus Budget. He says the Minute is notionally circulating in the higher regions of the Colonial Office, and that the matter ought to be settled quite soon'. At that point they were discussing a visit in late spring of that year. The file does indeed reflect this; on 18 January the Secretary of State for the Colonies, Sir Philip Cunliffe-Lister, was writing to propose a visit whose cost should be born by the Cyprus Budget.[36]

On 23 January Hill wrote to say that, if he were to be sent officially, he needed to supply 'a semi-official note explaining why it is desirable that I should go'; Buckler responded with an account of some of the problems that Hill could be asked to look into.

(1) The Nikosia museum, built in 1897–8,[37] is damp and in winter very cold; its lay-out, with an open court where antiquities in the course of repair were sitting about, struck me as primitive. After nearly 40 years, with but little change, such a structure is bound to be antiquated, and it seemed to me reasonable that Dikeos (*sic*), the curator, should complain of its defects.

(2) The sale of duplicate antiquities, though adding to the museum revenue, seems to me of doubtful expediency. It supplies food for gossip as to the integrity of diggers and especially of officials. I should (speaking for myself only) abolish it as unworthy of the government's prestige. The Pères Blancs practise it in their Carthage excavations, but I never heard of the Tunis government doing it in theirs. At any rate the practice deserves expert consideration.

(3) The care of the 'new' prehistoric palace at Vouni (see *Syria* XII, 1931, 60; *AJA* XXXVI, 1932, 408) becomes important as its greatness becomes better known. The reference to it in Jeffery's last report (p.29) shows that he is aware of its value, but does not convince one that his 'preservative treatment' is adequate.

(4) The whole 'Antiquities Law', which is I think about 25 years old, needs overhauling in the light of modern requirements.

To get two such heads as yours and Peers' put together on such problems is a heaven-sent opportunity. I hope devoutly that your authorities will regard you both as the new Castor and Pollux.'[38]

From private discussions and letters, it seemed clear that the visit of Hill and Peers would be welcomed in Cyprus; and on February 2 the Colonial Office sent a telegram to Cyprus, formally requesting that Hill and Peers should visit the island, at the expense of the Cyprus Government. But Stubbs, who had been so encouraging to the project when in England, was now facing the reality of the situation in Cyprus; the local government was in constant conflict with the Treasury over issues of finance, above all because of the notorious Turkish Debt Charge, which was an extra burden to a fragile economy, and had been one of the stimulants to the riots of 1931. The proposal met with a frosty response, in a telegram of 4 February. 'At this time when distress is widely prevalent this Government would be accused of wasting money on unnecessary things.'[39] The first response to this was to reduce the cost: ; the British Museum would pay for Hill, but Cyprus should pay for Peers, whose costs were estimated at £150–£175.[40] The Governor responded at length in a letter to Sir Philip Cunliffe-Lister of 20 February, in which he again welcomed the visit, but drew attention to the problems:

The British Museum Committee have of course no idea of the desperate poverty of this country and of the tiny sums which are all we can find for the protection of our antiquities. If they had, they would be as amazed as I am that Jeffery has been able to do so much.

The total sum available for 1933 was £500, of which

£300 covered Jeffery's salary, leaving £200 for all necessary works. The cost of a visit of inspection would therefore leave nothing at all to be spent that year. Stubbs also felt that the criticisms of Jeffery in Buckler's report might have stemmed from Gunnis, about whom he appeared to have no illusions; 'Gunnis is an amusing companion, and an expert conchologist, but he has no archaeological or architectural knowledge whatever and, to do him justice, doesn't pretend to any'.[41]

Stubbs therefore suggested to Cunliffe-Lister that the money for the visit should be raised privately, or from the learned societies. Cunliffe-Lister wrote to the First Commissioner of Works, William Ormsby-Gore, who was already involved in the question as being Sir Charles Peers' superior:

> can you ménager your artistic friends and colleagues into the right frame of mind to do what Stubbs wants?[42]

But there seemed to be little hope of success. On 4 April Dawe minuted the file, observing that it was now too late for Hill and Peers to go before the hot season. In September Peers was due to retire, after which his services would not be available free of charge.

> It looks, therefore, as if the whole proposal . . . has come to nothing . . . All this has been caused for the want of £150.

But the financial considerations were real. On 6th May Cunliffe-Lister minuted:

> I am satisfied that the Island is so poor that they could not in fact find the money. They will be hard put to financing the necessary relief works.[43]

The British political class had still failed to grasp the potential of cultural politics; but other governments were ready to fill the vacuum which this neglect was creating. In 1933 'the Ministry of Public Instruction in France' offered to give the government of Cyprus a substantial sum 'for the preservation and restoration of the French mediaeval monuments in the island', to be carried out by a French architect. The offer met with a cool reception; but it shows clearly how other European countries perceived the usefulness of ancient and medieval historical links in furthering modern claims.[44]

Meanwhile, however, Buckler continued to lecture on the frescoes of Asinou: to the Hellenic Society on 7 February; to the Oxford Clerical Society, 'on the invitation of old Canon Edwards', on 14 February; at Johns Hopkins University in Baltimore on 9 March, and the Fogg Museum, Boston on 23 March: and, back in England, on July 3rd, to the Society of Mural Decorators and Painters in Tempera, in Melbury Road, W.14. He was also corresponding with academic colleagues, such as the R. P. Delehaye, who wrote, clearly in response to a letter from Buckler about churches in Cyprus and their dedications: 'Je suis étonné du nombre de nouveaux saints que vous rapportez de Chypre. ὁ ἅγιος Στεφανίτης m'est complétement inconnu. Il faudra faire une nouvelle édition de mes *Saints de Chypre*'.[45]

Academic interest in the antiquities of Cyprus was continuing, while word of the government's parsimony had leaked out; eventually the academics decided to put further pressure on the authorities. On the 22nd September, 1933 *The Times* published a letter, subheaded 'The Antiquities of Cyprus: Byzantine Culture'; it was signed by William Buckler, W. D. Caroë, F. H. Marshall (Koraes Professor of Byzantine and Modern Greek, University of London), John L. Myres (Wykeham Professor, Oxford), Steven Runciman (Fellow, Trinity College, Cambridge), George Francis, Bishop in Jerusalem and Harold Gibraltar. The name of Norman Baynes (Professor of Byzantine History, University of London) also appeared, but a disclaimer, printed on 26 September, pointed out that he had not been a signatory.[46] The letter set out the importance of the Byzantine monuments in Cyprus, and drew attention to the problems.

> For lack of requisite funds and consequent well-considered attention most of that great inheritance is in dire jeopardy and rapidly going to pieces. Is it not time that Great Britain, which has inherited this responsibility with the direct control of the Island, should play her part as Italy is doing in Rhodes and Tripoli, and France in Syria, Algeria and Tunis? These may be hard times, but the loss of such priceless treasures of antiquity is likely in the long run to lead to a lack of prestige in the world of culture as irreplaceable as are the treasures themselves if allowed to founder.
>
> We press upon a Government, apparently callous in this important matter, a reconsideration of their negative attitude, pointing out that in Cyprus even a little money goes a long way. Building costs are remarkably favourable, with ample skilled labour available, owing to the hard times the Island is passing through. Thus only exiguous outlay under sound direction is needed. The responsibility for both should be shouldered by Great Britain before it is too late.

This letter was followed up by ones from Montagu J. Rendell (on 31 October) and by Sir Lionel Earle, who revealed in his letter of 3 November that the proposed visit of Peers had been called off because the Cyprus government had refused to pay.

It was apparently this correspondence which attracted the attention of Lord Mersey, a Liberal peer, who, although he had never visited Cyprus, knew the Middle East well. He had travelled in Turkey in 1895, and, on the strength of his local knowledge, was sent by *The Times* to Thessaloniki to cover the Turkish-Greek fighting in spring 1897; later that year he went to serve in the Embassy at Constantinople, with, among others, Maurice de Bunsen and W.-G. Max Müller (one a close friend and one a cousin of the Bucklers).[47] After several years in the Diplomatic Service, including attendance at the Versailles Conference, he had taken up a career in the city, including a directorship at the Ionian Bank (from 1925). In his memoirs, he attributes his interest in Cyprus to seeing the letter in *The Times*; but it also seems likely that he, Buckler and Hill will have been already acquainted with one another; one mutual friend, Sir Walter Lawrence, had been elected to the Dilettanti in the same year as Buckler (1930), and it may be that in fact he was approached as being clearly extremely well-placed to help matters along.

In early November Lord Mersey wrote to the Colonial Office offering to help. The letter has unfortunately not been preserved, but it was clearly extremely welcome to the Colonial Office and to the Cyprus Government, both feeling stung by the comments in *The Times*. During that autumn, with the encouragement of Cunliffe-Lister, a committee was formed to press for the points made in the letter, and to raise the money to make them possible. On 8th November Buckler 'lunched at Brooks' with Lord Mersey to talk about Cyprus'; on 23rd November William and Georgina dined with the Merseys. On 1 December Lord Mersey and Sir George Hill had a meeting with the new Governor-Designate, Sir Richmond Palmer; and on Tuesday 5 December 1933 the Committee on Cyprus Monuments met at the House of Lords, chaired by Lord Mersey, and with Sir Richmond in attendance.[48] The full membership was announced in a letter by Mersey to *The Times*, on 31 January 1934, accompanied by a letter of support by Cunliffe-Lister and backed up by a leading article; this was followed up by a brochure, issued in March 1934:

THE CYPRUS COMMITTEE

Archbishop of Canterbury	Rt. Hon W. Ormsby-Gore, M.P.
Marquess of Lansdowne	Hon. Francis Rodd
Earl of Onslow	Sir George Hill
Viscount Mersey, *Chairman*	Sir Akbar Hydari
Lord Balniel, M.P.	W.H. Buckler
Lord Howard de Walden	Steven Runciman

The above Committee has been formed to interest the public in the Antiquities of Cyprus, to take steps for their preservation, maintenance, discovery and examination and to collect funds for this purpose

The setting up of the Committee was welcomed by *The Guardian*: [49]

At last a strong committee, officially encouraged by the Secretary of State for the Colonies, has been formed to remedy our negligence. It is headed by Lord Mersey, and includes the Archbishop of Canterbury, the First Commissioner of Works, the Director of the British Museum and scholars who know the Levant. Naturally they asked for some money at once (which may be sent to the Cyprus Monuments Fund, Lloyds Bank, 6 Pall Mall, S.W.1) but their first step will be to arrange for a general inspection in the spring by Sir Charles Peers and, if possible, Sir George Hill.

A further article commented on the composition of the Committee, which included Mr Steven Runciman 'a young scholar whose writings on Byzantium and its times mark him out as fit to follow in the the the path along which Gibbon and Professor Bury have lead', and Sir Akbar Hydari, who 'will help his colleagues in dealing with Moslem owners of property and in work upon buildings which by intention or through changes have become connected with Islam'.

The first achievement of the Cyprus Committee was to provide the necessary finance for Hill and Peers to undertake their long-planned visit to Cyprus. Hill's expenses were to be paid (as already agreed) by the British Museum; Sir Charles Peers' expenses—and his fee, since he was now retired—were paid by the Committee. Sir Richmond Palmer, now established in Cyprus, wrote to Lord Mersey that the visit would be welcome, although the correspondence in *The Times* 'gave considerable offence here'.[50] There were other causes for concern; Sir John Myres wrote to the Colonial Office on 1 January 1934 to report that some antiquities which had just been sold at Sotheby's on behalf of Rupert Gunnis were quite clearly from the excavations at Poli (Marion).[51]

In February Buckler evidently wrote to George Hill, to ask if he and Vivian Seymer would still be wanted on such an official expedition: Hill answered on 24 February: 'The answer is most distinctly yes!'; and final arrangements were made at the Cyprus Committee meeting on 28 February. On 12 March 1934 the expedition set off. The official members were Hill and Peers, accompanied, at their own expense, by Mr. C. J. P. Cave as photographer, Vivian Seymer as chauffeur, and William Buckler as organiser and interpreter. 'Mr Buckler . . . was probably the first to draw attention to the danger to the monuments.'[52] The official world had therefore been forced to send an official team of inspection, whose recommendations it would not be easy to ignore. 'The releasing of the Director of the British Museum for this purpose of making a Colonial Report was unprecedented'.[53] It was Sir George Hill's first visit to the island which he had studied for so long, and whose historian he was to become.

The group embarked at Trieste on 14 March; it was a sign of the times which they noted, but perhaps did not fully appreciate, that the ship was taking large number of Jewish emigrants from central Europe to Palestine. The official party stayed in Cyprus from 18 March until 12 April, and visited a wide range of sites, particularly the Byzantine ones [PLATE 17.2].[54] They were considerably helped by Rupert Gunnis. One problem was coping with the sensibilities of the aged Jeffery: 'We visited the great Templars' tower at Kolossi with "old Jeffery" who proudly showed his restorations—some good & some very bad. The wife of the Commissioner (=préfet) has recently injured herself badly by falling 14 ft. down an open well & as most people think that Jeffery shd. have covered this with boards, it was a subject that had to be avoided!'[55] On the 8th of April they were joined by Lord Mersey, for the last days of their visit; by April 20th he was in London, setting out the situation to the Colonial Secretary.[56] Buckler and Seymer stayed on a few days longer than the official party, during which time they visited Palaiochori and Laghoudera.

On their return, Hill and Peers each submitted confidential reports to the Secretary of State for the Colonies, pressing for the establishment of a proper Directorate of Antiquities.[57] One of the points in Hill's report was that it would be particularly desirable to have a Director with an architectural training, although he was not optimistic that such a person could be found. The creation of a Directorate was now the focus of the Committee's attention. They met on 16 May, and on 19 May Lord Mersey wrote to the Colonial Office: 'we are now engaged in drafting our appeal. . . . We feel very strongly that it is of great importance that it should contain some definite indication of the certainty of an adequate service of inspection and maintenance in the future'.[58] By 28 May the Joint Archaeological Committee was forwarding a draft of a new Law of Antiquities to the Colonial Office.[59]

The Cyprus Committee met again on 12 June to discuss progress. Later in June 1934 Hill stayed with the Bucklers in Oxford for various purposes, including opening (in pouring rain) the buildings which he had financed, 'Marylands Green', for the Chislehampton Building Society; it seems likely that he, Peers and Buckler were also working on the public side of the follow-up to their visit.[60] In July 1934 the Report of Hill and Peers to the Cyprus Committee was made public, and attention was drawn to its conclusions in a letter to *The Times* from the Cyprus Committee, appealing for money for restoration of Bellapais, St.

Hilarion, Famagusta, the Bedestan of Nicosia, and some smaller monuments (Pyrga, Lambousa, Kouklia and 'several medieval Khans'), together with the excavation of Salamis. 'The Secretary of State for the Colonies has given an assurance that means will be taken to provide a permanent service for inspection and maintenance of the antiquities'.[61]

The search for a Director had already begun; Hill wrote to A. J. Dawe in June that he and Peers were looking for likely candidates: 'one or two promising people, like Kirwan and Megaw, have fallen out, being engaged for the next few years'.[62] The candidate eventually appointed in August 1934 was J. R. Hilton, a qualified architect with a First in Greats, who had done some work on Byzantine church architecture. It was also intended that at least one skilled restorer, from among those trained by Sir Charles Peers at the Ministry of Works, be seconded to the island; the man eventually appointed was Charles Bowler, who did much constructive work for Cyprus. The Colonial Office and the Cyprus Government continued to squabble over the costs, including the pension to be paid to Jeffery; this was eventually approved in 1934, only months before his death.[63]

The Committee kept up the pressure. On 5 November the Royal Empire Society gave a dinner and reception for the Fund, which was addressed by Sir Ralph Oakden and Sir Charles Peers on the future of Cyprus, and the care of its monuments: 'A start had been made with the appointment of a director of antiquities for the island'.[64] The Committee met on 18 December 1934; and on 16 January 1935 the Archbishop of Canterbury, Sir Philip Cunliffe-Lister and Lord Mersey spoke at a meeting hosted by the Lord Mayor of London, at the Mansion House, on 'The Island of Cyprus, its Trade Prospects and its Historic Monuments'; 'but we did not get much money. Gamon, the excellent secretary to the Lord Mayor, who

PLATE 17.2:
*Sir George Hill,
W. H. Buckler,
Sir Charles Peers
and C. P. J. Cave.*

deals with many such meetings, tells me that one can only reckon on getting 20 per cent of the people invited: we had invited 350, so he was exactly right'.[65]

'On 1st January, 1935, the new Department of Antiquities came into being. With the generous aid of £1,200 collected in England by the Cyprus Committee under the Chairmanship of Lord Mersey and of £1,000 from the Carnegie Trust . . . a beginning was made on the two urgent tasks of repairing the Monuments and reorganising the Museum'.[66] In June 1935 Malcolm MacDonald became Secretary of State for the Colonies, and J. H. Thomas Secretary for the Dominions; they exchanged these posts in November, and on 21st both met Lord Mersey, and on 26th W. H. Buckler to discuss Cyprus.[67] The Committee met on 28th of that month. Shortly afterwards, on 19 December, Lord Mersey entertained the prominent American diplomat Robert Bliss and his wife to tea at the House of Lords—another foreshadowing of the future connection of their foundation, Dumbarton Oaks, with the care of monuments in Cyprus.

As well as raising money, the Committee and the Joint Archaeological Committee continued to nag the government to get a new Antiquities Law into place. A first draft of proposals had been forwarded in May 1934, and the Colonial Office had approved it by the end of the year; but it was not enacted until 30 December 1935. A. J. Dawe minuted 'The delay is, to say the least, most disappointing, and seems to be another instance of the lack of tact and imagination which the Cyprus Government seems almost fated to display upon this subject'.[68]

Indeed, it is clear that reaction in Cyprus to all these developments was very mixed, and the situation was far from simple. The resultant victims were the young Hilton, who arrived in Cyprus with no experience of government service, and no established Department; Hilton 'was told nothing of his duties or what was expected of him'. Moreover, while he was a government servant, most of the money which he was spending came from the Cyprus Committee; but the Governor objected to the fact that he communicated directly with the Committee. To add to all this, Rupert Gunnis still held various responsibilities, and 'tended . . . to monopolise the work and to treat Mr. Hilton as less experienced than himself'. By July Hilton had had enough, and tendered his resignation on 29 July, to take effect from 31 December 1935. The Governor gave a lively defence of the Government position in letters to the Colonial Office: it was Hilton who 'didn't realise that the title of Director meant nothing', who refused to consult the right people and use the correct procedures; but A. J. Dawe eventually summed up the affair in a minute of July 1936: 'I do not from what I have heard (and it is a great deal!) entirely share Sir Richmond Palmer's view regarding the relations between Government and Mr. Hilton. I think the Government might have been much more forthcoming towards a young official who did not know the ropes'.[69]

Hilton went on to a distinguished career in the Diplomatic Service, and only died in 1994. The post was readvertised, and one of the candidates who had not been available in 1934, A. H. S. Megaw, then Assistant Director of the British School at Athens and a specialist in Byzantine architecture, was appointed Director of Antiquities.

Hilton's departure left a hiatus, during which Dikaios, as acting Director, and Bowler tried to keep things going. The situation was further complicated by a visit of David Talbot Rice to the island in spring 1936; in May he produced an unsolicited report, which he circulated widely, on the unsatisfactory situation of the Antiquities, criticising restoration techniques, and claiming that antiquities were being sold. He also criticised the anomalous role of Gunnis, whom he saw as partly responsible for undermining Hilton's position. This further irritated the Cyprus Government.

But all these reversals perhaps helped to attract the attention of the new Secretary of State for the Colonies, William Ormsby-Gore, who had of course been involved with the Cyprus question in his capacity as First Commissioner of Works. He became Minister in May 1936, and wrote to Sir Richmond Palmer in June, urging the need for the Government of the island to support the Director of Antiquities, and repeating, with more force, an old argument. 'We must show that we are not less civilised or progressive in this sphere than the French and the Italians. Recent events have brought home to us acutely the need for upholding our prestige in the Mediterranean as against the Italians.'[70] The Italians, of course, had attacked Abyssinia in the preceding October, flaunting all kinds of pseudo-historical justifications. The British were at last beginning to realise the possible uses of a cultural policy. The situation to which Megaw came was therefore a very sensitive one; but it would seem that by the time he arrived the Cyprus Government had at last learned that the care of the island's antiquities was a serious responsibility, and the British Government had come to rate such matters much more highly. In November 1936 Ormsby-Gore wrote again to Palmer: 'I am most anxious that it should be made clear that British Colonial Governments are as alive to the significance of these cultural matters as that of any foreign country'.[71]

In April 1937 Lord Mersey wrote to *The Times*, reporting on the progress of the Committee's work, on the occasion of the publication of the Committee's second report: 'It is now three years since we started, and in that time we have done a good deal.' Several monuments had been restored. 'In addition the committee have been largely responsible for the setting up by the local Government of an efficient antiquities department, with a director and trained staff.'. . . 'We have raised nearly £4,000, half of which has been supplied by about a dozen people, and we have been sending money to Cyprus at the rate of £1,200 a year.' He ends with a further appeal for support, and a list of the current members of the Committee: new Members since its foundation in 1933 were Lord Stanhope, Lord Gerald Wellesley, Sir Eric Maclagan, Sir Charles Peers, Colonel Vivian Gabriel, Mr. E.J. Forsdyke, Captain Alan Graham, M.P., and Mr. Geoffrey Peto; the Marquess of Lansdowne had died, and the Earl of Onslow had apparently resigned.

The Department was now safely established, and the crucial work was done. The Committee, however, seems to have continued in existence. Lord Mersey spoke on Cyprus in the House of Lords on 31 March 1943; 'Devonshire, who is Under-Secretary for the Colonies, thanked our Committee on behalf of the Government for what we had done in preserving the ancient buildings there'.[72] In October 1946 he reported 'a talk at the Colonial Office with the new Secretary of State, Mr. Creech Jones, who is inclined to be helpful about Cyprus, and wishes our Committee to continue its work. There is no fear, he says, of this government ever bartering away the island'.[73] His last mention of Cyprus suggests that the Committee was still in existence as late as 1947: 'Megaw makes an excellent chief of the Antiquities Department, and our Committee, of which I am still Chairman, has done excellent work in conserving buildings'.[74] I have been unable to discover when the Committee was finally wound up.

As for the Bucklers, their farewell to Cyprus was when they visited the island in March 1938—Georgina for the first time; the Megaws acted as their hosts and showed them round. They arrived on 10 March, and spent seven days in Nicosia, visiting a series of sites. They were welcomed and given coffee and quince jam by the Abbot of Stavrovouni; they went over the Museum with Mr. Dikaios; they visited the Bedestan, then undergoing repairs, and saw 13 Mevlevi Dancing Dervishes; they dined at 'the new Government House' (the old one having been burnt down during riots in 1931); and, on March 17, they saw Canon Malcolm Laurie Maxwell collated as Archdeacon of the Church of England in Cyprus, by Bishop George Francis of Jerusalem.

On March 18 they were joined by R. M. Dawkins, and all three set off to travel more widely. They saw the recently-uncovered mosaics of the House of Eustolios at Kourion, visited Paphos and the monastery of St. Neophytos, and then returned to Nicosia. The next day's Journal entry reads: 'Sunday, March 20. H(oly) C(ommunion) at 8. Motored to Nikitari with the Megaws, Prof. Dawkins, Mrs. Bardswell' (who had restored the paintings at St. Chrysostomos, Nicosia: her husband was the medical inspector of tuberculosis) 'and Mr. Bowler' who was then in charge of restoring the Bedestan. 'Walked to Asinou, with mules carrying one priest from Morphou & our lunch, which we ate in the enclosure round the church. The mukhtar and papas of Nikitari came with us. Tea with the Megaws.' On 23 March they motored down the Carpas peninsula and 'had tea with Miss Joan Taylor

at her excavations (Byzantine church) at Ayios Philon'; on 24 March, having parted from R. M. Dawkins, they 'motored with the Megaws to see the wild red tulips in the Kykko fields.' It was during this visit that Georgina Buckler and Elektra Megaw discussed Elektra's interests in painting and in flowers, and the possibility that they could be combined. On return to England Georgina sent Elektra a copy of Bentham and Hooker's *British Flora*, as an aid and an exemplar; and those conversations were the first stimulus to Elektra's *Wild Flowers of Cyprus*.[75]

King's College London

NOTES

1. The idea for this article came from documents and letters which I found in the *Journal Books* kept by my grandparents, Georgina and William Buckler. I am very grateful to several people for their advice and anecdotes: to Sir Steven Runciman, the last surviving member of the Cyprus Committee; to the present Lord Mersey, grandson of the Chairman of the Committee; to Lady Hilton, daughter of the very first Director of Antiquities in Cyprus; to Dr. Veronica Tatton-Brown, for checking the British Museum's records; to my colleague, Dr. Philip Carabott, who encouraged me to consult the very full records at the Public Records Office; and above all to the dedicatee of this volume, Peter Megaw himself, who was able to clarify a number of points: for that, and for so much else, many thanks.

    For the casual nature of excavation in Cyprus, Elizabeth Goring, *'A mischievous pastime' Digging in Cyprus in the nineteenth century* (Edinburgh 1988).

2. Sir George Hill, *Report on the condition of antiquites in Cyprus (Confidential)*, London, April 1934.

3. On all this see P. Dikaios, *A guide to the Cyprus Museum* (Nicosia 1961); V. Karageorghis, 'The Cyprus Department of Antiquities, 1935–1985', in V. Karageorghis ed., *Archaeology in Cyprus, 1960–1985* (Nicosia 1985) 1–10, 1–2; see also A. H. S. Megaw, 'The British School at Athens and Cyprus', *RDAC*, 1988.2, 281–6

4. Appointed 1911.

5. Sir Harry Luke, *Cyprus* (London 1957) 93-4; Luke served in the Colonial Service on Cyprus 1911–20. Jeffery was Curator of Ancient Monuments from 1903 to 1934; he died in 1935, aged 80. See an appreciation in *RDAC*, 1935, vii.

6. Sir Ronald Storrs, *Orientations* (London 1937), 493.

7. R. Storrs and B. J. O'Brien, eds., *The Handbook of Cyprus* (London 1930) 69.

8. Luke, *Cyprus*, 93.

9. H. D. Purcell, *Cyprus* (London 1969) 217.

10. Lord Mersey, *A Picture of Life* (London 1941) 382; I have not been able to find any mention of this offer in the biographies of Lawrence, suggesting, perhaps, that it was made informally.

11. Storrs, *Orientations*, 492.

12. His work was soon published as *The Byzantine Monuments of Cyprus* (Athens 1935).

13. On the Buxtons, see Charles Louis Buxton, *The Buxtons of Coggeshall* (London 1910); I am grateful to my colleague, Professor John Buxton, for information about them and for a loan of the volume.

14. G. Jeffery, *Historic Monuments of Cyprus* (Nicosia 1918) 284.

15. For Buxton's description of his visit see *Archeologia* (1933) 327–9.

16. C. Roueché, 'Georgina Buckler: the making of a British Byzantinist' in R. Beaton and C. Roueché eds., *The Making of Byzantine History, Studies dedicated to Donald M. Nicol* (London 1993) 174–96.

17. Buckler *Journal Book*.

18. See the prospectus, and the article in the *Oxford Times* for 31 October 1931.

19. Letter of 4 March 1932.

20. Letter of 27 March 1932.

21. Letter, undated (1932).

22. *Journal Book*, June 24, 1932; Miss du Plat Taylor was excavating in Cyprus; she became Assistant Curator of the Cyprus Museum.

23. W. H. Buckler, *Memoir* (unpublished).

24. *Historic Cyprus*, (London 1936); see also Storrs, *Orientations*, 492–3.

25. As is clear from the minutes of the Joint Archaeological Committee, 16 November, 1932, CO 67 248/12 Doc. 1.

26. 'The Church of Asinou, Cyprus, and its frescoes', *Archeologia* 83, 1933, 327–50.

27. 'The Frescoes at Galata, Cyprus', *JHS* 53 (1933) 105–10.

28. PRO records, CO 67.248/12, Minutes 2.

29. A copy survives at the PRO, CO 67 248/12, doc. 1, together with the minutes of the meeting.

30. CO 67 248/12 Minutes 6–7, November 1932.

31. Letter of 18 November, 1932.

32. Letter of 9 December 1932.

33. CO 67 248/12 Doc. 7.

34. CO 67 248/12 Doc. 8.

35. *Oxford Times*, 24 February, 1933.

36. CO 67 248/12 Doc. 23.

37. In fact, it was opened in 1909, as a memorial to Queen Victoria.

38. Letter of 24 January, 1933; this is also recorded as CO 67 249/11 Doc. 4.

39. CO 67/249/11, Docs 6 and 8.

40. Telegram of 11 February, CO 67 249/11 Doc. 9.

41. CO 67 249/11 Doc. 15.

42. Letter of 1 March 1933, CO 647 249/11 Doc. 16.

43. CO 67 249/11, Minutes.

44. This incident was reported to Hill by Mogabgab in a letter of August 1934; CO 67 253/2, Doc. 80.

45. Postcard of 22 December 1933. This particular issue was cleared up in further correspondence.

46. It is perhaps worth noting that Baynes and Marshall, one at University College and one at King's, did not describe themselves in that way, but as Professors of the University of London.

47. Lord Mersey (Charles Clive Bigham), *A Picture of Life* (London 1941) 53–60, 113–127; I am most grateful to his grandson, the present Vicount Mersey, for bringing this volume of reminiscences to my attention.

48. *Journal Book* entries; see also Mersey, *A Picture of Life*, 369; CO 67/249/11 Docs. 50 and 55.

49. 2nd February, 1934

50. Letter of 5th January, CO 67/253/1, Doc.7.

51. CO 67/253/1, Doc.8.

52. *Daily Telegraph*, announcing the expedition on 6 March 1934.

53. W. H. Buckler, *Memoir*.

54. The visit was described by W. H. Buckler in a volume of the *Journal of Hellenic Studies* dedicated to Sir George Hill on his 80th birthday: , 'A tour in Cyprus, 1934', *JHS* 66 (1946) 61–5. There was a report by 'a special correspondent', in *The Times*, 5 May 1934 (with a reference to 'Mr. W. H. Blackler'); and an article in *Ἐλευθερία* of 14 April 1934. In the same spring, an expedition from the Courtauld Institute, led by David Talbot-Rice also visited Cyprus: 'work was restricted to the icons or religious panel paintings of the Orthodox Church'. Both expeditions were reported in the *Illustrated London News*, 11 August 1934, 221–3; for the Courtauld trip see D. Talbot Rice, *The Icons of Cyprus* (London 1937), Courtauld Institute publications on Near Eastern Art 2, with a chapter by Rupert Gunnis.

55. W. H. Buckler, letter to Georgina Buckler, 3 April 1934.

56. *A Picture of Life*, 371–3, 375.

57. CO 67/253/1, Doc.30.

58. CO 67/253/1, Doc.35.

59. CO 67/253/1, Doc.357.

60. *Journal Book* 19-21 June 1934.

61. This was also reported in *Ἐλευθερία*, 10 October 1934. The Report was published by the Government Printing Office, Nicosia.

62. Letter of 26 June, CO 67/253/1, Doc.48.

63. CO 67/253/1, Doc.51, CO 67/253/2, Doc.75.

64. *The Times*, 6 November 1934.

65. Mersey, *A Picture of Life*, 384.

66. *RDAC* 1935, vii.

67. Mersey, *A Picture of Life*, 386; Buckler, *Journal Book*; Malcolm was the son of Ramsay MacDonald, with whom

          Buckler had had extensive dealings during the War.
68.   CO 67/259/7, Minute of 1.1.1936.
69.   Minute of 17 July 1936, from CO 67 264/8; cf. also CO 67
          264/9
70.   Letter of 18 June, CO 67 264/8, Doc. 74.
71.   Letter of 5 November 1936; CO 67 264/8, Doc.90.
72.   Mersey, *Journal and Memories* (London 1952) 28.
73.   Mersey, *Journal and Memories*, 66.
74.   Mersey, *Journal and Memories*, 72.
75.   E. Megaw and D. Meikle, *The Wild Flowers of Cyprus*
          (London and Chichester 1973).

18

Kite Aerial Photography for Archaeology: An Assessment and Short Guide

Richard C. Anderson

INTRODUCTION

I first participated on Peter Megaw's excavation of Saranda Kolones at Paphos in Cyprus in the spring of 1970 and in what spare time was available I made and flew a large kite just for fun. The coastal breezes that make Paphos an excellent place to fly kites had inspired me to pursue this old hobby of mine. The following winter, while I was at Dumbarton Oaks in Washington, DC, Peter asked me if I would develop a balloon supported system for taking aerial photographs of the castle and suggested that I contact Julian H. Whittlesey who was very active at that time taking archaeological photographs by balloon. Consequently, I met Julian Whittlesey and he generously suggested how an ultra-cheap balloon system might be developed using an eight-foot neoprene weather balloon. Having acquired what was necessary for the system which included the manufacture of my own aero-camera which is described in this article, I set out for Paphos early in 1971.

A spherical balloon cannot tolerate much wind, especially a fragile weather balloon tethered under a light cotton canopy, so after much waiting for zero wind conditions and two failed attempts where, after a balloon had been filled, a breeze arose which buffeted the balloon until it burst, I built a large kite that I was confident would lift the camera. So in the spring of 1971, after the excavation had finished and all the rest of the excavation team had gone home, the two of us flew my first aerial photographic system carried by a 2.75m paper box kite. Miraculously we managed to achieve four 4x5 inch negatives of Saranda Kolones. One of these photos was quite well aimed and reasonably sharp and it has been published several times.[1] I realized that in appropriate conditions, kite aerial photography was a powerful and practical tool for archaeology, and in the following years I developed my system considerably. The improved system flew many times at Peter's excavation at the Kourion Basilica in Cyprus, producing aerial photographs after each major campaign, though most of my flying was done over several Euphrates Valley sites in Syria. In the eighties, there were more flights over Saranda Kolones for Peter.[2] Without the initial impetus from Peter in 1970 and subsequent encouragement in 1971, I probably never would have become one of the founding members of the *Kite Aerial Photography Worldwide*

Association.[3] Peter is *imaginative* enough and *old* enough to believe in kites, though initially we were both more willing to trust a frail, neoprene balloon.

WHY KITES?

Scientific and Military Kiteflying

In August 1912 a *Grand Concours International de Cerf-Volants Scientifiques et Militaires* was held at the city of Spa in Belgium to judge entrants using kites for aero-photography, meteorology, marine life-saving and other serious applications. The contest also witnessed kite-supported, man-lifting observation systems sent by the armies of Belgium, France, Germany, Austria and Great Britain. This event was won by the host nation.[4] At that time it is clear that kites and kiteflying were being taken seriously as an effective means of carrying various apparatus and even people into the air for beneficial purposes. The achievements of kites up to then had been considerable, but three years had passed since Blériot had flown the English Channel and more ominously, 1912 saw the first military use of aeroplanes employed by the Greek Army and Navy in war against the Ottoman Empire.[5] By the outbreak of the First World War in 1914, almost all of the achievements of kites had been utterly superseded by aeroplanes. The kite was relegated to become a frivolous and, once placed in the hands of children, inevitably broken toy. After being so poorly used for eighty years and even after a considerable modern renaissance in kiteflying (largely led by deliberately unstable 'stunt' kites), the suggestion of sending an expensive camera up with a kite provokes a reaction of incredulity in most people.

If armies have stopped using kites, why might kites still be useful for archaeologists? The answer lies in scale. The military systems were developed for reconnaissance and the static, kite—or balloon—borne observer at a few hundred metres altitude could see very little compared to a mobile observer in an aeroplane at perhaps a thousand metres. Also the kite or balloon observer, along with the kites and particularly the balloons themselves, were vulnerable to enemy fire both from the ground and from the air, so it was clear that they must soon be abandoned. Despite their vulnerability, the systems were not abandoned immediately but continued to serve throughout the First World War because of their unique virtues of giving detailed reports of the battlefield, identifying targets and particularly informing gunners where their shells were landing. The kites and balloons carried field telephones which made it possible for the observer to immediately report this valuable information to the ground. This could not be done satisfactorily from aeroplanes at that time. Shooting down observation balloons was a high priority (and a great sport) for aviators on both sides, because these low-level, stationary observers were enormously valuable in seeing the *fine detail* of that *static, trench war*. Similarly, a modern kite or balloon supported photographic system can record the fine and subtle detail of a concise archaeological site in an inestimably valuable way. While the manned, free-flying aeroplane or helicopter is superior for discovering new things or providing vast, general views, the low-altitude, stationary kite or balloon supported camera will patiently record known sites with limitless thoroughness.

While the unmanned system is unlikely to discover a totally unknown archaeological site, a remote, aero-static camera can be lowered under great control to record the finest detail of a known site. It can be lowered to a point where the camera is below levels easily achieved with a photo-tower or even a ladder, but there will be no structure below the camera to obstruct the view and nothing even to cast a shadow except the camera itself. A remote system can also easily produce excellent stereo imagery which may be used for classic photogrammetry or for computerized digital stereo plotting systems.[6] It is this very low-level arial photography that remote systems are best at and which is most valuable for recording archaeological sites.

Aeroplanes are not useful for photography when flying at a few tens of metres any more than good pictures can be taken from a speeding car. Although helicopters can fly very low and be aero-static, when hovering they vibrate their most, and if they hover only a few metres above a dusty archaeological site the result is a dust storm.

Obviously, both kites and balloons can do the job of lifting a camera and each method has its advantages and disadvantages. In good conditions balloons undoubtedly provide a better, more stable 'sky hook' but kites are also adequately stable, cost nothing to fly and they require no (sometimes difficult or impossible to obtain) gas. Balloons are *best* but kites *have advantages!* An exhaustive comparison would be lengthy. The purpose of this article is to try to dispel the current poor opinion of kites and to provide some information on how and in what conditions modern kite aerial photographs are actually achieved.

SKILL AND EXPERIENCE

Wind sports today are legion: sailing, wind surfing, hang gliding, parachuting, to name a few, and all of these are acknowledged to require considerable skill. No person, child or adult, would think of doing any of these things without first some instruction from simple and safe first steps, a beginner, through practice and experience, will gradually advance to become competent or even expert. Kite flying is really no different except that a beginner with a good kite might at once fly very successfully. The skills that a kite flyer must nevertheless develop are to learn to select or make reliable kites and how to adjust them to fly safely in

FIG. 18.1: *Chart of The Beaufort Wind Scale with Wind Pressure Curve*[7]

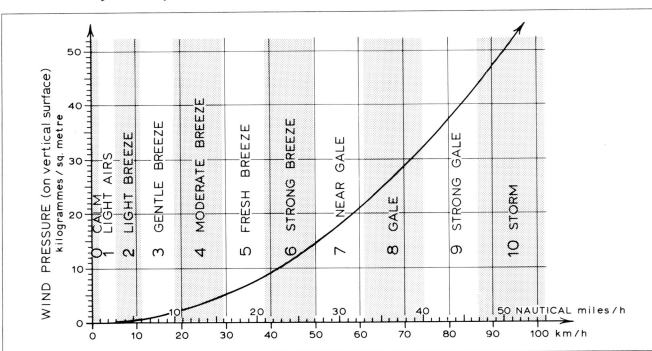

varying wind conditions. In common with the serious, even dangerous wind sports mentioned above, a foremost skill is to learn to judge the weather and wind correctly.

WEATHER AND KITES

Kite flying requires wind and a favorable wind is the most critical ingredient for success. Kite aerial photography can only be done when the wind is fairly stable and of moderate strength. A sailor cannot sail when there is no wind, and if there is too much wind, he or she would certainly prefer to be safely in port. So too with kite flying but with kites, the world is less forgiving. A sailor is quite safe when becalmed but if the wind ceases, a flying kite will immediately descend to the ground. In a storm, a sailor will reduce or lower altogether the sails of his or her ship to ride out the storm. Once flying, a kite cannot similarly be trimmed so if the wind speed dramatically increases, a kite or its tether might break or the kite become aerodynamically unstable and roar in descending circles in the sky, all of which spell disaster. A kite flyer must not fly unless he or she is quite certain that the weather will be satisfactory.

Wind is measured in the *Beaufort Scale* and in most places a wind forecast is obtainable from harbour or airport authorities or is broadcast on the radio. Kite fliers prefer about the same wind speeds as dinghy sailors: Beaufort four or five are perfect. FIG. 10.1 is an abbreviated chart of the Beaufort system together with a curve showing the pressure produced by the wind on a vertical surface.

It can be seen from the chart that the force of the wind increases in a parabolic curve rather than in a straight line. Wind speeds below Beaufort four are just not powerful to lift very much while speeds over Beaufort six are so powerful as to be daunting or dangerous. Kites can be designed to fly in practically any wind conditions but giant, super-lightweight kites for flying (and lifting a load) in Beaufort three, still cannot fly if the wind decreases nor can such a kite survive if the wind increases very much. Kites have also been designed to fly in conditions similar to hurricanes but these are not the best conditions for people. All kites will have a certain latitude between the minimum wind in which they will fly and the maximum wind that they will tolerate before becoming aerodynamically unstable (which may be the result of them simply breaking or tearing while in flight). Tension in the kite tether will similarly increase dramatically with wind speed so the tether must be strong enough (and anchored well enough) to withstand any wind that is likely to be encountered. Flying must only take place when the wind speeds are judged to be within *and remain within* the safe latitude imposed by the kite and its supporting equipment.

PHOTOGRAPHIC AND ENGINEERING SKILLS

In addition to a safely and efficiently flown kite, to achieve photographs from a kite requires a functional photographic rig which, as well as a camera, will probably include a radio control, which also might be used for aiming as well as for triggering the camera. Such rigs are not made commercially but are quite easily developed by practical, technically-minded people usually using radio equipment manufactured for radio controlled model aeroplanes. Thus, a kite aerial photographer will be a kiteflier, a photographer, to some extent a radio technician, and an engineer of sorts: skills that do not immediately come into the mind of a normally experienced person who first imagines kite aerial photography. In our minds we must replace the stereotypical image of a small child, a kite from a toy shop and a little ball of string, with an image of stalwart people, a large, powerful kite, sturdy windlasses, a quality camera, radio and other moderately expensive gadgetry. Successful kite photography requires a return to the same practical, intermediate technology exhibited at the event in Spa, where five of the world's great armies flew kites in the pursuit of their deadly business.

WHAT KITE TO USE?

Of the many kinds of kites, only a small repertoire of the most efficient and stable are used for kite aerial photography. FIG. 10.2 illustrates four which are, for light winds, the *delta*, a modern design; for moderate and strong winds, the *Sanjo Rokkaku*, a traditional Japanese design, and the *parafoil*, a fundamentally new, non-rigid design. For strong winds there are various types of *box kites* which were the workhorses of the turn-of-the-century scientific and military kitefliers. I show a famous 1893 design by Lawrence Hargrave, an Australian pioneer of aviation.

Of these kites, the current favorite among KAPWA members is the Rokkaku because it is powerful, efficient, easy to assemble, to fly and to disassemble, and especially because it flies very steadily in a fairly wide range of wind speeds. B. F. S. Baden-Powell, brother of the founder of the Boy Scouts, used a similar design for man-lifting in the 1890s and the Baden-Powell design was adopted by Guglielmo Marconi to lift the aerials for his experiments with radio including the first transatlantic broadcast in 1901.[8]

The parafoil was invented in 1963 in Boca Raton, Florida in the United States by a balloon and sailmaker, Domina C. Jalbert and about it I must quote the 'kite bible', *The Penguin Book of Kites* by David Pelham: 'Incorporating balloon, parachute, airfoil and kite features, it is the lightest, most efficient and economical non-mechanized lifting surface yet devised.'[9] I purchased a Jalbert J–45 (45ft² = 4.18m²) parafoil in 1972 at the suggestion of Julian Whittlesey and I have used it for all of my aerial photography ever since. On

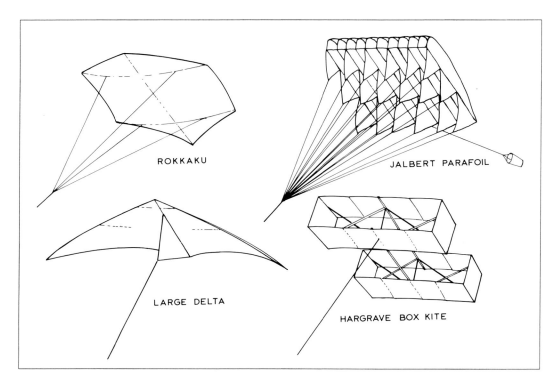

ROKKAKU

JALBERT PARAFOIL

LARGE DELTA

HARGRAVE BOX KITE

FIG. 18.2: *Types of Kites*

demonstrating this kite at a KAPWA event at Berck Plage in France in April 1987, Raoul Fosset, a KAPWA founder, judged it to be 'the only good parafoil'. Parafoils do not have such a good reputation for stability but mine is, in fact, remarkably stable, perhaps due to the fact that it is a non-sporty, older model. It is longer than it is wide being 7.5ft (2.29m) long while only 6ft (1.83m) wide. It does not fly in as light a wind as newer, wider-than-they-are-long versions but in such light wind, no airfoil will lift much payload. Once the wind is strong enough for me to fly, about 19km/hr, my J-45 performs very well and remains stable up to about 60km/hr at which time the tension on the tether will be about 70kg. Parafoils are the easiest of kites to transport and fly as they are simply unrolled from a little bag, held up into the wind to inflate and then fly. There are no rigid spars to break or bend or be too long to easily get into a car or on an aeroplane. Parafoils can still break their tethers, be torn by sharp objects, and get horribly tangled in trees or prickly bushes. There are a number of Jalbert or Jalbert-based designs on the market today and it is possible to make your own (though it is a long, precision sewing job) so unless you can obtain a 'good' parafoil, a similarly sized Rokkaku is probably a better bet.

Deltas offer the possibility of flying in slightly less wind than either a Rokkaku or a parafoil. KAPWA members will get out their large deltas if the wind seems safely in the Beaufort three to four range but it must be remembered that even a slight decrease in the wind will make an excellent, light delta be unable to lift its payload. Worse, as has been said before, an increase to Beaufort five (29km/hr) will place the kite in danger and create a lot of work to lower the kite from the sky. Light winds are particularly capricious, subject to changes in both speed and direction, so systems designed for light wind flying are really only reliable in the most stable conditions in the hands of experienced fliers. A small decrease or a significant increase in the wind means that the kite must be landed. Of course, in the event of an increase, the delta may be replaced by a Rokkaku, parafoil or box kite which will serve the higher wind speeds.

Box kites come in many forms and have an illustrious history.[10] They are not quite so common today because they are somewhat more time consuming and difficult to make, more awkward to transport and much trickier to assemble than simpler 'flat' kites or, of course, parafoils. I would not be surprised if a good Hargrave box kite, made of modern materials, was found to out-perform either a Rokkaku or a parafoil and continue to be stable through wind speeds up through Beaufort six. The serious kitefliers of the past were not fools nor were they lazy.

CAMERAS, STABILIZATION, AIMING AND OPERATION

While kites can lift very heavy objects into the air, such as people, the kite or kites required to actually accomplish this feat are very large and must be flown by teams of well trained and disciplined people, such as soldiers, probably aided by a mechanized windlass mounted on a truck or gun-carriage. Man-lifting is far removed from our kite stereotype. Kite aerial photography is somewhere in-between with light-weight and heavyweight versions resembling the simplicity of the child's kite or the complexity of the military system. Generally speaking, to achieve a higher image quality will require a heavier camera and hence, system. The selection will be made based on the type of photos to be produced: vertical, oblique, high altitude general views, low altitude details, large or mid-format, high resolution images, or small format 'snapshot' quality images. Different cameras weigh more or less and this weight will determine the size of kite that is required and the wind speeds that it will fly in.

Though the best quality images tend to be made by bigger and heavier cameras, there are exceptions. View-finder 35mm cameras are much lighter than single-lens reflexes but their image quality can be as good or better. Also, it is possible to *make* a large format (4x5 inch) camera that weighs less than the average 35mm SLR. In 1971 when I began, I decided to construct a 4x5 inch aero-camera because I felt that achieving the finest image quality was essential for archaeological aerophotography, which will inevitably be scrutinized for fine detail. This *Anderson Aero Camera* is illustrated in FIG. 10.3.

With a view camera there is no possibility of taking a second exposure until the film is changed and the shutter re-cocked so it is necessary to lower the camera to the ground after each exposure. A system to make this repeated lowering relatively easy was another suggestion given to me in 1972 by Julian Whittlesey when I told him I had abandoned balloons in favour of kites. He had done some experimenting with parafoil supported, large-format photography and again, he was most generous with information.[11] He suggested that the camera be carried on a separate 'camera' line passing over a pulley that is fastened to the kite tether a few metres below the kite. This line is controlled be a second windlass near the flying point of the kite and by winding this line in or out, the camera is raised or lowered while the kite continues to fly at full altitude in steady upper air. With an efficient, large diameter windlass and a ball-bearing pulley, this system performs with almost miraculous ease. An advantage of always

FIG. 18.3: *The 4x5 inch Anderson Aero Camera*
The camera was built to receive a standard 4x4 inch view camera lensboard with a 90mm, f/8 Schneider-Kreuznach 'Super Angulon' lens at the front and a standard sheet film holder at the back. (As I already owned a 4x5 inch view camera with this lens, it was an easy decision to make.) It is fixed-focus though a provision had to be made to allow it to be focussed initially and this was done by separating the front frame (holding the lens) and the back frame (holding the film) by threaded rods and a sliding cardboard 'bellows'. Temporarily placing a focussing screen from a view camera at the back, it was possible to focus the camera by carefully adjusting nuts on the threaded rods to bring the camera exactly into focus perhaps just short of infinity. Once completed, this operation need never be done again. The shutter was released originally by a clockwork darkroom timer but in 1972, I adapted the cheapest single-channel model aeroplane radio control which has served ever since.

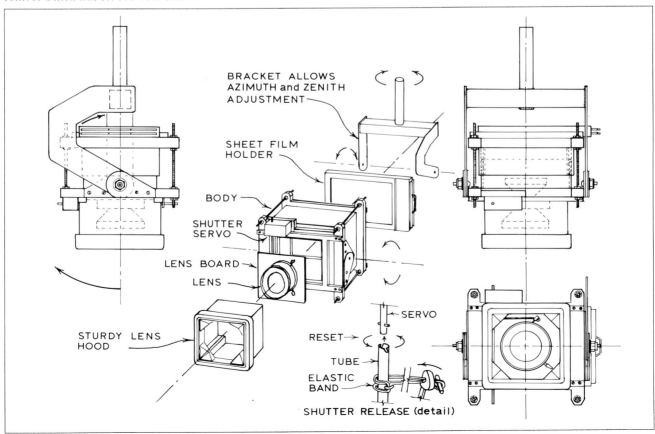

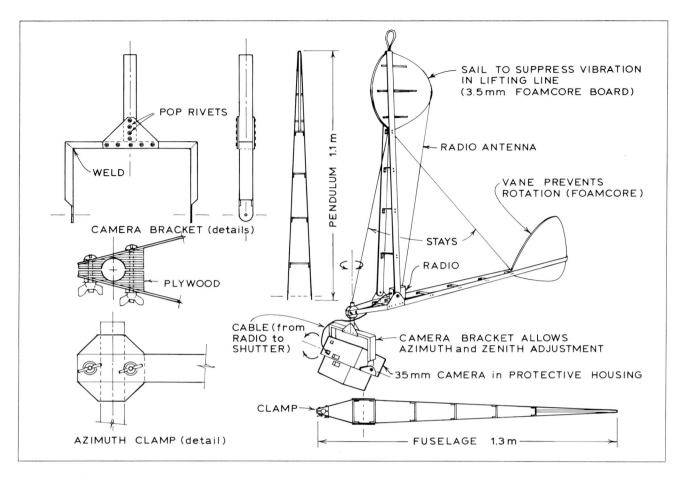

FIG. 18.4: *The Wind-Stabilized Frame*
The camera is held in an adjustable bracket that allows its azimuth and zenith (horizontal and vertical angle) orientation to be selected. This bracket is placed at one end of a horizontal 'fuselage' with a vertical vane at the other end. This unit is suspended at its balance point from a vertical element which, like a pendulum, allows gravity to orient the frame in two dimensions. The vane prevents rotation by always pointing the horizontal part into the wind like an arrow. I have built five of these frames over the years but the one that I illustrate is a composite of the earlier designs, two of wood and two of metal, and I am confident that it would perform as well as than any previous model. This design is quite simple to fabricate using aluminium extrusions, 'pop' rivets and some welding on the camera bracket.

returning the camera to the ground to change the film after each shot is that aiming and exposure can also be adjusted so there is little need for anything to be automatic other than the shutter release.

I invented my system for camera stabilization which I call a *wind-stabilized frame* in Syria in 1972. FIG. 18.4 shows a design of the mid-eighties.[12]

Suspending the camera at the bottom of a vertical pole is the almost universal approach taken by the members of KAPWA. This element, known as the pendulum, is usually attached directly to the kite tether; it is then raised or lowered simply by letting out or winding in this line. (It may be simple but it may not be easy if the kite is pulling very hard.) The pendulum or frame, as well as allowing the camera to be oriented in any direction, is intended to eliminate rapid local rotation or vibration that the camera might experience and which is most detrimental to image quality. The camera will still undergo lateral and vertical movement as the kite responds to changes in the speed and

direction of the wind and this larger, non–rotational, non–vibrational motion is dealt with in several ways. First, a relatively fast shutter speed must be used as with hand held (as opposed to tripod) photographs. Second, to improve the chances that a particular subject is actually framed in a photograph, a wide-angle lens makes 'aiming' much easier. The wide-angle lens will also 'see' much more for general views. A 28mm lens used with 35mm gives an angle of view of about 65° (on the long dimension) which I find very satisfactory. The 90mm lens used with the 4x5 inch camera gives an even greater coverage of about 67° which is excellent and with this kind of coverage, it is not too difficult to secure a desired result. The third, most vital ingredient for good image quality is to be able to actually make the exposure when the camera seems to be in a correct position and is reasonably stable. Here, some kind of remote control is essential which inevitably means a radio for high-level work but other systems such as infra-red, pneumatic, or mechanical are possible at a lower level. Almost all early kite photography or novice work more recently has begun by triggering the shutter with some kind of time delay, but when this is abandoned in favour of a remote control the number of successful exposures is increased dramatically, perhaps fourfold, and the standard of what is deemed to be successful also rises.

In 1978 I purchased an Olympus OM–1 with an f/2, 28mm lens plus the simplest motor-drive called a Winder–1. My choice was made because I believed that the slightly smaller Olympus might be lighter than other 35mm SLRs but also because the Winder–1 has miniplug socket for plugging-in a remote control. Direct, electrical control from the radio eliminated the need for a mechanical servo to physically push the shutter or cable release button which was necessary on all of the cheaper cameras then available. With this elegant triggering and the camera winding itself on, very easy remote aerial photography became a reality. Particularly for vertical shots where the camera need only be aimed initially straight down, a photo mission required only one launch of the camera, which was then gradually moved over the area to be photographed taking photos whenever the camera seemed to be in a good position. More recently I replaced the OM–1 with an OM–2 which has automatic exposure control albeit 'aperture priority'. 'Shutter priority' would be better. With the camera remaining in the air for longer periods without adjustments, varying light conditions such as passing clouds cease to be a problem.

As well as the ease of operation described above, the change to 35mm from large format brought an additional, significant advantage. The wider aperture lenses typically available with 35mm equipment allow any film to be used including the slowest and finest-grained colour and black-and-white materials. A bright sunlight exposure for Kodachrome 25 is 1/500s at f/4, which is still four f-stops inside a practical limit of 1/125s at f/2 which camera stabilization and the f/2 lens impose. Thus even Kodachrome 25 could be shot

FIG. 18.5: *Michel Dusariez's Motorized Rig*
The rig is made of aluminium extrusions and model aeroplane radio control parts. As the servos are not very powerful, it is essential that the design be carefully designed so that the camera turns almost exactly about its centre of gravity and with a minimum of friction. Normal servos rotate about 90° so one may serve directly for the zenith control. To achieve the 360° rotation required for the azimuth control, the motion of the servo must be geared up, which gives the opportunity to incorporate a much stronger bearing at the bottom of the pendulum than the bearing in the servo itself. Here the camera is triggered electrically by using a servo to close a microswitch. A similar cam device could also push a cable release or the servo itself can be positioned to directly push the shutter button of the camera. In order to maintain perfect balance, each different camera will require its own bracket that attaches to the zenith servo and an additional bracket if vertical format (oblique) pictures are desired (as shown on the left). For straight-down, vertical photos, the azimuth control will orient the format as required

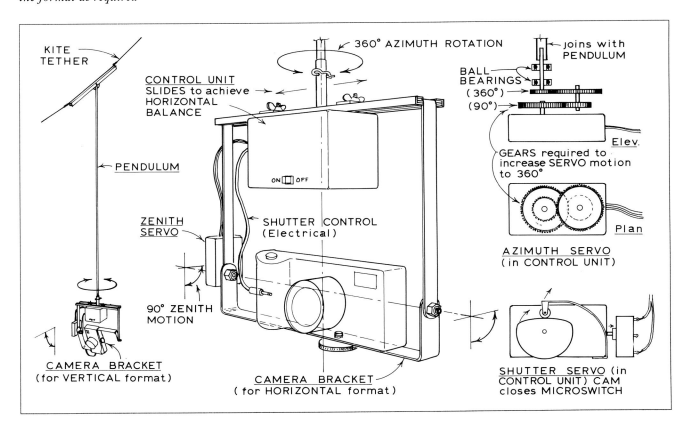

on a cloudy day or in attractive early morning or late afternoon light. My f/8 Super Angulon of the 4x5 inch camera is not satisfactorily sharp at its corners until it is stopped down to f/11 and the larger format is additionally, less tolerant of camera movement, so the same practical limit is perhaps 1/250s at f/11, which allows a minimum bright sunlight film speed of ISO 100. The standard film for large format colour photography is Ektachrome 64 which I have shot successfully in bright desert light conditions, but only in extreme bright light is this film satisfactory. To allow a significant margin for less-than—optimal light, I regularly shot Kodak Royal-X Pan, a vintage, press-corps workhorse black–and–white film rated ISO 1250. (I would now shoot Kodak T-Max 400 'pushed' to the equivalent speed of Royal-X Pan.) While these films are grainy, the large format negative is normally enlarged relatively little so the grain remains invisible and I still judge the image quality of Royal-X Pan, when shot with the 4x5 inch aero camera to be superior to any 35mm image I have achieved. My 4x5 inch camera could be improved by using a less elaborate lens than the Super Angulon. Being rigidly fixed-focus with no swings or tilts which are the virtue of a proper view camera, the super-wide image cast by the Super Angulon is wasted in the aero camera. I was once told that the simpler, lighter and slightly cheaper 100mm, f/5.6 Symmar–S, which can be used for classic photogrammetry, would serve the aero camera better as it would produce a substantially better image at full aperture.[13]

Countless compact, self-winding lightweight point-and-shoot or simpler 35mm cameras are available today on the new or secondhand market, any of which can be adapted for remote aerial photography. Auto focus is not required but few have sockets for plugging in a electrical remote control so most will require a servo for the shutter button. Current favorite cameras at KAPWA are the Canon T70, the Ricoh FF9 (also called Shotmaster) and the Konica Z-UP, all of which 'have an electronic shutter release switch'.[14]

Since a basic modern model aeroplane radio control unit has three controls (for rudder, elevator and motor speed), these units are perfect for adapting to control the aiming of an aero-camera from the ground. The servos are used to control rotation about the vertical axis (azimuth angle), rotation about the horizontal axis (zenith angle) and of course, the shutter. FIG. 18.5 schematically shows a camera mount developed by Michel Dusariez incorporating these features.[15] This mount is particularly well developed in that it is possible to know which way the camera is oriented from calibrations on the controls on the ground. (When a camera is very high, it is difficult to see which way it is pointing.) Almost everyone in KAPWA has some kind of multi-channel, aimable rig since it may not even be possible to buy a single-channel radio anymore. I have not built such a rig myself since my old single-channel radio continues to serve me well and my two-line system allows the return the camera to the ground for aiming and adjustment with reasonable ease.

FIG. 18.6: *Snatch-Pulley Operations*
(1) The snatch-pulley is placed on the main tether. (2) A person walks with it toward the kite until (3) the camera is lowered to the ground. For bringing down the kite itself, the person (or persons!) will at this stage (4) grasp the tether firmly with gloves and walk back toward the windlass towing the kite while the windlass operator winds in a section of the main tether which is no longer in great tension. If there is enough room, (5) the pulley might be taken right to the kite thus landing the kite in one operation and eliminating the need to so laboriously pull the kite forward as the line is wound in. If there are extra people, (6) the snatch-pulley may be held stationary while others pull sections of line back toward the windlass.

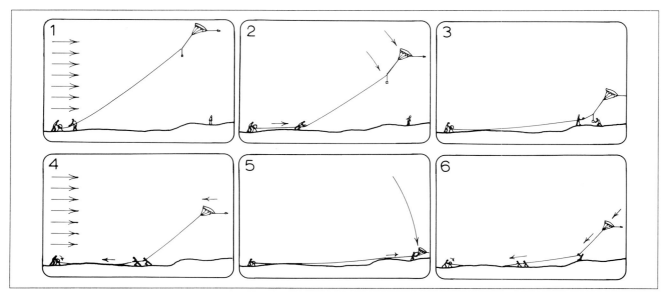

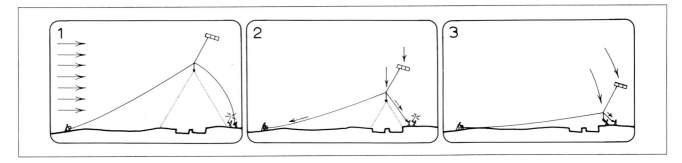

FIG. 18.7: *Control-Line Lowering System*
(1) A control line (or lines) is attached to the kite tether as the camera unit is attached and the lines are wound out until the camera reaches its desired maximum height. (2) The camera can be lowered and accurately positioned by winding in the control line (or lines) plus winding in or out (or repositioning) the main tether. (3) The camera can be lowered to the ground very safely for adjustment, film changing, etc.

It should be mentioned that the most dangerous part of any aircraft flight is the landing and kite-borne cameras do not escape this rule. Each time the camera is lowered, it must be caught and not be allowed to bump along on the ground. Because I lower my camera many times and sometimes it is not caught, I provide my cameras with some protection against minor impacts. The 4x5 inch camera simply has a sturdy, resilient lens hood while the more delicate Olympus is housed in a balsa wood box, also with a resilient lens hood. In my experience, the occasional missed catch has never seriously damaged a camera but I also do not doubt that some spectacular catches have occasionally saved the camera. There is no question of a free-fall for any equipment, even in the event of a sudden failure of the wind, because the kite, particularly a parafoil, will serve as an effective parachute. Normally, the camera windlass operators (with my system) will lower the camera slowly into the arms of a 'fielder'. If they see that no one is under the camera, they keep it in the air until someone is there to catch it. In the event of the camera windlass operators not being able to see where the camera is landing, great difficulties and substantial dangers arise. Some means of communication must be devised which is normally by using arm or flag signals but walkie-talkie radios are better if they are available and work properly.

Those who fly with the camera attached to the main kite tether do not have quite the same problem on landing because the camera is lowered by winding in the tether which will bring the camera directly down to the windlass. In open spaces, it is also possible to use a *snatch-pulley* to lower the camera. The case of a snatch-pulley can be opened to allow its sheave to be placed over a line at any point so it does not require an end of the line to be threaded through. It is placed over the tether at the windlass then held by a person who walks toward the kite. In so doing, the lower part of the kite tether, though still under full tension, will be brought parallel to the ground and of course, eventually the person will reach the camera which will have been brought to the ground. When a kite is pulling

very hard, a snatch-pulley is essential for lowering the kite itself because it is impossible for a manually operated windlass to wind in line under great tension. Many turns of line, wound in tension around a drum will also cause enormous crushing forces which will destroy all but the most carefully constructed windlass. Snatch pulley operations are illustrated in FIG. 18.6.

The snatch-pulley system eliminates the tension in a section of the kite tether making it possible for that section of the tether to be wound in. The sections must be short enough so that nothing will harm the tether as it lies along the ground. Again, as the pulley is going forward, the tether is still under the full tension of the kite and is subject to being caught by sharp objects or held in the bare hands of 'helpful' onlooking people who could have their hands seriously cut.

A third method of lowering the camera when it is directly attached to the kite tether is by means of a control line (or lines) attached to the tether near the camera. These lines are wound in, pulling the camera down from the sky. Here too, the camera is brought directly down to a person but, as with so many things involving large kites, it is easier said than done. The control windlasses must be strong and effective and again, the main tether will lie along the ground. FIG. 18.7 illustrates control-line operations.

MORE ON OPERATION: FIVE SYSTEMS

FIGS. 18.8 and 18.9 schematically show the major stages of kite photography missions; first with a one-line, pendulum system and second, with a two-line pulley system. These diagrams are not to scale but are compressed: my current main tether is 430m long which allows the camera to reach somewhat in excess of 200m above the ground. I seldom fly on the full length of the tether but I regularly used the full length of a 600m tether in Syria which is by no means a KAPWA record.

The Whittlesey system is unquestionably more difficult than a one-line system because it requires at

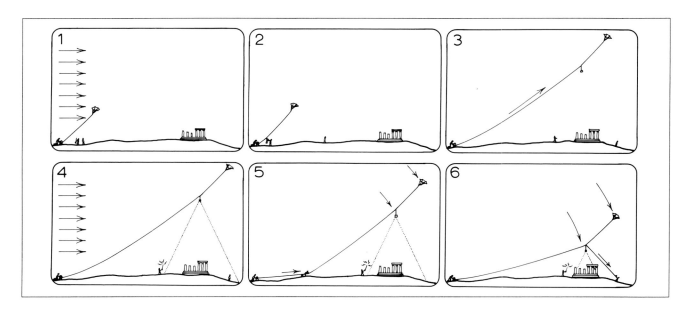

FIG. 18.8: *One-Line Pendulum System Diagram*
(1) The kite is launched and raised to a height where it is flying steadily. (2) The camera rig on its pendulum is attached and (3) more line is wound out until the camera reaches the desired height. (4) Using the radio control both to take photographs and aim the camera, photos are taken until it is judged that the objective is achieved. The camera is lowered by (ref. 3) winding-in the main tether (or) (5) using a snatch pulley (or) (6) using control lines.

least two people who must be able to communicate with each other though they might be separated by several hundred metres. Where catching the camera when it is lowered is made difficult by obstacles on the ground such as fences or archaeological trenches, still more people will inevitably be essential to cover landing zones separated by uncrossable barriers. Where the wind is unreliable or changes in the flying point will be required, two people must man the main tether windlass and two people are desirable on the camera windlass, one to work the windlass and one to observe and relay commands coming from the people under the camera. The kite windlass is simply hard work and it may require a lot of weight just to hold down. The camera windlass is not physically difficult but repeatedly winding in and out about 200m of line can be tiring and, particularly where signals are being used, an extra pair of eyes is very helpful.

The kinds of problems that have been encountered in the past have to do with the pulley becoming stiff or seizing entirely (due to an inadequate bearing) or the lines becoming wound together. This twisting can occur if the wind speed drops and the main kite tether below the pulley slackens to hang down in a great curve or 'belly', the uppermost part of which can be vertical. If the camera is hoisted above this curve, it is easy for it to pass in front of (in effect, over) the main tether which will result in a twist when the main tether becomes tight again. Similar twists will also result if the kite windlass passes in front of the camera windlass when the flying point is being moved. If several such twists occur, working the camera windlass can become very difficult and perhaps there is a danger of the

moving, camera line cutting the stationary main tether. It has never happened, nor has a seized pulley ever cut the camera line, but fears of these things terminated many early missions. These problems are avoided by using a ball-bearing pulley and having kite windlass operators who will wind in the main tether should it become slack and let it out again to it original length when suitable wind resumes.

There are also three other systems of kite aerial photography which should be mentioned briefly. First is the most obvious idea of attaching the camera directly to a kite. Such a system was used by Arthur Batut of Labruguière, Tarn in France to take the first known kite aerial photographs in June 1888[16] and as recently as the late 1970s by a system developed by Squadron Leader Don Dunford.[17] Doubtless most people initially visualize placing the camera on a kite but most experienced kiteflyers immediately dismiss it as impractical because they know that the turbulent air at ground level, into which a kite must be launched, will cause many minor, looping crashes. (Inexperienced kiteflyers too will be aware of the difficulty of the first few moments of a kite's flight and so they tend to rule out kite photography altogether.) Without a camera, a kite is picked up and launched again until it rises through this unstable air and flies steadily, but with a camera, even a normal little loop and bump at launch could be disastrous. Those who have successfully attached cameras directly to their kites are exceptionally skilled and probably are flying in extremely clean (non–turbulent) wind as on a wide, open plain or beach, or are, in fact, using a train of two or more kites, the camera being attached to the lowest so the upper kite

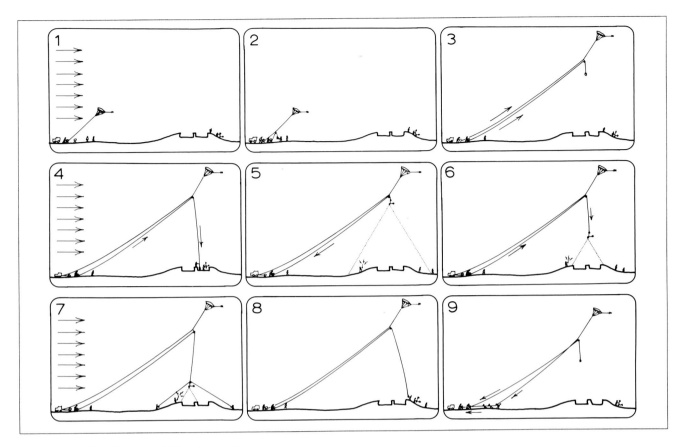

FIG. 18.9: *The Two-Line* Whittlesey *System*
(1) The kite is launched to fly steadily. (2) The pulley is attached with the second 'camera' line passing over it clipped to a plastic bucket. (3) Both lines are let out until the bucket reaches where it is desired to have the camera. (4) The camera line is let out more which lowers the bucket to the ground. The bucket is unclipped and replaced by the camera on its frame which (5) is raised to the desired height, up to the pulley or (6) lower as required. (7) For low-level photographs, control lines may be added which are used to move the camera horizontally and help to lower the camera directly to a person. To move the camera up or down wind, the main kite tether may be wound in or out, or the flying point may be moved. To move across the wind, only moving the the flying point will suffice though inevitable variations in the direction of the wind may be utilized to cover a considerable area from a single flying point. To terminate a flight, (8) the camera is lowered and replaced by the bucket and both lines are (9) wound in until the bucket and then the kite are landed. A snatch pulley is frequently (if not always) required to wind in the main kite tether.

or kites are already flying steadily and will help lift the camera-kite into the air. The Dunford system falls into this latter category and undoubtedly, a large and rigid kite (such as a Dunford Flying Machine) is an excellent means of stabilizing, if not orienting, a camera.

A second, interesting system is shown in FIG. 18.10. *Le Trolley Photographique* was a much-used and commercially marketed turn-of-the-century idea but I am unaware of modern practitioners.[18]

I say this system is interesting because no radio is required and it would seem to be quite easy, perhaps allowing rather spectacular, one-man operation. Imprecise aiming, camera vibration caused by the messenger reaching the stop, and uncontrolled camera descent are obvious problems but probably most of these could be solved. Here, as with attaching the camera directly to the kite, good wind is required right down to the ground because if there is a significant layer of relatively still air near the ground, the messenger will be difficult to start on its journey.

FIG. 18.11 shows a third, additional technique which is used to employ a manually operated trolley, such as several very clever and workable systems developed by Tom Pratt in the United Kingdom.[19]

Tom Pratt does not favour the use of a radio control, preferring to operate the shutter either with an additional, light control line or better, by using an additional pulley/loop line as half of the larger pulley/ loop system. In the United Kingdom it is necessary to obtain permission from the Civil Aviation Authority and to notify the local Air Traffic Controller if it is desired to fly a kite higher than 60m.[20] This procedure is not as onerous as it might seem, nevertheless it is a complication rather alien to kite flying. Furthermore, until recently, radio controls were supposed to be used strictly for flying models, so Tom Pratt, by not allowing

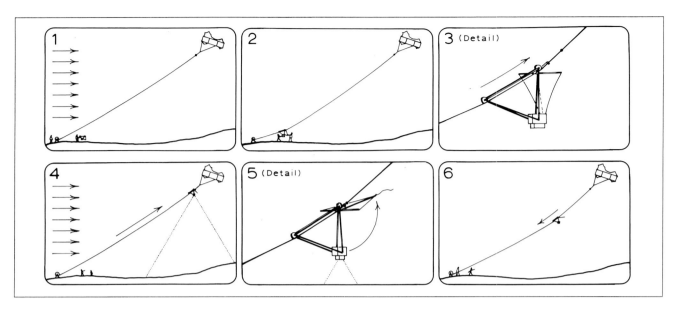

FIG. 18.10: *Le Trolley Photographique*
(1) The Kite is launched and flown to its full height. (2) The camera is attached to a messenger (detail 3) which runs like a trolley on the kite tether and it is (4) pulled up this line by a sail. When the messenger reaches a stop (5) placed below the kite, the impulse trips the shutter and also feathers the sail so (6) the trolley rolls back down the line to the ground. Systems also used a second, smaller messenger or a time delay (frequently a burning fuse) to trip the shutter.

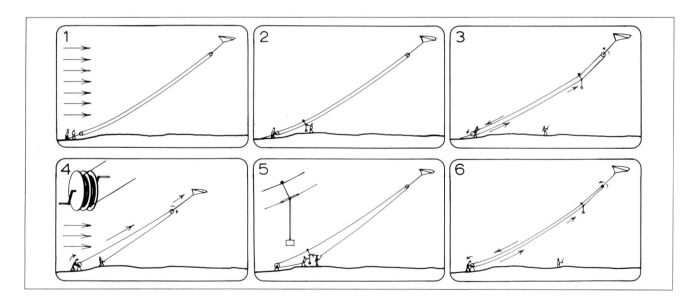

FIG. 18.11: *Manual Trolley / Pulley Systems*
For the simplest, (1) the kite is flown on an endless loop of line with pulleys both at the kite and at the ground. (2) The camera is attached to the lower line with a trolley to distribute its weight to the upper line. (3) By pulling the upper line, the camera is drawn up by the lower line as high as is required or until it reaches the upper pulley. Alternatively, instead of the lower pulley, (4) a two-reeled windlass is used, the two reels being fastened to turn together. The lines are wound in opposite directions around the adjacent reels so as one line is wound in, the other line is wound out. The kite is launched carrying its pulley as before but with only one of the lines passing over the pulley, the end of this line being kept at the ground. (5) When the kite is high enough, the end of the second line is attached to the end of the first and at this joint the camera is attached. From this moment, the system acts like an endless loop as before in that subsequent turning of the windlass will not affect the total length of the tether. (6) When the first line is wound in, the second line is wound out which action will draw the camera up toward the kite.

his kites to stray above 60m and by not using a radio control, remained completely legal. He is a champion of the unique ability of kite photography to achieve very well controlled, cheap, safe and efficient low-level aerial photographs. His systems would most admirably serve archaeologists who desire detailed, vertical or oblique views of their trenches. For great heights however, two-line trolley systems are likely to become clumsy or unworkable due to sag and stretch in the lines and the tendency of the lines to become twisted together.

CONCLUSION

The twentieth century arrived with kites seen as credible tools for lifting apparatus into the sky and the advent of KAPWA has assured that the century has ended with kites again regularly being used for taking kite aerial photographs. Archaeology is among the most perfect applications for kite aerial photography, largely for the same reasons that balloon aerial photography has firmly been established as a tool for archaeology. Low-level aerial photographs are of inestimable value for documenting and presenting archaeology; sites are frequently (but certainly not always) in suitable places for flying kites, and during surveys or excavations there is an available pool of manpower to fly a kite system. Kite photography unquestionably offers the cheapest means of obtaining low-level aerial photographs and these photos can be of superior quality to any taken by powered aircraft. Only balloons are really better at providing an equivalent vibration-free lifting system for a camera, but there is a substantial direct expense plus many problems associated with the gas, which kites are not subject to at all. If the conditions for flying kites are favourable and a few people from an archaeological survey or excavation team are present, excellent aerial photographs of a site can be provided for little more than the cost of the film itself. Kite aerial photography is not crazy, nor is it foolish or unrealistic, it is only perceived as such by people who do not know that kites are useful flying machines.

NOTES

1. A. H. S. Megaw, 'Supplementary Excavation on a Castle Site at Paphos, Cyprus, 1970–1971', *DOP* 26 (1972) 322–343, FIG. 1; F. G. Maier, V. Karageorghis, *Paphos: History and Archaeology* (Nicosia 1984) 305.

2. A. H. S. Megaw, 'Excavations at the Episcopal Basilica of Kourion in Cyprus in 1974 and 1975: A Preliminary Report', *DOP* 30 (1976) 345–371, fig.1; G. Buccellati, M. K. Buccellati, J. Knudstad, 'The Fourth Season: Introduction and Stratigraphic Record', *Terqa Preliminary Reports* 10 (Malibu 1979) pls. 1–5,10; Richard P. Harper, 'Excavations at Dibsi Faraj, Northern Syria, 1972–1974: A Preliminary Note on the Site and its Monuments', *DOP* 29 (1975) 319–338, figs. 4a, 8, 11, 14.

3. The *Kite Aerial Photography Worldwide Association* was formed in 1985 in Brussels by Michel Dusariez (founding President), Raoul Fosset and Comte Geoffroy de Beauffort with David P. Town as an associate in the United States. While not an officer, I participated in its foundation and was awarded the *KAPWA Challenge Annuel* trophy in 1987 for contributions to the art of kite aerial photography. (R. Fosset, M. Dusariez, 'Berck Plage Revisited', *KAPWA Magazine* 2–3 (July 1987) 4–8.) In its eight-year existence, KAPWA was joined by approximately 500 people in twenty countries and published 33 issues of a bilingual (parallel French and English) quarterly journal dealing entirely with kite aerial photography. Originally called *KAPWA Magazine*, in 1990 it was divided into two sections: *KAPWA News* and *KAPWA Technique*, the latter being detachable pages intended to produce a compact file dealing entirely with practical aspects of kite aerial photography. In 1994, it was decided that KAPWA had fulfilled its primary function of re-establishing kite aerial photography as a viable technique so the organization and journal have been suspended. In 1995, KAPWA published and excellent adn useful volume with both French and english versions: Geoffrey de Beauffort and Michel Dusariez, *Aerial Photographs Taken from a Kite: Yestereday and Today* (KAPWA-Foundation Publishing, 1995 [First English Edition - ISBN 2-9600048-3-3 Original Ediction in French: ISBN 2-9600048-2-5]).

4. Comte G. de Beauffort, 'The Great International Competition for Scientific and Military Kites in Spa', *KAPWA Magazine* 2–3 (July 1987) 11–13.

5. At the Hellenic War Museum in Athens there is a replica of the Army's aeroplane, *Daedalos*, the original of which flew in battle on 5 Dec. 1912. The Navy's aeroplane, *Nautilos*, flew reconnaissance missions against the Ottoman fleet before the battle of Cape Helles on 3 Dec. 1912. Both aeroplanes were built in France by Henri Farman.

6. J. H. Whittlesey, 'Elevated and Airborne Photogrammetry and Stereo Photography', in E. Harp, Jr. (ed.), *Photography in Archaeological Research* (Albuquerque 1975) 223–258. Digital, computerized systems of photogrammetry such as Elcovision 10 marketed by Wild Leitz Ltd., Heerbrugg, Switzerland are more recent than the Whittlesey article.

7. D. Dunford, MBE, *Kite Cookery* (Leafield, Oxford 1977) 47.

8. D. Pelham, *The Penguin Book of Kites* (Harmondsworth, Middlesex 1976) 42.

9. Ibid. 88.

10. Ibid. 8–109 (These pages: 'Part one: History' are rich in box kites.)

11. Whittlesey (n.6), 251.

12. My most recent design employs two oval-section telescopic legs from a lightweight video tripod which allows it to be transported in a large suitcase. I have found, however, that the asymmeticla, aeroplane-tail vane is a serious design fault. When such a tail is lifted very rapidly by a strong gust of wind, it is inclined to wobble from side to side. I had introduced the asymmetrical vane to avoid its lower fin being

photographed in downwind-oblique shots but this change proved to be responsible for the worst accident of my kite photographic career. At Al Andarin in Syria in 1998, an asymmetrical vane that I had added to a well-tested, wooden frame actually twisted and broke its spar which made the camera rig wildly unstable inthe air. Before the camera could safely be brought to the ground, the gyrations worked loose the azimuth clamp allowing the camera to free fall, smashing its housing to pieces. Amazingly, the housing completely protected the valuable Olympus f/2, 28mm lens and even the camera itself was possible to repair.

13. R. C. Anderson, 'A Kite Supported System for Remote Aerial Photography', *Aerial Archaeology* 4 (1979) 6.

14. M. Dusariez, 'A New Modular Rig', *KAPWA News* 7–1 (March 1992) 21. A good photographic dealer, especially one dealing in second hand equipment should be able to help in making a wise choice of camera based on image-quality, weight, price, availability, etc.

15. Ibid. 19–21. The *KAPWA News/Technique* magazine has numerous articles on camera rigs but unfortunately is held by very few libraries. The many possible combinations of cameras and radio controls, both often no longer in production, make the duplication of a 'published' design for a camera rig almost impossible. A good aero-model shop will provide the radio equipment required, possibly second-hand, as many simple, three-channel (or less) radios will have been made redundant by more sophisticated equipment that is better for flying aeroplanes. With the camera and radio equipment in-hand, it is possible for a good gadgeteer to produce a useful rig based on the ideas given here.

16. Comte G. de Beauffort, 'A Bit of History', *KAPWA magazine* 1–3 (July 1986) 5–17.

17. J. Cochrane, 'The Dunford Aerial Photographic System', *Aerial Archaeology* 4 (1979) 8–11.

18. Comte G. de Beauffort, 'Pictures from the Sky', *European Kiteflier* 1–3 (May 1979) 23–24.

19. T. Pratt, 'Kite Photography System: Just Add Kites!!', *The Kiteflier* 24 (June 1985) 7–1; 'Serious Photography from Kites', *KAPWA News* 7–4 (Dec. 1992) 27–28; 'The Loop—for Aerial Photography', *KAPWA News* 8–2 (June 1993) 37–38.

20. P. Lofting, 'Kite Law', *The Kiteflier* 28 (July 1986) 16–19.

Bibliography

A. H. S. Megaw

I. BOOKS

1. *Hermopolis Magna, Ashmunein: The Ptolemaic sanctuary and the basilica* (with A. J. B. Wace), Alexandria University, Faculty of Arts, (Alexandria, 1959).

2. *The Church of the Panagia Kanakaria at Lythrankomi in Cyprus, its mosaics and frescoes*, (with E.J.W. Hawkins), *Dumbarton Oaks Studies* XIV, (Washington, 1977).

3. *Kourion: The episcopal precinct* (in preparation).

4. *Saranda Kolones: A Crusader Castle excavated at Paphos* (with J. Rosser) (in preparation).

5. *The church of the Panagia Angeloktistos at Kiti and its mosaic* (with E.J.W. Hawkins) (in preparation).

II. ARTICLES

6. 'Researches at Isthmia : On the date of the fortifications', *BSA* 32 (1931–32), 69–79.

7. 'The chronology of some Middle-Byzantine churches', *BSA* 32 (1931–32), 90–130.

8. 'Byzantine architecture in Mani', *BSA* 33 (1932–33), 137–162.

9. 'The date of Hagioi Theodoroi at Athens', *BSA* 33 (1932–33), 163–169.

10. 'Archaeology in Greece', 1935–1936, *JHS* 56 (1936), 135–158.

11. 'Cypriot medieval glazed pottery' (with J. du Plat Taylor), *RDAC* 1937–39 (1950),1–13.

12. 'Three medieval pit-groups from Nicosia', *RDAC* 1937–39 (1950), 145–168, 224–226.

13. 'A seventh-century Byzantine Hoard', *RDAC* 1937–39 (1950), 210–211.

14. 'Three vaulted basilicas in Cyprus', *JHS* 66 (1946), 48-56

15. 'A Muslim tombstone from Paphos', *Journal of the Royal Asiatic Society*, Oct. 1950, 108–109.

16. 'The mosaics in the church of Panayia Kanakaria in Cyprus', *Atti dell'VIII Congresso di Studi Bizantini*, II, *Studi Bizantini*, VIII, 1953, 199–200 (summary).

17. 'Ninth international Congress of Byzantine Studies' (Saloniki 1953), *Archaeology*, 6, n°3, autumn 1953, 181–183.

18. Ἡ βασιλικὴ τῆς Ἑρμουπόλεως, *Πεπραγμένα τοῦ Διεθνοῦς Βυζαντινολογικοῦ Συνεδρίου* (Θεσσαλονίκη, 12–19 Ἀπριλίους 1953) Vol. I (Athens 1955), 287–295.

19. 'Early glazed pottery from Polis' (with A. I. Dikigoropoulos) *RDAC* 1940–48 (1957), 77–93.

20. 'A twelfth century scent bottle from Cyprus', *Journal of Glass Studies*, I (1959), 59–61.

21. 'Early Byzantine monuments in Cyprus in the light of recent discoveries', *Akten des XI. Internationalen Byzantinisten-Kongresses, 1958*, (Munich 1960), 345–351.

22. *Kyrenia Castle. A brief history and description of Kyrenia Castle* (Nicosia 1961), frequently reprinted.

23. 'The church of the Holy Apostles at Perachorio, Cyprus, and its frescoes' (with E.J.W. Hawkins), *DOP* 16 (1962), 279–348.

24. 'Notes on recent work of the Byzantine Institute in Istanbul', *DOP* 17 (1963), 333–372.

25. Preface to A. Stylianou, *Cyprus. Byzantine mosaics and frescoes*, (Paris, 1963).

26. 'The original form of the Theotokos Church of Constantine Lips', *DOP* 18 (1964), 279–298.

27. 'Twelfth century frescoes in Cyprus', *Actes du XIIᵉ Congrès International des Etudes Byzantines, Ochrid 1961*, Vol. III, (Belgrade 1964), 257–266.

28. 'Byzantine reticulate revetments', *Charistérion eis Anastasion K. Orlandon*, III, (Athens 1966), 11–22.

29. 'Glazed bowls in Byzantine Churches', *DChAE* 4 (Athens 1966), 145–162.

30. 'The Skripou Screen', *BSA* 61 (1967), 1–32.

31. 'Zeuxippus Ware', *BSA* 63 (1968), 67–88.

32. 'The castle of the Forty Columns at Paphos', *Proceedings of the VIII Scientific Meeting of the International Castles Institute* (Athens, Chambre technique de Grèce, 1968), 65-70.

33. 'Byzantine Pottery (4th–14th century)', *World Ceramics*, ed. R.J. Charleston, (London 1968), 100–106.

34. 'More gilt and enameled glass from Cyprus', *Journal of Glass Studies*, X, (1968), 88–104.

35. 'Excavations at Saranda Kolones, Paphos. Preleminary report on the 1966–67 and 1970–71 seasons', *RDAC* (1971), 117–146.

36. 'A glass vessel formerly attributed to Syria', *Alasia*, I, (Paris 1971), 134–145.

37. 'A fragmentary mosaic of the orant Virgin in Cyprus' (with E.J.W. Hawkins), *Actes du XIVᵉ Congrès des Etudes Byzantines*, Bucharest 1971, vol. 3, (Bucharest 1976), 363–366.

38. 'Supplementary excavations on a castle site at Paphos, Cyprus, 1970–1971', *DOP* 26 (1972), 321–343.

39. 'Background Architecture in the Lagoudera Frescoes', *Jahrbuch der Oesterreichischen Byzantinistik*, 21 (1972), 195–201.

40. 'Saranda Kolones: a medieval castle excavated at Paphos', *Πρακτικὰ τοῦ πρώτου Διεθνοῦς Κυπριολογικοῦ Συνεδρίου*, (Nicosia 1972), 173–182.

41. 'Byzantine architecture and decoration in Cyprus: metropolitan or provincial', *DOP* 28, (1974), 57–88.

42. 'An early thirteenth-century Aegean glazed ware', *Studies in Memory of David Talbot Rice*, (Edinburgh 1975), 34–45.

43. 'Excavations at the episcopal basilica of Kourion in Cyprus in 1974 and 1975: a preliminary report', *DOP* 30 (1976), 345–371.

44. 'The circumambulated presbytery in Cyprus', *Actes du XVᵉ Congrès des Etudes Byzantines*, (Athens, 1976), *Résumé des communications*, V, 85.

45. 'Interior decoration in early Christian Cyprus', *Actes du XVᵉ Congrès des Etudes Byzantines*, (Athens, 1976), (rapport préliminaire).

46. 'Aid for the British School of Archaeology at Athens', *Tribute to an Antiquary: Essays presented to Marc Fitch by some of his friends*, (London 1976), 21–26.

47. 'The Arts of Cyprus: Military Architecture', in K. M. Setton, *A History of the Crusades*, vol.4, ed. P. Hazard, (Madison 1977), 196–207.

48. 'A new basilica with trefoil sanctuary', *Byzantine Studies Conference* 4 (1978), 26–27 (summary).

49. 'The head and feet fragments and another stele from Marion', *Studies presented in Memory of Porphyrios Dikaios* (Nicosia 1979), 139–154.

50. 'The Atrium of the Episcopal Basilica at Kourion, a preliminary report', *RDAC* (1979), 358–365.

51. 'A twelfth-century Byzantine scent-bottle', *British Museum Occasional Paper* 10 (1980), 25–28.

52. 'Excavations at Ayios Philon, the Ancient Carpasia, Part II' (with J. du Plat Taylor), *RDAC* (1981), 209–250.

53. 'Spectrographic analyses of Byzantine and allied pottery', (with R. E. Jones) XVI. *Internationaler Byzantinistenkongress*, Résumés der Kurzbeiträge, (Vienna 1981) section 6.2.

54. 'Byzantine and allied pottery; a contribution by chemical analysis to problems of origin and distribution', *BSA* 78 (1983), 235–263.

55. 'A cemetery church with trefoil sanctuary in Crete', *Actes du Xᵉ Congrès International d'Archéologie Chrétienne (Thessalonique, 28 sept.– 4 oct. 1980)* vol 2 (Vatican-Thessaloniki 1984), 321–329.

56. 'Saranda Kolones : ceramic evidence for the construction date', *RDAC* (1984), 333–340.

57. 'Le fortificazioni bizantine a Cipro', *XXXII Corso di Cultura sull'Arte Ravennate e Bizantina*, (Ravenna 1985), 199–231.

58. 'Mosaici parietali paleobizantini di Cipro', *XXXII Corso di Cultura sull'Arte Ravennate e Bizantina*, (Ravenna 1985), 173–198.

59. 'Progress in early Christian and medieval archaeology, *Archaeology in Cyprus, 1960–1985*, (Nicosia 1985), 292–298.

60. '"Betwixt Greeks and Saracens"', *Acts of the International Symposium 'Cyprus between the Orient and the Occident'* (Nicosia 1986), 505–519.

61. 'The British School at Athens and Cyprus', *RDAC* (1988), part 2, 281–286.

62. 'Reflexions on Byzantine Paphos', *ΚΑΘΗΓΗΤΡΙΑ: Essays presented to Joan Hussey*, ed. J. Chrysostomides (Camberley 1988), 135–150.

63. 'Zeuxippus ware again', *Recherches sur la céramique byzantine*, ed. V. Déroche - J.-M. Spieser, *BCH Suppl.* XVIII, 1989, 259–266.

64. 'The episcopal basilica at Kourion and the evidence for its re-location', in *The Sweet Land of Cyprus, Papers given at the twenty-fifth Jubilee Spring Symposium of Byzantine Studies, Birmingham, March 1991*, eds A. A. M. Bryer and G. S. Georghallides, (Nicosia 1993), 53–67.

65. 'A castle in Cyprus attributable to the Hospital ?', *The Military Orders Fighting for the Faith and Caring for the Sick*, ed. M. Barber, (Aldershot 1994) 42–51.

66. 'The strategic role of the third Crusader castle at Paphos', *Proceedings of the XVIII meeting of the Scientific Council of the International Castles Institute (Paphos 10–14 Oct. 1992), IBI Bulletin 48, Western Defence strategies in the Mediterranean from the Crusader to the Siege of Vienna*, (The Hague, 1992) 17–22.

67. 'Reflections on the original form of St Mark's in Venice,' *Architectural Studies in Memory of Richard Krautheimer*, ed. C. L. Striker (Mainz 1996), 107–110 and pl. 53–55

68. 'The Soloi Basilicas Reconsidered,' *Third International Congress of Cypriot Studies, 16–20 April 1996* (Leukosia 2001), 171-80.

69. 'The Aegean connections of Cypriot church-builders,' in *Cyprus and the Aegean in Late Antiquity, Nicosia 8–10 December 1995* (Nicosia 1997), 343–52.

70. 'A Watchtower before the Paphos Castle' (with John Rosser) (to appear in *RDAC* 2002).

III. REPORTS

71. *Cyprus. Annual Report of the Director of Antiquities*: 1935 and annually to 1958, Nicosia 1948–1959.

72. 'Archaeology in Cyprus 1949-50', *JHS* 71 (1951), 258–260. Id. '1951', *JHS* 72 (1952), 113–117. Id. '1952', *JHS* 73 (1953), 133–137. Id. '1953', *JHS* 74 (1954), 172–176.

73. 'Archaeology in Cyprus 1954', *AR* 1955, 28–34. Id. '1955', *AR* 1956, 41–46. Id. '1956', *AR* 1956, 24–31. Id. '1957', *AR* 1957, 43–54. Id. '1958', *AR* 1958, 25–34

74. 'Archaeology in Greece, 1962–63', *AR* 1962–63, 3-33. Id. '1963–64', *AR* 1963–64, 3–30. Id. '1964–65', *AR* 1964–65, 3–31. Id. '1965–66', *AR* 1965–66, 3–24. Id. '1966–67', *AR* 1966–67, 3-28. Id. '1967-68', *AR* 1967-68, 3-26.

75. 'Excavations at Paphos, Cyprus, 1966', *AR* 1966–67, 27–28. Id. '1967', *AR* 1967–68, 25–26.

IV.

76. *St Hilarion Castle. A Guide* (Nicosia, no date), also frequently reprinted, (7th ed., Nicosia 1963).

77. *Buffavento Castle. A Guide* (Nicosia, no date).

78. *Kantara Castle. A Guide* (Nicosia, no date).

Index